Dear Student,

Reading. Writing. Speaking. Listening.

You communicate with other people in these ways every day. How? You use the English language, the tool that makes communication happen. It allows you to share thoughts, present ideas, and express feelings.

Because language is so important in your life, you will need to learn how to use it correctly. What you learn will help you when you read a book, write a story, speak to your friends, and listen to the world around you. This book, *Macmillan/McGraw-Hill Language Arts*, can help you become the best writer and user of language that you can possibly be.

We hope you enjoy learning the skills that will help you connect with those around you each and every day!

The Editors

MACMILLAN/McGRAW-HILL
Language Arts

6-Trait Writing **Study Guide and Practice**

Pages T2–T16

6-Trait Writing

Study Guide and Practice

- **Ideas and Content**
- **Organization**
- **Sentence Fluency**
- **Voice**
- **Word Choice**
- **Conventions**

Here are six key tools that help make your writing clearer.

Ideas and Content

Is your writing clear and detailed?

Your **ideas** are the heart of your writing. They can also be called the main idea or theme, and must be clearly presented. Your writing should include **details** that keep the reader's attention and show what is really important about your topic.

TIPS FOR BETTER WRITING

- You need to know a lot about your topic. Be sure to do your research.

- Does your writing have interesting details that surprise the reader and make your piece fun to read?

- Be sure to *show* what is happening ("Mary sped past the other runners and ran through the tape with her arms raised in victory.") rather than *telling* what happened ("Mary won the race.").

- When brainstorming, be sure that the topic is small enough so your writing will be focused and clear. ("The History of Dance" is a very big topic. You might narrow the topic to "The First Tango Dancers.")

Read Carl's **explanatory composition** below. Decide if you think his ideas are clear and if the details are well-chosen.

My father took me fishing for the first time last weekend.

> The opening paragraph states a focused topic.

Fishing is not as easy as it looks. It is important to have a boat without a motor because the fish are frightened by loud noise.

> There are many details that the readers may not know.

When we got to the location, I had to bait the hook with a lure. Lures are rubber or plastic bugs that look just like the kinds of things that fish eat.

> The writer uses interesting details that are fun to read.

I threw my fishing line forward and waited for hours before I finally got a bite. I reeled in my line, and at the end was a bright blue trout. I was thrilled because it is rare to catch a fish the first time you go.

> The writer shows *what happened* instead of telling *about it*.

THINK AND WRITE

- Why is it important to write about something you know a great deal about?
- What else could Carl have included in his composition to make it more interesting to the reader?

13

Writing

Organization

Is your writing well planned and easy to follow?

Organization is the **plan** or **pattern** you choose to put your ideas and details in order. Your plan may be to compare and contrast, state opinions and support them with facts, provide a time sequence, or any other clear pattern. The plan you choose should fit the main idea and details of your piece.

TiPS FOR BETTER WRITING

- Your beginning, or lead, should grab the reader's attention.

- All of your details add a little more information to your main idea or story. There is no extra information.

- The transitions between sentences and paragraphs create bridges from one idea to the next.

- Make sure to give the reader information in the right amounts at the right times. If you give too little information, the reader will get bored, and if you give too much, the reader might feel overwhelmed.

- Your ending makes a strong point and gives the reader something to think about.

Kate wrote a **personal narrative**. Read it and see what you think of its organization.

"I have a surprise for you," said Papa Jack when I got to his farm.

The opening sentence grabs the attention of the reader.

"What's my surprise?" I said. Papa Jack looked sad. "What's wrong, Papa Jack?" I asked. He looked at me for a minute and smiled.

Then he said, "Guess what I have for you." First, I guessed a cold glass of milk from the cows and some cookies. ~~Once I made chocolate chip cookies with my mother.~~

This sentence is not important to the main idea.

"No," he said. "Try again."

Before I could guess again, I heard a tiny "Peep." Then, I knew for sure.

Transitional phrases connect ideas.

"The chicks hatched!" I shouted. What a wonderful surprise.

The ending makes a strong point.

THINK AND WRITE

- How can you make sure that your ideas are connected in a logical way?
- How well did Kate organize her composition? What other ways could she have done it?

Sentence Fluency

Do you like the way your writing sounds when it is read aloud?

When you write, your sentences need to make sense, and they should sound like they fit together when read aloud.

TIPS FOR BETTER WRITING

- Check that your writing is easy to read aloud. It should sound natural and have an easy flow.

- Rewrite sentences that are hard to read aloud. Cut any words that seem to be extra.

- Use a variety of simple and complex sentences.

- Vary the beginnings of your sentences.

- Use words that show how your ideas connect.

As you read Horace's **persuasive letter**, ask yourself if it moves easily from sentence to sentence. Also, notice if the sentence structures vary.

Dear Franklin,

You should visit the San Diego Zoo. As soon as you can. I can tell you a lot of reasons to go there.

A good reason to visit is that they have koala bears. I know that's your favorite animal! Koalas look like bears. but they Koala bears are not bears. They eat the eucalyptus that grows in San Diego.

All in all, the San Diego Zoo has many wonderful qualities that will leave you wanting to go back. I think you will have a great time if you go.

Your friend,

Horace

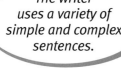

These sentences are fragments; they should be combined.

These sentences can be combined.

Transitional phrases help connect paragraphs.

The writer uses a variety of simple and complex sentences.

THINK AND WRITE

- What are some ways to check if a composition is written with good sentence fluency?

- Does Horace's letter have a natural flow to it? If not, what would you do to fix it?

Writing

Your paper should sound different from the way anyone else writes. When people read your paper, they should feel that you are talking right to them. When you really care about what you are writing, your personal stamp can be seen all the way through.

TIPS FOR BETTER WRITING

- Write about what you know and what you really care about.

- Be sure to write directly to the reader or audience.

- Don't be afraid to say what you really think.

- Write so the reader will feel just what you feel.

Look at Frank's **story** to see how this story is uniquely his.

The Lucky Dog

Gerardo was walking home from school when he spotted a small puppy. It seemed to be shivering. Gerardo gave the puppy a piece of his leftover sandwich. The dog was so happy that it began to follow Gerardo home.

As Gerardo was walking home, he began to think about his mother. She would certainly not approve of a dog in the house. She was sometimes short-tempered. When he got home, Gerardo got a huge surprise.

Instead of being angry, his mother asked Gerardo what they should name it. She said, "What about Lucky? He's lucky that someone as kind as you found him." Gerardo thought that would make a great name.

The writer addresses readers with details that will touch their feelings.

The writer knows about dogs and how they act.

You should say what you feel in a narrative.

It is plain that the writer likes Gerardo and his mother.

THINK AND WRITE

- How does the tone or voice of a written piece affect the reader?
- How do you think Frank felt about the story based on its voice?

Writing

Good **word choices** paint clear pictures in the reader's mind. They also help move the reader to feel and think the way you do. This doesn't mean you use a big vocabulary to impress the reader, but you use just the right word in the right place.

TIPS FOR BETTER WRITING

- Use very specific nouns that clearly name a person, place, or thing. (The word *hot rod*, *van*, *limousine*, *taxi*, or *station wagon* is clearer than just the word *car*.)

- Choosing vivid verbs shows the reader exactly what the action is. (The word *spring*, *bounce*, *hop*, or *leap* is a better choice than the word *jump*.)

- Good use of adjectives is more than just a descriptive list. Adjectives should tell the reader exactly how something looks, sounds, feels, tastes, or smells.

- Adverbs can make your verbs come alive. (Did the man *speak* to the clerk *politely*, *affectionately*, *angrily*, or *simply*?)

- Try to paint pictures so vividly that they stick in the reader's mind.

- Cut or revise sentences or phrases that seem flowery.

- Look for words that you repeat over and over again, and try to choose different words.

The more exact your word choice, the clearer your writing will be. Read this draft of Consuela's **expository composition** to see where she can improve her word choice.

Velcro is a great invention. Velcro is made of
two patches with connecting ~~things~~ *fibers* that grip each
other when placed together. This allows them to be
pulled apart. *Velcro is used in a wide variety of common objects.*
~~Velcro is used in sneakers, clothing, toys, household appliances, and watches.~~ With Velcro,
you can open and close something hundreds of
times, and you will not ~~mess up~~ *damage* the item.

Velcro is so useful that it is even used
aboard the space shuttle. The whole space
shuttle is ~~full of~~ *dotted with* Velcro patches!

There are things that we use every day that
have Velcro, and we don't even realize it.

> Use interesting and specific nouns.

> Instead of a long list of items, try to make one simple sentence.

> Try to use interesting and specific verbs.

> The word dotted *creates a picture that will stick in the reader's mind.*

THINK AND WRITE

- What resource can you use to find words to replace common or lifeless words?

- Where could Consuela have used other words to make her writing more specific and interesting?

T11

Writing

Conventions

Did you revise and proofread your writing carefully?

Here's an easy way for you to remember what to look for when you are proofreading your work: **CUPPS**. That stands for **C**apitalization, **U**sage, **P**unctuation, **P**aragraphs, and **S**pelling. These are the five **conventions** that need to be correct for your writing to be clear.

TIPS FOR BETTER WRITING

- For help with rules for capitalization, see Handbook pages 547–551.

- Usage means the rules of English language. For help with rules for usage, see Troubleshooter pages 512–523 and Handbook pages 530–543.

- The rules for punctuation can be found in the Handbook pages 552–557.

- Check that your paragraphs develop only one main idea.

- For help with spelling rules and strategies, see Handbook pages 582–585.

Read Joni's **comparative essay** to find where she can correct errors.

Pizza and tacos are very similar to each other.

pizza and tacos are made with a flat, thin bread.

cheese

They both also have ~~cheeze~~ and toppings.

> The first word of any sentence should be capitalized.

> Check spelling.

Even though pizza crust and flour tortillas look different, they are both made from whole wheat or white flour.

> Check punctuation.

Toppings can be added to both pizza and tacos. Like tomatoes, black olives, onions, fish, hamburger, and sausage.

> This sentence fragment can be combined with the previous sentence.

Pizza and tacos are two different ways of eating some of your favorite foods. I couldn't ~~not~~ even think of all the ways these foods can be prepared.

> Check usage.

THINK AND WRITE

- What are some ways to prevent errors in conventions *before* they happen?
- How could Joni have used books on CUPPS to help her avoid proofreading errors?

T13

Writing

✓ Checklist
Use the checklist to help you with your writing.

PREWRITE

✓ Ideas and Content
- ❑ Do I know what I want to say?
- ❑ Do I know a lot about this topic? Do I need to do more research?
- ❑ Have I listed details that will make my ideas come alive?

✓ Organization
- ❑ Do I have a clear plan or pattern for my writing?
- ❑ Do all the details in my plan connect to a main idea or theme?

✓ Voice
- ❑ Am I really interested in the topic?

DRAFT

✓ Ideas and Content
- ❑ Do I have enough supporting details to clearly explain or develop the main idea or theme?
- ❑ Can I picture events or objects in my head so my writing will *show* instead of *tell*?

✓ Organization
- ❑ Will the beginning grab the reader's attention?
- ❑ Do I have an idea for the ending?

✓ Voice
- ❑ Do I have a strong sense of who I am writing for?
- ❑ Can I say what the most exciting idea in my writing will be?

✓ Word Choice
- ❑ Do I know the meanings of any special vocabulary words well enough to use them in my writing?

REVISE

✓ Ideas and Content

- ❏ Can the reader easily tell me the point of my writing?
- ❏ Do all the details support the main idea or theme?
- ❏ Is there anything I could have shown instead of told?

✓ Organization

- ❏ Is there any information or details that seem extra?
- ❏ Is the order easy for the reader to follow?
- ❏ Does my ending give the reader something to think about?

✓ Sentence Fluency

- ❏ Does the writing sound natural and easy to read aloud?
- ❏ Did I use a variety of simple and complex sentences?
- ❏ Did I use words that show how my ideas connect?

✓ Voice

- ❏ Will the reader feel what I feel?
- ❏ Does my draft show that I really care about my topic?

✓ Word Choice

- ❏ Are the nouns specific and the verbs vivid?
- ❏ Do the adjectives involve the reader's senses?
- ❏ Do the adverbs create vivid pictures?
- ❏ Are there any words I used too often in my draft?

PROOFREAD

✓ Conventions

- ❏ Have I checked my writing for correct **CUPPS**?

Writing

Presentation is **how you share your writing**. It can be almost as important as what you have actually written. If your presentation is clear and attractive, your audience will want to pay attention to your words. If it is not, your audience may be distracted from your message.

TiPS FOR BETTER WRITING

- If your piece is handwritten, make sure your lettering and punctuation marks are easily readable.

- If you used a computer, make sure your font is easy to read and the margins and spacing are correct.

- Before reading aloud, practice to make sure that you do not stumble over words.

- For any presentation, consider using charts, graphs, pictures, headings, or other visual elements that might help make your meaning clear.

- Think about what other forms this piece of writing might take. Could it be a photo essay, a play, a postcard, or something else?

THiNK AND WRITE

- How might a visual presentation add to the effectiveness of what you are speaking about?
- Do you think that any one form of writing is easier than another? Why or why not?

McGRAW-HILL
Language
Arts

ACKNOWLEDGMENTS

The publisher gratefully acknowledges permission to reprint the following copyrighted material.

"The Big Storm" from *The Big Storm* written and illustrated by Bruce Hiscock. Copyright © 1993 Bruce Hiscock. Reprinted with the permission of Atheneum Books for Young Readers, an imprint of Simon & Schuster Children's Publishing Division.

"Can You Make a Rainbow?" Excerpt from the *McGraw-Hill Science*. Copyright © 2000 McGraw-Hill School Division, a Division of the Educational and Professional Publishing Group of The McGraw-Hill Companies, Inc. Reprinted by permission.

Excerpt from *Macmillan School Dictionary*. Copyright © 1990 by Macmillan Publishing Company. Reprinted by permission of the McGraw-Hill School Division.

"It's Our World, Too!" from *It's Our World Too!* by Phillip Hoose. Copyright © 1993 by Phillip Hoose. Used by permission of Little, Brown and Company.

"A Jar of Dreams" from *A Jar Of Dreams* by Yoshiko Uchida. Copyright © 1981 by Yoshiko Uchida. Reprinted with the permission of Margaret K. McElderry Books, an imprint of Simon & Schuster Children's Publishing Division.

"Koala" from *The World Book Encyclopedia*. Copyright © 1993 by World Book, Inc.

"Life in Flatland" from *Flatland: A Romance of Many Dimensions* written and illustrated by Edwin Abbott. Copyright © 1988 by Penguin Putnam, Inc. Used by permission.

"The Marble Champ" from *Baseball In April And Other Stories* by Gary Soto. Copyright © 1990 by Gary Soto. Reprinted by permission of Harcourt Brace & Company.

"Mariah Loves Rock" from *Mariah Loves Rock* by Mildred Pitts Walter. Text Copyright © 1988 by Mildred Pitts Walter. Published by Bradbury Press.

"Reaching the Americas" from *The Log Of Christopher Columbus* by Robert H. Fuson. Copyright © 1987 by Robert H. Fuson. Published by

International Marine, an imprint of TAB Books, a Division of McGraw-Hill Inc.

"The Sea Maidens of Japan" from *The Sea Maidens Of Japan* by Lili Bell. Used by permission of Ideals Children's Books, an imprint of Hableton-Hill Publishing, Inc. Text copyright © 1996 by Lili Bell. Illustrations copyright © 1996 by Hambleton-Hill Publishing, Inc.

"Spring Is Full of Wonders" by Gordana Danicic from *Have You Seen A Comet?* Copyright © 1971 by the United States Committee for UNICEF. Published by The John Day Company.

From *Wilma* by Wilma Rudolph and Bud Greenspan, copyright © 1977 by Bud Greenspan. Used by permission of Dutton Signet, a division of Penguin Putnam Inc.

Electronic Illustration

Function Thru Form

Photography

Page 115:

A. Steve Liss for Time for Kids

B. Courtesy Hillside Intermediate School

C. Bill Kostroun/AP

D. Ann States/SABA for Time for Kids

E. no credit

F. The Jackson Citizen Patriot

G. Phillip Greenberg for Time for Kids

H. Lori Cross/Nuckols Farm Elementary School

I. Phillip Greenberg for Time for Kids

J. Courtesy Hillside Intermediate School

K. Nina Berman/Sipa

L. Courtesy Hillside Intermediate School

M. Steve Liss for Time for Kids

N. MH Photography

Contributor

Time Magazine

Macmillan/McGraw-Hill Edition

McGRAW-HILL
Language Arts

AUTHORS

Jan E. Hasbrouck

Donna Lubcker

Sharon O'Neal

William H. Teale

Josefina V. Tinajero

Karen D. Wood

Mc Graw Hill **Macmillan McGraw-Hill**

New York   Farmington

Sentences and Personal Narrative

Theme: *Remember When*

Grammar *Spiral Review Every Day*

Sentences

Build Skills

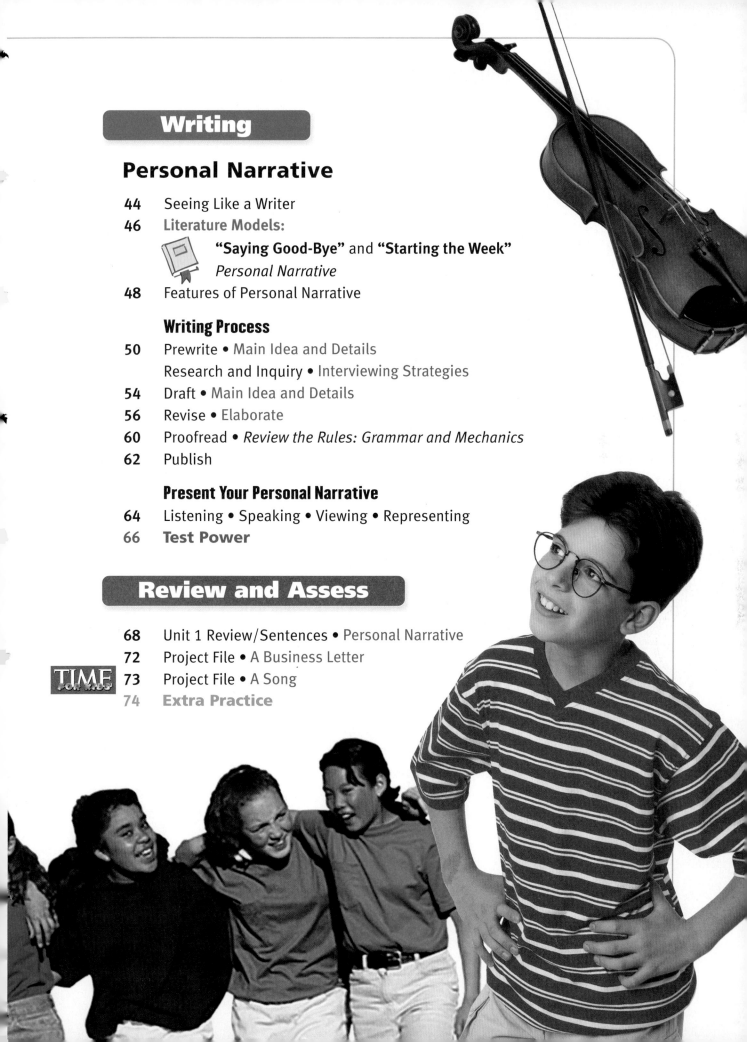

Writing

Personal Narrative

Review and Assess

UNIT 2 Nouns and Persuasive Writing

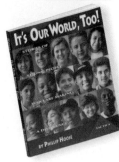

Theme: Join Hands

Grammar *Spiral Review Every Day*

Nouns

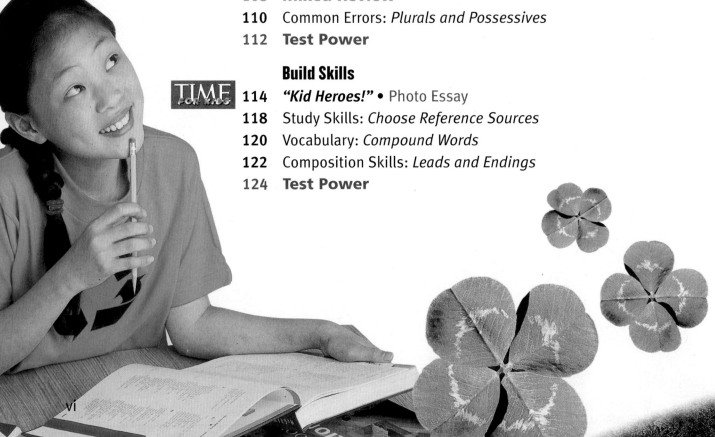

Writing

Persuasive Writing

Review and Assess

Theme: *Express Yourself*

Grammar *Spiral Review Every Day*

Verbs

Build Skills

Writing

Explanatory Writing

Review and Assess

Adjectives and Expository Writing

Theme: *Search and Discover*

Grammar *Spiral Review Every Day*

Adjectives

Build Skills

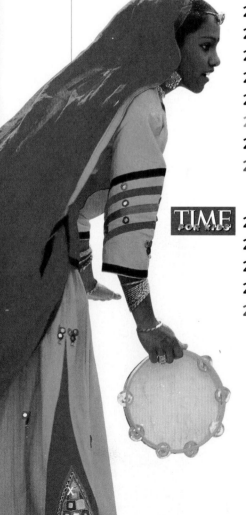

Writing

Expository Writing

Review and Assess

UNIT 5 Pronouns and Writing That Compares

Theme: *Thinking Power*

Grammar *Spiral Review Every Day*

Pronouns

Build Skills

Writing

Writing That Compares

Review and Assess

UNIT 6

Adverbs, Prepositions, Interjections, and Story Writing

Theme: *Decide on a Plan*

 Grammar   *Spiral Review Every Day*

Adverbs, Prepositions, and Interjections

Writing

Story Writing

Review and Assess

Sentences and Personal Narrative

In this unit you will learn about four types of sentences. You will also learn how to write a personal narrative, a true story about someone's experience.

Social Studies Link *Read about the unforgettable event that the great track-and-field star Wilma Rudolph calls "the absolute worst experience" of her life.*

When we got to the track, these girls from Georgia really looked like runners, but I paid them no mind because, well, I was a little cocky. I did think I could wipe them out because, after all, I had won every single race I had ever been in up to that point. So what happens? I got wiped out. It was the absolute worst experience of my life. I did not win a single race I ran in, nor did I qualify for anything. I was totally crushed. The girls from Georgia won everything. It was the first time I had ever tasted defeat in track, and it left me a total wreck. I was so despondent that I refused to go to any of the activities that were planned, including the big dance. I can't remember ever being so totally crushed by anything.

~ from ***The Story of Wilma Rudolph*** by Wilma Rudolph

Thinking Like a Writer

Personal Narrative In a personal narrative, the author writes about a true experience. Reread the passage.

- Why does Wilma say that she was "totally crushed" by the experience?

Sentences Wilma Rudolph uses long and short sentences to write her personal narrative. Read each sentence again.

QUICK WRITE How do her sentences make her writing flow more smoothly?

Sentences and Sentence Fragments

A **sentence** is a group of words that expresses a complete thought. Every sentence begins with a **capital letter** and ends with a **punctuation mark**.

Kelsey and Jamie listened to the thunder.

A **sentence fragment** is a group of words that does not express a complete thought.

Listened to the thunder.

THINK AND WRITE

Sentences

In your journal, write how you know if a sentence tells a complete thought.

When you write a sentence, be sure it expresses a complete thought and can stand alone. You can correct a sentence fragment by adding words or phrases to form a complete sentence.

Fragment	Sentence
The rain.	The rain was unexpected.
Canceled the class trip.	Our teacher canceled the class trip.

Guided Practice

Tell whether each group of words is a sentence or a sentence fragment.

EXAMPLE: Found an old photo album.
Sentence fragment

1. Grandmother came to visit.
2. Brought an old family album.
3. The two girls.
4. Grandmother explained each picture.
5. The girls enjoyed looking at old photographs.

REVIEW THE RULES

- A sentence is a group of words that tells a complete thought.

- Every sentence begins with a capital letter and ends with a punctuation mark.

- A sentence fragment is a group of words that does not tell a complete thought and cannot stand alone.

More Practice

A. Write *sentence* or *sentence fragment* for each group of words.

6. Told stories about their father.

7. Dad's hair was black and curly.

8. Baby pictures of Kelsey and Jamie.

9. One picture showed Grandma playing games with the girls.

10. Jamie took new pictures of us.

B. Add words to each fragment. Then write the new sentence.

11. Found her camera.

12. Grandma and Kelsey.

13. Posed together in silly hats.

14. Each of the two girls.

15. Enjoyed the rainy day after all.

C. [Spiral Review] **Write *sentence* if the words form a sentence. Rewrite each fragment as a sentence.**

16. Photographs remind us of happy times.

17. Family memories.

18. A picture of your friends.

19. Took a picture during their vacation.

20. A family album has special memories.

Extra Practice, page 74.

Handbook
page 526

Writing Activity A Diary Entry

Write a diary entry telling how you spent one rainy day. Organize your ideas to give the events in the order in which they happened.
APPLY GRAMMAR: Use only complete sentences in your diary entry. Proofread your work. Correct any sentence fragments.

3

Declarative and Interrogative Sentences

RULES

A **declarative sentence** makes a statement and ends with a **period**.

> *Plants produce oxygen.*

An **interrogative sentence** asks a question and ends with a **question mark**.

> *Why are plants important?*

THINK AND WRITE

Sentences

When would you use a declarative sentence? When would you use an interrogative sentence? Write your ideas in your journal.

Every sentence begins with a capital letter and ends with a punctuation mark. The punctuation mark you use depends on the kind of sentence you are writing.

	Declarative Sentence	**Interrogative Sentence**
Purpose	makes a statement	asks a question
End Mark	period (.)	question mark (?)
Example	Plants are important to people.	What types of plants do people eat?

Guided Practice

Tell whether each sentence is *declarative* or *interrogative*.

> **EXAMPLE:** How do we identify plants?
> *Interrogative*

1. Plants are important for many reasons.
2. Why are some plants green?
3. Plants make food through photosynthesis.
4. Do plants use carbon dioxide?
5. How do plants help us to breathe?

4

REVIEW THE RULES

- A **declarative sentence** tells something about someone or something. It ends with a period (.).

- An **interrogative sentence** asks a question. It ends with a question mark (?).

More Practice

A. Write each sentence. Then write whether the sentence is *declarative* or *interrogative*.

6. How are different plants classified?

7. Some plants are used to make medicine.

8. Plants need sunlight to grow.

9. Can you name a plant used in making medicine?

10. What are three ways plants help people?

B. Write each sentence. Add the correct end punctuation.

11. How do plants breathe

12. Are there any plants that don't produce seeds

13. A botanist is a scientist who studies plants

14. What information can a botanist learn from tree rings

15. Tree rings tell the age of a tree

C. Spiral Review Write the interrogative sentences as declarative sentences. Write the declarative sentences as interrogative sentences. Be sure to write complete sentences.

16. Do plants breathe in carbon dioxide?

17. Plants provide humans with oxygen and food.

18. Our forests are a great natural resource.

19. Are there many national forests in the United States?

20. Many forests are being destroyed.

Extra Practice, page 75.

Handbook
page 526

Writing Activity A Postcard

Imagine you are visiting a national forest. Create a picture postcard to send a friend. Choose exact words to describe your experience.

APPLY GRAMMAR: Label declarative and interrogative sentences.

 Art Link

5

Imperative and Exclamatory Sentences

— RULES —

An **imperative sentence** tells or asks someone to do something. An imperative sentence ends with a **period**.

Don't go outside.   *Please stay in the house.*

An **exclamatory sentence** expresses strong feeling. An exclamatory sentence ends with an **exclamation mark**.

Oh, look at this!   *How funny it is!*

What a lot of noise it makes!

THINK AND WRITE

Sentences

How do you know what punctuation to use at the end of a sentence? Write your thoughts in your journal.

Begin every sentence with a capital letter. End every sentence with a punctuation mark. Notice the punctuation mark that ends each of the sentences below.

	Imperative Sentence	**Exclamatory Sentence**
Purpose	tells or asks someone to do something	expresses strong feeling
End Mark	period (.)	exclamation mark (!)
Examples	Step inside. Please come with me.	What a great day it is! How happy I am!

Guided Practice

Tell whether each sentence is *imperative* or *exclamatory*.

> **EXAMPLE:** Watch your step.
> *Imperative sentence*

1. Please come into the tent.
2. Listen to the strange noise.
3. Oh, it's a skunk!
4. What a terrible smell there is!
5. How I wish we were somewhere else!

6

REVIEW THE RULES

- An **imperative sentence** gives a command or makes a request. It ends with a period (.).

- An **exclamatory sentence** expresses strong feeling. It ends with an exclamation mark (!).

More Practice

A. Write each sentence. Then write whether the sentence is *imperative* or *exclamatory*.

6. Let's leave this place.

7. Run for your life!

8. Don't be silly.

9. Please stay calm.

10. What a funny situation this is!

B. Write each sentence. Add the correct end punctuation.

11. Don't come any closer

12. Cross the street

13. Oh, look at that

14. How silly we are

15. Please go away

Handbook
page 526

C. **Spiral Review** Write the sentence in each pair. Label it *declarative*, *interrogative*, *imperative*, or *exclamatory*.

16. The skunk left the tent. Ran away.

17. Mother and baby skunk. How cute they are!

18. Like them better far away. What did they want?

19. Please put the food away. Smelled our picnic.

20. Disappeared into the trees. What a surprising day this has been!

Extra Practice, page 76.

Writing Activity A Paragraph

Write a paragraph about a time when you were surprised by someone or something. Use long and short sentences.

APPLY GRAMMAR: Use four types of sentences. Have a partner name each type of sentence you have written.

Combining Sentences: Compound Sentences

> **RULES**
>
> A simple sentence expresses one complete thought.
>
> *July 4 is a holiday.*
>
> A compound sentence contains two simple sentences joined by a comma and the word *and*, *but*, or *or*.
>
> *July 4 is a holiday, and everyone celebrates.*
>
> A conjunction joins words or groups of words. *And*, *but*, and *or* are conjunctions.

THINK AND WRITE

Sentences
How can knowing about compound sentences help you in your writing? Write your ideas in your journal.

You can form a compound sentence by joining two simple sentences that have similar ideas.

Our town has a parade.

The county puts on a fireworks display.

> *Our town has a parade, and the county puts on a fireworks display.*

The mayor makes a speech.

The fire chief does not.

> *The mayor makes a speech, but the fire chief does not.*

We can eat pizza.

We can eat hamburgers.

> *We can eat pizza, or we can eat hamburgers.*

Guided Practice

Tell whether each sentence is simple or compound.

EXAMPLE: Rain is predicted, but the sky is clear. *Compound*

1. Americans have holidays, and we honor important people.
2. Some people celebrate the Fourth of July with picnics, but others watch parades.
3. We watch fireworks, and we go to the park.
4. The fireworks are bright and colorful.
5. We can play games, or we can watch the parade.

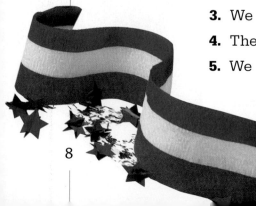

REVIEW THE RULES

- A compound sentence uses the conjunction *and*, *but*, or *or* to join two simple sentences with similar ideas.

- Use a comma before *and*, *but*, or *or* when you write a compound sentence.

More Practice

A. Write each compound sentence. Add the correct punctuation.

6. The flag stands for freedom and Americans display it proudly.

7. We sing the national anthem and we salute the flag.

8. I march in the parade or I watch with the crowd.

9. People eat chicken at picnics but we like pizza.

10. I play baseball and my sister plays volleyball.

B. Combine each pair of sentences to write a compound sentence. Use a comma and the word *and*, *but*, or *or*.

11. The Fourth of July is a special day. We have a family party.

12. We play games. We go to the carnival.

13. I like the fireworks. They are very loud.

14. People watch fireworks at the park. We watch from home.

15. Fireworks are exciting. I can't wait until next year.

C. **Spiral Review** Write each sentence. Add the correct punctuation. Then write whether each sentence is *declarative*, *interrogative*, *imperative*, or *exclamatory*.

16. We watched the fireworks and we played many games.

17. What amazing fireworks we saw and how loud they were!

18. Sit in the front or stand near the back.

19. Should we buy candy or should we buy popcorn?

20. I love the Fourth of July but my brother prefers Valentine's Day.

Extra Practice, page 77.

Handbook
pages 527,
554–555

Writing Activity A Journal Entry

Write a journal entry telling about the way you celebrate a special holiday. Begin with a strong topic sentence to introduce your main idea.

APPLY GRAMMAR: Use at least two compound sentences. Underline each compound sentence you use.

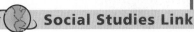

Social Studies Link

Sentence Punctuation

Grammar

RULES

Every sentence begins with a **capital letter**.

Our school is having a music concert.

A **declarative sentence** ends with a **period**.

I like to sing in the choir.

An **interrogative sentence** ends with a **question mark**.

Can you play the drums?

An **imperative sentence** ends with a **period**.

Please sing loudly.

An **exclamatory sentence** ends with an **exclamation mark**.

What a wonderful song you sang!

Use a **comma** before *and*, *but*, or *or* to join two sentences.

I sing, but my brother plays the drums.

THiNK AND WRITE

Sentences

How does knowing the rules for sentence punctuation help you with your writing? Write your ideas in your journal.

Sentences begin with a capital letter and end with a punctuation mark. Use a comma and a conjunction to join two sentences.

He plays the drums, and I play the flute.

capital letter   comma and conjunction   end punctuation

Guided Practice

Tell what punctuation is missing in each sentence and use correct capitalization.

EXAMPLE: what a beautiful sound that is
What a beautiful sound that is!

1. listen to the rhythm of the song

2. can some students dance to the music

3. how beautiful the music sounds

4. what time does the concert begin

5. i play the bells but I don't play the drums

10

B. **Join each pair of sentences to form a compound sentence. Write the new sentence. Use the correct capitalization and punctuation.**

11. the reporter is predicting rain. the sky is dark.

12. you could come in now. you could wait until it rains.

13. the lightning is dangerous. the thunder is loud.

14. mary turned on the radio. i watched the news.

15. spring rains are heavy. summer storms are fierce.

16. we stayed inside. we stayed away from the windows.

17. will there be strong winds? will there be tornadoes?

18. we practiced tornado drills. we stayed alert during the storms.

19. the bedroom is safe. the basement is safer.

20. my dog barks with fear. he hides downstairs.

C. **Challenge** **Write the sentences. Correct any errors in capitalization and punctuation. Circle all the conjunctions used to join compound sentences.**

21–25. a tornado can strike quickly and it can cause much damage people may not know it is coming or they may ignore the warnings. where is the best place to find shelter during a tornado a basement is the safest place but an enclosed room is also an option tornadoes can result in the loss of property and life

Writing Activity A Poster

Make a poster that describes what you would do in the event of a tornado. Use time-order words such as *first*, *next*, and *then* to organize your poster in a logical way.

APPLY GRAMMAR: Have a classmate proofread your poster to check for correct use of capital letters, commas, and end punctuation.

Science Link

Complete Subjects and Complete Predicates

RULES

Every sentence has a subject and a predicate.

The complete subject of a sentence includes all the words that tell *whom* or *what* the sentence is about.

> *The fifth-grade class* went to visit the White House.

The complete predicate of a sentence includes all the words that tell what the subject *does* or *is*.

> *All the students* rode in a bus.

Every sentence has two main parts: the subject and the predicate. The complete subject can be one word or many words. The complete predicate can be one word or many words. The complete predicate includes the verb of the sentence.

Complete Subject	Complete Predicate
The students	*learned about Congress.*

Guided Practice

Name the complete subject and the complete predicate of each sentence.

> **EXAMPLE:** Our class trip began yesterday.
> *Complete subject: Our class trip*
> *Complete predicate: began yesterday*

1. We learned about the three branches of government.
2. The United States Congress makes the laws.
3. The executive branch carries out the laws.
4. Judges on the Supreme Court interpret the laws.
5. Students and teachers like the Capitol Building.

REVIEW THE RULES

- The complete subject has all the words that tell *whom* or *what* the sentence is about. It can be one word or many words.

- The complete predicate has all the words that tell what the subject *is* or *does*. It can be one word or many words.

More Practice

A. Write each sentence. Draw one line under the complete subject. Draw two lines under the complete predicate.

6. The Constitution created the three branches of government.

7. James Madison and other leaders wrote the Constitution.

8. The first ten amendments are the Bill of Rights.

9. Congress added the Bill of Rights in 1791.

10. The writers wanted few changes to the Constitution.

B. Add a complete subject or a complete predicate to each group of words. Write the new sentence.

11. visited many famous buildings on our trip.

12. the House of Representatives.

13. saw the White House.

14. the president.

15. learned many things from the trip.

C. | Spiral Review | Write each sentence correctly. Draw a line between the complete subject and the complete predicate.

16. the president of the United States leads the country

17. people elect the members of Congress

18. the members of the House serve for two years

19. supreme Court judges hear important cases

20. our class trip taught us about government

Extra Practice, page 79.

Handbook
page 528

Writing Activity A Travel Article

Write about a class trip you have taken. Use the *I* point of view to describe what you saw.

APPLY GRAMMAR: Underline complete subjects once and complete predicates twice.

Simple Subjects

RULES

A simple subject is the main word or words in the complete subject. It tells exactly *whom* or *what* the sentence is about.

The students like their math class.

The simple subject tells you *whom* or *what* the sentence is about. Sometimes the simple subject is the same as the complete subject.

complete subject

Our math teacher loves numbers.

simple subject

complete subject

The students in the class learn about numbers.

simple subject

THINK AND WRITE

Sentences

In your journal, write how to identify the simple subject in a sentence.

Guided Practice

Name the simple subject in each sentence.

EXAMPLE: Some students finished their homework.
students

1. My fifth-grade class studies math.

2. Math is my favorite subject.

3. Many scientists work with numbers.

4. Some numbers are very large.

5. Rocket scientists use large numbers.

REVIEW THE RULES

- The main word in the complete subject is the simple subject.

More Practice

A. **Write the simple subject in each sentence.**

6. Our class learned about graphs.

7. A bar graph is one kind of graph.

8. Our task was to graph how many students wore red.

9. My friend Sam wore a red shirt.

10. Alexander's socks were red.

B. **Add a simple subject to each group of words. Write the new sentence.**

11. _____ drew a bar graph on the board.

12. _____ counted the number of red shirts.

13. _____ recorded the number on the graph.

14. _____ drew graphs in their notebooks.

15. _____ asked us to create our own graphs.

Handbook
page 528

C. **Spiral Review** **Add a complete subject to each sentence fragment. Write the new sentence. Draw one line under each complete subject and two lines under each simple subject.**

16. Shows numbers in picture form.

17. Use numbers to solve problems.

18. Explains the math lessons to the class.

19. Learned about many different types of graphs.

20. Is useful in everyday life.

Extra Practice, page 80.

Writing Activity A Paragraph

Write a paragraph about a topic for which you would like to create a graph. Tell why you chose the topic. Organize your reasons clearly.
APPLY GRAMMAR: Draw one line under each simple subject in your paragraph.

Math Link

Simple Predicates

The simple predicate tells you the action of the sentence. The simple predicate is also called the *verb*.

complete predicate

My softball team plays during the summer.

simple predicate

complete predicate

I hit three home runs last year.

simple predicate

THINK AND WRITE

Sentences

How can you identify the simple predicate in a sentence? Write your answer in your journal.

Guided Practice

Name the simple predicate in each sentence.

EXAMPLE: My team practices during the week.
Simple predicate: practices

1. My school has an annual softball game.
2. The fifth graders play against the teachers.
3. My entire school attends the game.
4. The crowd cheers for both teams.
5. The students receive the loudest cheers.
6. The teachers wear special T-shirts.
7. The students make their own T-shirts.
8. The students and teachers choose team names.
9. The team members meet before the big game.
10. Both teams are terrific.

REVIEW THE RULES

- The **simple predicate** is the main word or words in the complete predicate. It is always a verb.

More Practice

A. Write the simple predicate in each sentence.

11. The big game happened last week.

12. I pitched the entire game.

13. My friend Alex hit a home run.

14. The students shouted with excitement.

15. Mr. Rossi batted first for the teachers.

B. Write the complete predicate in each sentence. Underline the simple predicate.

16. The principal slid to second base.

17. We heard the cheers.

18. The custodian acted as our umpire.

19. Alice whacked a fly ball into the outfield.

20. Mrs. Anderson caught the ball with no trouble.

C. Spiral Review Add a complete subject or a complete predicate to each sentence fragment. Write the new sentence. Draw one line under the simple subject and two lines under the simple predicate.

21. Lasted for about an hour.

22. The score.

23. Tied the score with a home run.

24. The last batter.

25. Won the game.

Extra Practice, page 81.

Handbook
page 528

Writing Activity A Sportscast

Write a radio sportscast about a game you once played or saw. Give a clear play-by-play description of events.

APPLY GRAMMAR: Underline each simple predicate in your sportscast.

19

Combining Sentences: Compound Subjects

RULES

A compound subject has two or more simple subjects that have the same predicate.

> *Cities and suburbs are near each other.*

Compound subjects are joined by the word *and* or *or*.

> *Subways or trains take you home.*

You can combine two sentences with the same compound predicate by linking the subjects with *and* or *or*. Notice that the verb may change in the present tense.

> *Jay likes map puzzles. Carlos likes map puzzles.*

> *Jay and Carlos like map puzzles.*

THINK AND WRITE

Sentences

How can you tell if a sentence has a compound subject? Write your ideas in your journal.

Use the word *and* or *or* to join together the parts of a compound subject.

> *Maps show countries.*
> *Globes show countries.*

> *Maps and globes show countries.*
>   ↑   ↑
> compound subject

Guided Practice

Name the compound subject in each sentence.

EXAMPLE: Keys and symbols are found on maps.
Keys, symbols

1. Longitude and latitude help you locate places on a globe.
2. Mountains and valleys appear on a relief map.
3. The West or the South is the fastest-growing region of the United States.
4. Alice or Raynell lives in the Northeast.
5. Illinois and Iowa are in the Midwest.

REVIEW THE RULES

- A **compound subject** has two or more simple subjects that have the same predicate. Compound subjects are joined by the word *and* or *or*.

More Practice

A. **Write each sentence. Underline the compound subject.**

6. Rachel and Kim gave a report about natural resources.

7. Encyclopedias or the Internet gave them useful information.

8. Lumber and minerals are natural resources.

9. Oil, coal, and natural gas are fossil fuels.

10. Rachel or Kim wrote the report.

B. **Write each pair of sentences as one sentence with a compound subject.**

11. The students listened carefully. The teacher listened carefully.

12. Rachel worked hard. Kim worked hard.

13. Schools need to recycle. Businesses need to recycle.

14. Greg took notes. May took notes.

15. Mrs. Winton checks the notes. Mr. Hernandez checks the notes.

C. **Spiral Review** **Write the paragraph. Complete each sentence with a simple subject or a simple predicate, a compound subject or a compound predicate, or the correct punctuation mark.**

(**16.** ____) can help save our planet. People should also conserve water (**17.** ____) We (**18.** ____) water in order to live. (**19.** ____) can give us information about recycling and conservation. What an important goal this is (**20.** ____)

Extra Practice, page 82.

Handbook
page 529

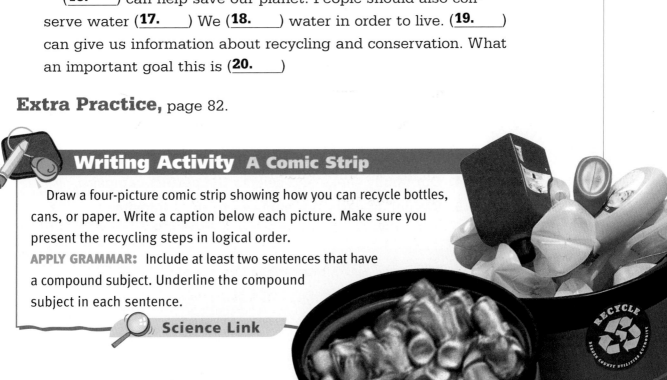

Writing Activity A Comic Strip

Draw a four-picture comic strip showing how you can recycle bottles, cans, or paper. Write a caption below each picture. Make sure you present the recycling steps in logical order.

APPLY GRAMMAR: Include at least two sentences that have a compound subject. Underline the compound subject in each sentence.

Science Link

Combining Sentences: Compound Predicates

RULES

A compound predicate has two or more simple predicates that have the same subject.

Emily jogs and hikes on trails.

Compound predicates are joined by the word *and* or *or*.

Our family skis or skates in the winter.

You can combine two sentences with the same subject by linking the predicates with *and*, *but*, or *or*.

Jim swims near camp. Jim fishes near camp.

Jim swims and fishes near camp.

THINK AND WRITE

Sentences

How does knowing about compound predicates help you combine sentences? Write your ideas in your journal.

Use the word *and* or *or* to join together the parts of a compound predicate.

My little brother stands and watches him.

↑   ↑

compound predicate

Guided Practice

Name the compound predicate in each sentence.

EXAMPLE: We plan and chart our route.
Compound predicate: plan, chart

1. We shop and choose special food for our trip.
2. We pack and check our bags before leaving.
3. Liana jokes and giggles in the car.
4. Our family seeks and selects the perfect campsite.
5. We pull or carry our supplies to the campsite.

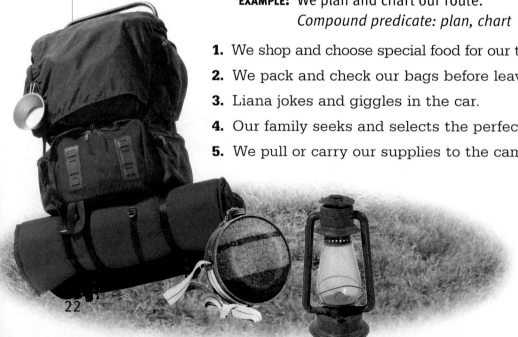

REVIEW THE RULES

- A **compound predicate** has two or more simple predicates that have the same subject and are joined by *and* or *or*.

More Practice

A. **Write each sentence. Underline the compound predicate.**

6. We hike or bicycle through the trails.

7. My mother hears and finds a rare bird.

8. We stop and notice a trail hidden by leaves.

9. My brother begs and pleads to follow the trail.

10. Our parents nod and agree to explore the path.

B. **Write each pair of sentences as one sentence with a compound predicate.**

11. We ride back to the campsite. We return to the campsite.

12. Everyone yawns after a tiring ride. Everyone sighs after a tiring ride.

13. Our family sings around the campfire. Our family talks around the campfire.

14. The bugs buzz around our heads. The bugs fly around our heads.

15. We rest peacefully under the stars. We dream peacefully under the stars.

C. **Spiral Review** **Write each sentence. Draw a line between the complete subject and the complete predicate. Circle compound subjects. Underline compound predicates.**

16. Everyone ran or jogged to the lake.

17. We saw two deer drinking from the stream.

18. My brother and I cleaned and swept the campsite.

19. My father filled and packed the car.

20. Family camping trips create wonderful memories.

Extra Practice, page 83.

Handbook
page 529

Writing Activity A Poem

Write a rhyming poem describing a family vacation or adventure. Use vivid words to create mental pictures for your reader.

APPLY GRAMMAR: Include at least one compound subject and one compound predicate in your poem.

Grammar

Correcting Run-on Sentences

— RULES —

A run-on sentence joins together two or more sentences that should be written separately.

> *My science class went on a nature hike my teacher led the way.*

You can correct a run-on sentence by separating two complete ideas into two sentences.

> *My science class went on a nature hike. My teacher led the way.*

You can correct a run-on sentence by rewriting it as a compound sentence. A compound sentence has two or more simple sentences that are joined by a comma and the word *and*, *but*, or *or*.

> *My science class went on a nature hike, and my teacher led the way.*

THINK AND WRITE

Sentences

How can correcting run-on sentences help you improve your writing? Write your responses in your journal.

Rewrite a run-on sentence as two separate sentences or as a compound sentence.

> *We walked one mile the park was still far away.*

> *We walked one mile. The park was still far away.*   or   *We walked one mile, but the park was still far away.*

Guided Practice

Tell which sentences are run-on sentences.

> **EXAMPLE:** The trail was rough we walked carefully.
> *Run-on sentence*

1. Mr. Simons asked us to look for wildflowers.
2. Selina found one flower Marcus found three.
3. Tricia saw poison ivy she did not touch it.
4. Some plants produce seeds inside their flowers.
5. We looked for dandelion seeds they were hard to find.

REVIEW THE RULES

- A run-on sentence joins sentences that should be written separately or as a compound sentence.

- Correct a run-on by writing it as two separate sentences or as a compound sentence.

More Practice

A. **Write *correct* or *run-on* for each sentence.**

6. Some seeds are carried through the air.

7. Butterflies pollinate some plants this helps the plant reproduce.

8. Mr. Simons pointed to a small flower.

9. A butterfly perched on a petal we saw the pollen.

10. Alberto sneezed loudly the butterfly flew away.

B. **Correct each run-on sentence. Write the new sentence.**

11. Mandy found acorns Mr. Simons said they were seeds.

12. The class followed the path the trees grew thicker along the way.

13. Plants were growing in the shade we identified some.

14. We collected leaves Krista decided to collect seeds.

15. We identified each leaf everyone planned to make books.

C. **Spiral Review** **Write the sentence in each pair. Then draw a line between the complete subject and the complete predicate.**

16. Mr. Simons and the class. Sean collected seeds.

17. We returned to school. Put our collections together.

18. Gave us supplies. The art teacher helped us.

19. Some students planned and organized their books. Others.

20. All of us learned from our hike. Enjoyed the trip.

Extra Practice, page 84.

Handbook
pages 526,
527, 528

Writing Activity A Journal Entry

Imagine that you are on a hike through the forest. Write a journal entry describing your hike. Include your feelings about the nature all around you. Let your voice come through.

APPLY GRAMMAR: Have a partner read your journal entry aloud. Correct any run-on sentences.

Mixed Review

- The complete subject of a sentence includes all the words that tell *whom* or *what* the sentence is about.

- The complete predicate of a sentence includes all the words that tell what the subject *does* or *is*.

- The simple subject is the main word or words in the complete subject.

- The simple predicate is the main word or words in the complete predicate.

- A compound subject has two or more simple subjects that have the same predicate. You can combine two sentences by using a compound subject.

- A compound predicate has two or more simple predicates that have the same subject. You can combine two sentences by using a compound predicate.

- A run-on sentence joins together two sentences that should be written separately. Correct a run-on by writing it as two sentences or by writing it as a compound sentence.

QUICK WRITE

Sentences
Write two sentences containing compound subjects and two sentences containing compound predicates.

Practice

A. Write each sentence. Draw a line between the complete subject and the complete predicate. Then draw one line under the simple subject and two lines under the simple predicate.

1. The United States began as thirteen colonies.

2. People came from many different countries.

3. Many early immigrants arrived on ships.

4. Each colony received a charter.

5. Native Americans lived in North America before the colonists.

B. **Write each sentence. Underline the part of the sentence that is named in parentheses.**

6. The Southern Colonies produced cotton. (simple subject)

7. The first settlers cut and assembled logs for cabins. (compound predicate)

8. Early settlers made their clothing with linen. (complete subject)

9. Furs and hides were also used to make clothing. (compound subject)

10. People cured themselves because doctors were scarce. (simple predicate)

11. Plants or roots were brewed for medicine. (compound subject)

12. Children attended classes in one-room schoolhouses. (simple predicate)

13. The blacksmith made shoes for horses. (complete subject)

14. The cobbler made shoes for people. (complete predicate)

15. Colonists developed many survival skills. (simple subject)

C. **Challenge** **Rewrite the following paragraph. Correct each run-on sentence. When you have finished writing, you should have five sentences.**

16–20. Colonial children lived a life different from the children of today they had very few toys. Many of their toys were made from common objects Girls would make dolls from corn husks boys would play with toys carved from wood.

Handbook
pages 526–529

Writing Activity A Diary Entry

Write a diary entry as if you were a young person living in colonial times. Describe what you would do on a typical day. Use different kinds of sentences to make your writing flow smoothly.

APPLY GRAMMAR: Include one sentence with a compound subject and one sentence with a compound predicate. Draw one line under the compound subject and two lines under the compound predicate.

🌐 **Social Studies Link**

Common Errors with Sentence Fragments and Run-on Sentences

Writing sentence fragments or run-on sentences is a mistake that writers sometimes make. This chart shows examples of sentence fragments and run-on sentences. Notice how you can correct each example to express a complete thought.

Common Errors	Examples	Corrected Sentences
The fragment does not have a predicate.	A democracy.	A democracy is a form of government.
The fragment does not have a subject or any punctuation.	Participate in the government	The people participate in the government.
Two sentences are joined with only a comma.	All adults should vote, people decide questions by voting.	All adults should vote. People decide questions by voting.
Two sentences are joined with no punctuation.	We vote for leaders they work for us.	We vote for leaders, and they work for us.

THINK AND WRITE

Sentences

In your journal, write how you can check if you have written complete sentences.

— REVIEW THE RULES —

SENTENCES

Every sentence has a subject and a predicate and expresses a complete thought.

- A sentence fragment does not express a complete thought.

- You can often correct a sentence fragment by adding a subject or a predicate.

- A run-on sentence has two or more sentences that should stand alone.

- You can correct a run-on sentence by rewriting it as two separate sentences or as a compound sentence.

- Remember Every sentence begins with a capital letter and ends with a punctuation mark.

More Practice

A. **Read each group of words. Write** *fragment* **if the words are a sentence fragment. Write** *sentence* **if the words are a complete sentence.**

1. Democracy is a form of government.

2. Began in Greece.

3. In a democracy, people have freedom of speech.

4. Many governments.

5. Choose their leaders.

B. **Rewrite each sentence fragment to make it a complete sentence. Use capitalization and end punctuation correctly.**

6. Democracy.

7. The citizens of a democracy.

8. Make decisions.

9. Have many opportunities.

10. Express their opinions.

C. **Rewrite each run-on sentence as two separate sentences or as a compound sentence. Use correct capitalization and end punctuation.**

11. Democracy began in ancient Greece it developed slowly.

12. Did kings and queens rule countries did presidents rule?

13. What terrible rulers some kings were how unhappy the people felt!

14. The Greeks threw out these rulers, the people decided to share the power.

15. This was the beginning of democracy it would not reach other countries for centuries.

Grammar Troubleshooter, pages 506–509

Handbook
page 526

Writing Activity **A Letter**

Write a letter to your congressperson describing what living in a democracy means to you. Be sure to use the correct form for a business letter.

APPLY GRAMMAR: Use complete sentences. Check for sentence fragments and run-on sentences. Begin each sentence with a capital letter and end with the correct punctuation mark.

 Social Studies Link

29

Mechanics and Spelling

Directions

Read the passage and decide which type of mistake, if any, appears in each underlined section. Choose the letter for your answer. If there is no error, choose "No mistake."

Sample

I'll always remember the first soccer goal I ever made. <u>the score of the big game was tied</u>. Everyone
(1)
<u>in the croud was cheering</u> as we moved down the field.
(2)
My teammate passed the ball to me. I took a <u>deep breath,</u>
(3)
<u>and I kicked the winning goal</u>. It's a day I'll never forget.

1 A Spelling

   B Capitalization

   C Punctuation

   D No mistake

2 F Spelling

   G Capitalization

   H Punctuation

   J No mistake

3 A Spelling

   B Capitalization

   C Punctuation

   D No mistake

Test Tip
When you come to a new section, read the directions carefully.

Grammar and Usage

Directions

Read the passage and choose the word or group of words that belongs in each space. Choose the letter for your answer.

Sample

Deep-sea monsters don't exist, or do they? Some people __(1)__ that giant squids are just such monsters. These ten-armed creatures can weigh as much as 2,000 pounds. They live deep in the ocean. People __(2)__ find them 600 to 1200 feet below the surface. Since these animals live in such deep water, very few people __(3)__ giant squids. That's probably why __(4)__ are sometimes referred to as "monsters of the deep."

Read the entire passage first. Then select the tense that fits here.

An adverb, not an adjective, tells more about a verb.

Verbs must agree with their subjects.

Pronouns must agree with the nouns to which they refer.

1 A think

  B thought

  C were thinking

  D had thought

2 F usual

  G usually

  H more usual

  J most usual

3 A has ever seen

  B have ever seen

  C is ever seeing

  D was ever seeing

4 F it

  G you

  H they

  J we

TIME FOR KIDS Writer's Notebook

RESEARCH

RESEARCH

I like to use **primary sources** when I research a story. I read newspaper accounts, watch TV news, and listen to interviews with people who were at the event. It's easier for me to understand what happened when someone tells about it firsthand.

COMPOSITION SKILLS

WRITING WELL

When I write, first I think of my **main idea**. That's the most important information to tell my readers. Then I think of the **details**—the facts, figures, and descriptions—to support my main idea. They bring my writing to life and keep my readers interested in what I write.

VOCABULARY SKILLS

USING WORDS

<u>First</u>, <u>next</u>, <u>then</u>, and <u>finally</u> are **time-order words**. They tell the order in which things happen. Time-order words help my readers keep track of the events I'm writing about. They also help me mark the start, middle, and end of a story. What time-order words can you think of?

Read Now!

As you read the photo essay, jot down the main idea. Also write down some supporting details that show what kind of a person and ballplayer Sammy Sosa is.

SOSA
21

TIME
FOR KIDS
PHOTO ESSAY

SLAMMIN' SAMMY

Baseball's Sammy Sosa thrilled fans with his home runs.

A HOME-RUN KING

One of the most exciting times in baseball history took place in 1998. Mark McGwire of the St. Louis Cardinals and Sammy Sosa of the Chicago Cubs were slugging it out to break the all-time home-run record set by Roger Maris in 1961.

First, McGwire would pull ahead. Next, Sosa would tie. It was like a seesaw on the field. Finally, at the end of the season, McGwire held the record of 70 home runs compared to Sosa's 66.

Everyone may know about Mark McGwire, but what about Sammy Sosa? As a boy, Sosa shined shoes and sold oranges in his home country, the Dominican Republic. Sosa had a talent for baseball, but his family was so poor that his first baseball glove was a milk carton turned inside out.

Sosa has had his ups and downs on the field. He had a lot of strikeouts. In fact, he led the league in them in 1997. "The reason I struck out so much is because I wanted to do everything myself," Sosa said. "Now I am willing to take a walk or a base hit. I'm having a lot of fun and I learned to be patient. I enjoyed each and every home run I hit in 1998. Each one was a gift."

Sosa slams another home run out of the park.

interNET CONNECTION Go to **www.mhschool.com/language-arts** for more information on the topic.

Sammy Sosa
warms up before
every game.

Brian Bahr/Allsport

Mark McGwire and
Sammy Sosa became
good friends during
their home-run race.

Vincent Laforet/Allsport

Jed Jacobsohn/Allsport

Write Now!

Although Sammy Sosa did not set the home-run
record, he came very close. He rose to the challenge
and showed his abilities. Write about a challenge you
have had in school or at home.

Note-Taking and Summarizing

Taking notes will help you remember what you have heard or read. When you take notes, write just enough words to help you remember the main ideas and the important facts or supporting details. Then **summarize** the information in your own words, using as few words as possible. A good way to take notes for a research report is to write on 3 x 5 index cards.

Look at the notes that a student took for a social studies report on Christopher Columbus's voyage to the Americas in 1492. The source that she used was a primary source—the log, or journal, of Christopher Columbus. The student wanted to know what the meeting was like between Columbus and the first people he saw in the Americas. She felt that his journal would give a firsthand account of his thoughts and feelings. Read Columbus's journal entry below. Then read the notes that the student took.

October 12

At dawn we saw . . . people, and I went ashore in the ship's boat. . . .

The people here call this island Guanahaní in their language, and their speech is very fluent, although I do not understand any of it. They are friendly and well-dispositioned people who bear no arms except for small spears, and they have no iron. . . .

They traded and gave everything they had with good will. . . .

The Log of Christopher Columbus, translated by Robert
H. Fuson, entry for Oct. 12, 1492

Question: What was the meeting like between Columbus
and the first people he saw in the Americas?

The meeting between Columbus and the first people he saw
went well. He thought that the people were smart , friendly,
and peaceful. Columbus says, "They traded and gave
everything they had with good will."

*Write the source of
your information in
order to refer to it in
your report or to go
back to it to look for
more information.*

*Summarize the
information in your
own words. Write
only the main ideas
and supporting facts
or details.*

Go to:
www.mhschool.
com/language-
arts **for more
information on
the topic.**

Practice

**A. Look at the journal entry and the notes. Write answers to
the following questions.**

1. On what source is the student taking notes?

2. Is the book a primary source? How do you know?

3. What question does the student want answered?

4. Why is it important to take notes?

5. Why do you need to summarize the notes you take?

**B. Read this paragraph from the autobiography of Olaudah
Equiano. Equiano was an 11-year-old boy living in West
Africa in 1756 when slave traders kidnapped him to take him
to North America. Take notes to answer the question below.**

The first thing I saw when I arrived at the coast was the sea
and the slave ship waiting to pick up its cargo. The sight of the
slave ship amazed me. My amazement turned to terror when I
was carried on board. . . . We were packed together in chains
so tightly we could hardly move or turn over. The cramped
surroundings and the deadly heat almost suffocated us.

**Question: What were conditions like on board a
slave ship?**

Writing Activity A Summary

Take notes on a primary source, such as a journal, a letter, or a newspaper article. Then write a summary paragraph of what you have read.

Vocabulary: Time-Order Words

DEFINITION

A time-order word or phrase tells when events happen and in what order.

first	last	as soon as	before
second	finally	one day	after
third	yesterday	the next day	now
next	today	last night	in the meantime
then	tomorrow	a long time ago	meanwhile

THINK AND WRITE

Time-Order Words

How can using time-order words help you organize events in your writing? Write your ideas in your journal.

Read the paragraph below. Look at the highlighted words.

Last summer, my family went on vacation to an amusement park. As soon as we arrived, I headed for the long line at the roller coaster. After several rides, my parents convinced me to see a show. Before lunch, I rode on a water ride and got soaking wet! Finally, it was time to head back to the hotel. The next day, I was first in line for the roller coaster.

Practice

A. Write the sentences. Underline the time-order words.

1. Before our vacation, I helped plan the trip.

2. First, we looked through travel brochures to find a location.

3. Then, I showed my parents the amusement park I wanted to visit.

4. Finally, we agreed that the park was the perfect destination.

5. My father called for hotel reservations the next day.

B. Choose a word or phrase from the Word Bank to complete each sentence.

before	second	next	someday	then
soon	last	tomorrow	yesterday	finally

6. I'm planning to go on a trip _____ .

7. _____ I wrote a list of items to pack for the trip.

8. I always check my packed belongings _____ I lock the suitcase.

9. This will be the _____ trip I take before school starts.

10. _____ it will be time to head for the airport.

C. [Grammar Link] **Write these sentences in the correct order. Punctuate each sentence correctly.**

11. At last, the car was fixed, and we arrived at our hotel ___

12. Next, we loaded the suitcases into the car and drove away ___

13. Yesterday was the first day of our trip ___

14. Oh, my, after several hours of driving, the car broke down ___

15. Before leaving home, I made sure we packed everything ___

Writing Activity A Journal Entry

Write a journal entry about something exciting that happened to you on a trip or a vacation. Tell how you felt about the trip and what made it a memorable experience. Include at least three time-order words or phrases in your writing.

APPLY GRAMMAR: Make sure that each of your sentences has a simple subject and a simple predicate.

Composition: Main Idea

A writer usually states the main idea of a paragraph in a topic sentence. The other sentences in the paragraph add details to develop or support the main idea.

GUIDELINES

- The main idea tells what a piece of writing is about.

- The main idea is usually stated in a topic sentence.

- In a paragraph, all the sentences should work together to support one main idea.

- Detail sentences support the main idea by giving examples, concrete details, facts, or opinions.

- Organize the main idea and supporting details in a logical order.

- Use time-order words, such as *first*, *next*, and *finally*, to connect ideas and to show the order, or sequence, of events.

THINK AND WRITE

Main Idea

Why is it important for a paragraph to have a main idea? Explain your answer in your journal.

Read this paragraph about a personal experience. Notice that the writer states the main idea and uses supporting details to develop that idea and make it clearer.

The topic sentence states the main idea of the paragraph.

A supporting detail helps to develop the main idea or make it clearer.

A time-order word helps to connect ideas and show the order of events.

I met my best friend Ashley in an unusual way. On the first day of summer vacation, Ashley and her family moved into the house next door. The day after they moved in, she and her brother were playing catch in their front yard. Ashley threw the ball too hard, and it sailed over her brother's head, right through my bedroom window! After that surprising introduction, we became best friends. Now we all play ball almost every day. However, these days we do our best to avoid windows.

Practice

A. Write the following paragraph. Circle the topic sentence. Underline each detail sentence.

1–5.   Winning the pie-eating contest was the most delicious victory I've ever had. I love cream pie, so my father suggested that I enter the pie-eating contest at the fair. Each contestant was given three pies to eat as quickly as possible. Then the judges blew a whistle, and everyone began to eat. A messy four minutes later, I was crowned the winner.

B. Write a sentence to state a main idea for each of the following topics.

   6. My Favorite Food

   7. My Best Performance

   8. The Most Exciting Game Ever

   9. My Favorite Summer Activity

   10. The Most Unforgettable Day at School

C.   **Grammar Link**   **11–15.** Write one detail sentence for each of the main-idea sentences you wrote for Practice B. Try to use one of each of these four types of sentences: declarative, interrogative, imperative, and exclamatory.

Writing Activity A Paragraph

   Write a paragraph about an unforgettable experience in your life. Be sure that all the sentences in the paragraph work together to develop and support the main idea.

APPLY GRAMMAR: Be sure that your paragraph includes at least one of each of the four types of sentences. Above each sentence, write *declarative*, *interrogative*, *imperative*, or *exclamatory* to show the kind of sentence it is.

Better Sentences

Directions

Read the passage. Some sections are underlined. The underlined sections may be one of the following:

- Incomplete sentences
- Run-on sentences
- Correctly written sentences that should be combined
- Correctly written sentences that do not need to be rewritten

Choose the best way to write each underlined section. If the underlined section needs no change, choose "No mistake."

> *If a sentence does not have a subject and a predicate, it is an incomplete sentence.*

> *Look for two sentences that are incorrectly joined. This group of words is a run-on.*

Sample

Our flag has changed many times. <u>One early flag had thirteen stars. And thirteen stripes</u>. As more states entered the **(1)**
Union, the flag was redesigned. <u>Today's flag shows thirteen red and white alternating stripes it has fifty white stars on a field of blue</u>. **(2)**

1 A One early flag had thirteen stars and thirteen stripes.

   B One early flag. Had thirteen stars and thirteen stripes.

   C There was one early flag. With thirteen stars and thirteen stripes.

   D No mistake

2 F Today's flag shows thirteen red and white alternating stripes. And fifty white stars on a field of blue.

   G Today's flag shows thirteen red and white alternating stripes, and it has fifty white stars on a field of blue.

   H Today's flag shows thirteen red and white alternating stripes, it has fifty white stars on a field of blue.

   J No mistake

> **Test Tip**
> Read all the answer choices carefully before you make a selection.

Vocabulary and Comprehension

Directions

Read the passage. Then read each question that follows the passage. Decide which is the best answer to each question. Choose the letter for that answer.

Sample

"We won't let rain ruin our vacation, Emmett!" exclaimed my dad as he looked out the window at the dripping sky. We had driven three hours to the beach, but it didn't look as if the weather would cooperate. My sister and I imagined being trapped in our hotel room.

My sister, Caryn, sat moping in our hotel room while I watched our parents pack picnic lunches. Dad grabbed the beach umbrella and headed for the door.

We started walking toward the beach. We were drenched in no time, but we were laughing. <u>Finally</u>, we arrived at the beach. We sat and ate under the beach umbrella. After lunch, we splashed and swam in the ocean. As we were leaving, the rain stopped.

"Don't worry," laughed Dad, "we won't let a little dry weather ruin our vacation!"

> *Time-order words can help you understand when story events take place.*

1 How do you think Emmett and Caryn felt when they first saw the rain?

  A afraid **C** disappointed

  B excited **D** happy

2 In this passage, the word *Finally* means—

  F now **H** soon

  G at last **J** next

Seeing Like a Writer

Imagine that you could step inside one of these pictures. Think about how you would feel. What would you write to a friend about your experience?

Mother and Child by Mary Cassatt

Writing from Pictures

1. Write a question about each picture. Then write a declarative sentence for each answer.

2. Imagine that you are one of the people in a picture. Write a caption about your experience. Use the *I* point of view to tell about your thoughts and feelings.

3. Choose two pictures. How do they show that adults can teach you important lessons? Write a paragraph to explain.

Apply Grammar: Include the four types of sentences. Above each sentence, write *declarative*, *interrogative*, *imperative*, or *exclamatory*.

Personal Narrative

Can you think of an interesting story to tell someone about yourself? A story that tells about a personal experience is called a personal narrative. A personal narrative brings to life a memorable event. It tells what happened and how the writer felt about the experience.

Learning from Writers

Read the following examples of a personal narrative. What stories do the writers share? Think about the words the writers use to tell the sequence of events. What did they say to show how they felt about the experience?

THINK AND WRITE

Purpose
Why do people like to write personal narratives? Why do other people like to read them? Jot down your thoughts in your journal.

Saying Good-Bye

The night before Aunt Waka left, Mrs. Sugar invited us all to her house for dinner. It was the first time we all got invited together, and Mrs. Sugar used her best china and her plated silverware and baked a big ham.

She gave Aunt Waka a beaded coin purse and several hugs and said she might even go to Japan someday to visit her.

And Aunt Waka said, "I'll be waiting for you," just the way she said she'd wait for me.

The next morning, Mama, Papa, Joji, and I took Aunt Waka to San Francisco to the same pier where we'd gone to meet her. Another big ship was berthed there, waiting to take her back to Japan.

—Yoshiko Uchida, from *A Jar of Dreams*

Starting the Week

I'm a pretty easygoing sort of person, and it takes a lot to get me upset. When I woke up yesterday, I had no idea of what was in store. There was a huge amount of math homework due, but I had done the work in no time. I was looking forward to the play rehearsal, too.

At school, the math teacher collected our homework. No wonder it had seemed so easy—I had done the wrong pages! The rest of the morning was fine, except I nearly sprained my jaw trying to eat the snack I had packed in my backpack. It turned out to be a rubber cookie that Wendy had slipped in.

At last it was time for our play rehearsal. "Break a leg," said Denise. The doctor laughed so hard when I told him the story that I almost kicked him with the plaster cast he had just put on my left foot.

—Markus Baker

PRACTICE AND APPLY

Thinking Like a Reader

1. In the correct order, name the sequence of events from "Saying Good-Bye."

2. Summarize "Starting the Week" by telling its beginning, middle, and end.

Thinking Like a Writer

3. What time-order words did the author use to tell you the order of events in "Saying Good-Bye"?

4. How did the author of "Starting the Week" use paragraphs to organize his personal narrative?

5. **Reading Across Texts** Compare the personal experiences of the two writers. Write about how their feelings might have been alike or different.

Personal Narrative

GUIDELINES

A personal narrative is a form of writing that tells what happened to you, including what you did and how you felt about the experience. A good personal narrative:

▶ tells a story from **personal experience**.

▶ expresses the writer's feelings by using the **first-person point of view**.

▶ has an interesting **beginning, middle**, and **end**.

▶ shares events in a **sequence** that makes sense.

▶ uses **time-order words** to connect ideas and show the sequence of events.

▶ A Personal Experience

Reread "Saying Good-Bye" by Yoshiko Uchida on page 46. Who is the narrative about? How do you think the writer felt?

> And Aunt Waka said, "I'll be waiting for you," just the way she said she'd wait for me.

The word *me* refers to the author, who is also the narrator. *Aunt Waka* refers to the author's aunt. These clues tell you that the narrative is about these two people.

▶ First-Person Point of View

Yoshiko Uchida's personal narrative uses this sentence to tell what happened during a family dinner. How do you know that the account is based on the author's personal experience? From whose point of view is the story being told?

> It was the first time we all got invited together, and Mrs. Sugar used her best china and her plated silverware and baked a big ham.

The word *we* indicates that the author was part of the action and is describing her personal observations.

▶ An Interesting Beginning, Middle, and End

A strong narrative needs to include an interesting beginning, middle, and end. Reread the following sentence from the final paragraph.

> Another big ship was berthed there, waiting to take her back to Japan.

What did you learn about the end of the visit?

▶ Sequence of Events

Yoshiko Uchida tells the events of her aunt's visit in a logical order. Notice that the first sentence tells the reader when the events in the paragraph begin.

> The night before Aunt Waka left, Mrs. Sugar invited us all to her house for dinner.

What phrase tells you when the event took place?

▶ Time-Order Words

To help your readers understand your experience from beginning to end, you can use time-order words and phrases. Some examples of time-order words are *first, before,* and *next.*

> The next morning, Mama, Papa, Joji, and I took Aunt Waka to San Francisco to the same pier where we'd gone to meet her.

What time-order phrase did the author use?

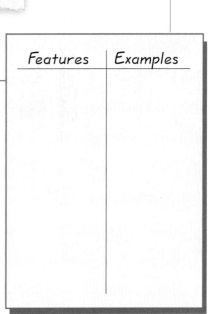

PRACTICE AND APPLY

Create a Features Chart

1. List the features of a good personal narrative.
2. Reread "Starting the Week" by Markus Baker on page 47.
3. Write one example of each feature of Markus's writing.
4. Write what you liked best about Markus's personal narrative.

Features	Examples

Prewrite

A personal narrative is a true story that describes an event or experience from your life. Writing a personal narrative allows you to share an experience with other people.

Purpose and Audience

The purpose of writing a personal narrative is to express your thoughts and feelings about an experience. It is also to interest and entertain your readers, or audience.

Before writing, you need to think about your audience. Who will be reading your personal narrative? How will you speak to your audience through your writing? How will you order your events and present your ideas?

Choose a Topic

Begin your writing by making a list of your memorable experiences. Think about which experience you would like most to share.

After choosing a topic, **explore ideas** by making a list of events or details that you remember about your experience. Also include some of your thoughts and feelings about the events. Later, you will organize these ideas.

THINK AND WRITE

Audience

How will your audience influence the topic you choose for your personal narrative? Write your ideas in your journal.

Here is how I explored my ideas.

Meeting My Summer Goal

Set a goal to swim across the lake at camp

Made a plan to meet my goal

Told my family about my plan

Asked the counselors to help me train

My favorite counselor's name was Derek

Trained for weeks

The water shined

People came to cheer me on

Linda videotaped the event

Someone rowed alongside me in a boat

I ended up meeting my goal

Organize • Main Idea and Details

A personal narrative develops from one main idea. You then add supporting details to the main idea to develop your narrative. To plan your personal narrative, you can use a main idea map. Some details may not be important to include in your story. What details from his list did the writer leave out of his chart?

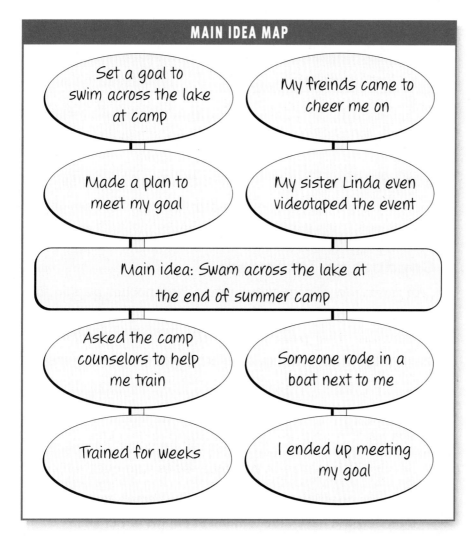

MAIN IDEA MAP

Set a goal to swim across the lake at camp

My freinds came to cheer me on

Made a plan to meet my goal

My sister Linda even videotaped the event

Main idea: Swam across the lake at the end of summer camp

Asked the camp counselors to help me train

Someone rode in a boat next to me

Trained for weeks

I ended up meeting my goal

Checklist ✓
Prewriting

- Did you think about your purpose and audience?

- Did you make a list of experiences?

- Did you choose a topic and explore ideas?

- Did you use a chart to organize your ideas?

- Did you support your main idea with important details?

- Do you need to do any research?

PRACTICE AND APPLY

Plan Your Own Personal Narrative

1. Think about your purpose and audience.

2. Brainstorm a list of memorable experiences.

3. Choose a topic and explore ideas about it.

4. Use a main idea map to organize your ideas.

Prewrite • Research and Inquiry

▶ Writer's Resources

You may have to do research to get more information for your personal narrative. Begin by writing a list of questions. Then decide what resources you need in order to answer each question.

What Else Do I Need to Know?	Where Can I Find the Information?
What is the name of the lake?	E-mail a counselor to find out.
Who rowed alongside me in the boat?	Watch home movie of that day at camp.
How long did I train?	Read my diary entries for that summer.

▶ Conduct an Interview

An interview is a conversation with another person for the purpose of gaining information. One person asks questions, and the other person answers. An interview can take place in person, in writing, on the telephone, or by e-mail.

STRATEGIES FOR INTERVIEWING

- Decide the information you need. Write your questions.

- Send the questions ahead of time. The person you interview will have time to think about his or her answers.

- Take clear notes and organize them right after the interview so you won't forget the information.

- Be polite and friendly. Always thank the person at the end of the interview.

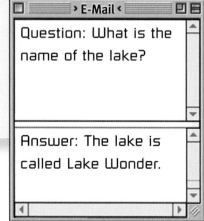

▸ E-Mail ◂

Question: What is the name of the lake?

Answer: The lake is called Lake Wonder.

▶ Study Personal Records

Souvenirs, photographs, journals, and home movies can be useful sources of information. Look for specific details in these sources that will help your readers "see" the event.

▶ Use Your Research

This writer learned something important in his e-mail interview. He also found information in his diary and in a video his sister made. How did he change his chart?

PREWRITE

DRAFT

REVISE

PROOFREAD

PUBLISH

Handbook
pages 564, 565, 574, 575

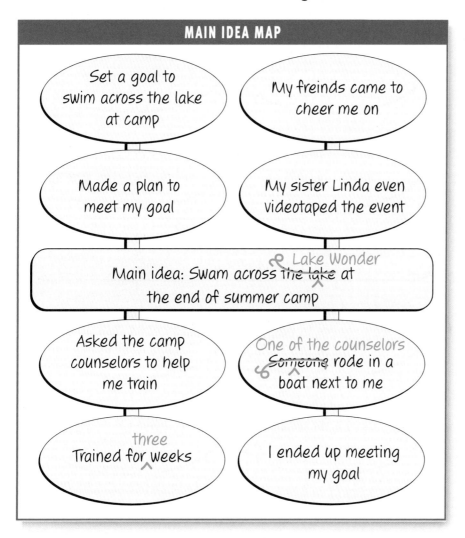

MAIN IDEA MAP

Set a goal to swim across the lake at camp

My freinds came to cheer me on

Made a plan to meet my goal

My sister Linda even videotaped the event

Main idea: Swam across the lake *Lake Wonder* at the end of summer camp

Asked the camp counselors to help me train

One of the counselors Someone rode in a boat next to me

Trained for *three* weeks

I ended up meeting my goal

PRACTICE AND APPLY

Review Your Plan

1. Look at your main idea map.

2. List questions you have about your topic.

3. Identify the resources you will need to find answers.

4. Add new information you gather to your chart.

Checklist ✓

Research and Inquiry

- ■ Did you write a list of questions?

- ■ Did you identify possible resources?

- ■ Did you take notes on the information you found?

- ■ Did you add the new information to your chart?

Draft

Before you begin writing your personal narrative, review your main idea map. Think about the paragraphs you could write to support the main idea. Include details in a logical order.

> *Main idea for first paragraph: Why I decided to swim across the lake.*

✓ Checklist

Drafting

- Does your narrative suit your purpose and audience?

- Did you include time-order words to show the sequence of events?

- Did you include your thoughts and feelings to make your writing personal?

- Did you use sensory details that will help your reader create a mental picture?

- Is your main idea clear, and do your details help your readers feel as though they were at the event?

MAIN IDEA MAP

Set a goal to swim across the lake at camp

My freinds came to cheer me on

Made a plan to meet my goal

My sister Linda even videotaped the event

Main idea: Swam across the lake at the end of summer camp   *Lake Wonder*

Asked the camp counselors to help me train

One of the counselors Someone rode in a boat next to me

three Trained for weeks

I ended up meeting my goal

> *Main idea for second paragraph: How I trained.*

> *Main idea for third paragraph: How I met my goal.*

Look at how this writer used the ideas in his map to write a first draft. He created paragraphs by telling his story in order and by using details.

DRAFT

Last summer, I went to camp. I go to the same camp every year. Last summer was diffrent. That was the summer I decided to swim across Lake Wonder.

> Main idea of first paragraph

I knew it wouldn't be easy. I made a plan to meet my goal. I asked the camp counselors to help me train. After three weeks of training in and out of the water, it was time. My freinds came to cheer me on as I jumped in and began to swim. My sister Linda even videotaped the event one of the counselors rowed in a boat next to me for safety. It wasn't easy, but I made it. Meeting my goal was the perfect end to the summer

> Supporting details tell how the writer trained for the swimming event.

> Supporting details tell about the events and how the writer felt about the experience.

PRACTICE AND APPLY

Draft Your Own Personal Narrative

1. Review your prewriting chart.
2. Write about the events in the order they happened.
3. Add details that tell about the main idea.
4. Use the *I* point of view throughout to tell about the events and your feelings.

TECHNOLOGY

Find out how to adjust line spacing on your computer. Double-space your draft so you will have more room to make revisions.

Revise

Elaborate

One way to improve your writing is to elaborate. When you elaborate, you add important ideas and details that might be missing from your writing. When you revise your personal narrative, you may need to tell more about your feelings.

The writer added details to let his audience know how he felt.

> After three weeks of training in and out of the
> *I finally felt ready*
> water, it ~~was time~~.

The writer added the name of the camp to give more true information to his story.

> *Camp Wilderness*
> Last summer, I went to ~~camp~~.

Word Choice

When you are writing, it is important to choose the right words for your topic and audience.

In a personal narrative, choose words that will help you tell the events of your story in order. This will enable your reader to "see" the events in the order in which they happened.

> *First,*   *Next,*
> I made a plan to meet my goal. I asked the camp
>   *Then,*
> counselors to help me train. After three weeks of
>   *I finally felt ready*
> training in and out of the water, it ~~was time~~.

TIME-ORDER WORDS

first

next

then

later

last

finally

now

one day

before

after

after that

as soon as

yesterday

today

tomorrow

56

Better Sentences

As you continue to revise your draft, check your sentences to make sure they fit together well and flow smoothly. Read the sentences aloud. How do they sound? Have you included different types of sentences? By using a variety of sentences, such as questions, exclamations, and commands, you can make your writing more interesting to read.

Sometimes you can use an exclamation to show emotion. Notice how the writer expresses his strong feelings about having achieved his goal.

> How excited I was when I made it across the lake
> ~~It wasn't easy, but I made it~~

PRACTICE AND APPLY

Revise Your Own Personal Narrative

1. Use time-order words to show the sequence of events.

2. Use vivid and exact words to create a clear image in the reader's mind.

3. Add important details that will make your writing clearer and more accurate.

5. **Grammar** Did you use different types of sentences to make your writing more interesting?

PREWRITE

DRAFT

REVISE

PROOFREAD

PUBLISH

Handbook
page 526

TECHNOLOGY

Review your draft to see if the sentences follow a logical order. Do the ideas flow smoothly? If not, try moving paragraphs or sentences around by cutting and pasting text.

Revise • Peer Conferencing

Take a break from your writing. Exchange your draft with a partner, and check each other's work. Your partner may be able to give you some new ideas or suggestions on how to improve your narrative.

This beginning makes me want to read more!

This helps me to see your plan.

You should describe the water so that your readers can see it.

I think you need a third paragraph.

Last summer, I went to camp. I go to the same camp every year. Last summer was diffrent.

That was the summer I decided to swim across Lake Wonder.

I knew it wouldn't be easy. I made a plan to meet my goal. I asked the camp counselors to help me train. After three weeks of training in and out of the water, it was time. My freinds came to cheer me on as I jumped in and began to swim. My sister Linda even videotaped the event one of the counselors rowed in a boat next to me for safety. It wasn't easy, but I made it. Meeting my goal was the perfect end to the summer

Conferencing for the Reader

- Are features of a personal narrative included in your partner's piece?
  - personal experience
  - first-person point of view
  - interesting beginning, middle, and end
  - logical sequence
  - time-order words
  - strong ending
- Be sure to tell your partner what's good about the piece as well as what needs improvement.

As you revise your personal narrative, consider the comments and suggestions your conferencing partner gave you. This writer made some changes based on his partner's suggestions.

PREWRITE

DRAFT

REVISE

PROOFREAD

PUBLISH

REVISE

The Perfect Summer Ending

Last summer, I went to camp. (Camp Wilderness) I go to the same camp every year. Last summer was diffrent.

That was the summer I decided to swim across Lake Wonder.

First, I knew it wouldn't be easy. I made a plan to meet my goal. Next, I asked the camp counselors to help me train. Then, After three weeks of training in and out of the shimmering blue water, ~~it was time.~~ I finally felt ready My freinds came to cheer me on as I jumped in and began to swim. My sister Linda even videotaped the event one of the counselors rowed in a boat next to me for safety. ~~It wasn't easy,~~ How excited I was when I made it across the lake ~~but I made it.~~ Meeting my goal was the perfect end to the summer

PRACTICE AND APPLY

Revise Your Own Personal Narrative

1. Read your draft aloud or have your partner read it to you. Listen to the way the words flow. How does it sound?

2. Add vivid words that describe.

3. Use the notes from your peer conference to help you revise your draft.

4. Add an interesting title that will "grab" your reader's interest.

Checklist ✔
Revising

- Does your story suit your purpose and audience?

- Did you describe a personal experience?

- Do you need to elaborate on any part of your narrative?

- Did you use colorful, exact words to describe the experience and your feelings about it?

- Did you use time-order words to tell when the events occurred?

- Do your sentences flow smoothly when read aloud?

- Did you add an interesting title?

Writing PROCESS

Proofread

After you have revised your personal narrative, you will need to proofread it to find and correct any errors in mechanics, grammar and usage, and spelling.

STRATEGIES FOR PROOFREADING

- **Reread your revised paper several times.** Each time you read, look for a different type of error. This will give you a better chance of catching your mistakes.

- **Reread for mechanics and usage.** Make sure you have used a capital letter to begin every sentence and the correct punctuation at the end of each sentence.

- **Check for commas.** Make sure you use a comma and the word *and*, *but*, or *or* to make compound sentences.

- **Check for spelling errors by reading your paper from the last word to the first word.** You will be able to concentrate on the spelling of the words instead of on the story.

Spelling

When choosing *ei* or *ie*, remember that *i* comes before *e*, as in *friend*, except after *c*, as in *receive*, or when sounded like /ā/, as in *neighbor* or *weigh*.

REVIEW THE RULES

GRAMMAR

- A compound sentence joins two complete sentences by using a comma and the words *and*, *but*, or *or*.

MECHANICS

- Every sentence begins with a capital letter.

- A declarative sentence ends with a period.

- An interrogative sentence ends with a question mark.

- An imperative sentence ends with a period.

- An exclamatory sentence ends with an exclamation mark.

- A run-on sentence joins together two or more sentences that should be written separately.

Look at the proofreading corrections made on the draft below. What does the symbol ⊙ mean? Why does the writer use it to end the last sentence?

PROOFREAD

The Perfect Summer Ending

Camp Wilderness
Last summer, I went to camp. I go to the same
, but   (SP) different
camp every year. Last summer was different.

That was the summer I decided to swim across

Lake Wonder.

First,
I knew it wouldn't be easy. I made a plan to meet
Next,
my goal. I asked the camp counselors to help me
Then,   shimmering blue
train. After three weeks of training in and out of the
I finally felt ready # (SP) friends
water, it was time. My freinds came to cheer me on

as I jumped in and began to swim. My sister Linda

even videotaped the event one of the counselors
⊙ ≡
rowed in a boat next to me for safety. It wasn't easy.

How excited I was when I made it across the lake!
but I made it. Meeting my goal was the perfect end

to the summer⊙

Checklist ✓
Proofreading

- Did you indent each paragraph?

- Did you group sentences about the same idea into a paragraph?

- Did you check the spelling of difficult words?

- Did you use a capital letter to begin every sentence and the correct punctuation at the end of each sentence?

- Did you combine any sentences or correct run-on sentences?

PROOFREADING MARKS

⌗ new paragraph
∧ add
⟋ take out
≡ Make a capital letter.
∕ Make a small letter.
(SP) Check the spelling.
⊙ Add a period.

PRACTICE AND APPLY

Proofread Your Own Personal Narrative

1. Find and correct misspelled words.

2. Include the correct ending punctuation for each kind of sentence.

3. Make sure you use a comma and the words *and*, *but*, or *or* to join compound sentences.

4. Know the meaning of each word you use.

Writing PROCESS

Publish

The last step before publishing your piece is to review your writing one last time. Use a checklist to help you keep track of what you have reviewed.

✓ Self-Check Personal Narrative

- ❑ What was my purpose? Did I describe a personal experience?
- ❑ Did I choose a topic that will interest my audience?
- ❑ Did I include a good title?
- ❑ Did I use a variety of sentences? Do my sentences flow together?
- ❑ Did I end each type of sentence with the correct punctuation?
- ❑ Did I correctly use compound sentences?
- ❑ Did I use time-order words to show the sequence of events?
- ❑ Did I include enough specific details so that the reader can easily visualize my experience?
- ❑ Did I proofread and correct all errors?

The writer used the checklist to review his personal narrative. Read "The Perfect Summer Ending" and discuss the writer's published piece with a small group. Do you think it was ready to publish? Why do you think so?

The Perfect Summer Ending

by Brad Lewis

Last summer, I went to Camp Wilderness. I go to the same camp every year, but last summer was different. That was the summer I decided to swim across Lake Wonder. I knew it wouldn't be easy.

First, I made a plan to meet my goal. Next, I asked the camp counselors to help me train. Then, after three weeks of training in and out of the shimmering blue water, I finally felt ready.

My friends came to cheer me on as I jumped in and began to swim. My sister Linda even videotaped the event. One of the counselors rowed in a boat next to me for safety. How excited I was when I made it across the lake! Meeting my goal was the perfect end to the summer.

TECHNOLOGY

Does your school have a Web site? Use your school's technology resources to publish your work on the Internet.

PRACTICE AND APPLY

Publish Your Own Personal Narrative

1. Check your revised draft one more time.

2. Make a neat, final copy.

3. Add a border, pictures, or a cover to your story.

4. Send your story to your school newspaper.

Present Your Personal Narrative

A good presentation requires careful planning. There are steps you can take to make sure your presentation is a success!

STEP 1

How to Tell Your Story

Strategies for Speaking As you present your personal narrative, remember that your purpose is to entertain the members of your audience. Think of ways to make them feel as if they are part of the experience.

- Decide on the best way to share your narrative. Focus on highlighting the main idea.
- Create an outline or use note cards to help you remember your story.
- Speak loudly so that a person in the back can hear you.

Listening Strategies

- Set a purpose. Are you listening for new information or enjoyment?

- Try to listen for the main idea and details.

- Visualize what the speaker is saying.

- Take notes on the important information in the speech. Jot down questions to ask later.

- Keep your eyes on the speaker. This will help keep you focused. It will also let the speaker know you are paying attention.

Multimedia Ideas

If the topic of your personal narrative was videotaped, you may wish to use footage of the experience in your presentation. You could play a piece of the tape at the beginning or end of your story.

How to Show Your Story

Suggestions for Visuals Make your presentation clearer and more interesting by adding visuals for your audience to look at as they listen.

- Photographs and drawings can be helpful to allow your audience to visualize parts of your story.
- A large poster or collage can get across your main idea and details.
- A diagram or map can help your audience "see" where your story happened.

How to Share Your Story

Strategies for Rehearsing The more you practice, the more comfortable you'll feel on the day of your presentation.

- Practice telling your story by pretending you are speaking in front of an audience.
- Work with a partner and give each other feedback on how well you present your story.
- Try experimenting with different ways of presenting your story. Rehearse several times to find the most effective way.

PRACTICE AND APPLY

Present Your Own Personal Narrative

1. Review your story and decide the best way to share it aloud.
2. Organize your thoughts on note cards or an outline.
3. Create a photo album, drawings, a poster, or a collage to help your audience visualize your story.
4. Practice rehearsing your story as if you were speaking in front of an audience.

TIP!

Viewing Strategies

- Carefully view the materials the speaker displays.
- Visuals may contain information the speaker does not tell you directly.
- Be careful with any items the speaker allows you to touch.

Writing Tests

A writing test requires you to write a composition in response to a prompt. A writing prompt presents a situation and tells you what kind of writing to do. Look for key words and phrases in the prompt that tell you what you should write about and how you should present your ideas.

Check for clues that name your audience.

Stories can inform, entertain, or influence an audience. Does this story have more than one purpose?

This phrase tells you to use "I" and to write in the first person.

> **Prompt**
>
> Reaching a goal can give you a feeling of pride and accomplishment.
>
> <u>Write a story about a time when you accomplished something.</u> <u>Tell what you did</u> to reach your goal and <u>how you felt</u> when you achieved it.

How to Read a Prompt

Purpose Sometimes a piece of writing can have more than one purpose. Look at the prompt again. Find key words that tell you the goal or goals of the writing. The words "Write a story about a time when you accomplished something" tell you that your purposes are to inform and entertain.

Audience Sometimes a prompt tells you who your audience is. If it does not, think of your audience as your teacher.

Personal Narrative When you are asked to write about your own experiences, you are writing a personal narrative. The phrases "Tell what you did" and "how you felt" show you that you should write about your own experiences and feelings.

Test Tip

Check your composition for errors in capitalization, punctuation, and spelling.

66

How to Write to a Prompt

Remember these tips when you are given a prompt on a writing test.

Before Writing **Content/Ideas**	• Think about the purpose of your writing. • Keep your audience in mind. • Make a list of things you know about the topic. • Stay focused on the exact assignment.
During Writing **Organization/** **Paragraph** **Structure**	• Begin with a good topic sentence. • Write your ideas in a logical order. • When you are writing a personal narrative, use time-order words to show the sequence of events. • End with an interesting conclusion.
After Writing **Grammar/Usage**	• Proofread your work. • Start each sentence with a capital letter. • End all sentences with the correct punctuation. • Spell all words correctly.

Apply What You Learned

When you read a writing prompt, look for words and phrases that tell you the purpose of your writing and your audience. Make a plan and decide how to organize your ideas in the most effective way.

> **Prompt**
>
> Learning a new skill can be a fun and exciting experience.
>
> Write a story about a time when you learned how to do something new. Tell what happened and how you felt during the experience.

Grammar and Writing Review

pages
2–3

Sentences and Sentence Fragments

A. Write each group of words. Next to each group write *sentence* or *sentence fragment*.

1. Planted a garden.

2. My grandfather helped us pull weeds.

3. My brother and I.

4. Watered it each day.

5. We had fresh vegetables at the end of the summer.

pages
4–7

Four Kinds of Sentences

B. Write each sentence. Then write whether the sentence is *declarative*, *interrogative*, *imperative*, or *exclamatory*.

6. I went to the library to find information for my report.

7. What a great selection of resources it had!

8. I found facts in books, magazines, and encyclopedias.

9. Isn't the library a wonderful place to find information?

10. Go to the library tomorrow.

pages
8–9

Combining Sentences: Compound Sentences

C. Combine each pair of sentences into one compound sentence. Use a comma and the word *and*, *but*, or *or* to connect ideas. Write the new sentence.

11. My grandfather makes kites. I love to fly them.

12. I usually watch the kites being made. Sometimes I help.

13. My grandfather cuts the wood. I help him tie the pieces.

14. I choose the fabric for the kite. I don't sew the pieces.

15. Should we build diamond-shaped kites? Should we build box kites?

16. The kites are brightly colored. They have long tails.

17. I love to fly our kites. The wind must be just right.

18. A breeze is not good for kites. A steady wind is perfect.

19. Our kites soar. They dip and twirl in the sky.

20. I love to fly kites. I love to spend time with my grandfather even more.

pages
10–11

Mechanics and Usage: Sentence Punctuation

D. **Write each sentence correctly. Add capital letters, end punctuation, and a comma where needed.**

21. i had trouble seeing the chalkboard in class

22. my teacher suggested that I move to the front of the room

23. what a difference that made

24. did I need to get eyeglasses

25. the eye doctor checked my vision and I needed glasses

pages
14–15

Complete Subjects and Complete Predicates

E. **Write each sentence. Draw one line under the complete subject. Draw two lines under the complete predicate.**

26. My sister and I wanted to earn some extra money.

27. Our parents suggested cleaning the garage.

28. The garage needed a complete overhaul.

29. My sister volunteered to help.

30. My job of sweeping the floor made me tired and dirty.

pages
16–19

Simple Subjects and Simple Predicates

F. **Write each sentence. Draw one line under the simple subject. Draw two lines under the simple predicate.**

31. My family rents a boat every summer.

32. We put the boat on the lake.

33. The waves are very strong.

34. My brother enjoys waterskiing.

35. Everyone on the boat wears a life jacket.

36. My father steers the boat through the choppy waves.

37. The water sprays our faces.

38. My grandmother likes fishing.

39. The motor hums quietly during the ride.

40. Trips on the boat create wonderful family memories.

Grammar and Writing Review

pages
20–21

Combining Sentences: Compound Subjects

G. **Combine each pair of sentences. Use the word *and* to make a compound subject. Write the new sentence.**

41. My friend decided to paint a mural. I decided to paint a mural.

42. Friends offered to help. Classmates offered to help.

43. Teachers gathered supplies. Parents gathered supplies.

44. Children worked together. Adults worked together.

45. Our friends were impressed. Our relatives were impressed.

pages
22–23

Combining Sentences: Compound Predicates

H. **Combine each pair of sentences. Use the word *and* to make a compound predicate. Write the new sentence.**

46. The players dribbled the ball. The players passed the ball.

47. The coach's whistle blew constantly. The coach's whistle rang in our ears.

48. The cheerleaders led us. The cheerleaders inspired us.

49. We cheered when our team scored. We also clapped.

50. The crowd whooped when our team won. The crowd hollered, too.

pages
24–25

Mechanics and Usage: Correcting Run-on Sentences

I. **Correct each run-on sentence by writing it as two sentences or by making it a compound sentence. Write the corrected sentence.**

51. Our class boarded the bus we headed for the campgrounds.

52. We hiked in the morning we took canoe trips in the afternoon.

53. Some students slept in cabins other students slept in tents.

54. We could sleep on the ground we could sleep on cots.

55. We had classes at the nature center we took walks by the lake.

56. I was worried about seeing bears I didn't see any.

57. At night we looked at stars the constellations were beautiful.

58. We listened for wolf howls all we heard were crickets.

59. We roasted marshmallows it was such fun.

60. Our trip was a great success it was the best part of the year.

pages
38–39
Vocabulary: Time-Order Words

J. **Write these sentences in the correct order. Use the time-order words and phrases in the sentences as a guide.**

61. Finally, I dusted and made my bed.

62. Next, I picked up all my scattered games and books.

63. Last Saturday, my mother asked me to clean my room.

64. First, I threw all my dirty laundry into the hamper.

65. When the floor was free of clutter, I vacuumed it.

pages
40–41
Composition: Main Idea and Supporting Details

K. **Write a sentence that states the main idea of each of these topics. Then write three supporting details for each main idea.**

66. A Family Vacation

67. An Unusual Pet

68. Learning to Ride a Bike

69. A Trip to an Amusement Park

70. A Favorite Book

71. My Good Deed

72. My First Trip on an Airplane

73. A Memorable Birthday

74. The Best Gift of All

75. The Silliest Thing I Have Ever Done

pages
50–65
Proofreading a Personal Narrative

L. **Write the following paragraph correctly. Be sure to correct 10 errors in capitalization, punctuation, grammar, and spelling.**

As long as I can remember, I have wanted to learn to play golf my aunt agreed to teach me but I had no idea how hard it would be. first, she showed me how to hold and swing the clubs then, she took me to the golf coarse for my first game. I tried to hit the ball I missed three times. Finally, I managed to strike the ball, but it went strait into the water. I felt ready to quit, but my aunt persuaded me to stick with the game. How glad I am that she did

Project File

A Business Letter

You will want to write a business letter sometime. A business letter has six parts to it. Think about why each part is needed.

> You will need to know the form of a business letter when you write your letter in the next unit.

543 Woltwood Drive
Amarillo, Texas 79107
September 25, 2002

> *Heading* Gives the writer's address and the date.

Chief Raymond Greer
Amarillo Police Department
29 Fourth Avenue
Amarillo, Texas 79107

> *Inside Address* Gives the name and address of the person or company to whom the letter is being written.

Dear Chief Greer:

> *Greeting* In a business letter the greeting is followed by a colon (:).

My fifth grade class has been learning about our local community. We are interested in finding out more about our police station and its police officers. Please send us any information you have about the police department in Amarillo.

> *Body* The main part of the letter.

Yours truly,
Robert Loza

> *Closing* Tells that the letter is about to end. In a business letter use one of these closings: Respectfully, Yours Truly, Sincerely.

> *Signature* The name of the person writing the letter.

For more information, see Handbook page 588.

72

Write to Request Information

Sometimes you will need to request information from a company or an individual. Imagine that you are writing a report about your local government. Write to a city official asking for information about your community. Before you write, be sure to outline all the information you are requesting. Look at the model on page 72 to make sure you include all the parts of a business letter.

ACTIVITY 2

A Song

Sammy Sosa worked hard to become a "home-run king." Do some research to find out more about Sosa's rise to the top. Then imagine you are Sammy Sosa as you think about all you have accomplished.

Sammy's Song Write lyrics to a song as if you were Sammy Sosa writing about your rise to baseball stardom. Include in your lyrics ideas from your research about the baseball player's life.

Sentences and Sentence Fragments

A. **Write *sentence* or *sentence fragment* for each group of words.**

1. Our teacher is testing our fitness.

2. Long and short distances.

3. We use stopwatches to record our running time.

4. Matthew and Nashema.

5. Tired from the long-distance run.

6. I enjoy running short sprints.

7. The teacher asked us to check our pulse.

8. Our fingers.

9. We recorded our pulse rates on a chart.

10. Our running time was recorded on a bulletin board.

B. **Add words to each sentence fragment to make it a complete sentence. Write the new sentence.**

11. Sit-ups and push-ups.

12. Fifty sit-ups.

13. Demonstrated how to do a pull-up.

14. Held ourselves for as long as we could.

15. Had trouble doing pull-ups.

16. Practice for next year.

17. Received a ribbon.

18. The number of times.

19. My best friend.

20. Jumped rope one hundred times in a row.

C. **For each pair, write the group of words that is a sentence. Then add words to the other group to make a complete thought. Write each new sentence.**

21. We were tired after the tests. The students.

22. Recorded all the results. We saw our scores.

23. I need to work on pull-ups. Learned about physical fitness.

24. I will practice every day. Next year.

25. My friends and I. We will be in great shape.

Declarative and Interrogative Sentences

A. Read each sentence. Then write whether the sentence is declarative (a statement) or interrogative (a question).

1. Claire and I went to see a movie.

2. What movie did you see?

3. Where did you sit in the theater?

4. The movie was a mystery.

5. The main characters solved mysteries at their school.

6. One of the detectives was a young girl.

7. What were the names of the main characters?

8. Where did the movie take place?

9. The first mystery involved a missing notebook.

10. How did the detectives solve the mystery?

B. Write each sentence. Then write whether the sentence is declarative or interrogative.

11. My friends and I decided to find a mystery to solve.

12. Where can we find a mystery?

13. Do we know of any mysterious situations?

14. Claire had an idea.

15. We made signs to advertise our business.

16. Where should we hang the signs we made?

17. Claire's little brother brought us our first mystery.

18. Claire's brother, Jimmy, tried to find his lost toy.

19. When did he last see his toy?

20. Was anyone else playing with it?

C. Write each sentence. Add correct punctuation.

21. Jimmy saw the family dog near his toy

22. Where is the dog's house

23. Who wants to look inside the doghouse

24. I looked inside the doghouse and found the toy

25. Our detective agency had solved its first case

Extra Practice

Imperative and Exclamatory Sentences

A. Read each sentence. Write whether the sentence is imperative (a request or command) or exclamatory (a strong feeling).

1. Listen to the sounds in the forest.

2. How beautiful they sound!

3. Sit and close your eyes.

4. Don't make any noise.

5. What amazing noises we can hear!

6. How loud the insects are!

7. Try to hear as many different sounds as you can.

8. What a good listener you are!

9. Write the names of the noises you hear.

10. Identify as many of the sounds as you can.

B. Write each sentence. Then write whether the sentence is imperative or exclamatory.

11. Share your list of nature sounds with a friend.

12. What a complete list of sounds you made!

13. Oh, listen to that scary sound!

14. What a frightening sound that was!

15. Let's follow that noise.

16. Walk quietly along the path.

17. Listen closely.

18. How loud the noise is getting!

19. Stop, look, and listen.

20. Try to find the source of the strange sound.

C. Write each sentence. Add correct punctuation.

21. Look by that big rock

22. What an amazing sight it is

23. Take a picture of that bullfrog

24. Write about our exciting discovery

25. What a perfect ending to the day we've had

Combining Sentences: Compound Sentences

A. Read each sentence. Write *compound* for each compound sentence. Write *simple* for each sentence that is not a compound sentence.

1. Our class decided to clean up the school grounds.

2. The teachers agreed, and our class formed a cleanup crew.

3. We divided into teams, and each group chose a job.

4. My group collected litter.

5. We carried garbage bags, and we wore gloves on our hands.

6. I found many candy wrappers, but I didn't find any soda cans.

7. My friend Kevin was on a different cleanup team.

8. His group planted flowers, or they chose to rake leaves.

9. Students dug the holes for the flowers.

10. Kevin decided to rake, but he changed his mind.

B. Write each sentence. Add the correct punctuation.

11. Our cleanup group pulled weeds and we worked hard.

12. There was much work to do and we decided to work both days.

13. We chose to plant flowers the second day and I was excited.

14. I love flowers but my family doesn't plant many at our house.

15. We could plant near the school or we could plant by the park.

16. I worked near the school and I planted ten flowers.

17. The flowers were many colors but I liked the red ones best.

18. We finished planting by lunch but we had to clean our tools.

19. We could eat first or we could clean our tools first.

20. Our group was hungry but we decided to clean our tools.

C. Combine each pair of sentences to write a compound sentence. Use a comma and the word *and, but,* or *or*.

21. We finished our work. We were very tired.

22. The cleanup was hard work. The school looked great.

23. We took pictures of our work. We sent them to the newspaper.

24. The principal held an assembly. He thanked us for our work.

25. The school looked beautiful. We were very proud of our work.

Extra Practice

Sentence Punctuation

A. Read each sentence. Write the name of the end punctuation mark used in each sentence.

1. Our class is doing experiments with plants.

2. How many different experiments will we do?

3. Put the dirt in each of the pots.

4. Which seeds will go in each pot?

5. Please add some fertilizer to each pot.

6. How messy this experiment is!

7. There are four different plants for our experiment.

8. Each plant will grow in a different place.

9. Will you record each location on the chart?

10. Now we need to select the locations for the plants.

B. Write each sentence. Use the correct capitalization and end punctuation.

11. place the first pot by the window

12. we put the second pot in the closet

13. can we place the third pot near the chalkboard

14. where should we put the last pot

15. richard thinks the pot should be placed in the hallway

16. what a wonderful idea he had

17. please take the pot into the hall

18. let's watch the plants during the next few weeks

19. someone will need to water the plants

20. you should add "watering plants" to our job chart

C. Combine each pair of sentences to form a compound sentence. Then write each new sentence. Use the correct capitalization and punctuation.

21. it has been three weeks. we should check the plants.

22. do you want to check growth? do you want to record results?

23. the plant by the window is growing. the plant in the hall is not.

24. plants need water to grow. don't water them too much.

25. look at the growth chart. compare how much each plant grew.

Complete Subjects and Complete Predicates

A. Write the complete predicate of each sentence.

 1. The students in our school present a play every year.

 2. Everyone works hard to prepare for the performance.

 3. The drama teacher selects the play we will perform.

 4. Many students audition for a part in the play.

 5. The auditions are held after school.

 6. The drama teacher asks for our ideas about casting decisions.

 7. The final cast list hangs on the gymnasium door.

 8. All the students gather around to see the names on the list.

 9. Everyone cheers for those chosen for the lead parts.

10. All students receive a role in the play.

B. Write each sentence. Draw one line under the complete subject. Draw two lines under the complete predicate.

11. Some students build the sets for the class play.

12. The sets require many hours of work.

13. The actors and actresses rehearse for several weeks.

14. The drama teacher helps students learn their lines.

15. Several parents volunteer to help make the costumes.

16. The music teacher works with students to select the music.

17. A group of students records a tape of sound effects.

18. The time for dress rehearsal arrives quickly.

19. All cast members are nervous.

20. The director sees problems at the dress rehearsal.

C. Add a complete subject or a complete predicate to each group of words. Write each new sentence.

21. Opening night

22. dressed in their costumes.

23. The audience

24. performed without a mistake.

25. Everyone in the gymnasium

Grammar

Simple Subjects

A. Write the simple subject in each sentence. The complete subject has been underlined to help you.

1. <u>Our teacher</u> suggested that each student set a personal goal.

2. <u>The goal</u> had to be set for a positive change.

3. <u>Some students</u> chose to set a goal in sports.

4. <u>My friend Olivia</u> wanted to score more goals in soccer.

5. <u>Her soccer coach</u> helped her develop a practice schedule.

6. <u>Her teammates</u> encouraged her to meet the goal.

7. <u>One boy</u> decided he would save money to buy a new bike.

8. <u>His parents</u> showed him how to open a bank account.

9. <u>The money</u> he earned was put into his account.

10. <u>The bicycle</u> was his in six months.

B. Write each sentence. Draw one line under the complete subject. Draw two lines under the simple subject.

11. My personal goal was to improve my spelling.

12. My teacher helped me develop a plan to meet my goal.

13. My first job was to keep a list of spelling words in my notebook.

14. The list included new words and words I had trouble spelling.

15. The spelling list was useful as I wrote stories.

16. My friends quizzed me on the school bus.

17. My father helped me practice the words during breakfast.

18. Another spelling strategy was to write the words each day.

19. Many hours were spent studying spelling words.

20. Spelling tests seem easy now.

C. Add a simple subject to each group of words. Then write the sentence.

21. thought of a personal goal.

22. gave us a goal to reach.

23. developed a plan to meet our goal.

24. kept track of our progress toward our goal.

25. were proud of the things we accomplished.

Simple Predicates

A. **Write the simple predicate in each sentence. The complete predicate has been underlined to help you.**

1. Thomas Jefferson studied history, architecture, and science.
2. Jefferson loved learning about nature as a boy.
3. He learned about nature in the forests by his home.
4. His sister Jane encouraged him to explore.
5. Thomas Jefferson played the violin.
6. He attended college in Williamsburg, Virginia.
7. The American colonies belonged to England at that time.
8. After college, Jefferson decided to become a lawyer.
9. He worked for five years in a friend's law office.
10. Jefferson achieved many of his goals.

B. **Write each sentence. Draw one line under the simple predicate.**

11. Thomas Jefferson designed the plan for his house.
12. He called his home Monticello.
13. The people of Virginia elected Jefferson to the House of Burgesses.
14. He represented the colony of Virginia.
15. Thomas Jefferson wrote the Declaration of Independence.
16. Jefferson finished the draft in two days.
17. He traveled to France to discuss the new United States.
18. Later, Jefferson served as the first Secretary of State.
19. In 1801, he became the third president.
20. Jefferson believed there were always new things to learn.

C. **Add a simple predicate to each group of words. Then write the sentence.**

21. Thomas Jefferson
22. The American Colonies
23. British troops
24. Some people
25. The United States

81

Extra Practice

Combining Sentences: Compound Subjects

A. Write each sentence. Underline the conjunction that joins the compound subject.

1. My aunt and uncle invite our family to their farm each year.

2. Their friends and neighbors are very nice.

3. Their son and daughter are the same age as my sister and I.

4. Chickens and ducks always come to greet us.

5. The pasture and barn are perfect places in which to play.

6. The stream and the lake are good for wading and fishing.

7. My sister and I help with work on the farm.

8. Apples and pears are ripe for picking.

9. My aunt or cousins help my uncle bale the hay.

10. My mother and father load the bales of hay onto the truck.

B. Write each sentence. Draw one line under the compound subject.

11. My aunt and uncle teach us how to make preserves.

12. Peaches or strawberries make the best preserves.

13. My sister and I have jobs on the farm.

14. Cows and pigs need to be fed.

15. The barn and chicken coop are cleaned every day.

16. The dog and cat are cared for every morning.

17. Roosters and ducks are noisy in the morning.

18. Crickets and frogs make noise at night.

19. Work and play make me tired on my farm visits.

20. My family and I look forward to spending time on the farm.

C. Write each pair of sentences as one sentence with a compound subject.

21. Horses live in the barn. Cows live in the barn.

22. The lofts are full of spiderwebs. The cellars are full of spiderwebs.

23. Apples are juicy and ripe. Pears are juicy and ripe.

24. The streams are full of fish. The lakes are full of fish.

25. Farms are interesting places. Ranches are interesting places.

Combining Sentences: Compound Predicates

A. **Write each sentence. Draw one line under the compound predicate.**

1. We select and play instruments during music class.

2. The music teacher discusses and demonstrates many choices.

3. We sit and wait for a chance to try each instrument.

4. We view and touch the stringed instruments.

5. We hold and carry the woodwind and brass instruments.

6. The students smile and laugh when they bang the drums.

7. Each student stops and thinks about which instrument to choose.

8. We question and consider which choice will be best.

9. We share and discuss our ideas.

10. Each person chooses and takes an instrument.

B. **Write the complete predicate of each sentence. Then write whether the predicate is *simple* or *compound*.**

11. The band teacher invites new members to join the group.

12. We attend practice sessions after school.

13. We learn and follow the rules of the class.

14. The teacher leads and directs each session.

15. The percussion players tap on their instruments.

16. The violinists use bows for their instruments.

17. People blow and toot the brass instruments.

18. The music teacher smiles and nods at the new players.

19. We clean and tune our instruments regularly.

20. We practice and play our instruments every day.

C. **Write each pair of sentences as one sentence with a compound predicate.**

21. The band practices together. The band plays together.

22. Our lessons begin on time. Our lessons end on time.

23. Beginning musicians practice. Beginning musicians learn.

24. The teacher directs the band. The teacher supports the band.

25. We respect our band teacher. We admire our band teacher.

Extra Practice

Correcting Run-on Sentences

A. Read each sentence. Write *run-on* for each run-on sentence. Write *correct* for each sentence that is correct.

1. My class decided to create a school newspaper.

2. Our teacher thought a newspaper was a great idea.

3. Students discussed story ideas we made a list.

4. Everyone read through the list some students had other ideas.

5. The top ten ideas were selected for further research.

6. Our teacher divided us into ten teams we began working on our lists.

7. Each team selected a topic to research and include in a report.

8. Members of one group chose sporting events they listed the top players.

9. Another team decided to write about school assemblies.

10. Members of another team chose to write about teachers they listed names.

11. The comic section was a popular choice I am not a good artist.

12. My team chose to write about current events.

13. The teacher told us we could change jobs throughout the year.

14. We thought taking turns was fair we knew waiting would be difficult.

15. The teams met to discuss how to begin they made a plan.

16. My team had four students we were all friends.

17. The team shared ideas we listed what needed to be done.

18. We needed several students to cover all the current events.

19. We decided to write two interesting news stories.

20. We knew there was much work to do we were excited.

B. Correct each run-on sentence by separating it into two sentences. Write *correct* if a sentence is correct.

21. I chose to write about the food drive my team approved.

22. Tanya wanted to write that story, but she let me do it.

23. The team members assigned me one more article that was okay with me.

24. They asked me to write a paragraph about our new school rules.

25. I thought about the information to include in my articles I wrote my ideas.

26. I wrote down a list of questions to answer.

27. The questions helped me organize my ideas I was ready to begin.

28. I finished one of my articles I needed help with the other one.

29. The principal answered questions about my second article.

30. My teammates edited my articles after I finished writing.

C. Correct each run-on sentence by separating it into two sentences or by forming a compound sentence. Write each new sentence.

31. The teacher monitored our work she helped us plan ahead.

32. We could type the articles we could write them neatly.

33. She collected the articles she organized them by topic.

34. We reviewed the pages we made some changes.

35. The teacher made copies we all received a newspaper.

36. We enjoyed reading our paper we wanted others to read it.

37. We passed out the newspapers they were gone quickly.

38. We asked readers for feedback we didn't know if anyone would respond.

39. We added a suggestion box many people sent notes.

40. The school liked our newspaper we can't wait to write more.

Nouns and Persuasive Writing

In this unit you will learn about the different kinds of nouns. You will also learn how to write a persuasive letter in order to convince others to accept your opinion or point of view.

Social Studies Link   *Read about how eleven-year-old girl Dwaina Brooks persuades her mother to turn their kitchen into a place that will help feed the homeless.*

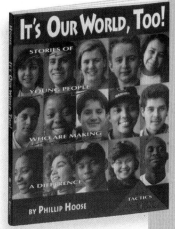

Dwaina tore into the house that night after school and found her mother, Gail. As usual, she was in the kitchen. "Mama," she said. "I need you to help me fix some stuff to take down to that shelter we call at school. Let's make up as much as we can. Sandwiches and chicken. Let's get everyone to do it. C'mon."

Gail Brooks looked at her daughter.... Make food for the homeless? Well, why not? They decided to prepare meals on Friday night.

〜 from ***It's Our World, Too!*** by Phillip Hoose

Thinking Like a Writer

Persuasive Writing Persuasive writing tries to influence the reader to agree with the writer's point of view. Sometimes it even moves people to take a course of action. Reread the passage.

• How does Dwaina persuade her mother to make meals for the homeless?

Nouns The author uses many kinds of nouns in his writing, including common and proper nouns and singular and plural nouns.

QUICK WRITE How can you recognize a proper noun? A plural noun?

Nouns

RULES

A **noun** is a word that names a person, place, thing, or idea.

The gardener planted. (person)

We visited the Tivoli Gardens. (place)

I learned about some unusual plants. (thing)

Their beauty amazed us. (idea)

A noun can be one word or two or more words used together. Nouns name things we can see as well as things we can only think about, such as ideas and feelings.

Things We Can See

Person	woman	child	Amy	Richard	doctor
Place	zoo		Mexico	school	city
Thing	computer	boots	cactus	dog	

Things We Can't See

Idea or Feeling	friendship	hunger	time	truth

THINK AND WRITE

Nouns

In your journal, write how you can recognize words that are nouns.

Guided Practice

Name the words in each sentence that are nouns.

> **EXAMPLE:** Some plants eat insects.
> *plants, insects*

1. Sticky leaves or flowers can trap bugs.

2. The leaves of a Venus's-flytrap can trap insects.

3. A bladderwort sucks mosquitoes through a trapdoor.

4. Special juices help it digest the insects.

5. These plants usually grow in swamps.

More Practice

A. **Write the sentences. Underline each noun.**

6. Many plants have their own protection.

7. A cactus has sharp thorns.

8. Nettles produce a juice that stings.

9. Cacti grow in the desert.

10. We get medicines from many plants.

B. **Write the nouns in each sentence. Next to each noun, write whether it names a person, place, thing, or idea.**

11. The baobab is a tree in Africa.

12. Cycads are tropical plants.

13. Scientists study fossils of wildlife.

14. The largest tree is the sequoia in California.

15. Books about strange plants satisfy my curiosity.

C. **Spiral Review** **Write each sentence. Write *N* above each noun. Draw one line under each complete subject and two lines under each complete predicate. Then circle the simple subject.**

16. Botanists study plants.

17. The largest flowers in the world grow in Asia.

18. One cactus looks like a rock.

19. The jackfruit produces huge fruit.

20. Certain leaves remind me of feathers.

Extra Practice, page 156

Handbook
pages 528,
530–531

Writing Activity An Advertisement

Write a newspaper advertisement for a plant nursery that sells unusual plants. Persuade people to visit the nursery. Use interesting and unusual details to catch and keep your reader's attention.

APPLY GRAMMAR: Write *person, place, thing,* or *idea* above each noun that you use.

Singular and Plural Nouns

RULES

A **singular noun** names one person, place, thing, or idea.

student   *country*   *key*   *wish*

A **plural noun** names more than one person, place, thing, or idea.

students   *countries*   *keys*   *wishes*

Most plural nouns are formed by adding *-s* or *-es*.

rabbit—rabbits   *day—days*   *bush—bushes*

THINK AND WRITE

Nouns

In your journal, explain how the spelling of a plural noun is different from the spelling of a singular noun.

The spelling of some nouns changes when they become plural. Remember these simple spelling patterns to form plural nouns.

Singular	Plural	Examples
Nouns that end in s, ss, x, ch, *or* sh	*Add* -es	*peach, peaches*
Nouns ending in a vowel and y	*Add* -s	*valley, valleys*
Nouns ending in a consonant and y	*Change* y *to* i *and add* -es	*party, parties*

Guided Practice

Name each noun. Tell whether the noun is singular or plural.

EXAMPLE: We watched a video about reptiles.
video, singular; reptiles, plural

1. The students wrote reports about animals.

2. Andrea read a book about birds in South America.

3. One report was about whales.

4. Group members studied the life of a penguin.

5. The twins reported on spiders.

REVIEW THE RULES

- **Singular nouns** name one person, place, thing, or idea.

- **Plural nouns** are usually formed by adding *-s* or *-es*. They name more than one person, place, thing, or idea.

More Practice

A. **Write the sentences. Draw one line under each singular noun. Draw two lines under each plural noun.**

6. Two students reported on the wallaby.

7. Wallabies are related to the kangaroo.

8. Wallabies and kangaroos are found in Australia.

9. A wallaby carries its baby in a pouch.

10. A law protects wallabies from hunters.

B. **List the singular nouns and plural nouns in each sentence. Then write the plural form of each singular noun.**

11. One student learned many facts about animals.

12. A baby deer is called a doe.

13. A monkey uses its toes like thumbs.

14. Chimpanzees can understand language.

15. An ostrich can run up to 40 miles per hour.

C. **Spiral Review** **Write the sentences. Use the plural form of the word in parentheses. Draw one line under the complete subject and two lines under the complete predicate.**

16. Flying (squirrel) live in many parts of the world.

17. These forest (creature) cannot really fly.

18. Such animals have a web of skin on both (side) of their body.

19. The skin on both sides works like a (parachute).

20. The (web) can be interesting.

Extra Practice, page 157.

Handbook
pages 528,
530–531

Writing Activity A Poster

Make up an idea for an event, such as a fair, to benefit endangered animals. Design a poster that will persuade people to come. Use persuasive language.

APPLY GRAMMAR: Circle singular nouns in red and plural nouns in blue.

Science Link

More Plural Nouns

RULES

There are special rules for forming the plural of some nouns.

To form the plural of some nouns ending in *f* or *fe*, you change the *f* to *v* and add -*es*.

half—halves   *knife—knives*

To form the plural of nouns ending in a vowel followed by *o*, just add -*s*.

video—videos   *radio—radios*

To form the plural of nouns ending in a consonant followed by *o*, add -*s* or -*es*.

solo—solos   *hero—heroes*

Some nouns have a special plural form that does not end in -*s*.

foot—feet   *mouse—mice*   *woman—women*

Some nouns stay the same whether singular or plural.

deer   *sheep*   *moose*

THINK AND WRITE

Nouns

In your journal, write strategies that can help you remember the spelling of nouns with special plural forms.

Remembering special plural forms takes practice. Check your dictionary until the forms are familiar enough for you to remember.

Guided Practice

Tell the plural form of each noun in parentheses.

EXAMPLE: Many (child) like to watch movies. *children*

1. My favorite pastime is watching (video) at home.

2. I enjoy watching movies about real-life (hero).

3. My favorite characters are men and (woman) from history.

4. I also like movies about earthquakes and exploding (volcano.)

5. Last week, I saw a true story about (tornado).

REVIEW THE RULES

- Change *f* to *v* and add *-es or -s* to form the plural of some nouns ending in *f* or *fe*.

- Add *-s* to form the plural of nouns ending in a vowel followed by *o*.

- Add *-s* or *-es* for nouns ending in a consonant followed by *o*.

- Some nouns have a special plural form that does not end in *s*.

- Some nouns stay the same whether singular or plural.

More Practice

A. Write each noun. Then write its plural form.

6. leaf **7.** tooth **8.** mouse **9.** rodeo **10.** piano

B. Write the sentences. Complete each sentence with the correct plural form of the noun in parentheses.

11. Our class visited Berkshire Television (Studio).

12. We wanted to see how they make (video).

13. The studio produces a program for (child).

14. It stars two (man) who dress like clowns.

15. Famous actors often make (cameo).

C. Spiral Review Write each sentence. Use the plural form of the word in parentheses. Underline the complete predicate. Circle the simple predicate.

16. The news set looked about four (foot) wide.

17. The (anchorwoman) read from scripts.

18. The (weatherman) stood in front of a blue screen.

19. Technicians are the real (hero) of the show.

20. I thought little (elf) made the show possible!

Extra Practice, page 158

Handbook
pages 528,
530–531

Writing Activity A Job

Imagine that you want a job as a student reporter at a local television station. Write a letter to the news director explaining why you would be the best person for the job.

APPLY GRAMMAR: Underline nouns with regular plural forms and circle nouns with special plural forms in your letter.

Common and Proper Nouns

RULES

A **common noun** names a person, place, thing, or idea.

leader   city   continent   book   harmony

A **proper noun** names a particular person, place, thing, or idea. Proper nouns begin with a capital letter.

Abraham Lincoln   Dallas   Liberty Bell   Renaissance

Remember that common nouns are general and proper nouns are specific. Compare the common and proper nouns below. The common nouns have a single line under them. The proper nouns have a double line.

Lisa Cunningham is a girl.

Pennsylvania Avenue is a street.

My dog's name is Champ.

Guided Practice

Name the nouns in each sentence. Tell whether each noun is common or proper.

EXAMPLE: Tim bought new boots at Shoe Village.
Tim: proper; boots: common; Shoe Village: proper

1. Our group is called the Big Pine Hiking Club.

2. Mr. and Mrs. Wills sponsor our club.

3. We planned a trip to Emerald Lake Park.

4. On Thursday, we made a grocery list.

5. Karen and Lydia prepared our sandwiches.

THINK AND WRITE

Nouns

In your journal, explain the difference between a common and a proper noun.

REVIEW THE RULES

- Common nouns name any person, place, thing, or idea.

- Proper nouns name particular people, places, things, or ideas.

More Practice

A. Write each word or phrase. Next to the word or words write *common noun* or *proper noun*.

6. Dr. Sanchez
7. Big Bend National Park
8. waterfall
9. canteen
10. ranger
11. Cloud Nine Campground
12. creek
13. chipmunk
14. month
15. April

B. Write each sentence. Draw one line under the common nouns and two lines under the proper nouns.

16. Mrs. Wills told us we might see deer, squirrels, and raccoons.
17. Tina found Coldwater Creek on the map.
18. Sam spotted a great campsite near the lake.
19. Mr. Wills read us a book of tales.
20. Tony said the trip was better than his vacation in Florida.

C. Spiral Review Combine each pair of sentences to make a compound sentence. Write the new sentence. Use correct sentence punctuation. Capitalize each proper noun.

21. We found a beautiful rock. It was too heavy for carlos to carry.
22. The campers put on a skit. mr. and mrs. wills sang a duet.
23. Can we climb mt. jackson now? should we wait until morning.
24. I saw a snake in coldwater creek. It didn't look dangerous.
25. Camping at emerald lake was great! I can't wait to return!

Extra Practice, page 159.

Handbook
pages 527, 531, 549, 552

Writing Activity A Letter to the Editor

Write a letter to the editor of your school or community newspaper. Explain why you think it is important to keep your local campgrounds safe and clean. Present your reasons clearly.

APPLY GRAMMAR: Use common and proper nouns. Draw one line under common nouns and two lines under the proper nouns.

Science Link

Capitalization

RULES

Capitalize days of the week, months of the year, and holidays.

> *Tuesday   June   Independence Day*

Capitalize names.

> *Jones   Guerrero   Chang   Frances*

Capitalize titles of people that precede names.

> *Mr. Chan   Mrs. Small   Dr. Jackson*

Capitalize the first, the last, and important words in titles of works.

> *The Wind in the Willows   Time   Twelfth Night*

THINK AND WRITE

Nouns

In your journal, explain how you know when a noun should begin with a capital letter.

If a proper noun has more than one word, capitalize each important word in the name.

> "Give My Regards to Broadway"

> *Beauty and the Beast*

Guided Practice

Name the words that should begin with capital letters.

> **EXAMPLE:** mr. huerta played the lead in *the sound* of *music*.
> *Mr., Huerta, The, Sound, Music*

1. mr. simms asked us to plan our dream vacation.

2. sid wants to visit disney world.

3. emily wants to see graceland, the home of elvis presley.

4. My dream is to see the white house on pennsylvania avenue.

5. The principal, ms. chee, suggested a trip to honolulu.

REVIEW THE RULES

- Capitalize days of the week, months, and holidays; capitalize family names, titles of people, and titles of works.

More Practice

A. **Write each sentence. Circle the letters that should be capitalized.**

6. On monday, leah will interview dr. evans for her career day.

7. lynn wants to spend halloween at mr. garcia's farm.

8. césar helps mrs. chu carry packages on tuesdays.

9. elaine heard beethoven's ninth symphony at dr. monroe's office.

10. mr. simms told us to have our reports ready by thursday.

B. **Write each sentence. Replace the underlined words with a proper noun.**

11. The teacher helped a student plan the car wash.

12. My friend invited me for the holiday.

13. Our teacher said he'd like to see a famous singer.

14. Two boys listened to a popular song.

15. We all thought a trip to an amusement park would be fun.

Handbook
pages 526–529,
548–550

C. **Spiral Review** **Write the sentences. Correct mistakes in capitalization and punctuation. Rewrite sentence fragments. Correct run-on sentences.**

16. Last week, my sister and i helped grandma clean out the attic.

17. we found old letters and even a medal

18. The medal had been given to aunt jean during the olympic games.

19. One letter had been written by mom to a famous actor it was dated december 17, 1975.

20. millions of memories. Found in old attics.

Extra Practice, page 160.

Writing Activity A Diary Entry

Imagine that you live in the past. Write a diary entry from a day in your life. Choose vivid words to describe your day.

APPLY MECHANICS AND USAGE: Capitalize important words in each proper noun that you use.

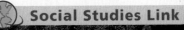
Social Studies Link

Mixed Review

REVIEW THE RULES

- A singular noun names one person, place, thing, or idea.

- A plural noun names more than one person, place, thing, or idea.

- Most plural nouns end in *-s* or *-es*, but some plural nouns have special forms.

- A common noun names any person, place, thing, or idea.

- A proper noun names a particular person, place, thing, or idea. It begins with a capital letter.

QUICK WRITE

Nouns

In your journal, write five common nouns. Then change three of the nouns to proper nouns.

Practice

A. Write a list of the singular nouns in each sentence. Next to each noun, write the plural form of the word.

1. My cousin visited us for the holiday.

2. We went to the lake or the library each day.

3. Every week we watched a video or went to a movie.

4. The hero of our favorite show was a lawyer.

5. We also weeded the garden for the woman across the street.

6. Our neighbor gave us each a baked potato with lunch.

7. We listened to the radio while we worked.

8. We also bought my sister a scarf.

9. My brother taught us to draw a monkey and wolf.

10. My uncle took us on a tour of the city.

B. Write each sentence. Draw one line under each common noun. Draw two lines under each proper noun. Correct mistakes in capitalization.

11. flowers grow along the highways in texas.

12. my cousin has never seen the alamo.

13. We rode the train and swam at barton springs.

14. i fed the ducks crackers from a box.

15. We visited a museum in the afternoon.

16. we went to see the texas state capitol.

17. We walked down congress avenue and bought some postcards.

18. The street reminded me of places in washington, d.c.

19. We even saw bats fly over town lake.

20. Next time we go to austin, I will bring my camera.

C. [Challenge] Rewrite the paragraph to correct the mistakes in plural forms and capitalization. You should find ten errors.

21–30. When ana returned to seattle, she wrote to thank us for the fun memorys. She wrote that austin is one of the best citys in the nation. She said that her brotheres wanted to come to texas during thanksgiving. I think my cousin and i will remember this summer for the rest of our lifes.

Handbook
pages 530–531,
532, 548–550

Writing Activity A Contest Entry

Write an essay for a "best hometown" contest. Explain what makes the place where you live a great hometown. Remember to write an introduction that makes your purpose clear and captures your reader's attention.

APPLY MECHANICS AND USAGE: Include common and proper nouns in your essay. Pay attention to correct capitalization of proper nouns.

Singular Possessive Nouns

A **possessive noun** is a noun that shows who or what owns or has something.

My brother's shirt is red and white.

The possessive form of most singular nouns end in an apostrophe and an *s* (*'s*).

Leo's hat   my guppy's food   James's scarf

To form the possessive of a singular noun, add *'s* to the noun.

the car that belongs to Ms. Hill	*Ms. Hill's car*
the work of the artist	*the artist's work*
the spots of the leopard	*the leopard's spots*
the book of the boy	*that boy's book*

THINK AND WRITE

Nouns

Why is it important to know how to form possessive nouns? Write your ideas in your journal.

Guided Practice

Tell the possessive form of each singular noun in parentheses.

EXAMPLE: My (cat) fur is black and white.
My cat's fur is black and white.

1. (Charles) dogs are Labrador puppies.
2. One (dog) coat is the color of chocolate.
3. Another (puppy) fur is golden.
4. Some of the (world) best dogs are retrievers.
5. This (breed) popularity began in England.

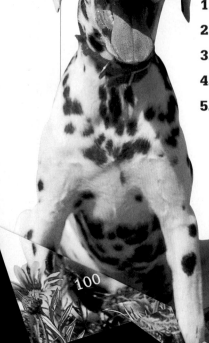

REVIEW THE RULES

- **Singular possessive nouns** show ownership, or possession.
- To form the possessive of most singular nouns, add *'s*.

More Practice

A. Write the possessive form of the noun in parentheses.

6. My best (friend) dog is a poodle.

7. (France) love of this dog has made the poodle famous.

8. (Ruth) favorite dogs are terriers.

9. (England) Yorkshire terrier has won many prizes.

10. My (brother) dog is a Dalmatian.

B. Write each sentence. Use the singular possessive form of the words in parentheses.

11. The Animal Expo is featuring (a pet that belongs to Jessica).

12. We like to watch (the chimpanzee that belongs to the zoo).

13. Kamal spends hours brushing (the coat of his horse).

14. (The mother of Nancy) is a dog trainer.

15. (The beagle that belongs to James) won a blue ribbon.

C. Spiral Review **Write each sentence. Add a singular possessive noun. Use the correct end punctuation. Then write whether the sentence is *declarative, interrogative, imperative,* or *exclamatory.***

16. Have you ever touched a _____ scaly skin

17. What a scare the _____ screech gave me

18. The _____ teeth are sharp and small

19. Hold the _____ leash

20. The _____ shell makes a good home

Extra Practice, page 161.

Handbook
pages 526–527,
530–531

Writing Activity A Speech

Write a speech that will persuade your parent to let you have a new pet. Give three reasons that will convince your mother or father.

APPLY GRAMMAR: Underline each singular possessive noun you use.

Plural Possessive Nouns

RULES

A **plural possessive noun** is a plural noun that shows ownership.

To form the possessive of a plural noun that ends in *s*, add only an apostrophe (').

> *two teachers' classes*   *ladies' night*   *three girls' pens*

To form the possessive of plural nouns not ending in *s*, add an apostrophe and *s* ('s).

> *children's toys*   *men's suits*   *two deer's tracks*

THINK AND WRITE

Nouns

In your journal, write how you know if a noun is a plural possessive noun.

To be sure you use the correct plural possessive form, ask yourself if the plural noun ends in *s*. If it does end in *s*, add only an apostrophe. If the plural noun does not end in *s*, add *'s*.

Guided Practice

Tell the possessive form of each underlined plural noun.

EXAMPLE: Please fold these <u>surgeons</u> gowns. *surgeons'*

1. All <u>doctors</u> training requires great dedication.
2. <u>Nurses</u> schooling is also challenging.
3. Students in each program learn about <u>children</u> illnesses.
4. Other training includes work on the <u>babies</u> ward.
5. The <u>patients</u> care always comes first.

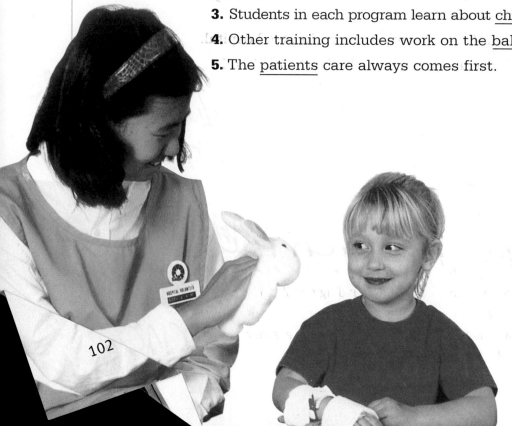

REVIEW THE RULES

- A comma follows the greeting and closing in a friendly letter.

- The greeting and the closing begin with a capital letter.

- A colon follows the greeting in a business letter.

- A comma separates the name of a city and state, and the day and the year in a date.

More Practice

A. Write the following phrases from business letters. Correct each mistake in capitalization or punctuation.

6. best regards   **7.** Dear Mr. Howe   **8.** Tallahassee Florida

9. July 28 2002   **10.** yours truly

B. Write the information that would be in each part of a letter from you to the principal at your school. Use correct letter punctuation.

11. heading   **12.** inside address   **13.** greeting

14. closing   **15.** signature

C. <u>Spiral Review</u> Write the letter. Add correct capitalization and punctuation. Correct fragments or run-on sentences.

16. Dear aunt Patricia

17. My parents are working on a very important project they are members of the Stop Pollution Now Committee. **18.** Yoko and I. Are making the posters and decorations for the Stop Pollution Fair. **19.** The fair will be like the one that was held on january 5 1999, in portland. I hope you can come.

20. love

   Elizabeth

Extra Practice, page 165.

Handbook
pages 544–546,
547–550, 552–555

Writing Activity A Business Letter

Write a business letter to an office supply store. Ask the company to donate computers to your school. Use persuasive language.

APPLY MECHANICS AND USAGE: Proofread for correct capitalization and punctuation.

Mixed Review

REVIEW THE RULES

- To form the possessive of most singular nouns, add 's.

- To form the possessive of a plural noun ending in s, add only an apostrophe (').

- To form the possessive of a plural noun not ending in s, add 's.

- Some sentences can be combined by joining nouns with the conjunction *and* or *or*.

- The greeting and the closing of a letter begin with a capital letter.

- A comma follows the greeting and closing in a friendly letter.

- A colon follows the greeting in a business letter.

- A comma separates the name of a city from the state, and the day of the month from the year.

QUICK WRITE

Nouns

Write the possessive form of five plural nouns ending in *s*.

Practice

A. Rewrite each sentence by using a possessive noun.

1. The class of Mrs. Donnally is starting a school news station.

2. They are studying the newscasts of the major TV channels.

3. Mrs. Donnally will listen to the ideas of her students.

4. She will help the class plan the format of the show.

5. The show will be broadcast from the library of the school.

B. Write the following sentences and phrases from business letters. Correct errors in punctuation and possessive nouns.

6. April 3 2001

7. Dallas Texas

8. Dear Ms. Mead

9. Thank you for helping with our schools news programs.

10. One reporter's camera was broken.

11. Their story's title is "How Our School Got It's Name."

12. I've included the reporters first assignment.

13. Will you be able to come to this Wednesdays meeting?

14. We look forward to hearing Chris suggestions.

15. Sincerely

C. **Challenge** Rewrite the part of the business letter shown below. Combine sentences with related nouns. Correct errors in capitalization and punctuation.

16. dear Coach Patel

17. I am a reporter for KSKL. I would like to interview Barry Jones. I would like to interview Coach Garza. **18.** The students are eager to hear about the big game. The teachers are eager to hear about the big game. **19.** Please let Mrs. Donnally know if you will be able to be on the program this friday.

    20. sincerely

          Lisa Simons

Handbook
pages 527,
528–529, 531,
544–546, 548–550,
552–556

Writing Activity A Letter

Write a business letter asking a leader in your community to speak at your school. Give three good reasons that will persuade him or her to speak. Use persuasive language.

APPLY MECHANICS AND USAGE: Use correct letter form. Circle the colons after the greeting and the commas in the address, the date, and the closing.

 Social Studies Link

Common Errors with Plurals and Possessives

A plural noun names more than one person, place, or thing. A possessive noun names who or what has or owns something. Although these kinds of nouns are different, writers sometimes confuse them. This chart shows examples of different kinds of mistakes writers make when using plural and possessive nouns. It also shows how to use these nouns correctly.

Common Errors	Examples	Corrected Sentences
Using an apostrophe in a plural noun	The Aztec Indian's built a great civilization in Mexico.	The Aztec Indians built a great civilization in Mexico.
Leaving out an apostrophe in a singular possessive noun	The emperors name was Moctezuma.	The emperor's name was Moctezuma.
Putting an apostrophe in the wrong place in a plural possessive noun	The childrens' training included religious education.	The children's training included religious education.

REVIEW THE RULES

PLURALS AND POSSESSIVES

- A plural noun names more than one person, place, or thing.

- A possessive noun shows who or what owns or has something.

- To form the possessive of most singular nouns, add an *apostrophe* and *s* (*'s*).

- To form the possessive of a plural noun that ends in *s*, add only an *apostrophe* (*'*).

- To form the possessive of a plural noun that does not end in *s*, add an *apostrophe* and *s* (*'s*).

- Remember Most plural nouns are formed by adding *s* or *es*.

More Practice

A. Write the underlined noun. Then write whether it is a singular possessive noun, a plural noun, or a plural possessive noun.

1. The Aztec <u>Indians'</u> civilization was mighty.

2. The largest <u>cities'</u> names were Tenochtitlán and Tlatelolco.

3. The <u>emperor's</u> palace was magnificent.

4. <u>Boys'</u> education included military training.

5. The <u>Spaniards</u> destroyed the Aztec empire in 1521.

B. Write each sentence. Use the possessive form of each underlined noun. Use apostrophes correctly.

6. The Aztec <u>Empires</u> capital was in the Valley of Mexico.

7. An Aztec <u>emperors</u> power depended on the council of nobles.

8. These <u>nobles</u> decisions limited the power of the emperor.

9. Can you imagine the <u>Spaniards</u> amazement when they first saw the Aztec capital?

10. The city was destroyed by the <u>invaders</u> attack.

C. Write each sentence. Use the correct form of the noun in parentheses.

11. Ditches were built to drain (farmers) land.

12. The (city) aqueducts brought water to the people.

13. Removable bridges halted the (enemy) advance.

14. Some Aztec (warriors) wore animal costumes.

15. Many Aztec (shields) were made of gold.

Grammar Troubleshooter, pages 510–511

Handbook
pages 530–531

Writing Activity An Editorial

Imagine that you are the editor of an Aztec newspaper. Write an editorial to try to convince the Spaniards that they should not destroy the Aztec Empire. Give three good reasons.

APPLY GRAMMAR: Be sure to use apostrophes correctly to form singular possessive nouns and plural possessive nouns.

Social Studies Link

Mechanics and Spelling

Directions

Read the passage and decide which type of mistake, if any, appears in each underlined section. Choose the letter for your answer. If there is no error, choose "No mistake."

Sample

I always turn to my grandmother when I need help with a problem. She knows what it's like to deal with challenging situations.

When she was twelve years old, my grandmother traveled alone from portugal to this country. She left her
(1)
parents and came to live with a cousin in Baltimore,
(2)
Maryland. At the age of thirteen, she persuaded a nearby restaurant owner to hire her for kichen duty.
(3)
Even at a young age, my grandmother showed determination and a willingness to work hard.

All proper nouns must begin with a capital letter.

Have you included a comma between the names of cities and states?

The /ch/ sound is often spelled tch when it follows a short vowel sound.

1 **A** Spelling

  B Capitalization

  C Punctuation

  D No mistake

2 **F** Spelling

  G Capitalization

  H Punctuation

  J No mistake

3 **A** Spelling

  B Capitalization

  C Punctuation

  D No mistake

Test Tip
When you have finished, reread all the answer choices to be sure you marked the choice you intended.

Grammar and Usage

Directions

Read the passage and choose the word or group of words that belongs in each space. Choose the letter for your answer.

Sample

The National Baseball Hall of Fame and Museum is located in Cooperstown, New York. This unique Hall of Fame __(1)__ outstanding baseball players of the past. The museum first __(2)__ its doors in 1939. Inside the museum are uniforms of famous baseball __(3)__ and other souvenirs.

Not every baseball player can be nominated for the National Baseball Hall of Fame. Candidates must be retired from professional baseball for at least five years, and __(4)__ must have played at least ten years in the major leagues.

The verb must agree with the subject of the sentence.

Be sure to use the correct tense. Look for clues in the sentence or passage.

Use the plural form of a noun when referring to more than one person, place, or thing.

Remember that the pronoun must agree with the noun to which it refers.

---

1 A honors

　B honor

　C are honoring

　D have honored

2 F will open

　G opens

　H opened

　J is opening

3 A play

　B players

　C player

　D playful

4 F he

　G I

　H you

　J they

TIME FOR KIDS Writer's Notebook

RESEARCH

RESEARCH

When I'm doing research on a topic, I think about the kind of information I need and choose the best **reference sources** for that kind of information. Whether it's a magazine, website, or encyclopedia, I know I'm giving my readers the most complete and accurate information I can get.

COMPOSITION SKILLS

WRITING WELL

"Congratulations; you are a winner!" I use that kind of **lead**, or opening sentence, as an attention-getter. I use **details** to paint a picture in my story. And I save my strongest arguments or facts as an **ending** for my story.

VOCABULARY SKILLS

USING WORDS

<u>Playground</u> and <u>somewhere</u> are **compound words**. They are made from two separate words. When I write, I use compound words to explain a specific idea. But remember: Not all words can be joined together to form compound words. What compound words can you think of?

Read Now!

As you read about some kids who are doing great things, think about each essay's lead and ending. Write down how each lead helped get you into the story and how each ending summed it up.

TIME

FOR KIDS

PHOTO ESSAY

SUPER KID

Kid Heroes!

THESE KIDS DID IT!

Here's a look at some kids who are real-life heroes. They are helping each other, helping the environment, or even saving lives!

Steve Liss for Time for Kids

Nina Berman/Sipa

"We Want Your Tired, Stinky, Old Sneakers!"

When kids at the Heritage Lakes School in Carol Stream, Illinois, decided to help the environment, they got off on the right foot. The students collected old rubber-soled shoes and sneakers that could be used to make bouncy, safe playground surfaces.

Many playgrounds cushion the ground with wood chips called mulch. The students learned they could recycle rubber from old shoes to make a safer, more Earth-friendly surface. The project saved trees by creating a replacement for wood chips. And it used old shoes which might have been dumped in landfills.

The class sent 471 shoes to be shredded into rubber mulch. The rubber mulch pads new playgrounds. Somewhere, kids are playing on Carol Stream's old shoes. And you can bet the Illinois students are getting a kick out of that!

inter NET CONNECTION Go to www.mhschool.com/language-arts for more information on the topic.

A Spot for Nature's Creatures

Many of New Jersey's natural habitats have been replaced with parking lots, malls, and houses. So some fifth-graders at Hillside Intermediate School in Bridgewater, New Jersey, decided to change that. They wanted to help protect the state's natural habitats. The kids wrote dozens of letters to businesses, government offices, and environmental groups to raise awareness about habitat loss.

The students then turned their school backyard into a wildlife-friendly nature preserve. They attracted birds to the area by planting trees and building birdhouses. They planted a wildflower meadow and a sunflower garden. "The environment can't protect itself," says Chris Sorace, a fifth grader. "It needs our help."

A Lucky Brake

When Larry Champagne III was 10, he hit the brakes on a runaway school bus. The St. Louis, Missouri, boy saved himself and 20 other kids on board from disaster.

It all happened in one big, scary flash. On the way to school, the bus driver suddenly blacked out. He slumped over the steering wheel. The bus started swaying, banging into the guardrails. The kids started to scream. But Larry ran to the front and stopped the bus.

"At first I thought, 'We're gonna die,'" says Larry. "But after I pressed the brake, I felt safe."

Write Now!

The Bridgewater, New Jersey, kids had to persuade people to help the environment. Think of an issue that concerns you. Then write to persuade people to get involved.

Choose Reference Sources

You can choose from a variety of **reference sources** to get information about a topic. Which reference book you use depends on the information you need. For example, if you need general information about a topic, use an encyclopedia. Encyclopedias come in book form, and many are also on-line. If you need to refer to a map for a social studies report, use an atlas. The chart below gives examples of the kinds of questions references answer.

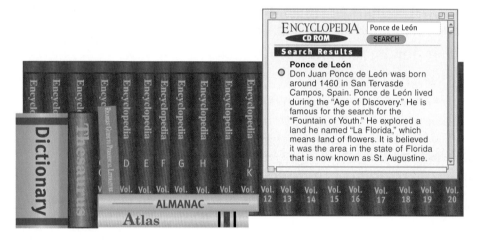

REFERENCE SOURCES

Sample Question	Where to Look
What does the word *superficial* mean?	A **Dictionary** gives the pronunciation, spelling, part of speech, and meaning of a word.
What is another word for *friendly*?	A **Thesaurus** lists words with the same or almost the same meaning.
When did Ponce de León first explore Florida?	An **Encyclopedia** has general articles on many topics.
Where is Kenya?	An **Atlas** has many kinds of maps.
Who were the gold medal winners in the last Olympics?	An **Almanac** has up-to-date information on events.
What have scientists just learned about asteroids?	The **Readers' Guide to Periodical Literature** lists recent articles from many different magazines.

Practice

A. **Write the reference source you would choose to answer each of the following questions.**

1. What does the word *conquer* mean?

2. What are five synonyms of the word *happy*?

3. In which magazine would you find a recent article about cave paintings?

4. Who are the current World Series champions?

5. Which countries border Lake Victoria in Africa?

B. **Write two reference books you would choose to answer each of the following questions.**

6. What is the capital of Indonesia?

7. What is a *wallaby*?

8. What is another word for *gloomy*?

9. What is the population of Bolivia?

10. When did Hernando Cortés live?

C. **Write a question you might look up in each of these reference sources.**

11. Almanac

12. The *Readers' Guide to Periodical Literature*

13. Encyclopedia

14. Dictionary

15. Atlas

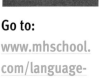

Go to:
www.mhschool.
com/language-
arts **for more
information on
the topic.**

Writing Activity **A Speech**

Think of a cause you would like to support, such as protecting the environment or saving sea mammals. Choose two reference sources that will give you facts about your cause. Take notes on the information you find. Use your notes to write a speech that will persuade your classmates to support your cause, too.

Vocabulary: Compound Words

DEFINITION

A compound word is a word made from two or more words that have been joined together. A compound word can be written as one word, as two or more words separated by a hyphen, or as two separate words.

birth + day = birthday   merry + go + round = merry-go-round

roller + coaster = roller coaster

fingernail	backpack
notebook	living room
double-park	space shuttle
fire truck	fishhook

THINK AND WRITE

Compound Words

Why do you think that most compound words are nouns? In your journal, explain your ideas in at least three sentences.

Read the paragraph below. Look at the highlighted words.

After dinner, Mom said that I needed to clear the table in the dining room, but I wanted to go outside to play. I decided to hurry and load the dishwasher as fast as I could. I worked so fast that I didn't notice I had put the pepper shaker in the dishwasher and the saltshaker in the sink! My effort wasn't exactly first-rate!

Practice

A. Use each pair of words to write a compound word. Use a dictionary if you need help deciding if a compound word should be written as one word, as a hyphenated word, or as two words.

1. dog   collar

2. back   yard

3. self   respect

4. butter   fly

5. table   cloth

B. Write the following sentences. Underline the compound words.

6. Dinnertime for the Ramirez family is usually at six.

7. The silverware is in the drawer.

8. Brandon eats cereal for breakfast.

9. The twins tried to use some double-talk to get out of making dinner.

10. Melissa used a double boiler to heat the milk.

C. **Grammar Link** Match a noun in Column *A* with a noun in Column *B* to make a compound noun. Write each compound noun and use it in a sentence.

Column A	Column B
stepping	speaker
loud	suit
jump	port
waiting	stone
air	room

11. stepping _____

12. loud _____

13. jump _____

14. waiting _____

15. air _____

Writing Activity A Speech

Write a short speech in which you try to persuade someone else in your family to do the dishes for you tonight. Include at least three strong reasons and three compound words.

APPLY GRAMMAR: Be sure to capitalize proper nouns correctly when you write your speech.

Composition: Leads and Endings

To focus a reader's attention, to persuade an audience to do something, or to draw a reader into a story, writers begin with a strong lead. A lead is the opening in a piece of writing. Its purpose is to "grab" the reader's attention. In the same way, endings must also be strong. An ending is the closing in a piece of writing. It summarizes the piece or draws a conclusion. It may even leave the audience with something to think about.

THiNK AND WRITE

Leads and Endings

Why is it important for a newspaper article to have a strong lead? Write your ideas in a brief paragraph.

GUIDELINES

- A lead is at the beginning of a piece of writing.

- A lead can use an "attention-getter," such as a question, a quotation, an anecdote, or a humorous brief story.

- A lead can include the writer's main idea.

- An ending is the last part of a piece of writing.

- An ending can summarize the piece or draw a conclusion. It can leave the reader with a question or with the feeling that it has tied up all the loose ends.

Read the paragraph. Notice how the author's lead and ending help the reader focus on the main ideas.

This lead makes the reader want to find out about the trip. ⟶ We've got to take that trip to Monterey! Our family would enjoy Monterey Bay. We all love to sail, and the bay and the wharf in Monterey are terrific. We could drive, and that would be less expensive than flying. Besides, Dad said *The ending summarizes the main idea of the paragraph.* ⟶ that he wanted us to see where he grew up. I think a trip to Monterey would be the perfect family vacation for us.

Practice

A. Write each sentence. Then write the word *lead* or *ending* to identify what each sentence is.

1. Have you ever gotten up on the wrong side of the bed?

2. We loved the adventure, but we were never so happy to be home.

3. What an adventure was about to unfold!

4. Chen put the money back in his wallet and thought he would remember this lesson forever.

5. As the report shows, these traits make the "Brandywine" tomato a great vegetable.

B. Write a lead sentence for each of these topics.

6. You Can Make a Difference

7. Animals Do Understand

8. Freedom Is More Than Just a Word

9. Why Moving Is an Adventure

10. How Seatbelts Save Lives

C. Grammar Link **11–15.** Write an ending for each of the topics in Practice B. Underline all the nouns in your sentences.

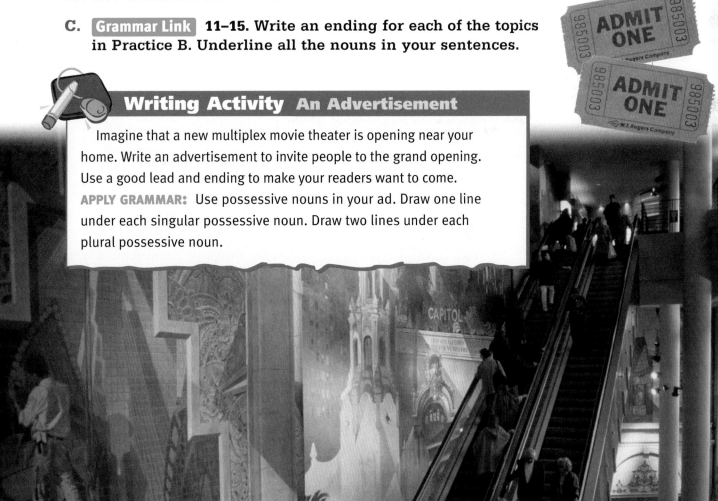

Writing Activity An Advertisement

Imagine that a new multiplex movie theater is opening near your home. Write an advertisement to invite people to the grand opening. Use a good lead and ending to make your readers want to come.

APPLY GRAMMAR: Use possessive nouns in your ad. Draw one line under each singular possessive noun. Draw two lines under each plural possessive noun.

Better Sentences

Directions

Read the passage. Some sections are underlined. The underlined sections may be one of the following:

- Incomplete sentences
- Run-on sentences
- Correctly written sentences that should be combined
- Correctly written sentences that do not need to be rewritten

Choose the best way to write each underlined section. If the underlined section needs no change, choose "No mistake."

> *Long sentences that have no punctuation may need to be written as two separate sentences.*

> *When sentences use the same words, combine ideas to make one sentence.*

Sample

A huge shopping mall was just about to open. The parking lot was jammed hundreds of people were lined up at the doors. The new mall contained more than 500 stores and 25 restaurants. People thought that the theater was the most exciting feature. People thought that the bowling alley was the most exciting feature.

(1)

(2)

1 A The parking lot was jammed hundreds of people were lined up. At the doors.

B The parking lot was jammed hundreds of people. Were lined up at the doors.

C The parking lot was jammed. Hundreds of people were lined up at the doors.

D No mistake

2 F People thought that the theater was the most exciting feature and the bowling alley.

G Some people thought that the theater was the most exciting feature, but other people thought that the bowling alley was the most exciting feature.

H People thought that the theater was the most exciting feature and they thought that the bowling alley was, too.

J No mistake

> **Test Tip**
> Read the entire passage first. Then go back and focus on the test items.

Vocabulary and Comprehension

Directions

Read the passage. Then read each question that follows the passage. Decide which is the best answer to each question. Choose the letter for that answer.

> **Sample**
>
> The men and women of our local volunteer fire department work hard to keep our community safe. They receive no money and little thanks for their brave work. Now it's our turn to show them how much we care.
>
> The Sunnydale Volunteer Fire Department is in desperate need of new equipment. Let's show our support. Help us raise money at the fair, which will be held on the <u>boardwalk</u>.

To define a compound word, look at the meaning of the two words that form the compound.

1 What is the author's purpose in writing this article?

A to tell the public about the life of a firefighter

B to thank firefighters for doing a great job

C to persuade the community to help buy equipment

D to tell about the dangers of fighting fires

2 What does the word *boardwalk* mean in this passage?

F a wide path made of boards

G to walk on boards

H a wood fence

J an old road

Seeing Like a *Writer*

What writing ideas do these pictures give you? How do these pictures persuade you to help save the environment?

Rooftop Garden by Mark Copeland

Writing from Pictures

1. What do you think is the message in each picture? Write three sentences that each include at least two nouns.

2. Choose one of the pictures. Write an attention-getting advertisement that will persuade others to take part in the activity.

3. Choose two pictures. What ideas about the environment do they share? Write a letter to a newspaper to support the message in the pictures. Give at least three strong reasons.

Apply Grammar: Include singular and plural nouns in your writing. Underline singular nouns and circle plural nouns.

127

Persuasive Writing

When you try to get people to agree with your point of view, you are trying to *persuade* them. Persuasive writing tries to persuade an audience to adopt the writer's opinion. Sometimes it even tries to persuade people to take action.

Learning from Writers

Read the following examples of persuasive writing. As you read, look for the authors' opinions. How do they make their arguments? Is each author convincing?

THINK AND WRITE

Purpose

Why does a writer use persuasive writing? Explain your ideas in a paragraph in your journal.

The Forecast: A Warmer World

According to a report by a United Nations scientific group, the earth's average temperature could rise as much as 6° F in the next 100 years! That would be a huge change. Over the past 100 years, the average temperature rose 1° F, and even that is considered to be a big change.

Even a small rise in the earth's temperature could have a big impact. The U.N. scientists predict that over the next century, polar ice caps and glaciers could melt, raising ocean levels as much as three feet. Low-lying land along seacoasts and in river basins could flood. Entire islands in the Pacific could be under water. Many people could have to move to higher ground. . . .

Global warming could also make weather less predictable, with extreme heat and cold, drought and more violent storms. Rainfall patterns could change. Some farm areas could be unable to grow crops.

What can we do? Most nations have taken small steps to control the release of gases that trap heat. Everyone agrees that stronger measures are needed. Scientists now know global warming can't be ignored much longer.

—from "The Forecast: A Warmer World," in *Time for Kids*

94 East 8th Street
Clover, MO 63805
May 17, 20__

Division Publishing Company
886 Third Avenue
New York, NY 10022

Dear Mr. Cisneros:

   I am writing you on behalf of the fifth-grade classes at the Whitney School. Everyone here loves your books, and in a recent student vote, you were chosen Author of the Year.

   Our language arts teacher noticed that you are on a lecture tour and will be speaking in Kansas City on June 21. The town of Clover is nearby, and I would like to invite you to stop here on your way to Kansas City. Everyone would be delighted if you could come and speak on any subject.

   Please let me know if you will be able to speak so that we can make arrangements for your stay.

                              Sincerely yours,
                              Tracy Dell

PRACTICE AND APPLY

Thinking Like a Reader

1. List the reasons that the author of "The Forecast: A Warmer World" is concerned about global warming.

2. Read Tracy Dell's letter again. Why does she want Mr. Cisneros to come to her school?

Thinking Like a Writer

3. How does the author of "The Forecast: A Warmer World" persuade the audience to agree with his opinion?

4. Where does Tracy place her strongest argument? Do you think it will persuade Mr. Cisneros to speak?

5. Reading Across Texts Compare the two literature models. Which one is more convincing? Why?

Features of Persuasive Writing

▶ An Opinion

Reread "The Forecast: A Warmer World" on page 128. What is the author's opinion about global warming?

> Scientists now know global warming can't be ignored much longer.

This persuasive conclusion summarizes the author's opinion about global warming.

▶ Convincing Reasons

The author states that global warming could cause flooding. What reasons are listed to convince the reader that the floods would be harmful?

> Low-lying land along seacoasts and in river basins could flood. Entire islands in the Pacific could be under water. Many people could have to move to higher ground....

The author gives a list of ways that flooding would hurt human beings and other species.

▶ Logical Order

To make a clear argument, it is important to give reasons or details in a logical order. Reread the first paragraph of "The Forecast: A Warmer World." Why are the details listed in this order? Does the writer begin with a strong lead?

> According to a report by a United Nations scientific group, the earth's average temperature could rise as much as 6° F in the next 100 years! That would be a huge change. Over the past 100 years, the average temperature rose 1° F, and even that is considered to be a big change.

The author begins with a strong lead. He uses the example of the 1° F change to show the impact of a 6° F change.

▶ Strongest Argument Last

The author's last argument is meant to leave a strong impression on the reader. This makes it a strong ending.

> Global warming could also make weather less predictable, with extreme heat and cold, drought and more violent storms.

The author's final argument is strong because it lists changes that would directly affect people.

▶ Opinion Words

The author uses opinion words to appeal to the way an audience thinks and feels.

> Everyone agrees that stronger measures are needed.

The author uses the words *Everyone agrees* to persuade the audience to adopt his point of view.

PRACTICE AND APPLY

Create a Features Chart

1. List the features of good persuasive writing.
2. Reread Tracy Dell's letter on page 129.
3. What is Tracy's most persuasive argument?
4. Write one example in Tracy's letter of three features of persuasive writing.

Features	Examples

Prewrite

Persuasive writing presents a writer's opinion about a topic and tries to persuade an audience to agree with that opinion. Persuasive writing may also influence an audience to take a certain plan of action.

Purpose and Audience

The purpose of persuasive writing is to persuade your reader to adopt your opinion. In persuasive writing, you must use convincing reasons and language that will persuade your audience to agree with your point of view.

When planning a persuasive letter, for example, you need to think about your reader. What is his or her opinion about your topic? What will you need to say to get your audience to think as you do?

Choose a Topic

Start by **brainstorming** a list of issues or topics that you feel strongly about. Choose the issue most important to you.

Next, **explore ideas** by making a list of at least three reasons that support your opinion. For each reason, give facts and opinions to support it. Later, you will put your reasons in a logical order.

THINK AND WRITE

Audience

How will your audience's opinion about your topic influence the way you plan and write your persuasive letter? Write your ideas in your journal.

Here is my list of reasons that support my opinion.

Why We Should Clean Up the Park

A clean park will be good for business.
   (Shoppers will like coming to the area.)
Litter looks bad.
Trash is not good for the environment.
Trash causes disease.
Cleaning up would be fun.
Cleaning up the park would make our
   community proud.
Cleaning up would help trash collectors.
Store owners and businesses should help.

Organize • Reasons and Explanations

To plan your persuasive letter, you need to include **facts** and **opinions** that support your position. A fact can be proved to be true. An opinion cannot. As you write your reasons and explain them, jot down whether each reason is a fact or an opinion. Which ideas from her list did the writer leave out?

PREWRITE

DRAFT

REVISE

PROOFREAD

PUBLISH

REASON-AND-EXPLANATION CHART

Position Statement:
Our community park should be cleaned up.   opinion

Reason: A clean park will be good for business.   opinion

Explanation: Shoppers will come to the area.   opinion

Reason: Litter is harmful to the environment.   fact

Explanation: Litter can pollute the water.   fact

Reason: Cleaning up the park would be a good experience.   opinion

Explanation: It's fun to work together with your friends.   opinion

Reason: Cleaning up the park will build community pride.   opinion

Explanation: People take care of their community when they are proud of it.   not sure

Conclusion: Business owners should help clean up the park.   opinion

Checklist ✓
Prewriting

- Did you think about your purpose and audience?

- Did you choose an issue and decide on your position?

- Did you list reasons and explanations that support your opinion?

- Did you organize your reasons in a chart?

- Did you arrange your reasons in a logical order?

- Do you need to find facts or do any research?

PRACTICE AND APPLY

Plan Your Own Persuasive Writing

1. Think about your purpose and audience.

2. Brainstorm a list of topics, and choose one.

3. Use the reason-and-explanation chart to organize your ideas.

Prewrite • Research and Inquiry

▶ Writer's Resources

You may need to do research to support your position in your persuasive letter. First, make a list of questions that your audience might have about your topic. Then decide which resources you will need to answer your questions.

What Else Do I Need to Know?	Where Can I Find the Information?
What conditions affect where people shop?	Interview shopkeepers and community leaders.
What problems does litter create in the environment?	Look in reference and other nonfiction books, and search the Internet.

▶ Use Parts of a Book

Nonfiction books are useful resouces for a writer. These books have different parts to help you find information. In the front of the book, the **title page** tells you the book's title, author, and publisher. The **copyright page** tells you the year the book was published. The **table of contents** lists the titles of the chapters or main sections and the page number on which each begins. In the back of the book, an **index** lists all the topics in the book in alphabetical order.

INDEX

Litter

clean-up campaigns, 148

effects on environment, 122–123

water pollution, 139

STRATEGIES FOR USING PARTS OF A BOOK

- Check the copyright page to make sure the information is current.

- Check to see if the table of contents contains the type of information you are looking for.

- If the table of contents is too general, look at the index for specific topics.

► Choose Reference Sources

It is important to think carefully about your topic when choosing reference sources. If you are writing about a local issue, you might want to ask your community leaders for information. If you need recent information to support facts and opinions, use the *Readers' Guide to Periodical Literature* to find current magazine or newspaper articles. The Internet can also help you find information to support your opinion or position.

► Use Your Research

After completing your research, add any new facts to your reason-and-explanation chart. This writer found information about neighborhood clean-up programs. She also found more details about litter and the environment. How did she change her chart?

PREWRITE

DRAFT

REVISE

PROOFREAD

PUBLISH

Handbook
pages 565, 566, 574, 575

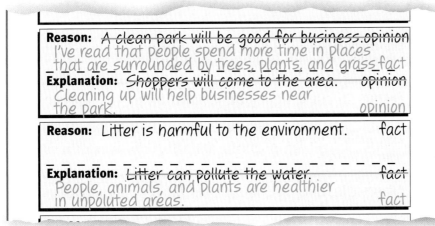

Reason: ~~A clean park will be good for business.~~ opinion
I've read that people spend more time in places that are surrounded by trees, plants, and grass. fact
Explanation: ~~Shoppers will come to the area.~~ opinion
Cleaning up will help businesses near the park. opinion

Reason: Litter is harmful to the environment. fact

Explanation: ~~Litter can pollute the water.~~ fact
People, animals, and plants are healthier in unpoluted areas. fact

Checklist ✓

Research and Inquiry

- ■ Did you list questions a reader might have?
- ■ Did you identify possible references?
- ■ Did you take notes and list your sources?

PRACTICE AND APPLY

Review Your Plan

1. Look at your reason-and-explanation chart.

2. Jot down questions a reader might ask about the ideas you listed in your chart.

3. Identify the resources you will need to find answers to your questions.

4. Add new facts that you gather to your chart.

Draft

Writing PROCESS

Before you begin writing your persuasive letter, review the chart you made. Think about writing a paragraph for each reason you listed. Include details, especially facts, that support each reason. Arrange your reasons in a logical order. Save your strongest reason for last.

Main idea for first paragraph: My position on cleaning up the park

REASON-AND-EXPLANATION CHART

Position Statement:
Our community park should be cleaned up.   opinion

Reason: A clean park will be good for business. opinion
I've read that people spend more time in places that are surrounded by trees, plants, and grass fact
Explanation: Shoppers will come to the area.   opinion
Cleaning up will help businesses near the park.   opinion

This reason is weak: I'll drop this.

Reason: Litter is harmful to the environment.   fact

Explanation: Litter can pollute the water.   fact
People, animals, and plants are healthier in unpoluted areas.   fact

Reason: Cleaning up the park would be a good experience.   opinion

Explanation: It's fun to work together with your friends.   opinion

Reason: Cleaning up the park will build community pride.   opinion

Explanation: People take care of their community when they are proud of it.   not sure   opinion

Conclusion: Business owners should help clean up the park.   opinion

Main idea for the last paragraph before my conclusion: My strongest reason for cleaning up the park.

✓ Checklist

Drafting

- Remember purpose and audience. Will your letter persuade your audience?

- Did you state your position clearly?

- Did you include facts and opinions to support your reasons?

- Did you save your strongest argument for last?

- Did you end with a logical conclusion?

Look at the way this writer used the ideas in her reason-and-explanation chart to write a first draft.

PREWRITE

DRAFT

REVISE

PROOFREAD

PUBLISH

DRAFT

Dear mr. Stanley

There is a lot of litter in Midtown Park. We students are hoping you can help us chang that for three reasons.

> *Opinion is clearly stated.*

I've read that people spend more time in places that are surrounded by trees, plants, and grass. Since there are stores next to the park, it would help business to clean up the land.

> *First reason is stated and supported by opinion.*

Also, litter is harmful to the environment. People, animals, and plants are healthier in unpoluted areas.

> *Second reason is stated and backed up by fact.*

Community pride is another good reason to help. When citizens work together, they feel pride and take care of their community

> *Third and strongest reason is stated and supported by opinion.*

If you don't mind, a volunteer will be calling soon to see if you can donate some materials. Remember: Your customers are depending on you to help. Your community is also depending on you to help.

Sincerly

Patricia Perez

PRACTICE AND APPLY

Draft Your Own Persuasive Letter

1. Review your prewriting chart.

2. State your position at the beginning of the letter.

3. Give your reasons in a logical order.

TiP!

TECHNOLOGY

Be sure that your reasons are written in a logical order with the strongest one last. If not, use the cut-and-paste features on your computer to arrange sentences or paragraphs in the order that will be most convincing to your audience.

Revise

Elaborate

One way to improve your writing is to elaborate. When you elaborate, you add important facts, reasons, opinions, and details that might be missing from your writing. When you revise your persuasive letter, you may need to include more reasons or details to prove your point. The facts and details that this writer added make her arguments more convincing.

> *Studies show* *clean downtown areas*
> ~~I've read~~ that people spend more time in ~~places~~
>
> that are surrounded by trees, plants, and grass.

The writer changed her wording to make her statement more forceful. She also added specific information to influence her reader.

> *your* *is*
> Since ~~there are~~ stores next to the park, it would
> *your*
> help business to clean up the land.

Word Choice

When you use persuasive writing, it is important to understand how the words you choose can influence your audience. In a persuasive letter, **opinion words** help make your statements more convincing.

> *Everyone knows that*
> People, animals, and plants are healthier in
>
> unpoluted areas.
> *the best*
> Community pride is ~~another good~~ reason to help.

OPINION WORDS

I believe

I think

in my opinion

obviously

everyone

no one

ought

should

most

best

least

Better Sentences

As you continue to revise your draft, check your sentences to make sure they fit together well. Read the sentences aloud. Have you combined sentences that repeat the same idea about two different nouns? By combining sentences with similar information about two different nouns, you can avoid writing short, choppy sentences.

Remember: Your customers are depending on you to help.

Your community is also depending on you to help.

Remember: Your customers and community are depending on you to help.

PRACTICE AND APPLY

Revise Your Own Persuasive Letter

1. Add facts and opinions to explain your reasons and make them more convincing.

2. Include opinion words that will influence your audience to accept your position.

3. Make sure that each paragraph introduces a new reason to support your argument.

4. Grammar Should you combine sentences that repeat the same idea about two different nouns?

TiP!

TECHNOLOGY

Find out if your classmates know how to use the automatic letter-formatting function or other word-processing shortcuts. Ask them to explain and demonstrate what they know.

139

Revise • Peer Conferencing

Writing PROCESS

Now that you have made your best first effort, exchange drafts with a partner. Your partner may have new ideas for making your letter more interesting and persuasive.

> You need an opening that gets the reader's attention.

> Interesting! Could you tell me more about your research?

> Time-order and opinion words could make your ideas flow better.

> Good point!

> What do you need? Be specific.

Dear mr. Stanley

There is a lot of litter in Midtown Park. We students are hoping you can help us chang that for three reasons.

I've read that people spend more time in places that are surrounded by trees, plants, and grass. Since there are stores next to the park, it would help business to clean up the land.

Also, litter is harmful to the environment. People, animals, and plants are healthier in unpoluted areas.

Community pride is another good reason to help. When citizens work together, they feel pride and take care of their community

If you don't mind, a volunteer will be calling soon to see if you can donate some materials. Remember: Your customers are depending on you to help. Your community is also depending on you to help.

Sincerly

Patricia Perez

Conferencing for the Reader

- Are the features of persuasive writing included in your partner's letter?
  - writer's opinion
  - convincing reasons
  - opinion words
  - reasons presented in a logical order
  - strongest argument last
- Discuss what you like about your partner's writing, as well as what needs revising.

When you revise your persuasive letter, think about your partner's suggestions. This writer used her partner's ideas to correct and improve several parts of her letter.

PREWRITE

DRAFT

REVISE

PROOFREAD

PUBLISH

REVISE

Dear mr. Stanley

~Have you noticed the~

~There is a lot of~ litter in Midtown Park. We students are

hoping you can help us chang that for three reasons.

First, studies show   clean downtown areas

I've read that people spend more time in ~places~

that are surrounded by trees, plants, and grass.

your   is   your

Since ~there are~ stores next to the park, it would help

business to clean up the land.

Second   Everyone knows that

Also, litter is harmful to the environment. People,

animals, and plants are healthier in unpoluted areas.

Third,   the best

Community pride is ~another good~ reason to help.

When citizens work together, they feel pride and take

care of their community

If you don't mind, a volunteer will be calling soon to

shovels, trash cans, gloves, and other

see if you can donate ~some~ materials. Remember: Your

and community

customers are depending on you to help. ~Your~

~community is also depending on you to help.~

Sincerly

Patricia Perez

Checklist ✔

Revising

■ Have you made your position clear?

■ Will your reasons persuade your audience to agree with you?

■ Have you included facts and opinions?

■ Did you include opinion words to make your arguments stronger?

■ Did you use different kinds of sentences in each paragraph?

■ Is your conclusion persuasive and logical?

PRACTICE AND APPLY

Revise Your Own Persuasive Letter

1. Use the notes from your peer conference.

2. Take out unnecessary information from your draft.

3. Check that you have used the correct letter form.

Proofread

Once you have revised your persuasive letter, you will need to proofread it to find and correct any errors in mechanics, grammar and usage, and spelling.

STRATEGIES FOR PROOFREADING

Read your revised letter more than once. Look for a different kind of error each time you read. Remember: It is easier to concentrate on one kind of error at a time.

- Check for correct capitalization in each part of your letter. Each name and title before it, greeting, and closing of a letter must begin with a capital letter.

- Check for correct punctuation in each part of your letter. Be sure that you have used a colon after your greeting and a comma after the last word in your closing.

- Check for spelling mistakes. Read slowly and carefully rather than reading at your normal rate.

Spelling

When the /j/ sound is spelled *g*, *g* is always followed by *e*, *i*, or *y*, as in the word *change*.

REVIEW THE RULES

GRAMMAR

- Sentences with similar information about two different nouns may be combined. Use the conjunction *and* or *or* to join nouns in a sentence.

MECHANICS

- The greeting and the closing of a letter must begin with a capital letter.

- A colon follows the greeting in a business letter.

- A comma follows the last word in the closing of a letter.

- In the inside address, a comma separates the name of a city and state and the day and year in a date.

Notice the proofreading marks on the draft below. What does the ∽ symbol mean? Why does the writer replace *places* with *clean downtown areas*?

PREWRITE

DRAFT

REVISE

PROOFREAD

PUBLISH

PROOFREAD

Dear mr. Stanley :

⌗ Have you noticed the

There is a lot of litter in Midtown Park. We students are

(SP) change

hoping you can help us chang that for three reasons.

First, studies show   clean downtown areas

I've read that people spend more time in places

that are surrounded by trees, plants, and grass.

your   is   your

Since there are stores next to the park, it would help .

business to clean up the land.

Second   Everyone knows that

Also, litter is harmful to the environment. People,

(SP) unpolluted

animals, and plants are healthier in unpoluted areas.

Third,   the best

Community pride is another good reason to help.

When citizens work together, they feel pride and take

care of their community⊙

If you don't mind, a volunteer will be calling soon to

shovels, trash cans, gloves, and other

see if you can donate some materials. Remember: Your

and community

customers are depending on you to help. Your

community is also depending on you to help.

(SP) Sincerely

Sincerly,

Patricia Perez

Checklist ✓
Proofreading

- Did you use correct letter capitalization and punctuation?

- Did you use correct end punctuation?

- Did you use the correct form for a business letter and indent your letter correctly?

- Did you spell all the words correctly?

PROOFREADING MARKS

⌗ new paragraph

∧ add

∽ take out

≡ Make a capital letter.

/ Make a small letter.

(SP) Check the spelling.

⊙ Add a period.

PRACTICE AND APPLY

Proofread Your Own Persuasive Letter

1. Correct spelling mistakes.

2. Check for correct letter form, including capitalization, punctuation, and formatting.

3. Use the Proofreading Checklist.

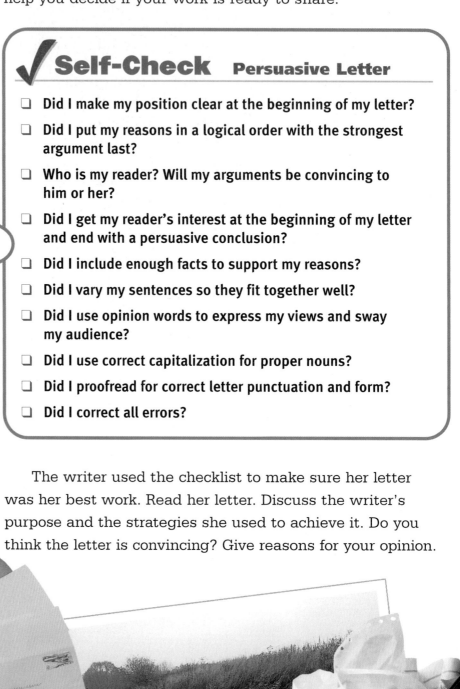

Publish

Review your persuasive letter one more time to see if you are ready to publish it. Follow the checklist below to help you decide if your work is ready to share.

Writing PROCESS

✓ Self-Check Persuasive Letter

❏ Did I make my position clear at the beginning of my letter?

❏ Did I put my reasons in a logical order with the strongest argument last?

❏ Who is my reader? Will my arguments be convincing to him or her?

❏ Did I get my reader's interest at the beginning of my letter and end with a persuasive conclusion?

❏ Did I include enough facts to support my reasons?

❏ Did I vary my sentences so they fit together well?

❏ Did I use opinion words to express my views and sway my audience?

❏ Did I use correct capitalization for proper nouns?

❏ Did I proofread for correct letter punctuation and form?

❏ Did I correct all errors?

The writer used the checklist to make sure her letter was her best work. Read her letter. Discuss the writer's purpose and the strategies she used to achieve it. Do you think the letter is convincing? Give reasons for your opinion.

Park Ridge School
4617 Cedar Drive
Bellaire, TX 77401
November 12, 20—

Central Hardware Company
3144 Bell Boulevard
Bellaire, TX 77401

Dear Mr. Stanley:

Have you noticed the litter in Midtown Park? We students are hoping you can help us change that for three reasons.

First, studies show that people spend more time in clean downtown areas that are surrounded by trees, plants, and grass. Since your store is next to the park, it would help your business to clean up the land.

Second, litter is harmful to the environment. Everyone knows that people, animals, and plants are healthier in unpolluted areas.

Third, community pride is the best reason to help. When citizens work together, they feel pride and take care of their community.

If you don't mind, a volunteer will be calling soon to see if you can donate shovels, trash cans, gloves, and other materials. Remember: Your customers and community are depending on you to help.

Sincerely,

Patricia Perez

PREWRITE

DRAFT

REVISE

PROOFREAD

PUBLISH

TECHNOLOGY

Learn to use your computer and printer to address an envelope. Select the envelope formatting option and type in the receiver's address and your return address. Ask someone to help you position the envelope in the printer.

PRACTICE AND APPLY

Publish Your Own Persuasive Letter

1. Check your revised draft one last time.

2. Make a neat, final copy of your draft.

3. Address an envelope and add your return address.

Present Your Persuasive Letter

To make a persuasive presentation, you need to plan every detail. There are several things you can do to make sure your presentation will be persuasive.

STEP 1

How to Give a Speech

Strategies for Speaking As you prepare to present your persuasive letter, remember that your purpose is to persuade your listeners to agree with you. Think of ways to make your audience care about your topic as much as you do.

■ On note cards, write each reason and one or more facts or opinions that support it.

■ Make eye contact with your audience and state your position with confidence.

■ Use your voice to stress your most important points.

Listening Strategies

■ Understand the speaker's purpose. Is the speaker trying to persuade you to agree with his or her opinion?

■ Grasp the main points. Jot down the list of reasons and explanations that the speaker gives.

■ Listen for persuasive language. If a statement contains opinion words and emotional language, decide whether the statement is supported by fact.

■ Jot down an opinion you don't agree with. Save your comments and questions for after the presentation.

Multimedia Ideas

You may want to create a computer slide show to give visual examples of the points you make. Showing slides on a slide projector is a good way to illustrate your arguments.

STEP 2

How to Show Your Letter

Suggestions for Visuals Make your persuasive presentation more powerful by showing pictures, diagrams, or graphs that your audience could look at as they listen.

- A slogan on a banner, a bumper sticker, or a poster is a good way to make your audience aware of your position.
- Holding up an object to show an important point will help your audience remember that idea.

STEP 3

How to Share Your Letter

Strategies for Rehearsing The more you practice, the more effective your persuasive presentation will be.

- Tape-record or videotape your presentation. Listen to it as if you were in the audience.
- Ask a friend to listen to your speech from across a large room. Have him or her give a signal if you are speaking too softly.

PRACTICE AND APPLY

Present Your Own Persuasive Letter

1. Refer to note cards to help you remember your main points and details.

2. Prepare banners, photographs, slides, diagrams, graphs, or other visuals to sway your audience to your point of view.

3. Give your speech only after rehearsing it for others.

4. Use gestures, emotional language, and eye contact to appeal to your audience.

TiP!

Viewing Strategies

- Make a note of opinion words the speaker has used in slogans or labels.
- Examine photographs and decide whether they support the speaker's opinions.
- Think about how objects and symbols relate to points the speaker is making.

Writing Tests

On a writing test, you are required to write a composition in response to a prompt. Remember to read the prompt carefully. Look for key words and phrases that describe the topic of your composition and explain how you should present your ideas.

Should your writing be formal or should it be friendly?

Are you writing to entertain, inform, or influence your audience?

This sentence tells you what type of information to include in your writing.

> **Prompt**
>
> You and your friends <u>want officials to know</u> about an unsafe intersection near your school. Write a letter to <u>convince the city government</u> that a traffic light is needed. <u>Give clear reasons</u>. Be sure to write about your ideas in detail.

How to Read a Prompt

Purpose Look at the prompt again. Look for key words that tell you the purpose of your writing. The words "convince the city government" tell you that your purpose is to influence someone to do something.

Audience This prompt tells you that your audience is the officials in the city government. If a prompt does not specify the audience, assume it is your teacher.

Persuasive Writing When you are asked to write a letter to influence the opinions of others, you are writing a persuasive piece. The phrase "Give clear reasons" tells you to include convincing reasons and arguments in your persuasive writing. You should usually save your strongest reason for last.

Test Tip
Before you begin writing, make a list of ideas to include in your composition.

How to Write to a Prompt

Here are some tips to think about while you complete a writing test.

Before Writing **Content/Ideas**	• Think about the purpose of your writing. • Consider the best way to present information to your intended audience. • Brainstorm what you know about the topic. • Stay focused on the assignment.
During Writing **Organization/** **Paragraph** **Structure**	• When you are writing to persuade, start with a good topic sentence that clearly states your opinion. • Put your ideas in a logical order. In a persuasive piece, you should usually save your strongest argument for last. • Use transition words to connect ideas. • Write a conclusion that summarizes your main idea.
After Writing **Grammar/Usage**	• Proofread your work. Correct any errors. • Capitalize proper nouns and titles of people. • If you are writing a letter, use correct letter punctuation. • Check that you have spelled each word correctly.

Apply What You Learned

When you read a prompt on a writing test, look for clues about your purpose and audience. Identify the topic and think about the best way to organize your ideas in your writing.

Prompt

Your school is considering a schedule change that would give students an extra thirty minutes of recess each day.

Write a letter to your principal, convincing him or her that extra recess time is or is not a great idea.

Grammar and Writing Review

pages
88–89

Nouns

A. Write the sentences. Underline each noun.

1. Our school needed a song.

2. Their teacher wrote a wonderful melody.

3. The principal asked our class to write the words.

4. My classmates practiced the tune in the auditorium.

5. Students sang it for parents and guests.

pages
90–91

Singular and Plural Nouns

B. Correct the sentences by replacing each underlined singular noun with its plural form. Write the new sentences. Then underline the plural nouns.

6. Many student competed in the sandcastle contest.

7. The event was held at several different beach.

8. Students persuaded their family to join in the fun.

9. Contestants from different country worked together.

10. The boy and girls worked together to build a huge castle.

pages
92–93

More Plural Nouns

C. Write the sentences. Complete each sentence with the correct plural form of the noun in parentheses.

11. We worked together to rake the neighborhood _____. (leaf)

12. The _____ purchased the supplies. (man)

13. The _____ organized jobs for everyone to do. (woman)

14. The _____ made lemonade for the workers to drink. (child)

15. People played _____ while they worked. (radio)

16. Some even watched _____ during their break. (video)

17. Everyone ate chicken _____ for lunch. (sandwich)

18. One group forgot to bring _____ to carve the chicken. (knife)

19. A photographer took _____ of the teams as they worked. (photo)

20. A reporter called the people _____ for cleaning up the neighborhood. (hero)

pages
94–95

Common and Proper Nouns

D. Write each sentence. Draw one line under each common noun. Draw two lines under each proper noun.

21. Our baseball team was saluting the town of River Oaks.

22. Citizens gathered for the celebration on Tuesday night.

23. Virgil and Bruce bought popcorn from a vendor.

24. The mascot, Koko the blue gorilla, clowned around on the field.

25. The players invited the crowd to the first game in April.

pages
96–97

Mechanics and Usage: Capitalization

E. Write each sentence correctly.

26. harley was invited to meet president clayton

27. He left for washington, d.c., on friday, july 1.

28. He and his mother had not seen much of the united states.

29. In fact, they had been outside california only once before, on thanksgiving.

30. During the trip, mother sang a song she wrote called "lend a helping hand."

pages
100–103

Possessive Nouns

F. Write each sentence. Change the underlined group of words to include a possessive noun. Then write whether the possessive noun is singular or plural.

31. The restaurant belonging to Clint held its first chili contest.

32. The brother of Joanie cooked his favorite recipe.

33. The friends of the family helped add spicy ingredients.

34. Yolanda tasted the chili belonging to her friend.

35. The chili recipes of the contestants were a secret.

36. The mouth of Joanie was burning after tasting one spicy recipe.

37. The mayor of the town gave Joanie some lemonade.

38. Mr. Ross won the blue ribbon for the division belonging to the men.

39. Another ribbon went to the division of the children.

40. Joanie smiled warmly as she shook the hand of the winner.

Unit 2 Review

pages
104–105

Combining Sentences: Nouns

G. **Rewrite each pair of sentences by combining them. Then underline the two nouns that are linked together in each new sentence.**

41. Tia organized a party for the retirement home. Tracy organized a party for the retirement home.

42. They prepared sandwiches. They prepared a salad.

43. The salad was made with spinach. The salad was made with lettuce.

44. Tia gathered party supplies. Tracy gathered party supplies.

45. Residents greeted the girls. Staff members greeted the girls.

46. Some musicians played ragtime. Some musicians played jazz.

47. Doctors persuaded people to sing. Nurses persuaded people to sing.

48. Tracy took pictures. Mr. Rivera took pictures.

49. The girls had a fantastic time. The residents had a fantastic time.

50. Tia promised to help them celebrate the holidays. Tracy promised to help them celebrate the holidays.

pages
106–107

Mechanics and Usage: Letter Punctuation

H. **Correct the punctuation in the following parts of a letter.**

51. Dear Mr. Jackson

52. March 16 2002

53. Best regards:

54. San Antonio TX

55. Dear Grandma

56. Dear Sir

57. Yours truly

58. Redwood City CA

59. Dear Sis

60. July 4 2003

pages
120–121

Compound Words

I. Form compound words by joining words in Column A with words in Column B. Write the compound words.

Column A	Column B
56. pop	conditioner
57. air	corn
58. school	uncle
59. wheel	teacher
60. great	chair

pages
122–123

Leads and Endings

J. Write a lead and an ending for each of the following topics.

61. Keeping Our Community Clean

62. Why Summer School?

63. Why Sports Are Important

64. How to Get a Bigger Allowance

65. Saving the Environment

pages
132–147

Proofreading a Persuasive Paragraph

K. Read the following paragraph. Look for mistakes in capitalization, punctuation, grammar, and spelling. Then write the paragraph correctly.

Dear Mr. Bradshaw

My name is pedro savalas, and I am writing to you as a concerned citizen of our community robertson park is downstrem from your factory and I have noticed that the park is getting damaged from your companies waste. Since october, when your company moved to our community, the wild life in the area has suffered. The fish in Slawson river have disappeared. Also, the leafs along the Riverbanks have turned brown. It worrys me to see this destruction. I am asking you to stop dumping chemical waste into the river. It's up to you to keep our community healthy and save.

Project File

A Poem

Poetry is a great way for you to experiment with word patterns, sound, rhythm, and language. You may use poetry to describe, persuade, explain, or tell a story.

> You will need to know the form for a poem when you write your own.

An Unexpected Treasure

In an unexpected place, one day,
A treasure you may find,
Filled with journeys, quests, and feats
Enough to stretch your mind.

Its covers may be leatherbound,
Or have a tattered look.
The adventures that I speak about
Are found within a book.

Topic Choose a topic that will be fun or interesting to write about.

Sound Decide on how you will use sound in your poem. Will your poem rhyme? Will it use sounds that repeat?

Form Think of the pattern, or form, for your poem. Some poems are divided into stanzas, or groups of lines that rhyme.

Descriptive Language Poets create word pictures. Use descriptive words that appeal to one or more of the reader's five senses.

For more information, see Handbook page 586.

154

Write a Persuasive Poem You hear persuasive poetry in many forms in your everyday life. Advertisers often use poetry in their commercials to persuade people to buy products and services. Imagine that you want to persuade someone to do something. Perhaps you would like people to exercise regularly. Maybe you want to persuade people to adopt a pet or eat healthy foods. Be creative, and write a persuasive poem encouraging people to do something. Look at the model on page 154 to give you some inspiration.

ACTIVITY 2

A Public Service Announcement

The kids at Heritage Lakes School collected rubber-soled shoes to be shredded into playground mulch. What are some other ways playgrounds are becoming more "friendly" to the environment? Do research to find out.

Now Hear This! Write a script for a public service announcement to be aired on the radio. The announcement should convince people in your town to use recycled materials to fix up your public playgrounds. Include reasons to explain why using materials that are "environmentally friendly" is important.

Extra Practice

Nouns

A. Read each sentence. Write whether each underlined noun is a person, a place, a thing, or an idea.

1. A medical <u>doctor</u> spoke to our science class.

2. She told us about the <u>body</u>.

3. The <u>heart</u> pumps blood to all parts of the body.

4. <u>Dr. Gilbert</u> let us listen to her heart through a stethoscope.

5. She told us about her work at a well-known <u>hospital</u>.

6. The hospital is in <u>Minnesota</u>.

7. This <u>clinic</u> is famous for medical research.

8. Many <u>people</u> go there to receive help.

9. Dr. Gilbert told us about performing <u>transplants</u>.

10. It takes <u>courage</u> to be a doctor.

B. Write each sentence. Draw one line under each noun.

11. We learned about the body in school.

12. Humans have more than 200 bones.

13. The skeleton helps to protect the organs.

14. Bones and muscles work together.

15. Nerves alert the body to danger.

16. Signals from the brain control the organs.

17. The senses help people adjust to their environment.

18. Lungs take in oxygen for the blood to use.

19. The blood carries nutrients throughout the body.

20. The skin is our largest organ.

C. Write the nouns in each sentence. Next to each noun, write whether it names a person, a place, a thing, or an idea.

21. The body is a complex machine.

22. Many systems work together to keep the body healthy.

23. Different doctors treat different parts of the body.

24. A cardiologist treats the heart.

25. The doctor from Minnesota is a cardiologist.

Singular and Plural Nouns

A. Read each sentence. Write whether the underlined noun is singular or plural.

1. A botanist is a scientist who studies <u>plants</u>.

2. The Egyptians built <u>gardens</u> to observe plants.

3. A Greek is the <u>father</u> of botany.

4. Plants have scientific <u>names</u>.

5. Some names of plants are more than 250 <u>years</u> old.

6. Plants vary from <u>country</u> to country.

7. People around the <u>world</u> use plants to treat illnesses.

8. Scientists make <u>medicines</u> from plants.

9. They are interested in plants from the <u>rain forests</u>.

10. <u>Scientists</u> believe medicines can be made from rare plants.

B. Write each sentence. Draw one line under each singular noun. Draw two lines under each plural noun.

11. Our neighborhood planted a garden.

12. The garden provides fresh fruits and vegetables all summer.

13. Every person works at least five hours a week.

14. Volunteers pull weeds almost every day.

15. The garden needs fertilizer often.

16. The lettuce and avocadoes must be washed.

17. The neighbors enjoy the harvest.

18. Salad tastes better when the tomatoes are fresh.

19. Large, fresh peppers taste good, too.

20. The pumpkins are also big this year.

C. Write the singular and plural nouns in each sentence. Then write the plural form of each singular noun.

21. A peach begins as a blossom on a tree.

22. A strawberry begins as a flower, too.

23. The flowering plants make our garden look pretty.

24. The bush looks beautiful in the yard.

25. What a terrible stain blueberries can make!

Extra Practice

More Plural Nouns

A. Write each noun pair by matching the noun in the left column with its correct plural form in the right column.

1. echo	women
2. woman	moose
3. half	calves
4. tomato	news
5. mouse	halves
6. news	mice
7. foot	sopranos
8. soprano	feet
9. calf	echoes
10. moose	tomatoes

B. Write each noun. Then write its plural form.

11. loaf   **16.** goose

12. cameo   **17.** wife

13. life   **18.** piano

14. ox   **19.** tornado

15. sheep   **20.** scarf

C. Write the sentences. Complete each sentence with the correct plural form of the noun in parentheses.

21. Some local _____ and women helped repair houses. (man)

22. They painted porches and patched _____. (roof)

23. A group of _____ helped clean up the yards. (child)

24. They raked lawns and bagged _____. (leaf)

25. We cooked fish and _____ to feed the volunteers. (potato)

Common and Proper Nouns

A. Write *common* if the underlined word in each sentence is a common noun. Write *proper* if it is a proper noun.

1. The <u>4-H Club</u> has two clubs in our town.

2. My brother belongs to the <u>club</u> led by Mr. Morello.

3. The club cleaned up the park last <u>Tuesday</u>.

4. Two young men from the club entered the <u>Olympics</u>.

5. The <u>mayor</u> honored the club for its work at the food bank.

6. The city council named the <u>leader</u> "Man of the Year."

7. Both clubs marched in the parade along <u>Third Avenue</u>.

8. The children sang a <u>song</u> for the town meeting.

9. The performance moved the <u>audience</u> to tears.

10. The <u>organization</u> is an asset to the Huntsville area.

B. Write each sentence. Draw one line under the common nouns and two lines under the proper nouns.

11. The 4-H Club was founded in the United States.

12. The organization sponsors camps all across the country.

13. Many young people participate in 4-H Clubs.

14. These clubs work with county governments.

15. Their emblem is a four-leaf clover.

16. The letters represent *head*, *heart*, *hands*, and *health*.

17. The 4-H Club is supported by Congress.

18. The National 4-H Council offers many programs.

19. This council gives courses in schools.

20. Boys and girls can join in many parts of the nation.

C. Write the nouns in each sentence. Next to each noun, write *common* or *proper*. Capitalize the proper nouns.

21. Volunteers for 4-H clubs donate time and money.

22. Leaders often drive more than 300 miles each year.

23. Another national club is the boy scouts of america.

24. The girl scouts of america is a well-respected organization.

25. Members sell cookies to raise money.

Extra Practice

Capitalization

A. Choose the word or group of words in each pair that should be capitalized. Then write it using the correct capitalization.

1.	april	raindrop
2.	doctor	dr. bradley
3.	valentine's day	heart
4.	novel	*charlotte's web*
5.	wednesday	tomorrow
6.	brother	gary
7.	woman	mrs. diego
8.	"you are my sunshine"	song
9.	poem	"what is pink?"
10.	birthday	sunday

B. Write the words that should begin with capital letters. Capitalize each word correctly.

11. Our club meets every tuesday.

12. The club leader is mr. parker.

13. We begin each meeting by singing "america."

14. Sometimes we read books such as *a taste of blackberries*.

15. Other days our club watches videos such as *runaway ralph*.

16. The club attended the ballet in january.

17. For st. patrick's day, we put on a play.

18. The smith family directed the play for us.

19. Next friday our club will go on a field trip to the theater.

20. We will watch actors perform in *the pied piper*.

C. Write each sentence. Write a proper noun to replace the underlined words.

21. We don't have school on a winter holiday.

22. The club will meet on a weekday because of the holiday.

23. To celebrate, we will sing a holiday song.

24. Then we will read a holiday story.

25. That holiday makes the month my favorite time of year.

Singular Possessive Nouns

A. Write the possessive form of each singular noun.

1. Rosa
2. painter
3. computer
4. Springfield
5. president
6. uncle
7. dog
8. city
9. Mrs. Stein
10. nurse

B. Write each sentence. Rewrite the words in parentheses to include a singular possessive noun.

11. The mural was (the idea of Willie).
12. We borrowed (the paints of Mr. Grogan).
13. It was (the idea of Gavin) to draw our ancestors.
14. I thought we drew (the sails of the boat) too short.
15. The trees covered up (the head of the sailor).
16. (The bristles of the paintbrush) kept falling out.
17. Ryan painted (the face of his grandfather).
18. (The landmarks of the town) were drawn last.
19. An aide from (the office of the mayor) visited when we had finished.
20. He said the mural showed (the pride of the city).

C. Write the paragraph. Complete each sentence with a singular possessive noun.

Have you ever visited (**21.** ___) oldest neighborhood? The buildings are covered with the (**22.** ___) artwork. One mural honors the (**23.** ___) contribution to the city. (**24.** ___) favorite restaurant is in that neighborhood. Be sure to order (**25.** ___) famous spaghetti if you go there.

Grammar

Plural Possessive Nouns

A. Write the possessive form of each plural noun.

1. scientists
2. orchestras
3. children
4. tuxedos
5. calendars
6. relatives
7. counties
8. women
9. musicians
10. sponsors

11. leopards
12. friends
13. mice
14. pianists
15. ambulances
16. plays
17. senators
18. deer
19. cousins
20. men

B. **Write the possessive form of each plural noun.**

21. ladies

22. trout

23. puzzles

24. teachers

25. conductors

26. boys

27. engineers

28. girls

29. magazines

30. bakers

C. **Write each sentence. Rewrite the words in parentheses to include a plural possessive noun.**

31. (The instruments of the musicians) were tuned, polished, and ready to be played.

32. (The performance of the players) was outstanding.

33. (The chairs of the spectators) were very comfortable.

34. (The help of the ushers) was appreciated by all the people in the audience.

35. (The solos of the students) received standing ovations.

36. Everyone enjoyed (the choir of children).

37. The program included (the names of the composers) and information about their lives.

38. (The seats of the balconies) were full.

39. (The batons of the conductors) looked like blurry lines.

40. (The families of the musicians) were proud of the students and their performance.

Combining Sentences: Nouns

A. Write the two nouns that are joined by a conjunction in each sentence. Include the conjunction in your answer.

1. Trees need good soil and water.

2. Trees and grass make their own food.

3. Bacteria and fungi cause decay.

4. Lakes provide food and shelter for animals.

5. Plants need light and water to grow.

6. Birds and butterflies migrate south for the winter.

7. Trees and flowers produce seeds.

8. People eat berries and nuts from trees.

9. Aspen trees and spruce trees grow in Colorado.

10. Rain and snow can cause flooding.

B. Write the two nouns you can join to combine each pair of sentences.

11. You can plant a tree. You can plant a garden.

12. Boys are cleaning up the beach. Girls are cleaning up the beach.

13. Glass can be recycled. Cans can be recycled.

14. Gardens make a community beautiful. Parks make a community beautiful.

15. I feed the birds in the winter. I feed the deer in the winter.

16. Some people live in cities. Some people live in towns.

17. We grow our own peaches. We grow our own tomatoes.

18. Schools can recycle paper. Businesses can recycle paper.

19. They reuse bottles. They reuse cartons.

20. Miguel joined the Sierra Club. Jon joined the Sierra Club.

C. Rewrite each pair of sentences by combining two nouns.

21. The club will recycle. The team will recycle.

22. Birds need clean water. Fish need clean water.

23. Pollution harms people. Pollution harms animals.

24. Shrubs need light. Shrubs need water.

25. People need food. People need shelter.

Letter Punctuation

A. Write the following words and phrases from business letters. Correct the five examples that contain errors in capitalization and punctuation.

1. Sincerely,
2. May 4, 2001
3. Dear Mrs. Johnson,
4. Yours truly,
5. Orlando Florida

6. Best wishes
7. respectfully,
8. Detroit, Michigan
9. Dear Ms. Torres:
10. September, 21 2002

B. Write the following phrases from business letters. Correct each mistake in capitalization and punctuation.

11. Yours truly
12. April 3 2001
13. Dear Governor Thompson
14. Phoenix Arizona
15. respectfully yours,

16. November 17 2002,
17. Dear Mr. Adolphus,
18. Baltimore Maryland,
19. best Wishes,
20. August, 23 2002

C. Write each numbered item or sentence in the following letter. Add the correct punctuation mark where needed.

21. 770 Chicago St
    Bronson, Michigan 49028
22. September 5 2000

Mrs. June Taylor
Bronson Floral Company
63 Douglas Avenue
23. Bronson Michigan 49028

24. dear Mrs. Taylor

The fifth-grade civics committee is visiting Fair Lawn Senior Home next month. We would like to give residents small bouquets. We are hoping you can help with a donation of flowers.

I believe your donations will bring smiles to many faces and will give you a way to dispose of old flowers. I will be calling soon to see if you can help. Thank you.

25. Sincerely
    Kenny Jones
    Kenny Jones

165

Verbs and Explanatory Writing

In this unit you will learn about verbs. You will also learn about writing that explains. Writing that explains gives you the opportunity to write clear directions or instructions. It also helps you explain to others how to do something that you know how to do well. For this reason, writing that explains is sometimes called "how-to" writing.

Social Studies Link *Read about Gary Soto's memorable character, Lupe Medrano. By taking lessons from her brother and by practicing, Lupe learns how to play marbles and becomes the marble champ.*

S he squeezed a rubber eraser one hundred times, hoping it would strengthen her thumb. This seemed to work because the next day her thumb was sore. She could hardly hold a marble in her hand, let alone send it flying with power. So Lupe rested that day and listened to her brother, who gave her tips on how to shoot: get low, aim with one eye, and place one knuckle on the ground.

"Think 'eye and thumb'—and let it rip!" he said.

from ***The Marble Champ*** by Gary Soto

Thinking Like a Writer

Explanatory Writing In "how-to" writing, the author explains how to do something or gives directions. Reread the passage.

- What steps in the game of marbles does Lupe's brother explain?

Verbs The author used action verbs to explain how to play marbles. Read the sentences again.

QUICK WRITE What are some of the action verbs that the author used to explain how to play marbles?

Action Verbs

RULES

An **action verb** is a word that shows action. It tells what the subject of a sentence *does* or *did*.

She bangs the drum.

She banged the drum.

An action verb tells what event or activity is happening or has already happened. Action verbs express many of the actions that people do every day. *Talk, walk, run, play, go,* and *make* are all common action verbs.

Guided Practice

Name the action verb in each sentence.

EXAMPLE: The band practiced a new march.
practiced

1. Our class played a song.
2. Caroline blew the whistle.
3. Sam banged a gong.
4. Noah rang the bell.
5. Ali struck the cymbal.
6. Karen practices the piano.
7. Noah and Ali write a song.
8. We rehearse for several days.
9. Karen sings the lead.
10. We perform on Tuesday.

REVIEW THE RULES

- An **action verb** tells what the subject of a sentence *does* or *did*.

More Practice

A. Write each sentence. Write *AV* above each action verb.

11. Kim raised the flag.

12. The bugle welcomes the day.

13. Mr. Wright twirled the baton.

14. The band played an anthem.

15. Our class recited the Pledge of Allegiance.

B. Write each sentence. Complete each sentence with an action verb.

16. Our school band _____ a talent contest.

17. We _____ new uniforms.

18. We _____ a march.

19. The judges _____ the winner.

20. Our band _____ a trophy.

C. **Spiral Review** Write the sentences. Complete each sentence with a proper noun, a common noun, or an action verb. Underline the simple subject in each sentence.

21. Our _____ brought their musical instruments.

22. Rick _____ the tuba.

23. _____ carried the saxophone.

24. Lauren _____ her trumpet.

25. Everyone enjoyed the _____.

Extra Practice, page 242.

Handbook
pages 528,
530–531, 532–533

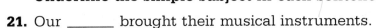

Writing Activity A Poster

Design a poster that tells the steps to learning how to play a musical instrument. The poster should include details such as the name of the instrument and how to hold it properly.

APPLY GRAMMAR: Use action verbs in your poster. Write *AV* above each action verb that you use.

♪♫ **Music Link**

Direct Objects

— RULES —

A **direct object** is a noun or pronoun that receives the action of the verb. It answers the question *whom?* or *what?* after an action verb.

*Brooke judges **dogs**.*

A **direct object** is in the predicate part of the sentence. It receives the action of the verb.

*Nikki gives **ribbons** to the winners.*

Guided Practice

Name the action verb and the direct object in each sentence.

EXAMPLE: We planned a pet show.
action verb: planned; direct object: show

1. My friends enter their pets.
2. Elaine and Brooke judge our show.
3. George shows his iguana.
4. I bring my gray cat.
5. Norma holds her parrot.
6. My cat chases her bird.
7. Thomas carries his snake.
8. A terrier performs tricks.
9. The judges award prizes.
10. George's iguana wears its ribbon.

THINK AND WRITE

Direct Objects
How can you recognize the direct object in a sentence? Write your ideas in your journal.

REVIEW THE RULES

- A **direct object** is a noun or pronoun that receives the action of a verb. It answers the question *what* or *whom* after the action verb.

More Practice

A. Write each sentence. Write *AV* above each action verb and *DO* above each direct object.

11. A beagle shows her skills.

12. Norma's parrot speaks many words.

13. My kitten fetches a ball.

14. Thomas holds his boa constrictor.

15. Two parakeets ring a bell.

B. Write each sentence. Choose a direct object to complete the sentence.

16. Some pets perform _____.

17. The dogs obey their _____.

18. Susan feeds her _____.

19. Richard carefully holds a _____.

20. One judge announces the _____.

Handbook
page 532

C. **Spiral Review** Complete each sentence by using an action verb. Draw one line under the direct object. Draw two lines if the direct object is a proper noun.

21. The owners _____ their pets.

22. Javier _____ his Saint Bernard.

23. The pets _____ their treats.

24. Brooke and Elaine _____ the show.

25. The iguana _____ a prize.

Extra Practice, page 243.

Writing Activity A Paragraph

Write a paragraph about the steps you once took to enter a contest. Be sure to include exact details to make your paragraph interesting.

APPLY GRAMMAR: Include direct objects in your sentences. Write *AV* above the action verbs and *DO* above the direct objects in the sentences.

Verb Tenses

— RULES —

The **tense of a verb** tells when something happens.

A verb in the **present tense** tells that something is happening now.

> *Keith explores caves.*

A verb in the **past tense** shows that something has already happened.

> *Yesterday Keith explored a small cave.*

A verb in the **future tense** shows that something is going to happen.

> *Tomorrow Keith will explore a large cave.*

THINK AND WRITE

Verbs

In your journal, explain how verb tenses show when an action takes place.

Present Tense	today or now
Past Tense	yesterday or sometime in the past
Future Tense	tomorrow or sometime in the future

Guided Practice

Name the verb in each sentence. Tell whether it is in the present, the past, or the future tense.

EXAMPLE: The cave looked dark.
> *looked, past tense*

1. Carrie shined a flashlight into the cave.
2. The flashlight revealed bats on the ceiling.
3. The bats clung to the rocks.
4. We watch the bats silently.
5. I hear a stream in the distance.
6. Crystallized rock gleams in the light.
7. The cave has stalactites.
8. Tomorrow we will climb to another part of the cave.
9. I will remember to take my binoculars.
10. The bright weather will help our attitude.

More Practice

A. Write each sentence. Write *present*, *past*, or *future* to show the tense of the underlined verb.

11. Explorers <u>discover</u> new places.

12. Christopher Columbus <u>made</u> his first voyage.

13. Edmund Hillary <u>climbed</u> Mount Everest in 1953.

14. Today, scientists <u>search</u> for ways to live in outer space.

15. Maybe someday people <u>will find</u> life on other planets.

B. Write each sentence by using the correct tense of the verb.

16. Next week, our class (explore) a cave.

17. Mrs. Adams (say) the trip will be an adventure.

18. Yesterday we (watch) a video about caves.

19. Tomorrow we (read) about cave safety.

20. Every day our class (learn) new things about caves and explorers.

C. **Spiral Review** **Write each sentence. Draw a line between the complete subject and the complete predicate. Describe the tense of each verb. Underline each plural noun.**

21. Long ago, explorers traveled in ships.

22. Today, they use space shuttles.

23. Scientists will discover new ways to travel.

24. Men and women will go to new places in the future.

25. Many people love adventure.

Extra Practice, page 244.

Handbook
pages 528, 532-533

Writing Activity A Log Entry

Pretend you are an explorer. Write a log entry to explain how to do a certain skill, such as use a compass. Use time-order words.

APPLY GRAMMAR: Include verbs in the present, past, and future tense. Write the tense of each verb you use.

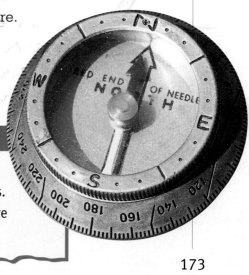

Subject-Verb Agreement

RULES

A verb must agree with its subject. A singular subject takes a singular verb. A plural subject takes a plural verb.

Singular: *Julie likes poetry about nature.*

Plural: *The girls like poetry about birds.*

If the subject is singular, the verb must be singular. Add -*s* to most verbs in the present tense if the subject is singular.

Tim enjoys poems about nature, too.

If the subject is plural, the verb must be plural. Do not add -*s* to the verb if the subject is a plural noun or if the subject is the pronoun *I* or *you*.

Poets create beautiful images with words.

I write poetry about the ocean.

THINK AND WRITE

Verbs

In your journal, write how you know if a sentence needs a singular verb or a plural verb.

Many verbs are singular with an *s* on the end, and plural without the *s*.

Singular Subject	Singular Verb	Plural Subject	Plural Verb
Nancy	writes	Philip and Jack	write

Guided Practice

Name the verb in parentheses that agrees with the subject.

EXAMPLE: Sara and Brenda (read, reads) poetry in the park.
read

1. New ideas (form, forms) in her mind.

2. Today she (see, sees) ducks in the pond.

3. They (play, plays) in the water.

4. The ducklings (follow, follows) the mother duck.

5. You (watch, watches) the ducks with her.

REVIEW THE RULES

- A singular subject takes a singular verb.
- A plural subject takes a plural verb.

More Practice

A. Write each sentence. Use the correct form of the verb.

6. Scott and Chris (visit, visits) a poet.

7. Scott (ask, asks) the poet questions.

8. Chris (write, writes) the answers in a journal.

9. The students (want, wants) to learn how to write poetry.

10. The poet (give, gives) them a book called *How to Write Poetry*.

B. Rewrite each sentence, using a verb from the Word Bank.

like	give	read	tell
likes	gives	reads	tells

11. I always _____ my friend a poem on her birthday.

12. My cousin _____ her toys or clothing.

13. My brother _____ poetry in his English class.

14. My poems _____ my friend why she is special.

15. My friend _____ my gift the best!

Handbook
pages 528, 530,
532–533

C. Spiral Review **Choose the noun in parentheses that agrees with the verb. Write whether the subject is singular or plural.**

16. (Actor, Actors) express feelings in different ways.

17. (A composer, Composers) write music.

18. (A musician, Musicians) plays songs.

19. (A mime, Mimes) shows feelings without saying anything.

20. (A poet, Poets) writes verses about different feelings.

Extra Practice, page 245.

Writing Activity Create a How-to Poster

Make a poster that shows and tells how to create something, such as a poem or a painting. Give the steps in the right order.

APPLY GRAMMAR: Be sure that subjects and verbs agree. Underline each subject once and each verb twice.

Art Link

Spelling Present- and Past-Tense Verbs

RULES

To form **present-tense singular verbs**:

- Add *-s* to most verbs. Add *-es* to verbs that end in *s, ss, ch, sh, x,* or *z.*

  Caitlin dances on her toes.
  Brian catches his dance partner.

- Change *y* to *i* before adding *-es* to verbs that end in a consonant and *y.*

  Amy carries her dance shoes everywhere.

To form **past-tense verbs**:

- Add *-d* or *-ed* to most verbs. Add *-d* to verbs that end in *e.*

  Steve watched and loved the performance.

- Change *y* to *i* before adding *-ed* to verbs that end in a consonant and *y.*

  Stacey hurried to the recital.

- In most cases, double the consonant before adding *-ed* to one-syllable verbs that end in one vowel and one consonant.

  Shannon scanned the audience.

THINK AND WRITE

Verbs

In your journal, write how knowing spelling rules for present-tense and past-tense verbs can help you in your writing.

Guided Practice

Name the verb in parentheses that is spelled correctly.

EXAMPLE: Meryl (wantted, wanted) to be a ballet dancer.
wanted

1. Meryl (pland, planned) for her future career.
2. She (studyed, studied) different ways to dance.
3. Now Meryl (teaches, teachs) ballet to children.
4. She (buzzs, buzzes) with excitement.
5. Meryl (smilees, smiles) all day.

REVIEW THE RULES

- Add -*s* or -*es* to form present-tense singular verbs. Before adding -*es* to singular verbs ending in a consonant and *y*, change *y* to *i*.

- Add -*d* or -*ed* to form past-tense verbs. To add -*ed* to verbs ending in a consonant and *y*, change *y* to *i*. To add -*ed* to one-syllable verbs ending in one vowel and one consonant, double the consonant.

More Practice

A. Write the correct form of the verb in parentheses. Use the tense indicated.

6. Lois (rush) to the ballet competition. *past*

7. She (worry) about her chances. *past*

8. Lois (hurry) through her warm-up exercises. *present*

9. She (watch) the judges carefully. *present*

10. Another dancer (slip) during her dance. *past*

B. Write each sentence. Use the past tense of the verb.

11. Maria (dress) for the performance.

12. She (clip) some barrettes in her hair.

13. Her mother (apply) her makeup.

14. She (like) her mother's help.

15. Maria's performance (amaze) the audience.

C. **Spiral Review** Write each sentence. Use the correct tense of the verb in parentheses. Write *proper* above each proper noun.

16. Yesterday, Carol and I (register) for a talent contest at school.

17. Next week, we (perform) a dance at the Buchanan Center.

18. Last week, we (pick) the music.

19. We always (pick) the music together.

20. Later, we (show) the dance to Miss Ames.

Extra Practice, page 246.

Handbook
pages 532–533

Writing Activity Write Instructions

Write instructions for how to do a dance you've created. Organize the "dance steps" in the best order.

APPLY GRAMMAR: Include both present-tense and past-tense verbs.

 Music Link

Commas

RULES

- A comma tells the reader to pause between the parts of a sentence.

- Use commas to separate three or more items in a series. Do not use a comma after the last word in a series.

    Sherry brought music, food, and games to the cast party.

- Use a comma or commas to set off a person's name when the person is spoken to directly.

    Sherry, I loved your party.

    I need directions to your house, Sherry.

    Your house, Sherry, is beautiful.

- Use a comma to show a pause after an introductory word such as *yes*, *no*, or *well*.

    Yes, I would like to come.

THINK AND WRITE

Commas

How can using commas make your writing clearer? Write your ideas in your journal.

Commas make sentences easier to understand. They signal a pause or separation between parts of a sentence.

Nick, Jake, and Bob went to the cast party.

Terry, are you going?

No, I can't go.

Guided Practice

Tell where a comma is needed in each sentence.

EXAMPLE: Sam Eric and Tina will audition for a play.
Sam, Eric, and Tina will audition for a play.

1. Mom can we be in the play?
2. The auditions are on Thursday Friday and Saturday.
3. Well I can sing and dance.
4. I know Tina that you have acted in other plays.
5. Please wear the fake beard Sam.

REVIEW THE RULES

- Use commas to separate three or more items in a series.

- Use a comma or commas to set off the name of a person who is directly addressed.

- Use a comma to show a pause after an introductory word.

More Practice

A. Write each sentence. Add a comma or commas where needed.

6. Mary will you attend the play?

7. Garth Tina and I won roles in the play.

8. Yes Eric will paint the scenery.

9. Oh we laugh at every rehearsal.

10. We will perform today tomorrow and Saturday.

B. Write each sentence. Use a comma or commas where needed.

11. Penny Al and Eli loved our play.

12. The audience stood and applauded.

13. Have you ever been in a play Nathan?

14. Aaron and I want to be in another play.

15. Well what did you think of the play?

C. ‖Spiral Review‖ **Write each sentence. Use the correct capitalization and punctuation, including commas.**

16. Miss nabors did you make all our costumes

17. She bought buttons fabric and ribbon.

18. Adam nancy and Josh helped miss nabors.

19. They worked on the costumes every monday wednesday and friday.

20. On presidents' day we will perform *young mr. lincoln*.

Handbook
pages 547–550,
554–555

Extra Practice, page 247.

Writing Activity Interview Questions

Write interview questions that you might ask a performer about how he or she prepares to be in a play. Organize your questions.

APPLY MECHANICS AND USAGE: Circle each comma you use.

Mixed Review

REVIEW THE RULES

- An action verb tells what the subject *does* or *did*.
- A direct object receives the action of the verb.
- A present-tense verb tells that something is happening now.
- A past-tense verb tells that something has already happened.
- A future-tense verb tells that something is going to happen.
- A singular subject must have a singular verb.
- Add *-s* or *-es* to form most present-tense singular verbs.
- A plural subject must have a plural verb.
- Add *-d* or *-ed* to form many past-tense verbs.
- Use the comma in a series, after an introductory word, and to set off the name in a direct address .

QUICK WRITE

Verbs

Write five sentences that use action verbs. Use two verbs in the present tense, two verbs in the past tense, and one verb in the future tense.

Practice

A. Write the sentences. Write *AV* above each action verb and *DO* above each direct object. Write whether the verb is in the present, the past, or the future tense.

1. Last year, José entered some diving contests.
2. He loved the challenge.
3. José won many events.
4. He even received medals.
5. Today, he still enters contests.
6. José's speed earns points.
7. The judge measures the distance.
8. José wins the event.
9. He will get a medal.
10. Someday, he will enter the Olympics.

B. **Write each sentence. Use the correct tense of the verb in parentheses. Add a comma or commas where needed.**

11. Yesterday the softball team _____ at the tournament. (arrive)

12. Everyone _____ her own glove ball and bat. (carry)

13. Well the tournament _____ right now. (begin)

14. Friends parents and grandparents _____ the seats. (fill)

15. The team _____ onto the field. (rush)

16. Alexis _____ a fast ball. (pitch)

17. Yes Robin _____ after a fly ball. (race)

18. Cindy always _____ about hitting the ball. (worry)

19. Alexis Cindy and Robin _____ runs every day. (score)

20. Mark _____ we will win the tournament. (guess)

C. **Challenge** **Write the following sentences. Correct the verb forms. Be sure that subjects and verbs agree. Add commas where needed.**

21. The races begins next week.

22. Wayne Billy and Travis plans to attend.

23. No Charlene can't go.

24. She slip on the stairs and broke her ankle.

25. She hope she can go next time.

Extra Practice, page 248.

Handbook
pages 532–533,
554–555

Writing Activity **A Magazine Article**

Write a short magazine article to tell how to organize a local event, such as a softball tournament. Be sure that your instructions are clear and easy for your readers to follow.

APPLY GRAMMAR: Use action words and direct objects. Write *AV* above each action word and *DO* above each direct object.

Main Verbs and Helping Verbs

The **main verb** in a sentence shows what the subject *does* or *is*.

Patty is writing a book about the space shuttle.

A **helping verb** helps the main verb show an action or make a statement.

Patty is writing a book about the space shuttle.

THINK AND WRITE

Verbs

Write in your journal how you know if a verb has a helping verb.

Helping Verbs: am, can, is, could, are, had, was, has, were, should, will, have, shall

Guided Practice

Name the main verb in each sentence. Then name the helping verb.

EXAMPLE: The hot-air balloons will rise into the air.
main verb: rise; helping verb: will

1. People are filling the balloons with helium.
2. Grace and I have watched them all afternoon.
3. Skydivers could perform, too.
4. Kevin could miss the whole event.
5. I will ride in a balloon later.

182

REVIEW THE RULES

- A main verb shows what the subject *does* or *is*.

- A helping verb helps the main verb.

More Practice

A. **Write each sentence. Draw one line under the helping verb. Draw two lines under the main verb.**

6. My family is going to the Kennedy Space Center.

7. We could meet an astronaut.

8. Heather has watched a space shuttle launch.

9. The Kennedy Space Center is located in Florida.

10. The Ruiz family will visit the Kennedy Space Center this fall.

B. **Write the sentences. Complete each sentence with a helping verb.**

11. Look, the space shuttle _____ getting ready to lift off!

12. I _____ hear the engines roar.

13. Mission control _____ started the countdown.

14. Soon the space shuttle _____ blast into space.

15. I _____ take a picture.

C. **Spiral Review** **Write each sentence correctly. Capitalize words and combine sentences as needed. Add helping verbs where necessary.**

16. Smitty learning to fly. jane is learning to fly.

17. They use more practice.

18. Jane invited mom to watch. Jane invited dad to watch.

19. mom and dad watch them tomorrow.

20. Smitty fly solo. jane fly solo.

Extra Practice, page 248.

Handbook
pages 529, 534, 547–550

Writing Activity Trivia Questions

Write trivia questions about traveling by air. Make sure your questions ask for specific answers and that your facts are correct. Use time-order words to organize your facts.

APPLY GRAMMAR: Underline main verbs and helping verbs.

Using Helping Verbs

RULES

- Forms of *be* can be used with a main verb ending in *-ing* to show action that is or was continuing.

    The judges are picking the winner.

    The contestants were waiting patiently.

- The verbs *has, have,* and *had* can be used with the past form of most verbs to show an action that has already happened.

    Dawn has created a new science project.

THINK AND WRITE

Verbs

How do helping verbs let you see how verbs can change to show time? Write your ideas in your journal.

Subject	*Be* plus *-ing* Form	*Has, Have,* or *Had* plus Past Form
I	am playing	have, had played
you	are playing	have, had played
he, she, it	is playing	has, had played
we, they	are playing	have, had played

Guided Practice

Name the helping verb that completes each sentence.

EXAMPLE: Myra (am, is) planning to join the science club.
  is

1. I (has, have) enjoyed the club for two years.
2. Venissa (has, have) served as president of the club.
3. The science club (is, am) meeting tomorrow.
4. We (are, have) discussing our science fair.
5. Ms. Matsuda (is, had) explaining the rules.

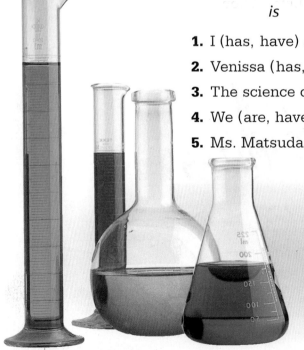

REVIEW THE RULES

- Use a form of the verb *be* with the *-ing* form of a verb.

- Use a form of the verb *have* with the past form of most verbs.

More Practice

A. Write the helping verb that completes each sentence.

6. I (is, am) excited about the science fair.

7. We (have, are) working on our projects.

8. Darnell (has, have) taken pictures all afternoon.

9. I (am, is) presenting a paper on water pollution.

10. Frank and Evelyn (has, have) won ribbons in the past.

B. Complete each sentence with a helping verb.

11. Mr. James _____ graded our science tests.

12. Clancy _____ scored the highest grade in the past.

13. Mr. James _____ calling my name.

14. I _____ scored the second-highest grade.

15. I _____ jumping for joy this very minute.

C. Spiral Review **Complete each sentence with the correct helping verb or punctuation mark.**

The judges (**16.** ____) awarding the science fair prizes. Julie, Dexter (**17.** ____) and Lisa won blue ribbons (**18.** ____) The judges (**19.** ____) presenting a blue ribbon to me, too. My mom (**20.** ____) buying me a present. It is in honor of my blue ribbon.

Extra Practice, page 249.

Writing Activity A Proposal

Write a science-project proposal. Choose a topic for your science project. Include general directions for how the project is done.

APPLY GRAMMAR: Include *-ing* and past forms of verbs. Draw one line under each helping verb and two lines under each main verb.

Science Link

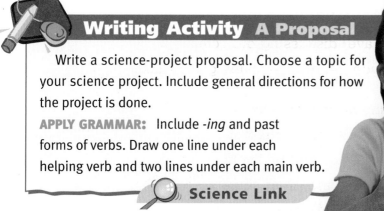

Linking Verbs

RULES

A linking verb links the subject to a noun or adjective. Linking verbs do not show action. Subjects and linking verbs must agree.

The noun that follows a linking verb renames or identifies the subject.

> subj.   LV   noun
> *Ms. Osorio is our teacher.*

The adjective that follows a linking verb describes the subject.

> subj.   LV   adj.
> *The choir seems large.*

A linking verb can also help to state a condition, such as the condition of where or when.

> *Choir rehearsal is tonight.*

THINK AND WRITE

Verbs

How does knowing about linking verbs help you write better sentences? Write your ideas in your journal.

Common Linking Verbs

be: *am, are, is, was, were, will be*				seem	appear
look	taste	smell	feel	become	

Guided Practice

Name the linking verb in each sentence.

> **EXAMPLE:** The spring concert will be tomorrow. *will be*

1. Dress rehearsal was this afternoon.
2. My glee club robe seems long.
3. My shoes feel big.
4. I am excited.
5. Our club members look wonderful.
6. We became nervous before.
7. Mr. Laska is the choir director.
8. The performance will be lively.
9. Some members are great singers.
10. Two former members were sopranos.

REVIEW THE RULES

- A linking verb links the subject of a sentence to a noun or an adjective in the predicate. The subject and the verb must agree.

- A noun that follows the linking verb renames or identifies the subject of the sentence. An adjective that follows the linking verb describes the subject.

More Practice

A. Write each sentence. Underline the linking verb.

11. Our spring concert will be in the town square.

12. Old town squares are interesting places.

13. The stage is red and blue.

14. The flowers smell sweet.

15. The air feels cool.

B. Complete each sentence with the correct form of the linking verb in parentheses. Underline the noun or adjective that this verb links to the subject.

16. The glee club director (seem) nervous.

17. The members of the audience (look) ready.

18. I (be) excited about singing.

19. The concert (be) a success.

20. We (feel) happy about our performance.

C. **Spiral Review** **Write each sentence. Draw a line between the complete subject and predicate. Underline each noun. Circle each linking verb.**

21. The play is tonight.

22. Lance and Pam are the singers.

23. Our club organized the event.

24. The scenery is spectacular.

25. I play the part of a prince.

Extra Practice, page 250.

Handbook
pages 528, 534, 552–555

Writing Activity   A Newscast

Write a television newscast about a special event at your school. Read the report aloud. Make sure your sentences flow together.

APPLY GRAMMAR: Draw one line under each linking verb.

 Drama Link

Irregular Verbs

RULES

An irregular verb is a verb that does not add *-d* or *-ed* to form the past tense or to use with *has, have,* or *had.* The form of a verb used with *has, have,* or *had* is called the past participle.

Present Tense: *Anna and Ethan begin their debate today.*

Past Tense: *Tod and Donna began their debate yesterday.*

Past Participle: *Kendra and Kyle have begun their debate already.*

THINK AND WRITE

Verbs

How can you tell if a sentence has an irregular verb? Write your ideas in your journal.

IRREGULAR VERBS

Present	Past	Past Participle	Present	Past	Past Participle
begin	began	begun	go	went	gone
bring	brought	brought	grow	grew	grown
do	did	done	make	made	made
drive	drove	driven	ride	rode	ridden
eat	ate	eaten	see	saw	seen
fall	fell	fallen	write	wrote	written

Guided Practice

Choose the correct form of the verbs in parentheses.

EXAMPLE: For years, political candidates have (wrote, written) speeches.   *written*

1. Political candidates have always (went, gone) to debates.

2. These debates (grew, grown) from the idea of democracy.

3. Through debates, people (saw, seen) the best candidate.

4. Abraham Lincoln's debates (make, made) him popular.

5. Today, candidates have (brought, brung) their debates to television.

REVIEW THE RULES

- **Irregular verbs** do not form the past tense and the past participle by adding *-d* or *-ed*. Instead, they have special spellings.

- The **helping verbs** *has*, *have*, and *had* are used with all verbs, including irregular verbs, in the past participle.

More Practice

A. Write the correct form of the verb in parentheses.

6. The debate at our school (began, begun) about 30 minutes ago.

7. Our team (went, gone) first.

8. The other team members (make, made) some interesting points.

9. They had (did, done) much research on the topic.

10. Their arguments (grew, grown) stronger and stronger.

B. Write each sentence. Use the correct form of the verb.

11. We (bring) my grandparents to watch my brother's debate.

12. My father had (drive) Mom's car.

13. My brother was almost (do) by the time we arrived.

14. We (see) he had done well.

15. They (make) my brother give the winner's speech.

C. **Spiral Review** Write each sentence. Use the correct form of the verb in parentheses. Underline each simple subject. Add correct punctuation.

16. Yesterday, our teacher (make) us practice our debate.

17. She (begin) by asking our team if we were for or against raising the voting age to 21

18. We (go) with the side to keep the voting age at 18.

19. Then we (write) our ideas about the topic on index cards.

20. By that time, our team had (grow) nervous

Extra Practice, page 251.

Handbook
pages 528, 535

Writing Activity Write Directions

Imagine that your school is holding a debate. Write a note to a relative that explains how to get to your school. Give your directions clearly. List the directions in the correct order.

APPLY GRAMMAR: Circle the irregular verbs that you use.

More Irregular Verbs

RULES

Irregular verbs do not add *-d* or *-ed* in the past tense or past participle.

Present Tense: *I speak to my friends.*

Past Tense: *Yesterday, I spoke to my friends.*

Past Participle: *I have spoken to my friends recently.*

Always use the helping verb *has*, *have*, or *had* with the past participle.

THINK AND WRITE

Verbs

How can knowing the correct form of an irregular verb make your writing clearer? Write your ideas in your journal.

SOME IRREGULAR VERBS

Present	Past	Past Participle	Present	Past	Past Participle
break	broke	broken	speak	spoke	spoken
choose	chose	chosen	swim	swam	swum
draw	drew	drawn	take	took	taken
drink	drank	drunk	teach	taught	taught
fly	flew	flown	throw	threw	thrown
know	knew	known	wear	wore	worn

Guided Practice

Choose the correct form of the verb in parentheses.

EXAMPLE: We (chose, chosen) to go to the county fair.
chose

1. My mother (took, taken) us there in her car.
2. We (knew, known) the fair would be crowded.
3. Leona had (wore, worn) shorts because of the heat.
4. I had (took, taken) my camera to shoot some pictures.
5. One woman (teach, taught) us some handicrafts.

REVIEW THE RULES

- Irregular verbs do not add *-d* or *-ed* in the past or past participle forms.

- The helping verbs *has*, *have*, and *had* are used with the past participles of irregular verbs.

More Practice

A. Write each sentence with the correct verb.

6. Kelly (threw, thrown) the baseballs to win a prize.

7. Her dad had (teached, taught) her.

8. Seth had (threw, thrown) two balls and missed.

9. The last ball (flew, flown) through the air.

10. He had (chose, chosen) the teddy bear as a prize.

B. Write each sentence. Use the correct past tense or past participle form of the verb in parentheses.

11. I would have (choose) to go swimming.

12. James had (take) swimming lessons yesterday.

13. Leona (know) we couldn't decide.

14. We (draw) names to make a choice.

15. Luckily, everyone had (wear) a swimsuit.

C. **Spiral Review** **Write each sentence. Use the correct past tense or past participle form of the verb in parentheses. Underline proper nouns. Write *HV* above the helping verbs.**

16. At the river, we (swim) for an hour.

17. Kelly had (teach) Seth how to do a back flip.

18. Afterward, we (fly) home as fast as we could.

19. We (choose) to eat dinner at a friend's house.

20. Terry had (know) his mother wouldn't mind.

Extra Practice, page 252.

Handbook
pages 534–535

Writing Activity A Postcard

Create a picture postcard that describes a warm-weather activity . Draw an illustration on one side. On the other side, use vivid words to describe the activity.

APPLY GRAMMAR: Draw one line under the irregular verbs you use. Circle the helping verbs.

 **Art Link**

Contractions with *Not*

> ### RULES
> A **contraction** is a shortened form of two words.
>
> *do not = don't*   *should not = shouldn't*

A *contraction* is often made up of a verb combined with the word *not*. An *apostrophe* (') shows where the letter *o* in *not* has been left out of the contraction. A few contractions do not follow this rule. In *can't*, both the *n* and the *o* are dropped. Also, the words *will not* become *won't*.

THINK AND WRITE

Contractions with *Not*

In your journal, write why you think it is important to know about contractions.

Contractions with the Word *Not*

are not	aren't	have not	haven't
cannot	can't	is not	isn't
could not	couldn't	must not	mustn't
did not	didn't	should not	shouldn't
do not	don't	was not	wasn't
does not	doesn't	were not	weren't
had not	hadn't	will not	won't
has not	hasn't	would not	wouldn't

Guided Practice

Name the contraction for each pair of underlined words.

EXAMPLE: We <u>must not</u> be late for the game.
　　　mustn't

1. We <u>did not</u> know the game was today.
2. The coach <u>cannot</u> start without me.
3. The team <u>does not</u> have enough players.
4. The softball league <u>should not</u> have changed the schedule.
5. I <u>have not</u> practiced all week.

REVIEW THE RULES

- A contraction can be formed from a verb and the word *not*.

- An apostrophe (') shows where the letter *o* in *not* has been left out.

More Practice

A. Write the contraction for each pair of underlined words.

6. We <u>had not</u> played their team before.

7. They <u>were not</u> afraid to play our team.

8. The crowd <u>must not</u> forget to applaud both teams.

9. Winning <u>is not</u> everything.

10. We <u>are not</u> giving up!

B. Write each sentence. Replace the underlined words with a contraction.

11. Our class <u>could not</u> decide on a mascot.

12. Mr. Mann <u>does not</u> like snakes.

13. We <u>did not</u> want to have a tiger.

14. Our school colors <u>are not</u> black and gold.

15. Our class <u>did not</u> have any good ideas.

C. [Spiral Review] Write the paragraph. Use a conjunction to combine sentences and a contraction to combine a verb with *not*. Draw one line under each contraction. Draw two lines under each conjunction.

16.–20. Matt raced to the park. Steve raced to the park. They were afraid they would not make the game! They ran to the snack bar too late. The boys were not disappointed, though. They ate a hot dog in the stands. Their team didn't disappoint them, either.

Extra Practice, page 253.

Handbook
pages 527, 553

Writing Activity Write Instructions

Write a paragraph to explain how to play baseball. Include only important information. Give the rules of the game in the best order. **APPLY MECHANICS AND USAGE:** Use contractions. Underline each contraction that you use.

Mixed Review

QUICK WRITE

Verbs

Write five sentences about verbs. Use linking verbs in two of them.

Practice

A. Write each sentence. Draw one line under the linking verb. Draw two lines under the noun or the adjective that follows the linking verb.

1. My parents are teachers.

2. Both of them are smart.

3. I will be a programmer someday.

4. That job looks difficult.

5. My grandfather was a doctor.

6. His parents were very proud.

7. My brother seems uncertain.

8. He was a salesclerk.

9. Now he is a student.

10. He will be successful.

B. Write each sentence. Use the correct form of the verb in parentheses. Draw one line under each helping verb. Draw two lines under each main verb. The main verb may be in either the past participle or *-ing* form.

11. Nicole and Ginger (am, are) entering a geography contest.

12. They each (has, have) chosen different continents.

13. Nicole (has, have) drawn a sketch of a world map.

14. Ginger (are, has) made a globe out of clay.

15. Their social studies teacher (has, have) taught the girls geography.

16. I (am, is) going to the contest, too.

17. We (have, could) ride to the contest together.

18. Nicole and Ginger (was, were) planning on this.

19. We (are, will) go to the competition early.

20. I (shall, were) enjoy the contest.

C. **Challenge** Write the following sentences. Use the words in parentheses to form contractions. Then draw one line under each linking verb. Draw two lines under each irregular verb.

21. Kelly has written a very funny story.

22. At first she (did not) want me to read it.

23. She threw the page near the trash.

24. Her story looked interesting.

25. I (could not) stop laughing.

Handbook
pages
532–535, 553

Writing Activity **A Travel Brochure**

Write a travel brochure that tells people what to see and do in a place you have visited or would like to visit. Give three interesting facts about the place, and provide photographs or illustrations and a caption for each. Choose the most exact words to describe your ideas.

APPLY GRAMMAR: Draw one line under each helping verb, two lines under each main verb, and three lines under each linking verb. Circle all irregular verbs.

Social Studies Link

Common Errors in Subject-Verb Agreement

Every sentence has a subject and a verb. A verb in the present tense must always agree with the subject of the sentence. This means that the subject and the verb must both be singular or both be plural. When you check your own writing, be sure that the subject and the verb agree. Look at the errors on this chart. See how you can correct the mistakes so that the subject and the verb work together.

Common Errors	Examples	Corrected
Using a singular verb with a compound subject joined by and	A nomad and a camel crosses the Sahara Desert.	A nomad and a camel cross the Sahara Desert.
Using the wrong verb with a compound subject joined by or	Dust storms or heat slow them down.	Dust storms or heat slows them down.

THINK AND WRITE

Verbs

In your journal, write how you know whether a compound subject takes a singular verb or a plural verb.

REVIEW THE RULES

SUBJECT-VERB AGREEMENT

- When the parts of a compound subject are joined by *and*, use a plural verb in the present tense.

    Ali and Barbara ride the camel.

- When the parts of a compound subject are joined by *or*, *either...or*, or *neither...nor*, the verb agrees with the subject that is nearer to it.

    Either antelopes or a gazelle roams the desert.

    Neither a tourist nor merchants travel there alone.

- Remember When a verb ends in a consonant and *y*, change the *y* to *i* and add -*es* to form a singular verb.

- Remember When a verb ends in a vowel and *y*, add -*s*. Do not change the spelling.

More Practice

A. For each sentence, write the verb in parentheses that agrees with the compound subject.

1. Wind or dust storms (blows, blow) in the desert.

2. Arabs and Berbers (live, lives) in the Sahara.

3. An oasis or a mirage suddenly (appear, appears).

4. Irrigation ditches or underground water (creates, create) pools of clear water.

5. Corn or cassava melons (grow, grows) on irrigated land.

B. Write each sentence. Choose the verb in parentheses that agrees with the compound subject.

6. Sand dunes and sand plains (stretch, stretches) across the desert.

7. Neither towns nor an oasis (come, comes) into the traveler's view.

8. The sun or the wind (dry, dries) the land.

9. Either a well or springs (produce, produces) water for an oasis.

10. Goats or donkeys (stay, stays) on green grass.

Handbook
page 533

C. Write each sentence. Use the form of the verb in parentheses that agrees with the compound subject.

11. Grass and trees _____ in the Sahara Desert. (exist)

12. Rare antelope or white gazelles _____ the sand dunes. (cross)

13. Gas deposits or oil _____ under the Sahara. (lie)

14. A camel caravan or a diesel truck _____ supplies. (carry)

15. Goats or sheep _____ the Sahara for water. (search)

Grammar Troubleshooter, pages 512–513

Writing Activity A How-to Manual

Write a how-to manual about how to survive in the Sahara Desert if you are out of food or water. Organize your ideas in a logical way.

APPLY GRAMMAR: Be sure that each verb agrees with the subject of the sentence. Spell all singular verbs correctly.

Science Link

Mechanics and Spelling

Directions

Read the passage and decide which type of mistake, if any, appears in each underlined section. Choose the letter for your answer. If there is no error, choose "No mistake."

Be sure to use commas to separate three or more words in a series.

Remember that you do not form the past tense of an irregular verb by adding -ed.

Remember to capitalize proper nouns.

Sample

Last night was the talent show at the county fair.

<u>Sue Nikki and Rick won</u> first place. <u>They sang a funny</u>
(1)

<u>song that Nikki writed, and they</u> performed a short skit
(2)

to go with it. The four friends had been practicing since

last summer so they were especially proud to receive a

first place ribbon. <u>In august, they are going to sing</u> at the
(3)

state fair.

1 A Spelling

  B Capitalization

  C Punctuation

  D No mistake

2 F Spelling

  G Capitalization

  H Punctuation

  J No mistake

3 A Spelling

  B Capitalization

  C Punctuation

  D No mistake

Test Tip

Read all the answer choices carefully before selecting your answer.

Grammar and Usage

Directions

Read the passage and choose the word or group of words that belongs in each space. Choose the letter for your answer.

> **Sample**
>
> Last month, Jeremy __(1)__ a collage in the school art contest. The title of his collage was *Around the World in Pictures*. He included pictures from several __(2)__ travel magazines and highlighted __(3)__ with a marker to add special details. He had worked on the entry for weeks. Jeremy said his collage represented the beauty of people from around the world. Art __(4)__ a good way to help us appreciate our differences.

To determine the correct tense, look for clues in the sentence or in the passage.

Decide the correct part of speech to use here.

Pronouns must agree with the nouns to which they refer.

Remember that the verb must agree with the subject of the sentence.

1 A will enter

　　B enters

　　C is entering

　　D entered

2 F different

　　G differ

　　H differently

　　J difference

3 A they

　　B their

　　C themselves

　　D them

4 F are

　　G were

　　H is

　　J am

TIME FOR KIDS Writer's Notebook

RESEARCH

RESEARCH

When I want to learn more about a subject, an **encyclopedia** is a great place to start. Whether I use an encyclopedia in book form, or on CD-ROM, subjects are listed alphabetically. At the end of each entry, I look for words that say "SEE ALSO." That tells me where I can find other related articles.

COMPOSITION SKILLS

WRITING WELL

To make sure my report comes out as good as it can be, I always **organize** my ideas. Using index cards helps me do that. I put each fact on an index card. That way, I can shuffle the cards and ideas around until I find the right order. Then I number the cards in order from start to finish.

VOCABULARY SKILLS

USING WORDS

A **prefix** is a group of letters I can add to the beginning of a word. A **suffix** is a group of letters I add to the end of a word. If I add <u>ful</u> to <u>wonder</u>, it's <u>wonderful</u>! If I add <u>pre</u> to <u>view</u>, it's <u>preview</u>! Suffixes and prefixes help me to be more specific in my writing. What prefixes and suffixes can you think of?

Read Now!

As you read the following photo essay, note how the story is organized. What facts from the story might you jot down on index cards?

TIME
FOR KIDS
PHOTO ESSAY

A PYRAMID'S BURIED SECRET

Who built the first great city of Mexico?

The Pyramid of the Moon in Teotihuacán, Mexico

SECRET AT THE HEART OF THE PYRAMID

In 1999, scientists were working in the ancient city of Teotihuacán, Mexico (Tay-o-tee-wuh-KAHN) when they first came upon a creepy room inside a pyramid. A human skeleton was resting in a seated position on the floor. Stone knives lay there as well. The skeletons of two young jungle cats were buried amid pieces of a wooden cage. Bones from seven large birds were covered in dirt.

Now scientists are figuring out who built Teotihuacán and its pyramids. They do know that the site was the first great city of an area that includes Mexico and Central America. It is almost 2,000 years old and was once home to more than 150,000 people.

Because the pyramid was built like an onion, in layer upon layer, much of it has yet to be explored. As experts carefully peel away the layers, the secrets of Teotihuacán—and the people who called it home—may finally be unwrapped.

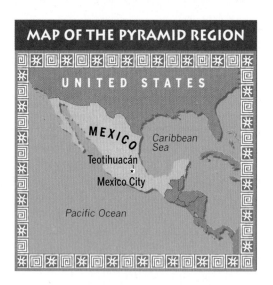

MAP OF THE PYRAMID REGION

UNITED STATES

MEXICO

Caribbean Sea

Teotihuacán

Mexico City

Pacific Ocean

A scientist holds one of the statues found in the pyramid.

Schoolchildren rest on the steps of Teotihuacán's Pyramid of the Moon. The giant Pyramid of the Sun looms in the distance. The Aztecs believed that the city was created by gods. (Teotihuacán means Place of the Gods.) Aztecs also believed that the city was where the sun and the moon were created.

 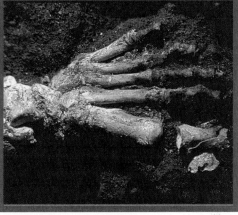

A scientist carefully removes dirt from the human skeleton found in the pyramid. The skeleton's hand is on the right.

Write Now!

Step by step, scientists removed layers of dirt to discover the pyramid's burial room. Think of the steps involved in something you do regularly. Write an explanation of the steps for a friend who may not know them.

Use an Encyclopedia

An **encyclopedia** is a reference that has general articles about people, places, things, events, and ideas. Most encyclopedias are made up of a set of books, or volumes. The articles are arranged in the volumes alphabetically by topic.

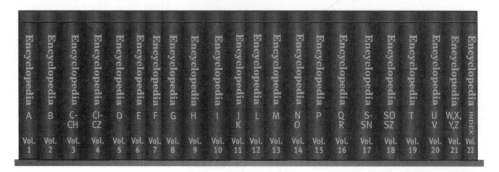

When you use an encyclopedia, you must have a **keyword** in mind. For example, for a research report about koalas, you would look under the keyword *koala* or *marsupial*. You might also look under *Australia*. The spine of each encyclopedia volume may have a word or a letter to tell you which part of the alphabet is in that volume. Encyclopedias also have volume numbers to help you find information.

The entry word *is the title of the article.*

A cross reference *leads you to other articles on the topic.*

Additional resources are books in which you can read about the same subject.

KOALA, *koh AH luh*, is an Australian mammal that looks like a teddy bear. It is sometimes called a *koala bear* or native bear, but the koala is not related to any kind of bear. Koalas have soft, thick fur; a large, hairless nose; round ears; and no tail. The fur is gray or brown on the animal's back and white on the belly. Koalas measure from 25 to 30 inches (64 to 76 centimeters) long and weigh 15 to 30 pounds (7 to 14 kilograms).

Koalas have sharp, curved claws; long toes; and a strong grip. They spend nearly all their time in trees and come down only to move to another one. Koalas are active mainly at night. They sleep most of the day in the fork of a eucalyptus tree. Koalas eat mainly the leaves and young bark of eucalyptus trees.

Koalas are *marsupials*. Female koalas give birth to tiny, poorly developed offspring. Like most marsupials, young koalas are carried in a pouch on the mother's belly until they develop more completely. A baby koala spends its first six months in the pouch and the next six months riding on its mother's back.

At one time, koalas were hunted for their fur. Since the 1920's, however, the killing of koalas has been prohibited by law.

Scientific Classification. Koalas make up the marsupial family Phascolarctidae. They are *Phascolarctos cinereus*.

SEE ALSO MARSUPIAL

Additional resources
Lavine, Sigmund A. *Wonders of Marsupials.* Dodd, 1979. For younger readers.

You can also find encyclopedia articles on-line. CD-Rom encyclopedias help you locate articles quickly. **Search** by typing in the key word. **Browse** by skimming the list of articles available. **Click** on the title that relates to your topic.

Another quick-and-easy way to find information in an encyclopedia is to use the **encyclopedia index**. The index is the last volume. It is also arranged in alphabetical order by subject.

*inter*NET
CONNECTION

Go to:
www.mhschool.
com/language-
arts for more
information on
the topic.

A	⟩ Entry Word
Australia A:891 *with pictures and maps*	
Dollar **D:253**	
International Trade **I:271**	⟩ Volume
Agriculture	
Bee (As an Industry) **B:162-163**	⟩ Page
Sheep **S:310**; (table) **S:312**	
Wheat (table) **W:228** with map	⟩ Subentries

Practice

A. Write each topic below. Then use the encyclopedia on the opposite page to write the number of the volume that would have an article about each of these topics.

1. how to play baseball

2. the early life of Abraham Lincoln

3. the Declaration of Independence

4. the history of Mexico

5. robots

B. Look up each of these topics in an encyclopedia. Write three sentences explaining what you have learned about each topic.

6. weather satellites   **9.** photosynthesis

7. parts of an orchestra   **10.** marsupials

8. how a volcano is formed

Writing Activity Directions

In an encyclopedia, find an article that explains how to play a sport or a game. Use the information to write directions to teach others how to play. Give the steps in order so that they will be easy to follow.

Vocabulary: Prefixes and Suffixes

DEFINITION

Prefixes and suffixes are word parts added to the beginning or ending of a base word, or root word. A prefix is a word part added to the beginning of a base word.

un- + happy = unhappy   *pre- + view = preview*

A suffix is a word part added to the end of a base word, or root word.

hope + -less = hopeless   *wonder + -ful = wonderful*

Prefix	Prefix Meaning
re-	again, back
un-, dis-, non-	not, the opposite of
mis-	wrongly, badly
pre-	before
bi-	having two of; twice
im-, in-	not, without, in, into

Suffix	Suffix Meaning
-ful	full of
-able, -ible	capable or worthy of, fit for
-ness	state, condition, or quality of
-less	without, not having
-ist	one who does or makes
-ment	the act, state, quality, or result of

Read the paragraph below. Look at the highlighted words.

Last night, I saw a preview of a new movie about the great artist, Picasso. This morning I read a critic's review of the movie. She said it shows an incomplete picture of the artist. I would like to see the movie to judge its worthiness

Practice

A. Write each sentence. Draw one line under words with a prefix. Draw two lines under words with a suffix.

1. Last night we watched a movie that was sheer nonsense.

2. I rode my bicycle to the video store to ask for a refund.

3. The clerk was inexperienced but helpful.

4. We had forgotten to rewind the tape.

5. The clerk still honored the "money back" agreement, even though the mistake had been ours.

B. Write each base word. Add a prefix or a suffix from the Word Bank to form a new word.

Prefix	Suffix
pre-	-ible
re-	-ful
non-	-able
im-	-ment

6. place

7. wonder

8. amaze

9. patient

10. flex

C. **Grammar Link** Write each of these verbs and add a prefix or a suffix to make a new word. Use the meaning of the prefix or suffix to figure out the definition of the new word.

11. behave

12. paint

13. agree

14. hope

15. pay

Writing Activity Directions

Write directions to your favorite movie theater. Include two words with a prefix and one word with a suffix.

APPLY GRAMMAR: Include action verbs to make your writing more vivid and interesting.

Composition: Organization

To produce a well-organized paragraph, writers must arrange their sentences in a clear and logical order. This means that all sentences in a paragraph will relate to the main idea.

GUIDELINES

- **Organization** in a paragraph shows a clear and logical connection of ideas.

- A **well-organized paragraph** presents sentences in a logical order.

- Two ways to **organize information** are by time order and spatial order.

- **Time order** uses words such as *first, next,* and *then* to show the order in which an activity should be done.

- **Spatial order** uses words such as *above, near, over, beside, next to,* and *on top of* to make directions clearer.

THINK AND WRITE

Organization

Why is it important for a paragraph to be organized in a clear and logical way? Write a brief paragraph to explain your ideas.

Read this explanation. Notice how the writer uses time-order words and spatial words to organize steps to make them clearer and easier to understand.

All sentences in the paragraph are organized around the main idea.

Time-order words help organize the paragraph by listing the steps in order.

Spatial words make the steps easier to follow.

Test the effects of sunlight on plants. First, gather seeds, potting soil, and two cups. Next, put some soil in each cup. After that, place some seeds in each cup and put soil over them. Then, place one cup in the sun and the other under a slide or in the shade next to a building. Finally, water each plant daily, and observe what happens.

Practice

A. **Write each sentence. Draw one line under the time-order words. Draw two lines under the spatial words.**

1. First, arrange shells in the bottom of a tray.

2. Then, mix the plaster of Paris.

3. Next, pour the mixture on top of the shells.

4. After the plaster hardens, remove the tray and shells.

5. Finally, you have "fossils."

B. **Write each sentence. Add time-order words to organize the steps of the activity in the correct order.**

6. Kara fills the pan with water.

7. She places the pan in the sun.

8. Kara uses white paper to "catch" the rainbow.

9. She leans a mirror at an angle in the pan.

10. Kara moves the mirror to reflect the light onto the paper.

C. Grammar Link **11–15. Organize all the sentences in Practice B into a paragraph that explains how to "catch" a rainbow. Add spatial words to help the reader understand the directions. Replace weak verbs with more vivid action verbs.**

Writing Activity A Recipe

Write a favorite recipe. Use time-order and spatial words to tell how to make the dish. Be sure all the steps are organized in the correct order.

APPLY GRAMMAR: Be sure that you use the correct verb tense for each of the steps in your recipe. Underline each verb and write above it whether it is in the present, the past, or the future tense.

Better Sentences

Directions

Read the passage. Some sections are underlined. The underlined sections may be one of the following:

- Incomplete sentences
- Run-on sentences
- Correctly written sentences that should be combined
- Correctly written sentences that do not need to be rewritten

Choose the best way to write each underlined section. If the underlined section needs no change, choose "No mistake."

Sample

It takes a long time to make a movie. First, someone thinks of an idea for a story. <u>After discussing the idea. A</u> **(1)** <u>screenwriter writes the script.</u> The script may be revised many times. Then, the producer and director hire the actors, designers, and crew. The director spends weeks shooting the film. After that, the film is edited. The sound and special effects are added next. <u>Finally, the</u> **(2)** <u>film is ready. It's ready for the theater.</u>

You can correct a sentence fragment by combining it with a sentence that comes before or after it.

Look for short, choppy sentences that might sound better if combined.

Test Tip

Read items carefully. If you work too quickly, you may make careless mistakes.

1 A After discussing. The idea a screenwriter writes the script.

B After discussing the idea, a screenwriter writes the script.

C After discussing the idea, a screenwriter. He writes the script.

D No mistake

2 F Finally, the film is ready, and it's ready for the theater.

G Finally, the film is ready, it's ready for the theater.

H Finally, the film is ready for the theater.

J No mistake

Vocabulary and Comprehension

Directions

Read the passage. Then read each question that follows the passage. Decide which is the best answer to each question. Choose the letter for that answer.

Sample

Try this easy recipe for a delicious snack. First, cover a cookie sheet with foil. Place a flour tortilla on the cookie sheet and sprinkle it with a few drops of water. Then, spread 1/3 cup of grated cheese on the tortilla. Next, place some green olives on the cheese. Set a flour tortilla on top. Ask an adult to bake your snack in a <u>preheated</u>, 375° oven. Your treat is ready when the cheese bubbles.

To define an unfamiliar word with a prefix or a suffix, think about the meaning of the base word first.

1 To make this snack, you should—

A Put a tortilla on a cookie sheet and sprinkle it with water.

B Put cheese on top of the olives.

C Bake the snack and then cover it with a tortilla.

D Place a tortilla on a cookie sheet and cover it with foil.

2 In this passage, what does the word *preheated* mean?

F Very hot

G Heated again

H Heated before

J The opposite of hot

Seeing Like a Writer

What information can you learn from these pictures? Imagine that you had to explain one of these inventions to your classmates. Think about how you would give clear details. In what order would you write the steps for making this invention?

Recycled Toy Motorcycle

Writing from Pictures

1. Write two sentences for each picture to explain what you see. Include at least one action verb in each sentence.

2. Write a title for one of the pictures. Use one of these words in your title to show place or location: *next to, near, above, below, around, in front of,* or *behind.*

3. Choose two of the pictures. What information do they have in common? Write a short paragraph that explains what you see. Use clear details to write your explanation.

Apply Grammar: Include verbs in your writing. Use one line under each action verb and two lines under each linking verb.

213

Explanatory Writing

Have you ever had to write down directions for someone? Have you ever had to explain how to do or make something? Your directions or instructions were an example of explanatory writing. Writing that explains, or explanatory writing, tells an audience how to do something by giving step-by-step directions. Sometimes this type of writing is called "how-to" writing since it explains how to do something.

Learning from Writers

Read the following examples of explanatory writing. What are the writers explaining? Notice the details that help you follow the steps of the explanation. As you read, look for spatial words that show location or distance.

THINK AND WRITE

Purpose

Why is it important to write a clear explanation? Write your ideas in your journal. Also tell why it is important to organize your steps in a logical way.

Can You Make a Rainbow?

Can you make a rainbow with a garden hose? If you've stood with your back to the sun and looked at the fine mist from a hose, fountain, or waterfall, you've probably seen a rainbow form.

You can also make a rainbow indoors. Fill a clear-plastic cup about halfway with water. Carefully place it on the edge of a table. A third of it should extend over the edge. Hold a piece of white paper directly behind the cup. Shine a flashlight vertically through the bottom of the cup. You should see a rainbow on the paper.

—from *a science textbook*

An Unusual Vegetable

Last year I amazed my friends when I showed them a cucumber inside a bottle. They all wondered how I had managed to get it in there, as the vegetable was much too big to fit through the bottle's narrow neck. Here's how I did it.

In May, I planted some cucumber seeds about six inches apart from one another. Because a cucumber plant is a vine, it will grow up a fence; or it can also be tied with string to a stake as it grows. I used an old stepladder and planted seeds on both sides.

Soon the vines started to grow up the stepladder, and there were small cucumbers starting to form. I chose one about one inch long, but I did not pick it. I slipped the vegetable on its stalk into the bottle. Several weeks later, when the cucumber was fully grown, I cut the stalk and showed my cucumber in a bottle to my baffled friends. —Adam Ling

PRACTICE AND APPLY

Thinking Like a Reader

1. Explain how to create a rainbow as described in "Can You Make a Rainbow?"

2. List in order the step-by-step directions for getting a cucumber inside a bottle as explained in "An Unusual Vegetable."

Thinking Like a Writer

3. What spatial words did the authors of "Can You Make a Rainbow?" include?

4. What time-order and spatial words did the author of "An Unusual Vegetable" use to organize his steps?

5. **Reading Across Texts** Compare the two literature models. Write about how they use step-by-step instructions to explain a task.

215

Features of Explanatory Writing

GUIDELINES

In **explanatory writing**, the writer gives directions or tells the audience how to do or make something, step by step. Good explanatory writing:

▶ **explains** or gives information on how to complete a specific task.

▶ presents **step-by-step instructions** organized in a logical way.

▶ gives **clear details** that are easy to follow.

▶ uses **time-order words** or **spatial words** to make instructions clearer.

▶ Explains or Gives Information

Reread "Can You Make a Rainbow?" on page 214. What will you know how to do after reading the directions?

> Can you make a rainbow with a garden hose?

The main idea of each paragraph suggests that you will learn how to make a rainbow.

▶ Step-by-Step Instructions

Reread the second paragraph of "Can You Make a Rainbow?" What is the last step in making a rainbow indoors?

> Shine a flashlight vertically through the bottom of the cup.

The next-to-last sentence in the paragraph explains the last step. The last sentence in the paragraph tells what will happen if you complete all the steps of the process.

▶ Clear Details

Details give specific information about the steps the writer presents in explanatory writing. The sentence below gives details that help the audience understand what to do.

> Fill a clear-plastic cup about halfway with water.

Notice how the authors tell the exact kind of cup to use as well as how much water to place in the cup.

▶ Time-Order or Spatial Words

Time-order or spatial words help you clearly understand how to complete the steps of the process.

> Hold a piece of white paper directly behind the cup.

What spatial words tell you where to place the paper? How do these words make the instructions clearer and easier to follow?

PRACTICE AND APPLY

Create a Features Chart

1. List the features of good explanatory writing.
2. Reread "An Unusual Vegetable" by Adam Ling, on page 215.
3. Write one example of each feature in Adam's writing.
4. Write a brief summary of the information Adam gives. List the steps in order.

Features	Examples

Prewrite

Explanatory writing gives the reader facts and information about a topic. This writing is sometimes called "how-to" writing because it often explains how to make or do something. Writing an explanation gives you the chance to let others know how to do something that you know how to do.

Purpose and Audience

The purpose of explanatory writing is to inform your reader by giving clear step-by-step instructions. Before writing, think about your audience. Who will your readers be? Also, think about how to present your ideas. What words will you choose to make the steps of your explanation clear?

Choose a Topic

Begin by **brainstorming** a list of things you know how to do well and could explain to others. You might think about explaining a science experiment or another project.

Next, look at your list and choose a topic.

Then, **explore ideas** by making a list of the steps in the experiment or project. Later, you will organize these steps in a flowchart.

Audience

How will your audience affect the way you explain how to do or make something? Write your ideas in your journal.

Here is my list of steps that will explain how to make frost.

How to Make Frost

The temperature needs to be cold.

Place ice in a plastic bag.

Add salt to keep ice cold.

Break ice into pieces.

Use ice pick or hammer.

Put layers of ice in a can.

Put layers of salt in the can.

Keep in a cool place.

Wait for an hour or two.

Watch the frost form on the can.

Organize • Sequence

Writing that explains usually presents instructions in a step-by-step order. To explain something step-by-step, you can use a flowchart to plan your writing. Not all your ideas may be needed, however. What ideas from the list did this writer leave out of her chart?

PREWRITE

DRAFT

REVISE

PROOFREAD

PUBLISH

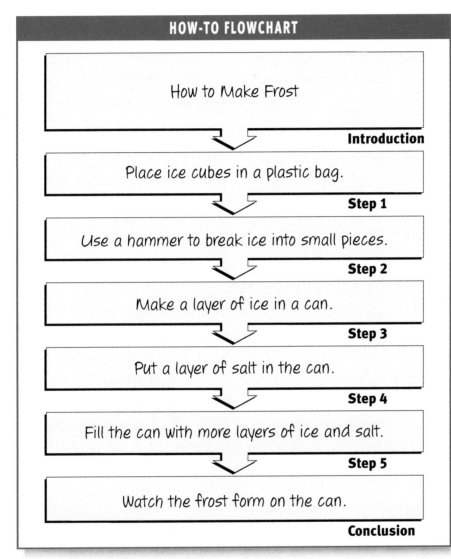

HOW-TO FLOWCHART

How to Make Frost

Introduction

Place ice cubes in a plastic bag.

Step 1

Use a hammer to break ice into small pieces.

Step 2

Make a layer of ice in a can.

Step 3

Put a layer of salt in the can.

Step 4

Fill the can with more layers of ice and salt.

Step 5

Watch the frost form on the can.

Conclusion

Checklist ✓
Prewriting

- Did you think about your purpose and audience?

- Did you make a list of the things you know how to do well?

- Did you choose an experiment, a project, or a skill that you can explain to others?

- Did you organize the steps of the experiment in a flowchart?

- Do you need to check facts or do any research?

PRACTICE AND APPLY

Plan Your Own Explanatory Writing

1. Think about your purpose and audience.

2. Brainstorm ideas for a topic to explain.

3. Choose an experiment, a project, or a skill, and explore ideas.

4. Organize your ideas in a flowchart.

Writing PROCESS

Prewrite • Research and Inquiry

▶ Writer's Resources

You may need to do research to get more information for your explanation. First, make a list of questions. Then, decide where you will go to find answers.

What Else Do I Need to Know?	Where Can I Find the Information?
What is frost?	Take notes from an online search or a talk with a scientist or science teacher.
Why does frost form?	Look in an encyclopedia in book form or on CD-Rom.

▶ Use an Encyclopedia

An encyclopedia has articles about many topics. These articles are arranged in alphabetical order. An encyclopedia can take the form of a set of books, a web site on the Internet, or a program on CD-ROM. Regardless of the kind of encyclopedia you use, you must have a keyword in mind to find information about your topic. For her explanation of frost, the student looked up the keyword *frost* in the *F* volume of a print encyclopedia.

Guide words help you find the article by giving the name of the first complete entry on the page.

The entry word is the title of the article. It is often the keyword of your topic.

A cross reference leads you to other articles that will give you more information.

FRONTIER

FRONTIER. See **PIONEER LIFE IN THE U.S**

FROST is one form of water. It is a pattern of ice crystals that forms when water vapor condenses on a surface, such as a windowpane. Frost usually occurs on cold, cloudless nights when the air temperature drops below 32°F. (0 C), the freezing point of water.

Frost and dew form in much the same way. At night, the drop in temperature causes the earth to cool. As the earth gets cooler, the water condenses, forming dewdrops on surfaces. Some of these dewdrops freeze when the temperature falls below freezing. When the frozen droplets get larger, they become frost crystals.

See also **DEW.**

220

► Search Online

National information services and online encyclopedias can help you check facts and find information. Search the Internet for these and other useful resources. Take notes or print out facts that will help you explain your topic. Write down the web address for each piece of information you find.

► Use Your Research

Review your flowchart, and add any new information you gained from your research. This writer discovered important information about how frost is made. How did she change her chart?

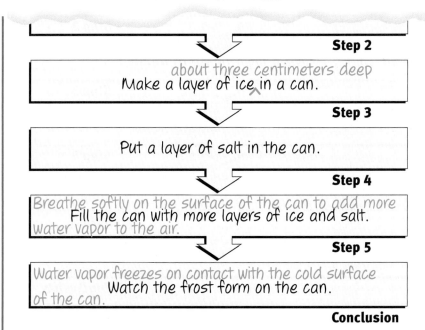

How to Make Frost
Frost is one form of water. It is made from water vapor.

Introduction

Step 2
about three centimeters deep
Make a layer of ice in a can.

Step 3
Put a layer of salt in the can.

Step 4
Breathe softly on the surface of the can to add more
Fill the can with more layers of ice and salt.
water vapor to the air.

Step 5
Water vapor freezes on contact with the cold surface
Watch the frost form on the can.
of the can.

Conclusion

Handbook
pages 565, 567, 574

PREWRITE

DRAFT

REVISE

PROOFREAD

PUBLISH

Checklist ✓

Research and Inquiry

- ■ Did you list your questions?

- ■ Did you identify possible resources?

- ■ Did you take notes or print out useful information?

PRACTICE AND APPLY

Review Your Plan

1. Look at your flowchart.

2. List questions you have about your topic.

3. Identify the resources you will need to find answers.

Draft

Before you begin writing your explanation, review the flowchart you made. Think about making a paragraph for your introduction, for the steps in the middle of your draft, and for your conclusion. Include details that support your step-by-step explanation.

HOW-TO FLOWCHART

The first paragraph should explain what I am going to show how to make.

How to Make Frost
Frost is one form of water. It is made from water vapor.

Introduction

Place ice cubes in a plastic bag.

Step 1

Use a hammer to break ice into small pieces.

Step 2

The steps will make a good second paragraph. I may need to add details to make the steps clearer.

about three centimeters deep
Make a layer of ice in a can.

Step 3

Put a layer of salt in the can.

Step 4

Breathe softly on the surface of the can to add more
Fill the can with more layers of ice and salt.
water vapor to the air.

Step 5

Water vapor freezes on contact with the cold surface
of the can. Watch the frost form on the can.

Conclusion

The last paragraph should show what will happen if I follow all the steps.

✓ Checklist

Drafting

- Does your explanation fit your purpose and audience?

- Are the steps organized in the right order?

- Have you included all the steps so that your audience can do the experiment?

- Do you need to add any important information or details?

- Do you begin and end your explanation in an interesting way?

Look at how this writer used the ideas on her chart to write a first draft. She opened with a question that would get her readers' attention. Then she used time-order words to help show the steps her audience would need to follow in order to do the experiment.

PREWRITE

DRAFT

REVISE

PROOFREAD

PUBLISH

DRAFT

Have you ever notised the frost that forms on windows in the Winter? Did you know that you can make frost? frost was one form of water. It is made from another form of water called water vapor.

First place ice cubes in a plastic bag. Use a hammer to break the cubes into small pieces. Next make a layer of ice about three centimeters deep in a can. Then add a thin layer of salt. Repeat layers of ice and salt until the can is full The surrounding air must contain water vapor for frost to form. Finally, breathe softly on the surface of the can to add more water vapor to the air.

Watch as frost appears on the can. The frost form when the water vapor freezes on contact with the cold surface of the can.

First paragraph tells what the audience will learn how to make.

Second paragraph explains how to do this experiment. Time-order-words connect the steps.

Third paragraph states the conclusion.

PRACTICE AND APPLY

Draft Your Own Explanatory Writing

1. Review your prewriting flowchart.

2. Write about how to make or do something.

3. Put the steps of the experiment in order and use time-order words.

4. Tell the outcome of the experiment in the conclusion.

TECHNOLOGY

You can use the cut-and-paste feature on your computer to put the steps of your explanation in a better order.

Revise

Elaborate

One way to improve your writing is to elaborate. When you elaborate, you add important ideas and details that you might have left out. When you revise your writing, you may need to explain in more detail.

The writer changed some of her directions to make them easier to follow.

> First place ice cubes in a plastic bag. *and seal tightly*

The writer added a better description of where to place the first layer of ice.

> *place*
> Next ~~make~~ a layer of ice about three centimeters
> *at the bottom of*
> deep ~~in~~ a can.

Word Choice

When you are writing, it is important to choose just the right words for your topic and audience.

In an explanation, you need to use spatial words that will help your reader do exactly what is needed to complete each step.

> *inside*   *and seal tightly*
> First place ice cubes ~~in~~ a plastic bag. Use a hammer
> *place*
> to break the cubes into small pieces. Next ~~make~~ a
> *at the bottom of*
> layer of ice about three centimeters deep ~~in~~ a can.
> *on top of the ice*
> Then add a thin layer of salt. Repeat layers of ice
> and salt until the can is full

SPATIAL WORDS

inside
outside
next to
through
on top of
at the bottom of
above
below
near
far
across

Better Sentences

As you continue to revise your draft, check the way your sentences sound. Read them aloud. Do your subjects and verbs agree?

When you check for subject-verb agreement in your writing, find the subject of the sentence first. Then find the predicate, or the verb, of the sentence. Remember: If the subject is singular, the verb must be singular. If the subject is plural, the verb must be plural. Add -s to most verbs if the subject is singular in the present tense.

> forms
> The frost ~~form~~ when the water vapor freezes on
>
> contact with the cold surface of the can.

PREWRITE

DRAFT

REVISE

PROOFREAD

PUBLISH

Handbook
page 533

PRACTICE AND APPLY

Revise Your Own Explanatory Writing

1. Add details or information that will make it easier for your reader to do the activity.

2. Use spatial words to help your reader understand the process.

3. Add details or information that will make your writing clearer and more interesting.

4. **Grammar** Check for subject-verb agreement in your explanatory writing.

TECHNOLOGY

Some of your classmates may know word-processing tips that you might like to know. Ask them to explain and demonstrate these tips by using steps that you can understand.

Revise • Peer Conferencing

Take a break from your writing. Exchange drafts with a partner. Your partner may have some good suggestions to give you. Remember: If your partner can't follow your steps, your audience probably won't be able to follow them either.

> **Your question gets me interested right away.**

> **What materials do you need?**

> **Time-order words help me see the steps.**

> **Add another word to connect the last paragraph.**

Have you ever notised the frost that forms on windows in the Winter? Did you know that you can make frost? frost was one form of water. It is made from another form of water called water vapor.

First place ice cubes in a plastic bag. Use a hammer to break the cubes into small pieces. Next make a layer of ice about three centimeters deep in a can. Then add a thin layer of salt. Repeat layers of ice and salt until the can is full The surrounding air must contain water vapor for frost to form. Finally, breathe softly on the surface of the can to add more water vapor to the air.

Watch as frost appears on the can. The frost form when the water vapor freezes on contact with the cold surface of the can.

Conferencing for the Reader

- Are features of explanatory writing included in your partner's writing?
  - informs or explains
  - step-by-step instructions
  - clear details
  - time-order and spatial words
- Make sure to tell your partner what's good about the piece, as well as what needs improvement.

When you revise your explanatory writing, consider your partner's comments. This writer made changes based on her partner's ideas.

REVISE

How to Make Frost

Have you ever notised the frost that forms on windows in the Winter? Did you know that you can make frost? frost was one form of water. It is made All you need are ice cubes, a plastic bag, a hammer, an empty coffee can, from another form of water called water vapor. and salt.
inside   and seal tightly.
First place ice cubes in a plastic bag. Use a hammer to break the cubes into small pieces. Next make a layer of
place
at the bottom of
ice about three centimeters deep in a can. Then add a
on top of the ice
thin layer of salt. Repeat layers of ice and salt until the can is full The surrounding air must contain water vapor for frost to form. Finally, breathe softly on the surface of the can to add more water vapor to the air.
Now   forms
Watch as frost appears on the can. The frost form when the water vapor freezes on contact with the cold surface of the can.

Checklist ✓

Revising

- Does your explanation suit your purpose and audience?

- Do you need to elaborate on any of your steps?

- Did you describe each of your steps clearly?

- Did you use spatial words to make your steps clearer?

- Did you write your steps in the correct order?

- Did you add a good title?

PRACTICE AND APPLY

Revise Your Own Writing That Explains

1. Read your notes from the peer conference.

2. Add information that will make your steps clearer.

3. Take out information from your draft that isn't necessary.

4. Add a clear, simple title.

Proofread

After you have revised your explanatory writing, you will need to proofread it to find and correct any errors in mechanics, grammar and usage, and spelling.

STRATEGIES FOR PROOFREADING

- **Read your revised explanation several times, each time looking for a different type of error.** This will give you a better chance of catching all mistakes.

- **Read each sentence again to make sure each verb is in the proper tense.** Be sure that verb endings are spelled correctly.

- **Reread for mechanics and usage.** Make sure that your writing is clear and makes sense.

- **Check for spelling mistakes.** Use a dictionary or the spell checker on your computer.

Spelling

When *c* represents the /s/ sound, *c* is always followed by *e*, *i*, or *y*, as in *noticed*.

REVIEW THE RULES

GRAMMAR

- **Present-tense** verbs tell that something is happening now.

- **Past-tense** verbs tell that something has already happened.

- **Future-tense** verbs tell that something is going to happen.

- Be sure that subjects and verbs agree.

- Add *-s* or *-es* to form most singular verbs in the present.

- Add *-d* or *-ed* to form the past tense of many verbs.

- An **irregular verb** does not add *-d* or *-ed* to form the past tense or past participle.

MECHANICS

- Use a **comma** after a time-order word, such as *first*, *next*, and *finally*, and to separate three or more items in a series.

Look at the proofreading corrections made on the draft below. What does the symbol ⌗ mean? Why does the writer want to start a new paragraph?

PROOFREAD

How to Make Frost

noticed (SP)

Have you ever noticed the frost that forms on

windows in the Winter? Did you know that you can

is

make frost? frost was one form of water. It is made   All you

need are ice cubes, a plastic bag, a hammer, an empty coffee can,

from another form of water called water vapor.   and salt.

inside   and seal tightly.

⌗ First, place ice cubes in a plastic bag. Use a hammer to

place

break the cubes into small pieces. Next, make a layer of

at the bottom of

ice about three centimeters deep in a can. Then, add a

on top of the ice

thin layer of salt. Repeat layers of ice and salt until the

can is full. The surrounding air must contain water vapor

for frost to form. Finally, breathe softly on the surface

of the can to add more water vapor to the air.

Now   forms

Watch as frost appears on the can. The frost form

when the water vapor freezes on contact with the cold

surface of the can.

Checklist ✓

Proofreading

- Did you spell all the words correctly?

- Did you insert commas after time-order words?

- Did you correct any problems with verb tenses?

- Did you end each sentence with the correct punctuation mark?

- Did you indent each paragraph?

PROOFREADING MARKS

⌗	new paragraph
∧	add
℘	take out
=	Make a capital letter.
/	Make a small letter.
SP	Check the spelling.
⊙	Add a period.

PRACTICE AND APPLY

Proofread Your Own Explanatory Writing

1. Correct spelling mistakes.

2. Add missing commas.

3. Correct problems with verb tenses.

4. Indent paragraphs.

Publish

Writing PROCESS

Before you publish, review your writing one more time. Use a checklist to help you focus on your work.

✓ Self-Check   Explanatory Writing

❏ **Who was my audience? Did I write in a way that will interest them?**

❏ **What was my purpose? Will my audience understand my explanation?**

❏ **Did I write a strong introduction and conclusion?**

❏ **Did I present my steps in the right order?**

❏ **Did I choose the best spatial words to make my instructions clear?**

❏ **Are my sentences varied? Do they fit together well?**

❏ **Did I use verb tenses and subject-verb agreement correctly?**

❏ **Did I use commas correctly?**

❏ **Did I proofread my writing and correct all the errors?**

This writer used the checklist to review her explanation. Read "How to Make Frost," and discuss the writer's published work. Do you think her writing was ready to publish? Why do you think so?

How to Make Frost

by Emily Chambers

PREWRITE

DRAFT

REVISE

PROOFREAD

PUBLISH

Have you ever noticed the frost that forms on windows in the winter? Did you know that you can make frost? Frost is one form of water. It is made from another form of water called water vapor. All you need are ice cubes, a plastic bag, a hammer, an empty coffee can, and salt.

First, place ice cubes inside a plastic bag and seal tightly. Use a hammer to break the cubes into small pieces. Next, place a layer of ice about three centimeters deep at the bottom of a can. Then, add a thin layer of salt on top of the ice. Repeat layers of ice and salt until the can is full. The surrounding air must contain water vapor for frost to form. Finally, breathe softly on the surface of the can to add more water vapor to the air.

Now watch as frost appears on the can. The frost forms when the water vapor freezes on contact with the cold surface of the can.

TiP!

TECHNOLOGY

Experiment with different type fonts for your title. Be sure to use a large font size and a style that suits your subject.

Practice and Apply

Publish Your Own Explanatory Writing

1. Check your revised draft one more time.

2. Print out or write a neat, final copy of your revised draft.

3. Add pictures that show the steps you have explained.

Present Your Explanatory Writing

To make a good presentation, you need to plan. Use these suggestions to make your presentation a success.

Listening Strategies

- Set a purpose. What will you do to help you listen for information?

- Try to picture what the speaker is explaining.

- Take notes to help you remember how to do the experiment.

- Keep your eyes on the speaker. Pay attention and listen for details.

- Don't interrupt. Jot down your questions to ask later.

STEP 1

How to Explain Your Experiment

Strategies for Speaking When you are preparing your explanatory writing, remember that your purpose is to explain how to make or do something. Try to help your audience understand that they need to follow the steps in order to do the experiment. If possible, demonstrate your experiment as you speak.

- Write the important ideas and key words for each step on note cards to help you remember them.
- Make eye contact with your audience as you speak.
- Stress important words or steps.
- Speak so that everyone can hear you.

Multimedia Ideas

If a live demonstration is difficult, you might want to videotape a demonstration of your experiment to play as you speak. Practice your speech while watching the tape so that your words match the actions in the video.

232

How to Show Your Explanation

Suggestions for Visuals Add visuals to your presentation to help show the steps in your demonstration.

- Make a large poster that illustrates each step in order, or do a type of storyboard that shows each step.
- Add clear labels or captions to explain each illustration.
- If you make illustrations, indicate in your notes when you might want to point to or display each picture.
- If you do a demonstration, check to be sure you have all the items you will need to complete the experiment.

How to Share Your Explanation

Strategies for Rehearsing The more you practice, the better your presentation will be in class.

- Tape-record or videotape your presentation at home. As you listen to or watch it, check for ways to improve your presentation.
- Ask friends or family members to watch your presentation. Have them offer suggestions on how to improve your performance.

PRACTICE AND APPLY

Present Your Own Explanatory Writing

1. Practice saying your explanation aloud.
2. Choose visuals that will help you explain each step in the experiment.
3. Make note cards and use them to rehearse your presentation.
4. Present your writing when you are sure that you can demonstrate each step with confidence.

TIP!

Viewing Strategies

- Be sure you can see the speaker and all the visuals clearly.
- Write down information about the visuals.
- Examine visuals more closely after the presentation.

Writing Tests

On writing tests, you are asked to write a composition in response to a prompt. Be sure to read the prompt carefully. Look for key words and phrases that describe your topic and how you should present it.

Look for words and phrases that name the audience.

Look for clues that tell you the purpose of your composition.

This phrase tells you how to organize your points.

> **Prompt**
>
> **Think of a game that you enjoy playing. Write a composition that <u>gives directions</u> for playing the game. Be sure to <u>present step-by-step instructions</u>.**

How to Read a Prompt

Purpose Look at the prompt again. The words "gives directions" tell you that your purpose is to inform. Your goal is to tell your audience how to play the game.

Audience Sometimes a prompt describes your audience. If a prompt does not state who your audience is, write for your teacher.

Explanatory Writing When you are asked to give instructions or to tell how to do something, you are writing an explanation. The phrase "present step-by-step instructions" tells you that in explanatory writing you should place directions in a logical order. Time-order words will help make your directions easy to follow.

Test Tip

Reread the prompt to be sure you are staying focused on the task.

234

How to Write to a Prompt

Remember these tips when you are given a prompt on a writing test.

Before Writing **Content/Ideas**	• Think about the purpose of your writing. • Keep your audience in mind. • If you are writing an explanation, make a list of steps to include. • Stay focused on the assignment.
During Writing **Organization/** **Paragraph** **Structure**	• Begin with a good topic sentence. • In explanatory writing, place your steps in a logical order. • Use time-order words and words that describe place or location to make your explanation clear. • End with an appropriate conclusion.
After Writing **Grammar/Usage**	• Proofread your work. • Check for subject-verb agreement. • Use commas in a series or after introductory words. • Spell all words correctly, including irregular verbs.

Apply What You Learned

Always determine the purpose and audience when you read a prompt for a writing test. Before writing, decide the best way to organize your ideas.

> **Prompt**
>
> Think of something that you know how to make, such as a birdhouse, a cake, or a kite.
>
> Write a composition that explains how to make the item. Be sure to present your instructions in a logical order.

Grammar and Writing Review

pages
168–171

Action Verbs and Direct Objects

A. Write the sentences. Draw one line under the action verbs. Draw two lines under the direct objects.

1. Abby whistles a tune in the morning.
2. She greets her elderly neighbors every day.
3. She walks their dogs.
4. Abby also carries their groceries.
5. She waves her hand at everyone.

pages
172–173

Verb Tenses

B. Write the sentences. Then write *present*, *past*, or *future* after each sentence to describe the tense of the underlined verb.

6. Terry studies science.
7. Last month, she tracked temperature changes.
8. Next, she will study the life cycle of a butterfly.
9. I like life science, too.
10. Someday, I will discover a new animal species.

pages
174–175

Subject-Verb Agreement

C. Write each sentence. Use the correct form of the verb in parentheses.

11. Nina and Charles (create, creates) comic strips.
12. Charles (write, writes) the dialogue.
13. Nina (draw, draws) the scenes.
14. They (collect, collects) ideas for their stories every day.
15. Charles (read, reads) newspapers and magazines.
16. Nina (watch, watches) people and television.
17. These students (discuss, discusses) their ideas.
18. Charles (plot, plots) the text for each frame.
19. Nina also (sketch, sketches) scenes to go with the text.
20. Nina (complete, completes) the final draft.

Unit 3 Review

pages
176–177

Spelling Present- and Past-Tense Verbs

D. Write each sentence. Use the past-tense form of the verb in parentheses. Then rewrite each sentence in the present tense.

21. Royce (hurry) to get the paper.

22. He (look) quickly through the advertisements.

23. Royce (clip) part of the page.

24. The page (list) guitar lessons.

25. Royce (study) each listing carefully.

pages
178–179

Mechanics and Usage: Commas

E. Write each sentence. Add a comma or commas where needed.

26. Maggie where are you going?

27. We are going to walk shop and eat.

28. Charlene Bob and Laurel are coming with me.

29. Will you come with us Peter?

30. No I can't come today Maggie.

pages
182–183

Using Main Verbs and Helping Verbs

F. Write each sentence. Use the correct form of the verb in parentheses. Then draw one line under the helping verb. Draw two lines under the main verb.

31. Duane is (run) for class president.

32. I am (serve) as his campaign manager.

33. We will (have) a meeting this afternoon.

34. The election can (go) either way.

35. Toshiro and I have (make) the campaign posters.

36. Duane could (give) a speech to the class.

37. He has (work) on the speech since Saturday.

38. Everyone has (participate) in the election.

39. We are (plan) a victory party.

40. Mr. Newton shall (count) the ballots.

Unit 3 Review

pages
186–187

Linking Verbs

G. **Write each sentence. Draw one line under the linking verb.
Circle the word that describes the subject of the sentence.**

41. The dance competition is fantastic.

42. Our teams are great.

43. The competition will be stiff.

44. No one seems nervous, however.

45. I am happy about our chances.

pages
188–191

Irregular Verbs

H. **Write each sentence. Use the correct past-tense form of the
verb in parentheses.**

46. Rick (ride) his bike down the street.

47. He (take) his new baseball glove.

48. He and his friends (begin) to play ball.

49. Rick (throw) the ball to Sally.

50. Coach Jacobs (teach) him to pitch.

51. The team (choose) red as the color for their uniforms.

52. Rick (grow) tall over the summer.

53. He (swim) every day after practice.

54. The team (eat) hot dogs after each game.

55. It (make) the state finals.

pages
192–193

Mechanics and Usage: Contractions with *Not*

I. **Write the contraction of the underlined word or words in
each sentence.**

56. We <u>have not</u> been at camp very long.

57. My mom <u>must not</u> worry about me.

58. I <u>should not</u> wait too long to write her.

59. I <u>cannot</u> think of anything to say.

60. I <u>will not</u> write today.

pages
206–207

Vocabulary: Prefixes and Suffixes

J. **Write the words that have a prefix or a suffix. Underline the prefix or the suffix part in each word.**

61. I am writing about an unimportant movie.

62. I saw a preview of the movie last night.

63. One character was a careless baker.

64. Another was a great artist.

65. The story seemed endless.

66. The plot was impossible.

67. I rewrote my article several times.

68. Movies often give me enjoyment.

69. This movie was complete nonsense.

70. Even the producer should ask for a refund.

pages
208–209

Composition: Organization

K. **Write these sentences in the correct order. Use the time-order words and spatial words in each sentence to help you.**

71. Then, I eat my breakfast.

72. Next, I pour my juice.

73. Finally, I wash my bowl and cup.

74. First, I prepare my cereal.

75. Every morning, I go into the kitchen.

pages
218-233

Proofreading Explanatory Writing

L. **Write the following paragraph correctly. Correct 10 mistakes in capitalization, punctuation, grammar, and spelling.**

I have a favoirte way of making a tuna sandwich. First, I melt butter in a pan on the stove. Next, I adds a slice of bread. Then, I pile on tuna and sprinkle it with salt and pepper. After that, I cover it with a slice of cheese. Finally, I put another piece of bread on top after all these steps are complete, i used a spatula to mash the layers together then, I dont wait. I carefully flipped over the sandwich to brown on the other side.

Project File

A Research Report

You will need to write many research reports in your school career. Writing a research report takes careful thinking and planning. For a research report, you do research on a topic and gather important information from several sources. Then you organize that information in a way that your reader can understand.

You will need to know the features of a report when you write your report in the next unit.

Antarctica: The Harsh Continent

Title *States what your report is about.*

Antarctica is the coldest continent on Earth. Nearly the entire continent is covered by ice, some of which is 7,000 feet thick.

Antarctica plays an important part in the world's weather. This landmass acts like a giant refrigerator for the rest of Earth. By studying the conditions in Antarctica, scientists can make predictions about the weather around the world.

Main Idea *Tells the main idea of the paragraph.*

Supporting Details *Give facts that support the main idea of the paragraph.*

Antarctica is a frigid place that greatly affects Earth's weather. Its conditions are vital in weather prediction.

Conclusion *Summarizes your facts and information.*

List of Sources:
Antarctica by G. Kupperstein
Earth and Weather by Catherine Nelson
The Frozen Continent by Alejandro Vargas

List of Sources *Is at the back of the report and tells the reader where you found your information.*

240

Write a Research Report Choose an animal that you would like to know more about. Write questions you have about the animal. Research your animal using at least three sources. Take notes on your sources to find answers to your questions. Group the information you find into categories such as *what the animal looks like, where it lives,* and *what it eats.* Keep in mind that these categories will become paragraphs for your report. List the sources you used at the end of your notes.

ACTIVITY 2

An Explanatory Paragraph

Scientists, such as those described in "A Pyramid's Buried Secret," must make careful plans and do much study before beginning an archaeological "dig." Do research to find out how scientists prepare for an upcoming dig.

How-to Write a paragraph that gives step-by-step instructions on how to prepare for an archaeological dig. Draw simple diagrams to illustrate any steps that could be shown with pictures.

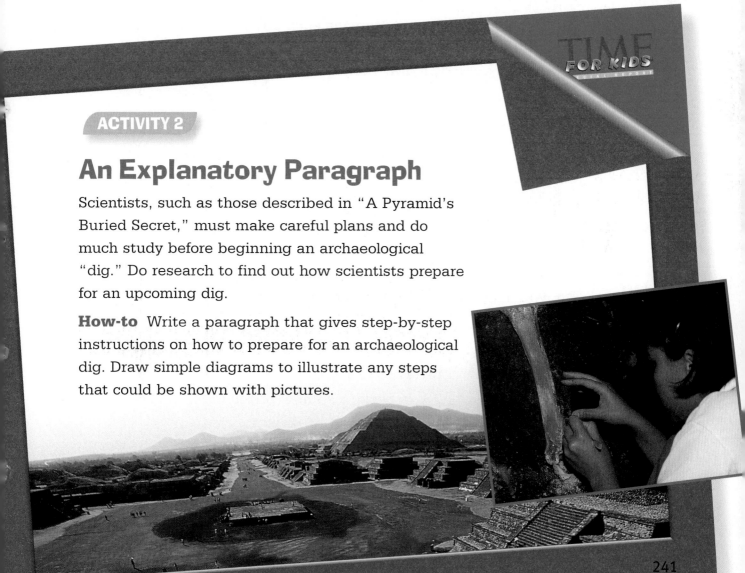

Extra Practice

Action Verbs

A. Write the action verb in each sentence.

1. Our family drove to the state fair.

2. Jamie watched the rodeo.

3. Andrew ate two corn dogs.

4. Jenna rode the merry-go-round.

5. My mother sewed a quilt for the quilt show.

6. The quilt won a blue ribbon.

7. Our family played carnival games.

8. My dad threw basketballs.

9. Jamie pitched pennies.

10. We stayed until after dark.

B. Write each sentence. Replace each underlined action verb with a different action verb.

11. A little girl rode a gray pony.

12. A clown made funny faces.

13. Artists carved statues.

14. People toured the exhibits.

15. I chose cotton candy for a snack.

16. Firefighters demonstrated safety techniques.

17. The crowd loved the parade.

18. My family watched a concert.

19. The musicians sang country songs.

20. We rode home after midnight.

C. Write each sentence. Complete each sentence with an action verb.

21. I _____ my little sister in a wagon.

22. My brother _____ a backpack full of prizes.

23. My parents _____ us every year.

24. We _____ a lot of treats.

25. Everyone _____ the fair.

Direct Objects

A. **Write the direct object in each sentence.**

1. These pets perform tricks.
2. The collie fetches the ball.
3. The kitten climbs a rope.
4. A parakeet rings a bell.
5. A monkey rides a tricycle.
6. Two mice run a race.
7. The gerbil spins the wheel.
8. A retriever catches a Frisbee.
9. The beagle climbs a ladder.
10. The animals eat their treats.

B. **Write the sentences. Choose a direct object to complete each sentence.**

11. The dog owners entered a _____.
12. The shepherd wears a _____.
13. The labrador fetches some _____.
14. The beagle digs a _____.
15. A girl called her _____.
16. A boy commanded his _____.
17. A woman washed her _____.
18. A poodle circled a _____.
19. The judge blew a _____.
20. The winner received a _____.

C. **Use each word as the direct object in a sentence. Write each new sentence.**

21. beagle
22. brush
23. trophy
24. collar
25. ball

Verb Tenses

A. Write *present*, *past,* or *future* to name the tense of the underlined verb.

1. Tomorrow we will explore the forest.

2. Curtis finds the trail.

3. Carrie packs carefully for the trip.

4. I packed my flashlight and compass.

5. We will hike most of the day.

6. Curtis climbs very quickly.

7. Carrie asked me to hold her pack.

8. I examine the wildflowers in the field.

9. The flowers will bloom soon.

10. The sun shone brightly.

B. Write each sentence. Complete each sentence with the correct tense of the verb in parentheses.

11. Yesterday, I (see) a woodpecker in a tree.

12. Now, an eagle (fly) overhead.

13. Soon, we (walk) carefully around the boulder.

14. At this time of day, the tree (provide) shade.

15. Two hours ago, we (eat) our lunch under a pine tree.

16. Curtis (clean) up now.

17. Tomorrow, Carrie (lead) the way through the forest.

18. Last night, I (find) a pinecone.

19. Tonight, we (stay) at a campsite.

20. All of us (enjoy) ourselves on our last trip.

C. Write the sentences. Underline each verb. Write *present*, *past,* or *future* to describe the tense of the verb you underlined.

21. Tomorrow, we will explore the lakeshore.

22. I saw many birds there last year.

23. Curtis wants to go this time.

24. Last night, Carrie asked her cousin about hiking trails.

25. Now everyone packs his or her own supplies.

Subject-Verb Agreement

A. Write *singular* or *plural* to show if the underlined subject and verb in each sentence are in the singular or plural form.

1. <u>Julie enjoys</u> plays.

2. <u>Tim likes</u> the stage.

3. <u>They write</u> plays together.

4. <u>Amelia watches</u> the people around her.

5. The <u>people give</u> her ideas for plays.

6. <u>Tim reads</u> Amelia's work.

7. <u>Julie and Amelia give</u> Tim some ideas.

8. <u>Tim makes</u> suggestions for changes.

9. His <u>suggestions help</u> them improve their writing.

10. <u>They work</u> together.

B. Write each sentence. Use the correct form of the verb.

11. Our drama teacher (ask, asks) us to put on a play.

12. Owen (choose, chooses) a play about a Viking ship.

13. He (enjoy, enjoys) sailing as a hobby.

14. Chris and Scott (read, reads) the narration.

15. The theatergoers (clap, claps) after the introduction.

16. Nancy (read, reads) her lines with a lot of emotion.

17. I (recite, recites) my part with feeling, too.

18. The play (remind, reminds) me of social studies class.

19. My friends (clap, claps) for me when I finish.

20. We (enjoy, enjoys) listening to our friends.

C. Write each sentence. Choose a word from the Word Bank.

| write | writes | like | likes | demonstrate |
| place | places | take | takes | demonstrates |

21. I _____ plays for my mother.

22. My mother _____ the plays about our family the most.

23. She _____ photos while I perform.

24. Mother _____ the photos in frames.

25. The plays _____ that I care about my family.

Spelling Present- and Past-Tense Verbs

A. Write *present* or *past* to name the tense of each verb.

1. dances

2. watched

3. tries

4. learned

5. spins

6. carried

7. sees

8. cheered

9. wishes

10. hurries

B. Write each sentence. Use the present-tense form of the verb in parentheses.

11. Paula (rush) to dance class.

12. She (slip) on the studio floor.

13. Antoine (carry) Paula across the floor.

14. The teacher (examine) her ankle.

15. She (notice) that something is wrong.

16. Paula (worry) about her injury.

17. Everyone (agree) that she is okay.

18. Paula (try) to stand up.

19. She (walk) carefully across the floor.

20. The dancers (applaud) when she is done.

C. Write each sentence. Use the past-tense form of the verb in parentheses.

21. Our class (attend) a dance recital.

22. The audience (buzz) with excitement.

23. The dancers (sail) onto the stage.

24. The lights (dim) as the music began.

25. The people (clap) at the end of a solo performance.

Commas

A. **Write each sentence. Place a comma or commas where they are needed in each underlined phrase.**

1. <u>James Amy and Shelby</u> want to perform.

2. <u>James what</u> do you think about a puppet show?

3. The characters could be a <u>frog a toad and an owl</u>.

4. <u>Shelby make</u> a green-and-blue frog.

5. <u>Ricardo let's</u> paint the stage.

6. <u>Yes Amy that's</u> a good idea.

7. Can we practice <u>Saturday Sunday and Monday</u>?

8. <u>Monday Tuesday and Wednesday</u> can be the days to perform.

9. <u>Yes Shelby</u> can be there.

10. <u>Okay let's</u> get started.

B. **Write each sentence. Add a comma or commas where needed in each sentence.**

11. Mom may we borrow some paint?

12. Oh let's ask Hugh to help us.

13. We'll need socks fabric and glue for the puppets.

14. The toad will be yours to make Amy.

15. Yes I'll make the owl.

16. We will need the frog the toad and the owl by today.

17. Do you want a pair of scissors a needle and some thread?

18. Let's invite parents grandparents and friends.

19. Well Ricardo is finished.

20. The show will be today tomorrow and the next day.

C. **Write each sentence. Use a comma or commas where needed. Write *correct* if the sentence is correct.**

21. Ricardo where is your puppet?

22. We know Amy that you are ready.

23. Hugh brought cookies and juice for snacks.

24. Terry Tina and Andrew came to watch.

25. Yes they really enjoyed our performance.

Main Verbs and Helping Verbs

A. Write the main verb in each sentence. Notice that each helping verb is underlined.

1. My family <u>will</u> attend an air show.

2. We <u>have</u> waited all year.

3. My dad <u>has</u> planned our trip.

4. The trip <u>will</u> take two hours.

5. We <u>can</u> stop for lunch at noon.

6. I <u>shall</u> talk to my friends about the show.

7. Tony <u>was</u> telling me about last year's show.

8. Many planes <u>were</u> soaring through the sky.

9. Five planes <u>were</u> flying in formation.

10. One pilot <u>could</u> perform amazing tricks.

B. Write each sentence. Draw one line under the helping verb. Draw two lines under the main verb.

11. The air show is starting in one hour.

12. The crowd was feeling anxious.

13. The pilots were working on their airplanes.

14. One woman was preparing her parachute.

15. A biplane can carry an extra person.

16. This person will walk on the wing.

17. Five jets will fly upside down.

18. The pilots have practiced for years.

19. The planes are flying close together.

20. The jets are making incredible turns.

C. Write the sentences. Complete each sentence with a helping verb.

21. My mother _____ leaving before the crowd departs.

22. Mom _____ taken the long way home.

23. We _____ hoping to attend the air show next year.

24. I _____ learn to be a pilot.

25. I _____ study hard.

Using Helping Verbs

A. Write the helping verb in each sentence.

1. Taylor is joining the science club.

2. Kazuko has asked about the meetings.

3. I have belonged to the club for a month.

4. Kazuko has suggested a field trip.

5. The club is planning a trip to the science museum.

6. We are discussing the trip.

7. The museum is featuring exhibits on sound.

8. I am looking forward to the field trip.

9. We are raising money for admission.

10. The club is going to go on Saturday.

B. Write the helping verb that completes each sentence.

11. The man (has, have) taken our tickets.

12. Vern (is, are) going to this exhibit first.

13. He (is, are) expected to learn about the ear.

14. I (am, is) observing a drawing of a sound wave.

15. Vern and Vanessa (is, are) viewing a demonstration.

16. The demonstration (has, have) shown how sound travels.

17. Two people (was, were) holding a piece of ribbon.

18. Popsicle sticks (was, were) glued across the ribbon.

19. One person (was, were) tapping the first stick.

20. The rest of the sticks (was, were) moving like a wave.

C. Write the sentences. Complete each sentence with a helping verb.

21. I _____ looking forward to my next visit.

22. Vanessa _____ attended this museum before.

23. Vern and his father _____ coming back tomorrow.

24. Vern _____ hoping to speak to a sound expert.

25. Vanessa _____ asked her parents to return with her.

Grammar

Linking Verbs

A. **Write each sentence. Draw one line under the linking verb.**

1. We are good singers.

2. Sandra's voice sounds good.

3. She is ready to reach the highest notes.

4. I am a baritone.

5. My voice is soft sometimes.

6. Our voices are harmonious.

7. Sandra seems nervous today.

8. The audience looks large.

9. A school newspaper reporter will be in the front row.

10. He appears restless.

B. **Write each sentence. Choose the correct linking verb in parentheses.**

11. Sandra (is, are) a good soloist.

12. She (feel, feels) confident in her ability to sing.

13. The conductor (is, are) ready to begin.

14. The crowd (grow, grows) noisy.

15. The bright lights (become, becomes) hot.

16. We (is, are) certain of our talents.

17. Singing (is, are) a hobby for me.

18. Sandra and Tamesha (is, are) professional singers.

19. The audience members (seem, seems) pleased with our efforts.

20. The reporter (look, looks) happy, too.

C. **Write each sentence. Use the present-tense form of the linking verb in parentheses. Then draw one line under the descriptive word that the linking verb connects to the subject.**

21. The concert _____ successful. (be)

22. Sandra _____ grateful to the people in the audience. (feel)

23. All the people _____ cheerful. (seem)

24. They _____ overjoyed with our performance. (look)

25. The reporter _____ enthusiastic, too. (appear)

Irregular Verbs

A. Write the past-tense verb in each sentence.

1. My friends and I went to a cooking class.

2. We made cookies during our first class.

3. We ate on the way.

4. Evan's mother drove us to class.

5. The teacher began the class on time.

6. We wrote recipes on note cards.

7. We brought an apron with us.

8. Carmen had two or three cookies.

9. I saw a picture of next week's recipe.

10. The cake made me hungry.

B. Write the past tense and the past participle of these verbs.

11. eat

12. drive

13. bring

14. ride

15. go

16. write

17. begin

18. see

19. do

20. make

C. Write each sentence. Use the correct past-tense or past-participle form of the verb in parentheses.

21. I (write) the recipes clearly and carefully.

22. Mother (drive) the van to pick us up.

23. Bart (ride) in the passenger seat.

24. We would have (grow) restless if we had waited any longer.

25. We should have (bring) something to read.

Grammar

More Irregular Verbs

A. Write the past-tense verb or the past participle in each sentence.

1. We chose the bumper cars as our next ride.

2. Kelly and I had spoken to the girl behind us.

3. We flew around the track.

4. I took three photos from the car.

5. Luckily, I had worn a sweater.

6. I knew a lot of people at the amusement park.

7. An artist had drawn a caricature.

8. He taught drawing classes during the week.

9. Kelly and I threw basketballs in a bushel basket.

10. We drank cold soda pop, too.

B. Write each sentence. Choose the correct verb in parentheses.

11. Earlier that day we had (took, taken) the bus downtown.

12. My friends (chose, chosen) to go swimming.

13. I (wore, worn) my swimsuit under my clothes.

14. My mother had (swam, swum) with us last year.

15. We (threw, thrown) our towels over the fence.

16. I had (took, taken) a step on the diving board.

17. The lifeguard (spoke, spoken) to me.

18. He (knew, known) I was a good swimmer.

19. He has (knew, known) me for a long time.

20. In minutes, I had (threw, thrown) myself into the water.

C. Write each sentence. Use the correct past-tense or past-participle form of the verb in parentheses.

21. The lifeguard (teach) Anthony how to swim.

22. Shelly could have (wear) her new red swimsuit.

23. I should have (teach) Anthony how to dive.

24. Anthony (know) what to do.

25. He (take) three steps before the dive.

Contractions with *Not*

A. Write the contraction in each sentence.

1. I didn't have any money for the soccer match.

2. My father said that I wouldn't need any money.

3. The match hasn't started yet.

4. It won't start until this afternoon.

5. I can't be sure who will win.

6. It doesn't look as if the Flames will be victorious.

7. My friends don't play on that team.

8. The goalie mustn't hurt his arm.

9. There won't be an empty seat in the stands.

10. It isn't going to be a boring game.

B. Write the contraction for each of the underlined words.

11. There were not many fans for the other team.

12. I have not eaten any popcorn yet.

13. Dad had not remembered to bring his hat.

14. I did not know where the hat was.

15. We could not find a place to sit.

16. My brother can not play until next year.

17. The coach does not need any more players.

18. I do not want to play softball.

19. I have not tried to play it yet.

20. The team has not lost any matches recently.

C. Write each sentence. Replace the underlined word with a contraction that is formed from that word and the word *not*.

21. I will be playing soon.

22. My brother was interested in softball.

23. I will miss next week's match.

24. It could be the last match of the season.

25. The coach does know the score.

Unit 1 Sentences

A. Write each sentence correctly. Add capital letters, end punctuation, and commas where needed. Write if the sentence is *imperative*, *declarative*, *exclamatory*, or *interrogative*.

1. where will your family travel this year

2. we will be going to the Grand Canyon

3. i like camping but my sister likes amusement parks

4. please give us directions

5. what a great vacation this is

6. we may go to Florida, or we may visit my aunt in Utah

7. do you have a choice

8. tell me where you want to go

9. what an incredible view this is

10. our family will have a good time

B. Write each sentence. Draw a line between the complete subject and the complete predicate. Then, draw one line under the simple subject and two lines under the simple predicate.

11. A new girl joined my class.

12. Rebecca draws beautiful pictures.

13. The whole class admires her work.

14. She paints with oils.

15. One painting shows a lake.

16. This picture won a prize.

17. Rebecca helps me during art class.

18. I welcome her help.

19. She gave a painting to the principal.

20. The painting hangs in the hall.

C. Combine the sentences to make a compound subject, a compound predicate, or a compound sentence. Write each new sentence. Underline each conjunction.

21. I want to go to the game. I want to go to a movie.

22. Margie plays softball. I play softball.

23. I am the pitcher. José is the catcher.

24. Zachary wants some popcorn. He has no money.

25. Margie likes soccer. Margie plays soccer.

D. Write whether the sentence is a *fragment*, a *run-on*, or a *complete sentence*. Rewrite the fragments and run-ons to make correct sentences.

26. Was very rainy that day.

27. The weather was unusual this morning.

28. It was stormy the clouds were everywhere.

29. A bright and spectacular rainbow.

30. We thought the clouds were a beautiful sight.

Unit 2 Nouns

A. Write whether each noun names a person, a place, a thing, or an idea. Then write *singular* or *plural* to show the form of each noun. Finally, write the noun in its possessive form.

31. children

32. insect

33. boxes

34. cities

35. freedom

36. babies

37. woman

38. radios

39. wolf

40. wolves

B. Write each proper noun, title, or abbreviation correctly.

41. "america the beautiful"

42. park avenue

43. george washington

44. yosemite national park

45. charlie and the chocolate factory

46. dr vargas

47. independence day

48. mississippi river

49. tuesday, february 10

50. maple road

C. Capitalize and punctuate the parts of a letter correctly. Write your answers.

51. january 5 2001

52. dear governor johanson

53. dear ms mayor

54. 10905 royal ridge avenue

55. sincerely yours

Unit 3 Verbs

A. Write each sentence. Write *AV* above each action verb and *DO* above each direct object.

56. The camp teaches our class about pioneers.

57. We learn survival skills.

58. One group twists rope from twine.

59. Darnell churned butter.

60. Daria created a corn-husk doll.

61. Some campers sew buckskin pouches.

62. We dried beef.

63. The blacksmith hammered metal bars.

64. One group performed a dance.

65. We wore woolen costumes.

Grammar

B. **Change the underlined verb to its past-tense form. Add commas where needed.**

66. I <u>buy</u> ice cream bowls and spoons for the party.

67. Yes Kevin I <u>give</u> the money to the teacher.

68. Thomas <u>walks</u> to school on Monday Tuesday and Friday.

69. Marva <u>studies</u> for her science test.

70. The test <u>covers</u> the topics of heat light and sound.

71. I <u>help</u> Marva before class.

72. We <u>bring</u> a book our notes and a pen.

73. I <u>write</u> important facts.

74. Marva we <u>know</u> our scores.

75. Marva Greg and I <u>pass</u> the test easily.

C. **Choose the correct verb from the pair in parentheses. Change the underlined words to a contraction. Be sure that subjects and verbs agree.**

76. Tomorrow, I will (finish, finishing) my work, but today I <u>cannot</u>.

77. Yesterday, Dad (saw, sees) a bear that <u>was not</u> in a cage.

78. Her homework <u>will not</u> get easier if she (waits, wait) until later.

79. Today, Hillary <u>does not</u> (get, gets) to school on time.

80. I (thinks, think) this is the way, but I <u>do not</u> know for sure.

81. I shall (go, goes) to the store, and I <u>should not</u> be long.

82. He can (get, gets) markers, but he <u>is not</u> going to the store now.

83. Hillary is (work, working) on a poster with me, but we <u>must not</u> be messy.

84. I was (hope, hoping) to be done, but we <u>are not</u> finished yet.

85. We <u>could not</u> have (chose, chosen) the topic without your help.

Adjectives and Expository Writing

In this unit you will learn about adjectives. You will also learn about expository writing. Expository writing is a type of writing that gives facts and information.

Science Link *Read about the violent spring storm that Bruce Hiscock tracked by gathering information from a variety of sources. This storm moved with "lightning" speed from the Pacific Coast, where it began as a rainstorm, through Texas and the Midwest, where it brought killer tornadoes, to New York and New England, where it became the worst April blizzard in history.*

Barometers measure the pressure of the air directly overhead. Air, like water, has weight, and tons of air press down on the earth. This force, called barometric or atmospheric pressure, changes constantly as air moves.

Forecasters pay close attention to these changes, for they help predict the weather to come. High pressure usually brings fair skies. Low pressure means storms, and the lower the pressure, the stronger the storm.

THE BIG STORM

written and illustrated by
BRUCE HISCOCK

⌒ from **The Big Storm** by Bruce Hiscock

Thinking Like a Writer

Expository Writing Expository writing gives facts and information about a specific topic. Reread the passage.

• What important information does Bruce Hiscock give in each paragraph?

Adjectives The author used adjectives to add more exact information to his writing. Read the sentences again.

QUICK WRITE How do the adjectives *high, low,* and *fair* help you picture the information in the paragraph?

259

Adjectives

RULES

An adjective is a word that describes a noun or pronoun. Many adjectives tell *what kind* or *how many*.

> *Encyclopedias have accurate information. (what kind)*

> *A library has several dictionaries. (how many)*

An adjective can appear before the noun it describes, or it can follow a linking verb, such as *is*, *seems*, or *appears*.

> *The article was important.*

THINK AND WRITE

Adjectives

How can knowing about adjectives make your writing more interesting? Write your ideas in your journal.

Adjectives often appear before the nouns they describe. Two or more adjectives used before a noun are usually separated by a comma. A comma is not needed when one of the adjectives tells *how many*.

what kind
↓   ↓
Nick read a *long, difficult* article on lasers.

how many   what kind
↓   ↓
You can learn *many fascinating* facts from an encyclopedia.

Guided Practice

Name the adjective or adjectives in each sentence. Then tell which noun each adjective describes.

EXAMPLE: You can find interesting facts in an encyclopedia.
Adjective: interesting   Noun it describes: facts

1. Encyclopedias have several volumes.
2. One volume is the index.
3. The index gives important information.
4. It tells you where to find interesting articles.
5. Some articles have colorful pictures.

- **Adjectives** describe nouns or pronouns. Many tell *what kind* or *how many*.

- **Adjectives** can come before the nouns they describe, or they can come after a linking verb.

More Practice

A. **Write the sentences. Draw one line under each adjective. Draw two lines under the noun it describes.**

6. Gail used an electronic encyclopedia for her research.

7. She used the keyword *lion* to search through several topics.

8. The search showed a good picture of a lion.

9. Gail clicked on the image and heard a loud, ferocious roar.

10. The article stated new facts about lions.

B. **Write each sentence. Add an adjective.**

11. Akira found an _____ encyclopedia article on comets.

12. He also found _____ articles on related space topics.

13. Akira thought the articles were _____.

14. He used some of the information to write a _____ report.

15. Akira's classmates were _____ with his report.

C. **Spiral Review** **Write each sentence. Add an adjective. Then rewrite each underlined singular noun as a plural noun. Write whether the sentence is declarative, interrogative, imperative, or exclamatory.**

16. Which _____ country did you read about?

17. Did you find _____ information about the historic landmark?

18. Try the other _____ resource.

19. The _____ atlas may be another place to check.

20. What a _____ map this atlas has!

Extra Practice, page 328.

Handbook
pages 530–531,
536–537

Writing Activity An Encyclopedia Article

Write an encyclopedia article about an interesting sight in a country you have studied. Use vivid adjectives to interest your readers.

APPLY GRAMMAR: Circle adjectives that tell *what kind* or *how many*.

 Social Studies Link

Articles

RULES

Articles are special kinds of adjectives. The words *a*, *an*, and *the* are articles.

> *a* truck   *an* airplane   *the* shoe factory

You often use *a*, *an*, or *the* before nouns.

Use *a* and *an* to refer to any person, place, thing, or idea. *A* is used before words beginning with a consonant sound. *An* is used before words beginning with a vowel sound.

> *A* leader is speaking against air pollution.

> *An* agency is working to stop pollution.

Use *the* to refer to a particular person, place, thing, or idea. *The* can refer to plural nouns.

> *The* pollution of air, water, and land must be stopped.

THINK AND WRITE

Adjectives

How do you know when to use the article *a*, *an*, or *the*? Write your ideas in your journal.

The article you choose depends on the word it precedes and the sense of the sentence.

Refers to any person, place, thing, or idea	Refers to a particular person, place, thing, or idea
a: consonant	*the*: consonant or vowel
a project	*the* project
an: vowel	*the* activities
an activity	

Guided Practice

Name the correct article to complete each sentence.

EXAMPLE: Which of (a, the) products do you recycle? *the*

1. How much daily trash does (a, an) person throw away?
2. Think of all (a, the) wrappers, boxes, and cans you use.
3. There is (a, an) overflow of trash at our dumps.
4. Each person must make (a, an) effort to recycle.
5. People should recycle (a, the) items they use.

N.Y.C. Department of Sanitation
Curbside Recycling

REVIEW THE RULES

- *A, an,* and *the* are special adjectives called articles.

- Use *a* or *an* to refer to any person, place, thing, or idea. Use *the* to refer to a specific item or items.

Handbook
page 536

More Practice

A. Choose the correct article to complete each sentence. Then write the sentence.

6. What can (a, an) individual do to help reduce waste?

7. Buy (the, a) products with less packaging.

8. Use (a, the) type of merchandise that can be reused.

9. Find (an, a) way to repair things, or use them differently.

10. Start (a, an) recycling program at your school or in your neighborhood.

B. Write each sentence. Use the correct article.

11. Plastic takes _____ long time to decompose.

12. Discarded plastic remains in _____ environment for hundreds of years.

13. Recycling is _____ important issue for everyone.

14. There are _____ few ways to reuse plastic.

15. What are some of _____ ways that you can reuse plastic?

C. **Spiral Review** **Complete each sentence with a common noun, an action verb, or an article.**

We should (**16.**_____) our natural resources. Aluminum is (**17.**_____) material that we can recycle. Yet it is not (**18.**_____) only one. (**19.**_____) can also be recycled. People can (**20.**_____) articles to be recycled.

Extra Practice, page 329.

Writing Activity A Commercial

Write a television commercial that explains how to recycle. Include facts that explain why recycling is important. Let your own voice come through as you "talk" to your audience.

APPLY GRAMMAR: Underline the articles that you use.

Drama Link

263

Demonstrative Adjectives

Adjectives

Why is it important to know the difference between *this* and *that*? Between *these* and *those*? Write your ideas in your journal.

Use *this* and *that* with singular nouns. Use *these* and *those* with plural nouns.

Singular noun — *this* image (nearby)
— *that* mirror (farther away)

Plural noun — *these* images (nearby)
— *those* mirrors (farther away)

Guided Practice

Name the demonstrative adjective in each sentence.

> **EXAMPLE:** You can make a kaleidoscope with these directions.
> *these*

1. This experiment requires three small mirrors.
2. Tape those mirrors together to form a triangle.
3. Make sure this side faces toward the center.
4. Pour these clear plastic shapes into the triangle of mirrors.

REVIEW THE RULES

- A **demonstrative adjective** tells *which* one or *which ones*. *This*, *that*, *these*, and *those* are demonstrative adjectives.

More Practice

A. Write the demonstrative adjective in each sentence.

6. The surface of that lens bulges out.

7. Those lenses curve inward.

8. This lens is called a magnifying glass.

9. You can use a magnifying glass to look at these objects.

10. Can you make out those words under the magnifying glass?

B. Write each sentence. Use *this*, *that*, *these*, or *those*.

11. _____ light shining near me looks white.

12. _____ prisms on the shelf over there can make rainbow patterns.

13. _____ crystals in my hand can make rainbow patterns, too.

14. Notice how I hold _____ prism in the light.

15. Look at _____ beautiful rainbow on the wall!

C. Spiral Review Use *this*, *that*, *these*, or *those* for each blank. Then combine each pair of sentences. Write the new sentence. Use the correct punctuation.

16. _____ prisms split light into different colors. Crystals split light into different colors.

17. _____ prisms over there refract light. They do not reflect light.

18. He used _____ light near me to make shadows. He used the same light to make rainbow patterns.

19. You can use _____ small mirrors. You can use large mirrors.

20. She made _____ light patterns on the wall. They changed as the mirrors moved.

Extra Practice, page 330.

Handbook
pages 536–537

Writing Activity A Paragraph

Write a paragraph to explain what rainbows are. Organize your ideas clearly and give them in a logical order.

APPLY GRAMMAR: Use at least three demonstrative adjectives. Circle the demonstrative adjectives that you use.

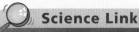

Science Link

Proper Adjectives

RULES

A **proper adjective** is formed from a proper noun. A proper noun names a certain person, place, thing, or idea.

We listened to Hawaiian songs.

A **proper adjective** begins with a capital letter.

Spanish **guitars**   *French* **horn**

You can change many proper nouns into proper adjectives. Sometimes you need to change the spelling of proper nouns to change them into proper adjectives. Here are the most common spelling changes.

Proper Noun	Ending	Proper Adjective
Japan	*-ese*	Japanese
Africa	*-n*	African
Egypt	*-ian*	Egyptian
Italy		Italian
England	*-ish*	English

Guided Practice

Name the proper adjectives. There may be more than one in each sentence.

> **EXAMPLE:** Drums are important in South American music.
> *South American*

1. Cuban music has an interesting sound.
2. Spanish melodies are often used in Mexican music.
3. African rhythms can also be heard in some Caribbean songs.
4. You might even hear a French melody.
5. Many cultures have influenced Latin American music.

THINK AND WRITE

Adjectives
In your journal, explain why you think a proper adjective begins with a capital letter.

REVIEW THE RULES

- A proper adjective is formed from a proper noun.

- A proper adjective begins with a capital letter.

More Practice

A. Write the proper adjective in each sentence.

6. One of the most popular Scottish songs is "Auld Lang Syne."

7. The Japanese national anthem was the first anthem written.

8. One of the longest musical pieces is a German opera.

9. Some Austrian composers have written beautiful classical music.

10. An American orchestra performed the longest classical concert.

B. Complete each sentence with a proper adjective formed from the proper noun in parentheses. Use your dictionary if needed.

11. The _____ composer Vivaldi wrote *The Four Seasons*. (Italy)

12. The _____ composer Haydn wrote beautiful music. (Austria)

13. Tchaikovsky is an important _____ composer. (Russia)

14. Drums are an important part of _____ music. (Native America)

15. _____ music has an interesting melody. (India)

Handbook
pages 536–537

C. Spiral Review **Write the sentences. Capitalize each proper noun and proper adjective. After each sentence, write whether the verb tense is *past*, *present*, or *future*.**

16. Long ago, chinese music came to europe.

17. The middle eastern melodies are quite old.

18. Rattles play a part in some native american music.

19. Many people enjoy east indian music.

20. british rock music will be popular forever!

Extra Practice, page 331.

Writing Activity A Flyer

Imagine that an international music festival is being held in your town. Create a flyer for the event. Be sure the flyer is well organized.

APPLY GRAMMAR: Underline the proper adjectives in your flyer.

♪♫ **Music Link**

Mixed Review

REVIEW THE RULES

- An **adjective** is a word that describes a noun or pronoun. Many adjectives tell *what kind* or *how many*.

- An **article** is a special kind of adjective. The words *a*, *an*, and *the* are articles.

- A **demonstrative adjective** tells *which one* or *which ones*. The words *this*, *that*, *these*, and *those* are demonstrative adjectives.

- A **proper adjective** is formed from a proper noun and begins with a capital letter.

QUICK WRITE

Adjectives

Write four sentences about a topic of your choice. Use a different demonstrative adjective in each sentence.

Practice

A. Write each sentence. Underline adjectives that tell *what kind* or *how many*. If an adjective is a proper adjective, write *proper* above it.

1. A warm climate is found in some parts of the world.

2. Mexican winters are mild.

3. Indian dust storms can be fierce.

4. In Saudi Arabia, many people suffer from the great heat.

5. African weather is dry.

6. The Greek islands have perfect summers.

7. Hawaiian breezes feel cool in the winter.

8. Australian winters are hot and sunny.

9. The Samoan islands are beautiful all year.

10. Jamaica is a wonderful place for a holiday.

B. **Write each sentence. Use the correct article or demonstrative adjective in parentheses.**

11. (A, The) climate in Siberia is harsh.

12. (A, The) people must be prepared for extreme temperatures.

13. (A, An) Alaskan winter is also very cold.

14. (This, Those) freezing temperatures are a problem for people in some northern countries.

15. Would you like to visit (those, that) country?

16. Maybe you should visit (a, the) country of Iceland in July.

17. Wouldn't you rather visit (the, a) country with the warmer climate?

18. You may prefer (these, that) countries: Greece, Jamaica, or Kenya.

19. Perhaps you don't mind (the, a) colder regions of the world.

20. If you could take (the, a) perfect vacation, where would you go?

C. **Challenge** **Rewrite the following sentences. Write each proper adjective correctly. Use correct capitalization and punctuation in each sentence.**

Handbook
pages 536–537

21. the south american climate varies

22. is the climate in brazil hot and tropical

23. look up information about the peruvian climate

24. how amazing that the temperature is so much cooler in the mountains of peru

25. is the climate in colombia like the bolivian climate

Writing Activity A Weather Report

Write a weather report for a country you have read about. Make sure your writing flows smoothly from one idea to the next.

APPLY GRAMMAR: Circle each proper adjective that you use. Make sure it begins with a capital letter.

Science Link

Comparative and Superlative Adjectives

RULES

Comparative adjectives compare two nouns or pronouns. Add *-er* to most adjectives to compare two people, places, things or ideas.

> *Sugar is sweeter than honey.*

Superlative adjectives compare more than two nouns or pronouns. Add *-est* to most adjectives to compare more than two people, places, things or ideas.

> *That is the sweetest cake of the three cakes on the table.*

THINK AND WRITE

Adjectives

How does knowing the rules for using adjectives that compare help you in your speaking and writing? Write your ideas in your journal.

For adjectives ending in *e*, drop the *e* before adding *-er* or *-est*.

$$\text{wide} \xrightarrow[\text{add } \textit{-er} \text{ or } \textit{-est}]{\text{drop } e,} \begin{array}{l} \text{wid}\textit{er}, \\ \text{wid}\textit{est} \end{array}$$

For adjectives ending in a consonant and *y*, change the *y* to *i*.

$$\text{funny} \xrightarrow[\text{add } \textit{-er} \text{ or } \textit{-est}]{\text{change } y \text{ to } i,} \begin{array}{l} \text{funn}\textit{ier}, \\ \text{funn}\textit{iest} \end{array}$$

For one-syllable adjectives that have a single vowel before the final consonant, double the final consonant.

$$\text{sad} \xrightarrow[\text{add } \textit{-er} \text{ or } \textit{-est}]{\text{double final consonant,}} \begin{array}{l} \text{sad}\textit{der}, \\ \text{sad}\textit{dest} \end{array}$$

Guided Practice

Name the correct adjective that compares.

EXAMPLE: Split pea soup is (thicker, thickest) than chicken soup.
thicker

1. Salsa is (hotter, hottest) than ketchup.

2. Blueberry cheesecake is (sweeter, sweetest) than pumpkin pie.

3. Lemon meringue pie is the (sweeter, sweetest) of all.

4. Steaks are often (tougher, toughest) than lamb chops.

5. Fudge may be the (chewier, chewiest) candy.

REVIEW THE RULES

- Add *-er* to most adjectives to compare two nouns.

- Add *-est* to most adjectives to compare three or more nouns.

More Practice

A. Choose the correct adjective in parentheses.

6. That Italian pizza is (bigger, biggest) than this one.

7. Which of the two cheeses is (older, oldest)?

8. This is the (simpler, simplest) recipe for tea cakes I have ever tried.

9. Italian ice is (colder, coldest) than American lemonade.

10. That spicy Polish sausage is the (hotter, hottest) of all.

B. Write each sentence. Use the correct form of the adjective.

11. Irish stew is (thick) than Japanese soup.

12. Jalapeño peppers are the (spicy) peppers in the Spanish market.

13. Chinese rice is (sticky) than Spanish rice.

14. Watermelons are the (large) melons grown.

15. German apple strudel is usually (sweet) than American apple pie.

Handbook
pages 528–529
536–537

C. | Spiral Review | **Write each sentence. Use the correct form of the adjective in parentheses. Draw a line to divide the complete subject from the complete predicate. Circle the nouns.**

16. This restaurant has a (wide) variety of dishes than that cafeteria.

17. The dinner rolls are (soft) than the French bread.

18. My mother thought the Caesar salad was the (tasty) she had ever eaten.

19. The onion rings were the (crunchy) food we ordered.

20. I had a (large) meal than my brother.

Extra Practice, page 332.

Writing Activity A Report

Find out information about the history of your favorite food. Write the information in a brief, clear report. Focus on the food's country of origin.

APPLY GRAMMAR: Circle the adjectives you use to compare.

 **Social Studies Link**

Comparing with *More* and *Most*

RULES

Use *more* or *most* to compare with most adjectives that have two or more syllables.

Use *more* to compare two nouns or pronouns. Use *most* to compare three or more people, places, things, and ideas.

> *The San Diego Zoo is* more colorful *than the London Zoo.*

> *Is the San Diego Zoo the* most colorful *zoo in the world?*

When you use *more* or *most*, do not use the *-er* or *-est* form of an adjective.

For most adjectives that have two or more syllables, add the word *more* or *most* to compare. Never use *-er* or *-est* when using *more* or *most*.

Incorrect:	The Bronx Zoo is more bigger than the Central Park Zoo.
Correct:	The Bronx Zoo is bigger than the Central Park Zoo.
Incorrect:	This is the most splendidest zoo I've ever seen.
Correct:	This is the most splendid zoo I've ever seen.

Guided Practice

Choose the correct form of the adjective in parentheses.

> **EXAMPLE:** San Francisco may be the (more beautiful, most beautiful) city in California.
> *most beautiful*

1. It is (more harder, harder) to fly to Taos than to Houston.

2. Flights are (more numerous, numerouser) on Fridays.

3. El Paso is the (more unusual, most unusual) city of all.

4. This city is (closer, more closer) to Mexico than to Dallas.

5. The (most splendid, more splendid) Mayan art of all is in Mexico.

REVIEW THE RULES

- Add *more* and *most* to adjectives with two or more syllables. Use *more* to compare two nouns or pronouns. Use *most* to compare three or more.

More Practice

A. Write the correct form of the adjective in parentheses.

6. New York City's traffic is (more terrible, most terrible) than Boston's.

7. The (more horrible, most horrible) traffic may be in Los Angeles.

8. Traffic signs are (more difficult, most difficult) to read in Wales than in England.

9. The language of Wales is the (more unusual, most unusual) in Great Britain.

10. That language has the (longest, most longest) words of all.

B. Write each sentence. Use the correct form of the adjective.

11. Tokyo is the (crowded) city in the world.

12. Rome has (unusual) buildings than a newer city.

13. San Francisco is (attractive) than that European city.

14. San Francisco is one of the (popular) tourist spots of all.

15. New York may be the (entertaining) city in the world.

C. `Spiral Review` **Write each sentence correctly. Capitalize the proper nouns.**

16. Many people think the plays in london is the outstandingest.

17. Do you think rome is the interestingest city of all?

18. Some people believe that paris is most exciting than New york.

19. Museums is most plentiful in chicago than in denver.

20. Your city are the more beautiful city of all.

Extra Practice, page 333.

Handbook
pages 531,
536–537, 548

Writing Activity   A Travel Brochure

Write a travel brochure about your city or town. Include facts about its history, businesses, and places of interest.

APPLY GRAMMAR: Include comparisons with *more* and *most*. Have a partner underline the adjectives that compare.

Social Studies Link

Comparing with *Good* and *Bad*

RULES

The word *good* has two forms for comparing: *better* and *best*. Use *better* to compare two nouns or pronouns. Use *best* to compare more than two people, places, things, or ideas.

> *Today's weather was good. Yesterday's weather was better.*

> *Last week's weather was the best of the month.*

The word *bad* has two forms for comparing: *worse* and *worst*. Use *worse* to compare two nouns or pronouns. Use *worst* to compare three or more.

> *That storm was bad. It was worse than the one last summer.*

> *Some people thought it was the worst storm of all.*

THINK AND WRITE

Adjectives

How does knowing when to use *good* and *bad* help you write clearer sentences? Write your ideas in your journal.

To decide which form of *good* and *bad* to use, look at the nouns or pronouns being compared. When using forms of *good* and *bad*, do not use *-er* or *-est*, or *more* or *most*.

Only one thing	good	bad
Comparing two things	better	worse
Comparing three or more things	best	worst

Guided Practice

Name the correct form of *good* or *bad* in each sentence.

EXAMPLE: A hailstorm is (worst, worse) than a heavy rainstorm.
worse

1. A tornado is (worst, worse) than a hailstorm.
2. A hurricane is the (worse, worst) storm of all.
3. Fog is (worse, worst) for driving than a light rain.
4. A steady rain is (better, best) for plants than a quick, hard downpour.
5. Sunshine is the (better, best) weather of all.

REVIEW THE RULES

- Use *good* to describe one noun. Use *better* to compare two nouns. Use *best* to compare more than two nouns.

- Use *bad* to describe one noun. Use *worse* to compare two nouns. Use *worst* to compare three or more nouns.

More Practice

A. Write each sentence. Use the correct word in parentheses.

6. A thermometer is the (better, best) of all measuring tools.

7. Satellites are (better, best) than ships for detecting weather conditions.

8. Meteorologists make the (better, best) weather forecasters.

9. A slight sprinkle may lead to (worse, worst) weather.

10. Some of the (worse, worst) storms have destroyed homes.

B. Write each sentence. Use the correct form of the adjective.

11. During a tornado, it is (good) to be in a ditch than under a tree.

12. A cellar is the (good) shelter during a tornado.

13. Some tornadoes are (bad) than others.

14. This is one of the (bad) tornadoes we have ever had.

15. The (good) thing you can do is to stay clear of tornadoes.

C. Spiral Review Correct each run-on sentence by writing two sentences. Use the correct form of the adjective that compares. Underline the action verbs.

16. Heavy rains cause floods some floods are (bad) than tornadoes.

17. Is a raincoat (good) than an umbrella I think so.

18. Don't drive in bad weather icy roads are (bad) than snow-covered roads.

19. In hot weather, wear cotton clothes they're (good) than wool.

20. The weather isn't bad it is (good) today than yesterday.

Extra Practice, page 334.

Handbook
pages 526–527,
528–529, 532, 537

Writing Activity A Log Entry

Imagine that you are a sailor at sea. Write a log entry describing a storm. Use the *I* or *we* point of view.

APPLY GRAMMAR: Underline forms of the adjectives *good* and *bad*.

275

Combining Sentences: Adjectives

When you combine two sentences, leave out the words that repeat.

Troy lost his binder.

His binder was blue.

Troy lost his blue binder.

Lana found a small kitten.

It was a striped kitten.

Lana found a small, striped kitten.

THINK AND WRITE

Adjectives

In your journal, write how knowing how to use adjectives to combine sentences can help you avoid repeating words and ideas.

Guided Practice

Tell how you would combine each pair of sentences to make a new sentence.

> **EXAMPLE:** Tori lost her baseball cap. It was her favorite cap.
> *Tori lost her favorite baseball cap.*

1. Tori looked in her room. Her room was cluttered.

2. She then searched under the bushes. The bushes were brown.

3. Ted helped her search for the cap. It was a red cap.

4. Tori looked behind a tree. The tree was tall.

5. She saw a raccoon chewing her cap. The raccoon was wild.

REVIEW THE RULES

- You can use an adjective to combine two sentences that tell about the same person, place, thing, or idea.

- When you combine two sentences, leave out words that repeat.

More Practice

A. Combine each pair of sentences. Write the new sentence.

6. We looked for our cat in the shed. It is a storage shed.

7. We heard a meow. It was a loud meow.

8. We saw something on the blanket. It was a plaid blanket.

9. We had a surprise. It was a wonderful surprise.

10. Our cat had given birth to kittens! She had given birth to five kittens!

B. Add an adjective to the second sentence of each pair. Then combine the two sentences. Write the new sentence.

11. We found a trunk in the attic. It was a(n) _____ trunk.

12. We saw several photographs. They were _____ photographs.

13. We came across a letter. It was a(n) _____ letter.

14. We found clothing. The clothing was _____.

15. We returned the trunk to its hiding place. The hiding place was _____.

Handbook
pages 530–531,
534–535, 536–537

C. Spiral Review **Combine each pair of sentences. Draw one line under the nouns. Draw two lines under the linking verbs.**

16. The boy is scared. The boy is little.

17. He was lost in the store. The store was huge.

18. There are many aisles in the store. The aisles are long.

19. Is that his mother with the salesclerk? The salesclerk is tall.

20. The boy and his mother were both happy. The boy was young.

Extra Practice, page 335.

Writing Activity A Newspaper Article

Imagine that you have just found a treasure chest. Write a news article to tell about your "find." Include important details.

APPLY GRAMMAR: Use adjectives to combine similar sentences.

Abbreviations

RULES

An abbreviation is a shortened form of a word.

J. Smith   *Randall Parker, Jr.*   *Mon.*   *Jan.*

Most abbreviations begin with a capital letter and end with a period.

Mr.   *Mrs.*   *Ms.*   *Dr.*   *Oct.*

THINK AND WRITE

Adjectives
Why is it important to know how to use abbreviations correctly?

Abbreviations are often used in addresses, in lists, and in titles before and after names. Here are some common abbreviations. Abbreviations for states are in the Handbook.

Abbreviations

Titles	Mister	Mr.	Doctor	Dr.	Governor	Gov.
Days	Monday	Mon.	Thursday	Thurs.	Sunday	Sun.
	Tuesday	Tues.	Friday	Fri.		
	Wednesday	Wed.	Saturday	Sat.		
Months	January	Jan.	April	Apr.	October	Oct.
	February	Feb.	August	Aug.	November	Nov.
	March	Mar.	September	Sept.	December	Dec.
Streets	Street	St.	Drive	Dr.	Avenue	Ave.
	Road	Rd.	Place	Pl.	Boulevard	Blvd.
Others	before noon (*ante meridiem*)	A.M.	Post Office	P.O.		
	after noon (*post meridiem*)	P.M.	foot	ft.		
	Incorporated	Inc.	Meter	m		

Guided Practice

Spell the correct abbreviation for each underlined word below.

EXAMPLE: The letter was sent to 320 Bryant <u>Avenue</u>.
Ave.

1. <u>Governor</u> Ward <u>Otis</u> Long

2. <u>Mister</u> Omar Blanchard

3. 9:30 <u>in the morning</u>

4. <u>Doctor</u> Rita Green

5. <u>Thursday</u>, <u>September</u> 20

REVIEW THE RULES

- An abbreviation is a shortened form of a word.

- Most abbreviations begin with a capital letter and end with a period.

More Practice

A. Write the correct abbreviations for the underlined words. Use the correct punctuation.

6. Farmers, Incorporated, will speak about farm wages.

7. Owen Martin, Junior, is going to talk about crop failure.

8. Mister Martin has rented an office on Pewter Street.

9. Questions can be sent beforehand to Post Office Box 427.

10. Monday, August 27 is the deadline for questions.

B. Write each sentence. Rewrite the underlined words as abbreviations. Use correct capitalization and punctuation.

11. Doctor Martin Luther King's birthday is celebrated in January.

12. Thanksgiving is the fourth Thursday in November.

13. Labor Day falls on the first Monday in September.

14. We celebrate Valentine's Day in February.

15. Daylight savings time ends in October.

Handbook
pages 531, 544–546, 547–550

C. **Spiral Review** Write each sentence using the correct capitalization and punctuation. Use abbreviations correctly for underlined words.

16. kathleen p sullivan will celebrate st. patrick's day in march.

17. what will happen on february 2, groundhog day

18. I gave mrs prince a birthday card on saturday.

19. mister blum is going to visit the white house on presidents' day.

20. where will doctor berry spend new year's day?

Extra Practice, page 336.

Writing Activity An Essay

Write an essay about the history of your favorite holiday. Be sure your sentences connect and flow naturally.

APPLY GRAMMAR: Use abbreviations to state the day and the month of the celebration.

Social Studies Link

Mixed Review

- **Comparative adjectives** compare two nouns or pronouns. Add *-er* to most one-syllable adjectives that compare.

- **Superlative adjectives** compare more than two nouns or pronouns. Add *-est* to most one-syllable adjectives that compare.

- Use *more* or *most* before some longer adjectives used to compare nouns. Use *more* to compare two nouns or pronouns. Use *most* to compare three or more.

- The words *good* and *bad* have special forms: *better*, *best* and *worse*, *worst*. Use *better* and *worse* to compare two nouns or pronouns. Use *best* and *worst* to compare three or more.

- Two sentences that tell about the same noun can be combined by adding an adjective to one of the sentences.

- An **abbreviation** is a shortened form of a word. It usually begins with a capital letter and ends with a period.

QUICK WRITE

Adjectives

Write a poem of 3-5 lines in your journal that uses at least three adjectives that compare.

Practice

A. Write each sentence by using the correct adjective in parentheses.

1. Lemon juice is one of the (more, most) important of all sources of citric acid.

2. It may also be the (more, most) amazing natural cleanser.

3. Lemon juice is (more, most) effective than another popular cleanser.

4. It can even make pennies (shinier, shiniest) than before.

5. The acid in the lemon juice will make the pennies the (brighter, brightest) coins in your pocket.

B. **Complete the sentences by using the correct form of** *good* **or** *bad*. **Combine each pair of sentences to form one sentence. Then write the sentence.**

6. Lemons may be the (good) product you can buy. Lemons are fresh.

7. Lemon juice is a cleanser. It is one of the (good) cleansers of all.

8. It makes a (good) bleach than another bleach. The other bleach is bottled.

9. It is also one of the (good) preservatives for fruit. The fruit is ripe.

10. Lemon juice is the (good) cleanser for mildew. The mildew is common.

11. Lemon juice smells (good) than vinegar. The vinegar is white or red.

12. Vinegar smells (bad) than lemons. The lemons are fragrant.

13. The rind is the (bad) tasting part of the fruit. The fruit is a lemon.

14. Lemons make water taste even (good) than before. The lemons are sliced.

15. The (good) use of lemons is for making treats. The treats are delicious.

Handbook
pages
536–537, 544–546

C. **Challenge** **Rewrite the following sentences. Combine similar sentences to avoid repeating words and ideas. Correctly use abbreviations and adjectives that compare.**

16. Mrs Ng showed us an experiment with lemon juice. It was an interesting experiment.

17. We did the experiment on wed of last week.

18. Dr. Long said he would be interested in seeing it. He is our wonderful principal.

19. I think he will find this experiment most interesting than the other one.

20. This is the most excitingest experiment we have ever done!

SOFTENS WATER
TO PREVENT
SPOTTING

Writing Activity A Poster

Make a poster that describes the many uses for lemons. Use vivid words to capture your audience's attention.

APPLY GRAMMAR: Include adjectives that describe and compare. Create images that will appeal to your reader's senses.

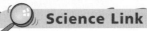

Science Link

Common Errors with Adjectives

Writers often use adjectives to compare two or more people, places, things, or ideas. Yet they sometimes make mistakes when they use adjectives that compare. This chart shows two errors that writers make when comparing with adjectives. Notice how each mistake can be corrected.

Common Errors	Examples	Corrected Sentences
Using -er or -est instead of more or most	I read the interestingest book about China.	I read the most interesting book about China.
Using -er or -est with more or most	China is more older than Japan.	China is older than Japan.

THINK AND WRITE

Adjectives

In your journal, write how you know when to use -er and -est instead of more and most.

REVIEW THE RULES

ADJECTIVES

- For most short adjectives, add -er to compare two nouns and -est to compare more than two.

- For long adjectives, use more to compare two nouns and most to compare more than two.

- Remember When an adjective ends in e, drop the final e before adding -er or -est.

- Remember When an adjective ends in a single vowel and a consonant, double the consonant before adding -er or -est.

- Remember When an adjective ends in a consonant and y, change the y to i before adding -er or -est.

More Practice

A. **Write the adjective that compares in each sentence.**

1. China is the world's largest country in population.

2. It is also the third biggest country in size.

3. Its civilization is also the oldest in the world.

4. In China, it is easier to travel on the rivers than on the roads.

5. Flood controls, such as dikes, make the rivers more predictable.

B. **Write each sentence. Choose the correct form of the adjective in parentheses.**

6. The Chang is China's (longer, longest) river.

7. The inland waterways are (more important, most important) than roads.

8. These waterways are inland China's (importantest, most important) means of transportation.

9. Railroads eventually became (more useful, most useful) than China's Grand Canal.

10. The Grand Canal is (larger, more large) than any other artificial waterway in the world.

C. **Write these sentences. Use the correct form of the adjective in parentheses.**

11. China has one of the _____ governments in the world. (strong)

12. Its people are among the world's _____. (busy)

13. Years ago, the Great Wall of China made the country the _____ of all to invade. (difficult)

14. The T'ang dynasty was _____ than the Shang dynasty in China. (powerful)

15. Chinese art is among the _____ in the world. (beautiful)

Grammar Troubleshooter, pages 516–517

Handbook
page 537

Writing Activity **A Paragraph**

Choose an animal, a machine, or something else that is the biggest, smallest, fastest, or slowest of its kind. Write a report that gives important information about the topic. Include a main idea and strong facts and details to support it.

APPLY GRAMMAR: Be sure that you use -er and -est or more and most correctly. Check the spelling of your adjectives that compare.

Science Link

Mechanics and Spelling

Directions

Read the passage and decide which type of mistake, if any, appears in each underlined section. Choose the letter for your answer. If there is no error, choose "No mistake."

Capitalize the main words in a proper noun.

Use an apostrophe in a contraction.

When a word ends in a vowel and one consonant, double the consonant before adding -ing.

Sample

When Milo Mottola was asked to design a new merry-go-round for a park in <u>new york city, he decided</u> to **(1)** be creative. He <u>didnt want his merry-go-round to have</u> **(2)** <u>horses</u>. He wanted different kinds of animals. He asked neighborhood children to draw pictures of the animals they would like to see on the merry-go-round. Mr. Mottola got 1,000 drawings. He chose 32 of the best. His merry-go-round <u>is now spining around with a zebra,</u> **(3)** a kangaroo, birds, and sea creatures on it. Under each animal is the name of the boy or girl who designed it.

1 A Spelling

B Capitalization

C Punctuation

D No mistake

2 F Spelling

G Capitalization

H Punctuation

J No mistake

3 A Spelling

B Capitalization

C Punctuation

D No mistake

Test Tip
Ruling out answers that you know are wrong can help you determine the correct answer.

Grammar and Usage

Directions

Read the passage and choose the word or group of words that belongs in each space. Choose the letter for your answer.

Sample

Wolves are very intelligent animals, and __(1)__ have

amazing endurance. They are part of the canine family,

which includes dogs, coyotes, and foxes. Only two

species of wolves, the gray wolf and the red wolf, exist

in the world. Most wolves are gray wolves. Gray wolves

include timber wolves and tundra wolves. Gray wolves

used to be one of the __(2)__ animals found in North

America. Their numbers decreased, however, when people

__(3)__ into their environment. The number of red wolves

has also dramatically decreased. At one time, red wolves

freely roamed the southern states. Today, the red wolf is

nearly extinct. Only a few hundred red wolves __(4)__ .

> *Choose a pronoun that agrees with the noun to which it refers.*

> *Do not use* most *and the* -est *form of an adjective when comparing more than two things.*

> *Context clues tell whether a verb should be in the present, past, or future tense.*

> *The subject and the verb of the sentence must agree.*

1 A it

   B he

   C they

   D we

2 F common

   G more common

   H most common

   J most commonest

3 A moved

   B move

   C are moving

   D will move

4 F remains

   G is remaining

   H was remaining

   J remain

RESEARCH

RESEARCH

A **time line** can show how history unfolds more easily than mere words. With a time line, I can place events in the order they happened. Time lines give me the "big picture" of history at a glance.

COMPOSITION SKILLS

WRITING WELL

An **outline** helps me organize what I want to write. I use an outline to list all my questions. It helps me remember everything I want to include so I can write a better story.

VOCABULARY SKILLS

USING WORDS

Amusing, comical, and funny are **synonyms**, or words that mean the same thing. Sad and somber are **antonyms** of funny because they have the opposite meaning. Synonyms and antonyms make my writing more varied and interesting for my readers. Can you think of some synonyms and antonyms?

Read Now!

As you read about quilt codes, think about the main idea of each of the three paragraphs. Then write a simple outline of the photo essay.

TIME FOR KIDS

PHOTO ESSAY

Quilt Codes

Slaves may have stitched secret messages into quilts!

Patchwork Messages

Like a patchwork quilt, history is pieced together from many different stories, not all of them written. That's what Jacqueline Tobin, a professor and writer, discovered one day in a Charleston, South Carolina, market. There she met Ozella McDaniel Williams, who was selling blankets and quilts. "Did you know that quilts were used by slaves to communicate on the Underground Railroad?" Williams asked Tobin.

Williams told an amazing tale that she had heard from her grandmother. The colors, patterns, designs, and stitches of quilts formed a secret code. The code was used by slaves to guide them safely along the Underground Railroad before the Civil War. The Underground Railroad was a system of escape routes to freedom and liberty for slaves. The routes led from states in the South to states in the North or to Canada.

According to Williams, slaves used quilt patterns as "visual maps" to help them remember directions and warnings on their long journey. Slaves also used quilts to send secret messages to one another. Each pattern had a meaning. "The quilts show that slaves crafted their own way of escape and helped some avoid capture," says Tobin.

Secret message? A quilt hangs from a window.

Ozella McDaniel Williams revealed the secret messages in quilts.

All photos: Raymond Dobard

interNET CONNECTION Go to www.mhschool.com/language-arts for more information on the topic.

Since geese fly north in the spring, this pattern gave fleeing slaves two important instructions: Head north, and travel in the spring. It is called Flying Geese.

This pattern held a helpful warning: Slaves were to travel in a zigzag pattern in order to avoid leaving a straight, clear path for slave catchers to follow.

This popular quilt design is known as the Star or the Evening Star. According to the code, escaping slaves were told to follow the North Star.

Write Now!

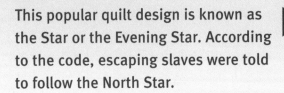

Write a paragraph about quilts using the information you just read. Include details such as the ones on these pages to make your paragraph interesting to a reader.

Use Time Lines and Historical Maps

A **time line** is a diagram of a series of events in time. Time lines show events in the order in which they happened. Dates are marked on a time line to identify these events. Putting events in correct time order helps you to see how events are related.

Look at this time line for a social studies report about the Inca. It shows what happened to the Inca empire.

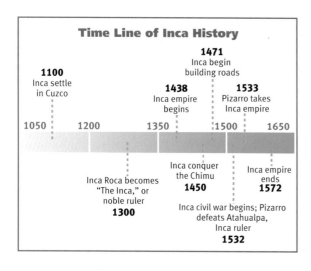

Time Line of Inca History

1100
Inca settle in Cuzco

1438
Inca empire begins

1471
Inca begin building roads

1533
Pizarro takes Inca empire

1050   1200   1350   1500   1650

Inca Roca becomes "The Inca," or noble ruler
1300

Inca conquer the Chimu
1450

Inca civil war begins; Pizarro defeats Atahualpa, Inca ruler
1532

Inca empire ends
1572

CONQUEST OF THE INCA, 1531-1533

Central America

Panama City (1531)

Quito (1532)

Cajamarca

Atahualpa is defeated, 1532

Cuzco

SOUTH AMERICA

Pizarro takes Inca empire, 1533

ATLANTIC OCEAN

PACIFIC OCEAN

0   500   1,000 Miles
0   500   1,000 Kilometers

Strait of Magellan

⊛ Inca capital
▮ Inca empire
← Pizarro's forces
← Atahualpa's forces
• Other city
⊛ Battle

Another way to study events from the past is to use a historical map. **Historical maps** show information about the past or where past events took place. Look at the historical map above. It shows the conquest of the Inca, from 1531 to 1533.

Practice

A. **Look at the time line. Write how many years separate the following events.**

1. Inca settle in Cuzco and Inca Roca becomes the noble ruler
2. Inca empire begins and Inca conquer the Chimu
3. Inca conquer the Chimu and begin building roads
4. Pizarro takes Inca empire and Inca empire ends
5. Inca empire begins and ends

B. **Use the historical map to write answers to these questions.**

6. What is a historical map?
7. Where was the Inca empire located? How do you know?
8. In which direction did Pizarro's forces travel? How can you tell?
9. How do you know that Quito was part of the Inca empire?
10. How can reading historical maps be useful to you?

C. **Use the time line and the historical map to answer these questions.**

11. What information does a time line show?
12. How is a time line like a historical map?
13. What information about the Inca do both the time line and historical map tell you?
14. What is the main difference between a time line and a historical map?
15. What are some things that reading time lines and historical maps can help you to do?

*inter***NET**
CONNECTION

Go to:
www.mhschool.
com/language-
arts for more
information on
the topic.

Writing Activity A Paragraph

Write a paragraph that will explain a series of events from American history. Then create an accurate time line or historical map that will help support and explain your ideas. Share your work with one or more of your classmates.

Vocabulary: Synonyms and Antonyms

— DEFINITION —

A **synonym** is a word that has the same or almost the same meaning as that of another word. **Antonyms** are words with opposite meanings.

Synonyms	Antonyms
large—big	large—small
move—travel	up—down
below—under	rise—fall
change—alter	hot—cold
end—finish	hard—soft
vapor—gas	gas—liquid

THINK AND WRITE

Synonyms and Antonyms

How can using synonyms and antonyms help make your writing clearer and more exact? Explain your answer in your journal.

Read the paragraph below. Look at the highlighted words.

Both *large* and *small* bodies of water are part of the water cycle. In the water cycle, water *moves* from the earth to the air. It then *travels* back to the earth again. The sun heats liquid water into a *vapor* or *gas*. Water vapor *rises* into the clouds and then *falls* to earth as rain, snow, hail, or sleet.

Practice

A. **Write each pair of words. Then write *synonym* or *antonym* next to each pair.**

1. cool—warm

2. wet—moist

3. bright—dark

4. clear—cloudy

5. cheerful—happy

B. **Write each sentence. Replace the underlined word with an antonym.**

6. The rain fell <u>slowly</u> to the ground.

7. The <u>quiet</u> thunder could be heard in the distance.

8. There was <u>less</u> rain today than yesterday.

9. The clouds made the sky look <u>dark</u>.

10. The air smelled <u>stale</u> after the storm.

C. **Grammar Link** **Write the paragraph. Replace each underlined adjective with a more vivid synonym from the Word Bank. Then write the paragraph again to use antonyms from the Word Bank in place of the synonyms.**

warm	moist	huge	small	cool
dry	marvelous	powerful	weak	terrible

11–15. The weather had been <u>hot</u> and <u>humid</u> for many days. Then a <u>wonderful</u> break in the temperature came. At first, only a few <u>tiny</u> drops fell from the sky. Within an hour, however, the gentle sprinkles had become a <u>strong</u> hurricane.

Writing Activity **An Eyewitness Report**

Imagine that you are a weather "spotter"—someone who watches the weather. Write an eyewitness report of a severe storm in your area. Use synonyms and antonyms to tell about the storm.
APPLY GRAMMAR: Use vivid adjectives to describe what the storm looked, sounded, and felt like.

Composition: Outlining

Writers make outlines as a way to organize their main ideas and put their ideas in order.

GUIDELINES

- An outline is a plan that organizes ideas about a specific topic.

- Outlines group facts into related categories.

- An outline can be used to plan the introduction, body, and conclusion of a piece of writing.

- Use Roman numerals to list main ideas and capital letters to list the supporting details below each main idea.

- Use a variety of sources to find facts and details for your outline.

THINK AND WRITE

Outlining

Why is it important to know how to make an outline? List three reasons in your journal.

Look at the outline of the life of William Clark. Clark was one of the explorers who took part in the Lewis and Clark expedition. Notice how the writer organizes the ideas.

Each Roman numeral shows a main idea.

Each main idea will become a paragraph in the report.

A capital letter indicates a supporting detail.

William Clark

I. Clark's Early Life

   A. Born in Virginia in 1770

II. Lewis and Clark Expedition (1804–1806)

   A. Explored Louisiana Purchase with Meriwether Lewis

   B. Mapped routes, kept journal, made sketches

   C. Helped hire Sacajawea, a Shoshone guide

   D. Gathered materials and published records of journey

III. Clark's Later Years

   A. Became governor of the Missouri Territory

Practice

A. Read the following incomplete outline. Answer the questions.

Meriwether Lewis

I. Lewis and Clark Expedition (1804-1806)

   A. Explored Louisiana Purchase with his friend William Clark

   B. Collected plants, animals, and minerals along the way

   C. Faced many dangers but saw amazing sights

   D. Paved the way for settlers to go West

1. What is the topic of the outline?

2. What main idea is listed?

3. How many details support the main idea?

4. How many paragraphs would develop from this outline?

5. The body of this outline is shown here. What two important parts are missing from the outline?

B. Determine which word or words in the following series are the main ideas. Create outlines showing the main idea and supporting details.

6. map symbols, using a map, mileage scale

7. Rocky Mountains, Pacific Ocean, features of the west

8. skills of a good explorer, observation skills, note-taking skills, survival skills

9. wagons, boats, transportation, trains

10. hiking boots, hiking equipment, knapsack, compass, maps

C. **Grammar Link** **11–15.** Use one of the outlines from Practice B to write a paragraph. Include a main-idea sentence, detail sentences, and a concluding sentence. Use adjectives to describe.

Writing Activity A Journal Entry

Imagine you are Lewis or Clark. Write a journal entry explaining what you saw in one day. Outline your entry beforehand.

APPLY GRAMMAR: Include adjectives in your journal entry. Draw one line under each adjective and two lines under the word it describes.

Better Sentences

Directions

Read the passage. Some sections are underlined. The underlined sections may be one of the following:

- Incomplete sentences
- Run-on sentences
- Correctly written sentences that should be combined
- Correctly written sentences that do not need to be rewritten

Choose the best way to write each underlined section. If the underlined section needs no change, choose "No mistake."

> **Sample**
>
> In 1988, the space shuttle *Discovery* launched into space. <u>The goal of the mission was to place a satellite</u> **(1)** <u>into orbit</u>. However, this mission was not the first time that American astronauts had traveled into space, nor was it the last. The first NASA program included seven male pilots. <u>In 1978, some women were finally chosen</u> **(2)** <u>to be astronauts. There were six of them.</u>

Some long sentences are correct and do not need to be changed.

Some sentences that describe the same thing or idea can be combined.

Test Tip

Read the directions more than once so you understand the exercise.

1 A It was the goal of the mission. To place a satellite into orbit.

B It was the goal of the mission it was to place a satellite into orbit.

C The goal of the mission. It was to place a satellite into orbit.

D No mistake

2 F In 1978, some women were finally chosen to be astronauts, and there were six women.

G In 1978, six women were finally chosen to be astronauts.

H In 1978, some women, and there were six, were finally chosen to be astronauts.

J No mistake

Vocabulary and Comprehension

Directions

Read the passage. Then read each question that follows the passage. Decide which is the best answer to each question. Choose the letter for that answer.

Sample

The Republic of Singapore is in Southeast Asia. The country consists of a large island and more than 50 smaller islands. The main island is called Singapore, just like the country. The capital city on the main island is also called Singapore, but the city of Singapore has its own special name, too. It is known as the Lion City.

The island of Singapore provides many opportunities for businesses. It is the home of one of the busiest ports in the <u>region</u>, and many corporations have located their Asian headquarters there.

What word can replace region, without changing the meaning of the sentence?

1 Which statement is <u>not</u> a fact about Singapore?

  A Singapore is in Southeast Asia.

  B The city of Singapore is known as the Lion City.

  C Singapore has the best fishing in the world.

  D Singapore has a busy port.

2 Which word is a synonym for *region*?

  F area

  G country

  H capital

  J world

Seeing Like a Writer

Look at these pictures. What ideas for writing do they give you? Notice the details in each picture. How do the details help you understand what the picture is about?

Kwiaguith Totem Pole by Calvin Hunt

298

Writing from Pictures

1. List the details in each picture. Use adjectives to describe each detail.

2. List facts about one picture. Write a conclusion based on those facts and on what you may already know about the subject of the picture.

3. Choose two pictures. What main idea do they share? Use the main idea as a title for both pictures. Then write a paragraph that explains the idea.

Apply Grammar: Use comparative and superlative adjectives. Underline comparative adjectives and circle superlative adjectives.

Expository Writing

Have you ever written interesting facts about a person, place, or thing? Your factual account was an example of expository writing. Expository writing gives readers important information about a topic.

Learning from Writers

Read the following examples of expository writing. What important facts do they tell about the topic? As you read, notice how each author introduces the main idea and develops it with facts and supporting details.

THINK AND WRITE

Purpose
Why do you think it is important to give facts and information in a magazine article? Write a brief explanation.

"Catching Up with Lewis and Clark"

Lewis and his best friend, Clark, left St. Louis in May 1804 with a party of 42 men. They never found the water route, but they became the first U.S. citizens to see many of America's wonders—the endless Great Plains, the jagged Rocky Mountains, and the glistening Pacific. They faced many hardships and dangers, including bear attacks and bitter cold. In Great Falls, Montana, they carried heavy canoes for weeks around waterfalls under the hot sun. At times they had little food to eat and almost starved.

More than 500 days and 4,000 miles after they had set out, Lewis and Clark reached the Pacific. "Ocían in view! O! the joy!" wrote Clark in his journal. (Clark was smart and brave, but not a very good speller.)

The explorers kept superb maps and diaries. They were the first to describe 122 kinds of animals and 176 plants, and to meet many native tribes. But they left barely a trace behind at their campsites. That makes it hard for historians to say "Lewis and Clark were here!"

—from "Catching Up with Lewis and Clark,"
in *Time for Kids*

The Lewis and Clark Expedition

Traveling across a land with no roads and no maps, two young men explored a vast unknown territory. After two and a half years, the young adventurers returned from their eight-thousand-mile journey. Lewis and Clark had tales to tell.

Thomas Jefferson chose Lewis and Clark to lead an expedition of 42 men to explore the land west of the Mississippi. The group left St. Louis in May, 1804.

The explorers struggled hard; however, in November of 1805 they reached the Pacific Ocean. After spending the winter there, they began their return trip.

The members of the expedition had been given up for lost, but they arrived back at St. Louis in September of 1806. They brought with them glowing reports of the land and the Native American groups who had helped them on their journey.   —Teresa Jiménez

PRACTICE AND APPLY

Thinking Like a Reader

1. What is the main idea of each paragraph in "Catching Up with Lewis and Clark"?

2. What is the most important information in "The Lewis and Clark Expedition"?

Thinking Like a Writer

3. How did the author of "Catching Up with Lewis and Clark" support his main ideas?

4. How did the author of "The Lewis and Clark Expedition" summarize her information in the conclusion?

5. **Reading Across Texts** Compare the introductions and the conclusions of the two literature models. How are they alike and different?

Features of Expository Writing

Expository writing gives facts and information about a topic. Good expository writing:

▶ introduces the **main idea** and develops it with facts and **supporting details.**

▶ gives **important information** about a specific topic.

▶ summarizes information from a **variety of sources.**

▶ uses **transition words** to connect ideas.

▶ draws a **conclusion** based on the facts and information presented.

▶ Main Idea and Supporting Details

Reread "Catching Up with Lewis and Clark" on page 300. What is the main idea of the article? What facts and supporting details tell about the main idea?

> Lewis and his best friend, Clark, left St. Louis in May 1804 with a party of 42 men.

This sentence from the first paragraph tells you the main focus of the selection. The facts and details in the rest of the selection help explain what happens to the explorers after they leave St. Louis.

▶ Important Information

You can use expository writing to share important information with your audience. What important information does the author share in this sentence?

> They were the first to describe 122 kinds of animals and 176 plants, and to meet many native tribes.

This sentence gives you specific information about the discoveries that Lewis and Clark made during their journey.

▶ A Variety of Sources

To present the most accurate and complete information about your topic, it is important to summarize facts and details from a variety of sources. Where might the author have found this information?

> "Ocían in view! O! the joy!" wrote Clark in his journal.

The author could have used encyclopedias, books, documentaries, and Clark's own journal to gather information.

▶ Transition Words

To help your readers clearly understand important information, you need to use transition words that connect the events and ideas in your writing. Words such as *at times, after,* and *however* help you connect ideas.

> More than 500 days and 4,000 miles after they had set out, Lewis and Clark reached the Pacific.

What transition word did the author use?

▶ A Conclusion

The author ends "Catching Up with Lewis and Clark" by drawing a conclusion.

> That makes it hard for historians to say "Lewis and Clark were here!"

On what information does the author base this conclusion?

PRACTICE AND APPLY

Create a Main Idea and Supporting Details Chart

1. Reread "The Lewis and Clark Expedition" by Teresa Jiménez on page 301.

2. Create a Main Idea and Supporting Details chart.

3. Write the main idea of the piece at the bottom of the chart. Then list the supporting details.

4. What kinds of sources do you think Teresa used to find her information?

Details
_____
_____
_____
_____

Main Idea

Prewrite

Expository writing presents facts about a particular topic. You can use expository writing to share important information with your readers. Often, this information is in the form of a research report.

Purpose and Audience

The purpose of expository writing is to give your readers information. In this way, expository writing lets you share important facts and ideas with your audience.

Before you begin to write, think about your audience. How will you present your ideas? Once you have chosen your topic, consider what your audience already knows about it. This will help you decide the kind of information to include in your report.

Choose a Topic

Start by **brainstorming** a list of topics. Focus on topics you have read or heard about in school or at home, or have seen on a television news program. Consider both past and current events. Then choose a topic.

Once you have chosen your topic, **explore ideas**. Make a list of facts. Later, you will organize these facts in an outline.

THINK AND WRITE

Audience
What kind of information will you give an audience who knows something about your topic? Write your ideas in your journal.

This is how I explored my ideas.

The First Thanksgiving

Thanksgiving is a national holiday in November.

Pilgrims had the first Thanksgiving.

Pilgrims traveled from England to New England.

They wanted to be free to practice their religion.

They wanted a better life.

They had a hard time living in New England.

Native Americans helped the Pilgrims.

Pilgrims had a feast to celebrate their harvest.

They shared the feast with Native Americans.

Organize • Outlining

The facts and details in expository writing are organized around an introduction, a body, and a conclusion. The introduction tells the main idea of the topic. The body develops the topic, and the conclusion summarizes the information. Notice that the writer does not include all the items on his list.

OUTLINE

The First Thanksgiving

I. Introduction

   A. Pilgrims had the first Thanksgiving.

II. Moving to New England

   A. Pilgrims traveled from England to New England.

      1. Settled Plymouth Colony

   B. They wanted a better life.

III. Life in New England

   A. Pilgrims had a hard time living in New England.

      1. Not enough food

   B. Native Americans helped the Pilgrims

IV. Conclusion

   A. Pilgrims had a feast to celebrate their harvest.

   B. They shared the feast with Native Americans.

Checklist ✓
Prewriting

- Did you think about your purpose and audience?

- Did you choose a topic that will interest your readers?

- Did you identify the main points you want to present?

- Did you group together similar facts and details?

- Did you organize your ideas in an outline?

- What kind of research do you need to do to gather important information?

PRACTICE AND APPLY

Plan Your Expository Writing

1. Think about your purpose and audience.

2. Brainstorm a list of possible topics.

3. Choose a topic, and explore ideas.

4. Use an outline to organize facts and ideas.

Prewrite • Research and Inquiry

▶ Writer's Resources

To get more information for your report, you will have to do research. First, write questions to guide you. Then decide which resources you will need to answer them.

What Else Do I Need to Know?	Where Can I Find the Information?
When did the first Thanksgiving take place?	Read a historical time line.
Why did the Pilgrims start a new colony?	Watch documentaries and videos about the topic.

▶ Use a Time Line

You can discover when an event took place by looking at a time line. A time line is a diagram that shows when a series of events took place. Time lines help you keep track of the order of events.

The time line below shows some of the important events that led to the Pilgrims' decision to start the Plymouth Colony. It also shows the events that led to the celebration of the first Thanksgiving.

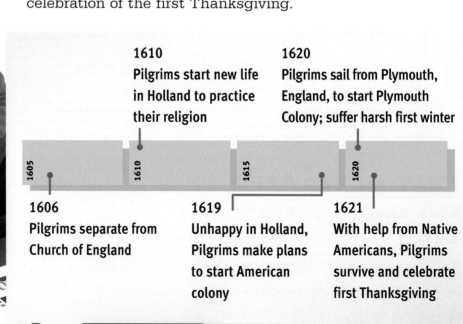

1610
Pilgrims start new life in Holland to practice their religion

1620
Pilgrims sail from Plymouth, England, to start Plymouth Colony; suffer harsh first winter

1606
Pilgrims separate from Church of England

1619
Unhappy in Holland, Pilgrims make plans to start American colony

1621
With help from Native Americans, Pilgrims survive and celebrate first Thanksgiving

▶ View Documentaries and Videos

Documentaries and videos can be helpful sources of information. These visuals can provide important facts and interesting details to include in your writing. Be sure to take notes or draw quick sketches of what you see.

▶ Use Your Research

After completing your research, add any new facts to your outline. This writer learned important information from the time line. He also learned about the Pilgrims' first year in New England by looking at historical videos and documentaries.

PREWRITE

DRAFT

REVISE

PROOFREAD

PUBLISH

Handbook
pages 568, 575

I. Introduction
   A. Pilgrims had the first Thanksgiving. *in 1621*
II. Moving to New England
   A. Pilgrims traveled from England to New England.
      1. Settled Plymouth Colony
      2. Landed in 1620
   B. They wanted a better life.
      1. Freedom to practice their religion
III. Life in New England
   A. Pilgrims had a hard time living in New England.
      1. Not enough food
      2. Many Pilgrims died.
   B. Native Americans helped the Pilgrims
      1. Met Squanto in March 1621
      2. He taught Pilgrims to fish and plant crops.

Checklist ✔

Research and Inquiry

- Did you list questions about your topic?

- Did you identify possible resources?

- Did you take notes about the facts you read?

PRACTICE AND APPLY

Review Your Plan

1. Look at your outline.

2. List questions you have about your topic.

3. Identify the resources you will need.

4. Gather facts from a variety of sources.

5. Add new facts to your outline.

Draft

Before you begin writing your report, review the outline you have made. Plan to make a paragraph for each idea that is indicated by a Roman numeral. The facts marked with capital letters and the details indicated by numbers should support the main idea of each paragraph.

Main idea for report: Pilgrims had the first Thanksgiving

Main idea for second paragraph: Moving to New England

Main idea for third paragraph: Life in New England

OUTLINE

The First Thanksgiving

I. Introduction   in 1621

   A. Pilgrims had the first Thanksgiving

II. Moving to New England

   A. Pilgrims traveled from England to New England.

      1. Settled Plymouth Colony
      2. Landed in 1620

   B. They wanted a better life.

      1. Freedom to practice their religion

III. Life in New England

   A. Pilgrims had a hard time living in New England.

      1. Not enough food
      2. Many Pilgrims died.

   B. Native Americans helped the Pilgrims

      1. Met Squanto in March 1621
      2. He taught Pilgrims to fish and plant crops.

IV. Conclusion

   A. Pilgrims had a feast to celebrate their harvest.

      1. Three-day feast

   B. They shared the feast with Native Americans.

The last paragraph will be my conclusion.

✓ Checklist

Drafting

- Remember your purpose and audience.

- Give important information about a specific topic.

- Be sure that your facts and details in each paragraph support the main idea.

- Write a strong introduction, body, and conclusion.

- Draw a conclusion based on the facts and details you presented.

This writer used the ideas in his outline to write a first draft. He stated the main idea of his report in a topic sentence. The writer added details about Squanto and the Pilgrims. He referred to a video to show the source of his facts.

PREWRITE

DRAFT

REVISE

PROOFREAD

PUBLISH

DRAFT

Many experts beleive that the first Thanksgiving took place in the Plymouth colony in 1621.

In the video <u>Journey to Freedom</u>, Robert Nang explains how the Pilgrims made the long journey to New England in 1620. It was a hard journey.

Mr Nang shows that the Pilgrims worked hard in the Plymouth colony to make a new life. Unfortunately, with little food or help, many Pilgrims died. In March of 1621, help arrived. A Native american man named Squanto taught the Pilgrims how to fish. He taught them how to plant corn and other new crops. With Squantos help, the fall brought a great harvest

The Pilgrims were thankful for the harvest. They held a three-day feast. They invited some Native Americans to help them celebrate.

Topic sentence of report

Includes facts from a reliable source

Main idea of paragraph: Life in New England

Supporting details tell how Squanto helped the Pilgrims to survive.

PRACTICE AND APPLY

Draft Your Expository Writing

1. Review your prewriting outline.

2. State the main idea of the report in a topic sentence.

3. Write events in the order in which they happened.

4. Use facts and details to support your main ideas.

TECHNOLOGY

If you typed the outline on the computer during prewriting, use the same document to begin your writing. Be sure each item in the outline is a full sentence in your draft.

Revise

Elaborate

One way to improve your writing is to elaborate. When you elaborate, you add important ideas, facts, and details that might be missing from your writing. When you revise your expository writing, you may need to tell more information about key events.

The information that this writer added lets the reader know when an event happened.

Unfortunately, with little food or help, many Pilgrims
  that first winter
died.

The writer added a fact to make clear which Native Americans were invited to the celebration.

  Squanto and some of his friends
They invited ~~some Native Americans~~ to help them celebrate.

Word Choice

When you are writing an expository piece such as a research report, it is important to choose the right words for your topic and audience.

In expository writing, you need to find words that will help you order your information and connect your ideas. These words are called *transition words*.

In March of 1621, help arrived. A Native american man

named Squanto taught the Pilgrims how to fish. He

taught them how to plant corn and other new crops.

In fact,
With Squantos help, the fall brought a great harvest

TRANSITION WORDS

however

yet

in fact

for example

as a result

because

therefore

so that

fortunately

now

then

finally

Better Paragraphs

As you revise your draft, check your paragraphs to make sure they fit together well. Read the paragraphs aloud. Do the details in each paragraph support the main idea? Does the information flow from one paragraph to the next? Rearranging paragraphs or changing parts of a paragraph may improve the overall flow of your report.

You can add, take out, move information, or add transitions to connect the ideas in one or more paragraphs.

PREWRITE

DRAFT

REVISE

PROOFREAD

PUBLISH

In the video Journey to Freedom, Robert Nang explains how the Pilgrims made the long journey to New England in 1620. It was a hard journey.

Mr Nang shows that the Pilgrims worked hard in the Plymouth colony to make a new life. Unfortunately, *that first winter* with little food or help, many Pilgrims died. In March of 1621, help arrived.

TECHNOLOGY

Review your draft for logical order. Do the ideas flow smoothly? If not, try moving paragraphs or sentences around by cutting and pasting text.

PRACTICE AND APPLY

Revise Your Expository Writing

1. Add facts and details that will support the main idea of each paragraph and give more information to the reader.

2. Use transition words to connect ideas.

3. Change or rearrange information so that ideas "build up" from beginning to end.

4. **Grammar** Should you combine any sentences by moving adjectives?

Revise • Peer Conferencing

Take a break from your writing. Exchange first drafts with a partner. Listen to all your partner's suggestions. Take notes. Make those changes with which you agree.

Writing PROCESS

Combine the adjectives in these two sentences.

You should add why the Pilgrims came to New England.

You should combine these two sentences into one.

Say that this was the first Thanksgiving.

Many experts beleive that the first Thanksgiving took place in the Plymouth colony in 1621.

In the video Journey to Freedom, Robert Nang explains how the Pilgrims made the long journey to New England in 1620. It was a hard journey.

Mr Nang shows that the Pilgrims worked hard in the Plymouth colony to make a new life. Unfortunately, with little food or help, many Pilgrims died. In March of 1621, help arrived. A Native american man named Squanto taught the Pilgrims how to fish. He taught them how to plant corn and other new crops. With Squantos help, the fall brought a great harvest

The Pilgrims were thankful for the harvest. They held a three-day feast. They invited some Native Americans to help them celebrate.

Conferencing for the Reader

- Are features of expository writing included in your partner's piece?
  - introduces a main idea and details
  - summarizes information from different sources
  - draws a conclusion
  - uses transitions
- Discuss with your partner things that you like about his or her writing, as well as things that you think need revising.

Think about the comments and suggestions your conferencing partner gave you. Use the ideas to revise your report. This writer made some changes based on his partner's ideas.

REVISE

How Thanksgiving Came to Be

Many experts beleive that the first Thanksgiving took place in the Plymouth colony in 1621.

In the video <u>Journey to Freedom</u>, Robert Nang explains how the Pilgrims made the long ^hard journey to New England in 1620. ~~It was a hard journey.~~

Mr Nang shows that the Pilgrims worked hard in
practice their religion and
the Plymouth colony to make a new life. Unfortunately,
that first winter
with little food or help, many Pilgrims died. In March of 1621, help arrived. A Native american man named Squanto taught the Pilgrims how to fish. ~~He taught~~ and
~~them how to~~ plant corn and other new crops. With In fact, Squantos help, the fall brought a great harvest
and
The Pilgrims were thankful for the harvest. They
Squanto and some of his friends
held a three-day feast. They invited ~~some Native~~
That feast was probably the first Thanksgiving.
~~Americans~~ to help them celebrate.

PRACTICE AND APPLY

Revise Your Expository Writing

1. Read the notes from your peer conference.

2. Use your partner's suggestions to improve your draft.

3. Take out any unimportant facts or details.

4. If you need to add important facts, do more research.

Checklist ✓
Revising

■ Does your report suit your purpose and audience?

■ Does your topic sentence clearly state the main idea of your report?

■ Do you need to elaborate on any part of your report?

■ Did you write the events in the right order?

■ Did you check your facts in more than one source?

■ Do your sentences and paragraphs flow smoothly?

■ Did you write a title that explains the topic?

Proofread

After you have revised your expository writing, you will need to proofread it to find and correct any mistakes in mechanics, grammar and usage, and spelling.

TECHNOLOGY

It is often easier to catch mistakes on paper than on a computer screen. For proofreading, print out your work, mark the corrections on paper, and then enter the corrections to the file.

STRATEGIES FOR PROOFREADING

- **Read your revised report more than once.** Look for a different kind of error each time. You'll have a better chance of catching all errors.

- **Check each sentence for correct capitalization.** Remember to capitalize proper nouns and proper adjectives.

- **Reread for correct punctuation.** These include commas, apostrophes, and end marks.

- **Check for spelling mistakes by reading your paper backward, from the last word to the first.** This will help you focus on the spelling of each word.

REVIEW THE RULES

GRAMMAR

- An adjective is a word that describes a noun or a pronoun and tells *what kind, which one,* or *how many.* You can use an adjective to combine two sentences that tell about the same noun or pronoun. When you combine two sentences, leave out words that repeat.

MECHANICS

- A proper adjective is formed from a proper noun. Proper adjectives always begin with a capital letter.

- An abbreviation is a shortened form of a word. Most abbreviations begin with a capital letter and end with a period.

Look at the proofreading corrections made on the draft below. What does the symbol / mean? Why does the writer need to use a small letter?

PROOFREAD

How Thanksgiving Came to Be

⁜ Many experts ~~beleive~~ that the first Thanksgiving took place in the Plymouth colony in 1621.

In the video Journey to Freedom, Robert Nang explains how the Pilgrims made the long journey to New England in 1620. ~~It was a hard journey.~~

Mr. Nang shows that the Pilgrims worked hard in practice their religion and the Plymouth colony to make a new life. Unfortunately, that first winter with little food or help, many Pilgrims died. In March of 1621, help arrived. A Native american man named Squanto taught the Pilgrims how to fish. ~~He taught them how to~~ plant corn and other new crops. With Squanto's help, the fall brought a great harvest.

The Pilgrims were thankful for the harvest. They held a three-day feast. They invited ~~some Native~~ Squanto and some of his friends

That feast was probably the first Thanksgiving.

~~Americans~~ to help them celebrate.

PRACTICE AND APPLY

Proofread Your Expository Writing

1. Correct spelling mistakes.

2. Check for correct use of commas, apostrophes, and other punctuation marks.

3. Be sure that proper nouns and proper adjectives begin with a capital letter.

4. Indent paragraphs.

Checklist ✓
Proofreading

- Did you spell all the words correctly?

- Did you use correct punctuation?

- Did you capitalize proper nouns, proper adjectives, titles, and the beginning of every sentence?

- Did you indent each paragraph?

PROOFREADING MARKS

⁜ new paragraph

∧ add

ℐ take out

≡ Make a capital letter.

/ Make a small letter.

ⓢⓟ Check the spelling.

⊙ Add a period.

Publish

Before you publish your report, check your writing one last time. You can use a checklist to help you focus on the review of your work.

✓ **Self-Check** Expository Writing

❑ Who was my audience? Did I give them enough information about my topic?

❑ What was my main topic? Did I include enough facts and details to support it?

❑ Did I begin in a clear and interesting way? Did I summarize my ideas at the end?

❑ Did I present my information in the best order? Did I use the right transition words to connect my ideas?

❑ Did I combine sentences? Do my sentences flow together?

❑ Are my paragraphs fully developed with important information? Do I have a clear introduction, body, and conclusion?

❑ Did I proofread and correct all errors?

The writer used the checklist to review his report. Read "How Thanksgiving Came to Be" and discuss the writer's published piece. Jot down your thoughts about the report. Did the writer include enough information? Do you think the report was ready to be published? What else would you like to know about the topic?

How Thanksgiving Came to Be

by Jamal Travers

Many experts believe that the first Thanksgiving took place in the Plymouth Colony in 1621.

In the video *Journey to Freedom*, Robert Nang explains how the Pilgrims made the long, hard journey to New England in 1620. Mr. Nang shows that the Pilgrims worked hard in the Plymouth Colony to practice their religion and make a new life.

Unfortunately, with little food or help, many Pilgrims died that first winter. In March of 1621, help arrived. A Native American man named Squanto taught the Pilgrims how to fish and plant corn and other new crops. In fact, with Squanto's help, the fall brought a great harvest.

The Pilgrims were thankful for the harvest, and they held a three-day feast. They invited Squanto and some of his friends to help them celebrate. That feast was probably the first Thanksgiving.

PRACTICE AND APPLY

Publish Your Expository Writing

1. Check your revised draft one more time.

2. Write or input a neat, final copy of your draft.

3. Add pictures, a Thanksgiving border, or a cover.

TIP!

TECHNOLOGY

There are many fonts and borders you can use to make your published piece clearer and more attractive. Experiment with different styles and sizes before making your final decision.

317

Present Your Expository Writing

To make a good presentation, you need to plan ahead. Here are some things you can do to make your presentation a success.

STEP 1

How to Explain Your Report

Strategies for Speaking As you prepare to present your report orally, remember that your purpose is to inform your listeners.

- List your outline on note cards to remember your main ideas, facts, and details.
- As you give your report, look up from your notes and make frequent eye contact with your audience.
- Don't race through your report. Pause after important points.

TiP!

Listening Strategies

- Set a purpose for listening. Form questions about the topic and see if they are answered in the speech.
- Pay attention to transition words. They show that the speaker is moving from one point to the next.
- Think about what is being said. Does it support or contradict facts you know?
- Don't interrupt the speaker. Save your questions for after the presentation.

Multimedia Ideas

You may want to show a short **video** clip from one of the videos you looked at while researching your report, or from another video. Check your local library or video store for documentaries or videos about your topic. If you have the equipment, you can also make a video of your own!

STEP 2

How to Show Your Report

Suggestions for Visuals Make your presentation clearer and more interesting by adding visuals for your audience to look at during your presentation.

- A large map or globe can help your listeners focus on the places mentioned in your report.
- A time line will enable your audience to connect events.
- Photographs of historic re-creations, for example, can give your audience more information.

STEP 3

How to Share Your Report

Strategies for Rehearsing The more you practice, the more comfortable you'll be when presenting your report.

- Practice in front of a mirror. Look at how you use facial expressions and gestures.
- Rehearse in front of friends or family members.
- Tape-record or videotape your report. Review what you say and how you say it.

PRACTICE AND APPLY

Present Your Expository Writing

1. Look at your note cards occasionally to remember your main ideas, facts, and details.

2. Use large maps, globes, time lines, illustrations, or photographs to help explain information.

3. Practice saying your report out loud. Vary your voice, body movement, and facial expressions to decide on the best way to deliver your report.

4. Pace your speech, and save time for a question-and-answer session at the end.

TiP!

Viewing Strategies

- Look carefully at the visuals the speaker displays. Move closer to get a better look.
- Look for connections between what you see and hear during the presentation.
- Read all labels and captions included in the display. Take notes on what you see.

Writing Tests

On a writing test, you are asked to write a composition in response to a prompt. Remember to read the prompt carefully. Look for key words and phrases that describe the topic of your composition and explain how you should present your ideas.

What goal will be accomplished by writing this piece?

Check for words or phrases that tell you about your audience.

This phrase tells you what type of information to include in your writing.

> **Prompt**
>
> Think about what you've seen and heard about the effects of too much sun. What <u>important information</u> do you think people should know about the possible dangers of the sun?
>
> Write an article for your <u>local paper</u> explaining the effects of too much sun. Be sure to include <u>facts and details</u> about the topic.

How to Read a Prompt

Purpose Read the prompt again. Look for key words that tell you whether your purpose will be to inform, influence, or entertain your readers. For example, the words "important information" and "Write an article" tell you that your purpose will be to inform.

Audience Often a writing prompt will identify your audience. Since you're writing an article for the local paper, your audience is the adults in your town.

Expository Writing When you are asked to present information about a specific topic, you are writing an expository composition. The phrase "include facts and details" tells you that you should develop your main idea with information known to be true about the topic.

Test Tip

Brainstorm ideas on paper to help organize your composition.

How to Write to a Prompt

Here are some tips to think about as you respond to a prompt on a writing test.

Before Writing **Content/Ideas**	• Think about your reasons for writing. • Choose a style that suits your audience. • List what you know about the topic before you begin writing the composition. • Plan what you will include in each paragraph of your composition.
During Writing **Organization/** **Paragraph** **Structure**	• State your main idea in a topic sentence. • If you are writing an expository composition, give facts and details to support your main idea. • Present your ideas in a logical order. • Draw a conclusion based on the facts and information presented.
After Writing **Grammar/Usage**	• Proofread your writing for errors in punctuation. • Make sure that each proper noun and proper adjective begins with a capital letter. • Use the correct comparative and superlative forms of adjectives. • Check that you have spelled all words correctly.

Apply What You Learned

When you read a writing prompt, look for clues about your purpose and audience. Identify the topic and think about the best way to organize your ideas.

> **Prompt**
>
> Imagine that your state is preparing a travel brochure for visitors.
>
> Write an article for the brochure about your town or city. Include facts and details about important sights to visit and the history of your town.

Unit 4 Review

Grammar and Writing Review

pages
260–261

Adjectives

A. Write the sentences. Underline the adjective in each sentence.

1. Artificial satellites orbit the earth.

2. Meteorologists can spot hurricanes on colorful photographs.

3. Industrial pollution can be spotted by satellites.

4. Satellites track the warm currents of El Niño.

5. What excellent detectives satellites are!

pages
262–263

Articles

B. Write each sentence. Use the correct article in parentheses.

6. (An, The) archaeologists dig carefully at the site.

7. (A, The) ruins contain decorated pottery.

8. (A, An) ancient burial site is discovered.

9. The ancient people left (a, an) rich legacy.

10. Exploring old ruins can be (a, an) slow job.

pages
264–265

Demonstrative Adjectives

C. Write each sentence. Use the correct demonstrative adjective in parentheses.

11. May I see (this, that) letter over there?

12. I wonder who wrote (this, that) letter you have just handed to me.

13. I don't recognize (that, these) initials.

14. Maybe we can search for answers in (this, these) scrapbook.

15. (That, This) signature matches that one.

16. I don't think I know the person who wrote (this, those) letter.

17. Let's look in (these, those) books in the other room.

18. Please get (this, that) album from the shelf over there.

19. Look at (that, those) signature on the painting.

20. (This, These) letter was written by my great-aunt.

322

pages
266–267
Proper Adjectives

D. **Write the sentences. Complete each sentence by using the correct proper adjective that is formed from the proper noun in parentheses.**

21. Henry Morton Stanley, a (Europe) explorer, traveled throughout Africa.

22. (Scotland) missionary David Livingstone explored the same area.

23. He had fought in the (America) Civil War before going to Africa.

24. Stanley was asked to find Livingstone on the (Africa) continent.

25. Stanley also saved a (Germany) explorer trapped in remote Africa.

pages
270–271
Comparative and Superlative Adjectives

E. **Write these sentences. Complete each sentence by using the correct form of the adjective in parentheses.**

26. Modern computers are the (great) way to find information.

27. Cherisse used the (new) computer she could find to research lions.

28. She discovered that lions are (bold) than cougars.

29. Some lions live in (cool) climates than other cats.

30. Lions are also (big) than cats we keep as pets.

31. Lions sleep (long) hours than other animals, too.

32. They are also (slow) than many other cats.

33. The cheetah is the (fast) land animal.

34. The lion and tiger are the (large) members of the cat family.

35. Cherisse found a (large) variety of facts than she had expected.

pages
272–275
Comparing with *More*, *Most*, *Good*, and *Bad*

F. **Write the sentences. Use the correct adjective in parentheses to complete each sentence.**

36. Fruit is (better, best) for your teeth than candy.

37. Brushing and flossing your teeth regularly are the (more, most) important things you can do to prevent cavities.

38. The (better, best) thing about jogging is being outdoors.

39. Exercise and a good diet will help you live a (best, better) life.

40. (More, Most) people are hiking today than ever before.

Unit 4 Review

pages
276–277

Combining Sentences: Adjectives

G. **Combine each pair of sentences to form one sentence. Then write the new sentence.**

41. We went on a safari. The safari was thrilling.

42. A guide drove our van. The guide was knowledgeable.

43. The road was bumpy. It was a dirt road.

44. Our guide pointed out birds. The birds were singing.

45. We noticed plants. The plants were colorful.

46. The elephants stomped nearby. The elephants were noisy.

47. The lion cubs played under a tree. The tree was tall.

48. We discovered a pond. The pond was small.

49. Gazelles drank the water. The gazelles were thirsty.

50. We saw many animals. The animals were wild.

Mechanics and Usage: Abbreviations

pages
278–279

H. **Write each group of words. Abbreviate the underlined word in each group.**

51. Phoenix, Arizona

52. Doctor Joy Smith

53. Monday, June 23

54. October 9, 1959

55. 18420 Austin Road

56. Governor Robert Johnson

57. Michael James, Junior

58. 1785 Hillside Avenue

59. Mister Oscar Moreno

60. Rock Collectors, Incorporated

Unit 4 Review

pages 292–293

Synonyms and Antonyms

I. Write *synonyms* or *antonyms* for the words in each pair.

61. bold   timid

62. joyful   happy

63. confused   puzzled

64. hilly   flat

65. brave   courageous

66. horrible   pleasant

67. sensational   dull

68. grateful   appreciative

69. temporary   permanent

70. achieve   accomplish

pages 294–295

Outlining

J. Think of a main idea to go with each set of details. Then write the main idea and details in the form of an outline. Use Roman numerals for main ideas. Use capital letters for details. Remember to capitalize the first letter of the first word for each item in the outline.

71. math, science, language arts, social studies

72. flies, mosquitoes, ants, moths

73. diamond, sapphire, ruby, amethyst

74. cantaloupe, watermelon, honeydew

75. wolves, foxes, coyotes, dogs

pages 304–319

Proofreading an Expository Paragraph

K. Read the following paragraph. Look for 10 mistakes in capitalization, punctuation, grammar, and spelling. Then write the paragraph correctly.

Mount everest is the famousest mountain in the world. It is located on a border between Tibet and Nepal and its the higher point on the earth. Because of the cold climate and lack of oxygen, very few plants and animals can survive in that surroundings. The peek makes the Himalayas a popular spot for climbers in fact, in 1953, two climbers from a british team were the first to reach the top of Mount Everest. On May 16, 1975, a Japan climber, Junko Tabei, became the first women to reach the top of the mountain.

Project File

A News Article

Millions of people read newspapers every day to find out what is happening in their city or town, in the nation, and in the world. The following example shows some basic features that you should include in a news article.

New Grocery Store to Open

SILVER CREEK, Sept. 15—Silver Creek residents will be able to shop for groceries closer to home in November. The Apple King grocery chain is building a new 10,000-square-foot store in the Silver Lake Center. The store will be the largest in the area.

Nick Goodwin, manager of the new Apple King, is eager to open. "We are thrilled to be opening a store in this area. We know there are many young families in Silver Creek, and we hope we can help them save money."

Silver Creek residents are also very happy about the news. Kim Gilbert, a local mother of two, says, "I only wish the store would open sooner. We drive over ten miles just to buy milk and bread. The new store will be very convenient."

Headline *Summarizes the news article and catches the reader's attention.*

Dateline *Tells where and when the story was written.*

5 W's *Answers the questions Who? What? Where? When? and Why? usually in the first paragraph.*

Direct Quotations *Make the news article more interesting.*

Write a News Article If you look around and ask the right questions, you will find that someone or something in your school or neighborhood is making news. Has an academic club or sports team done something exciting? Has a local business done something good for your community? Write a news article telling about someone or something happening at your school or in your neighborhood. Look at the model on page 326 to make sure you include all the parts of a news article.

ACTIVITY 2

A Report

In "Quilt Codes" members of the Underground Railroad had to communicate by code in order to pass on information. Do research to find out other times in history that codes have been used. What were the reasons that the codes were needed?

Speaking in Code Explain one code you have researched and tell about its history. Be sure to include why it was made, when it was made, and who used it. Also include how the code works.

327

Extra Practice

Adjectives

A. Write the noun that each underlined adjective describes.

1. King James I sent about a <u>hundred</u> settlers to North America.

2. The king hoped to find gold and <u>other</u> riches.

3. The settlers left on a <u>cold</u> day in December of 1606.

4. Christopher Newport was the commander of the <u>three</u> ships.

5. The <u>small</u> vessels were named *Susan Constant*, *Godspeed*, and *Discovery*.

6. On May 14, 1607, the colonists sailed up the <u>marshy</u> James River.

7. The colonists settled in a <u>swampy</u> area they called Jamestown.

8. Jamestown was a <u>bad</u> location for a settlement.

9. Native tribes frequently attacked the <u>poor</u> colony.

10. <u>Many</u> settlers starved.

11. The <u>supply</u> boat arrived too late to save most of them.

12. In 1608, Captain John Smith became the <u>new</u> leader.

13. Smith was a <u>strong</u> captain who helped the settlers survive.

14. The winter of 1609 was <u>harsh</u> for the settlers.

15. Lord De La Warr became governor of the <u>new</u> settlement.

16. In 1614, a <u>wealthy</u> settler married Pocahontas.

17. Their marriage brought Jamestown eight <u>peaceful</u> years.

18. The <u>main</u> resources of the colony were tobacco, corn, and hogs.

19. Jamestown established the <u>first</u> legislature in North America.

20. It was the first permanent <u>British</u> settlement there.

Adjectives

B. **Write the sentences. Draw one line under each adjective. Draw two lines under the noun that the adjective describes.**

21. England was not the first country to colonize North America.

22. Brave colonists came from England, Scotland, Wales, and Ireland.

23. Some settlers came from France, Germany, and Spain.

24. Many colonists traveled to the Americas voluntarily.

25. However, slaves and orphans were forced to make the long journey.

26. Native Americans were already settled in the vast land.

27. The colonists traded various goods with them.

28. The adventurous British arrived later.

29. By the end of the colonial period, the British controlled North America.

C. **Write the sentences. Complete each sentence with an adjective.**

30. The colonists were _____ to settle in North America.

31. _____ people from different countries settled there.

32. People had _____ reasons to leave their homeland.

33. The colonists wanted _____ opportunities.

34. North America offered _____ land.

35. The colonists suffered _____ hardships to make their lives better.

36. _____ weather was one problem.

37. A _____ supply of food and water was another challenge.

38. Some colonists survived, but _____ colonists died.

39. The colonists learned _____ skills in order to survive.

40. Colonists worked together to build a _____ life.

Extra Practice

Articles

A. **Write the sentences. Choose the correct article to complete each sentence.**

1. How many types of clouds do you see in (a, the) sky?

2. What is (an, the) air temperature at the top of Mount Everest?

3. The Greenhouse Effect occurs when (a, the) atmosphere traps solar heat.

4. Ozone is (a, an) form of oxygen present in Earth's atmosphere.

5. Scientists believe that primitive Earth had (a, an) great deal of carbon dioxide in its atmosphere.

6. The stratosphere's upper boundary lies at (a, an) altitude of approximately 30 miles.

7. Earth has more oxygen than (a, the) other planets.

8. Volcanic dust in (the, a) atmosphere blocks sunlight.

9. What is (a, an) aerosol, and how does it affect the atmosphere?

10. (The, A) ionosphere reflects radio waves back to Earth.

B. **Rewrite each sentence by using the correct article.**

11. _____ thousand years ago, Iceland had a warmer climate.

12. Fossil fuels release carbon dioxide into _____ air.

13. Meteorologists can forecast the development of _____ hurricane.

14. A huge hurricane hit Galveston, _____ island off the Texas coast.

15. Do you know how cold fronts affect _____ weather?

16. Satellites are one of _____ tools meteorologists use to study weather.

17. _____ weather balloon can carry instruments 20 miles into the sky.

18. Stratus clouds are formed less than 6,000 feet from _____ earth.

19. _____ altostratus cloud has a smooth appearance.

20. During springtime, fog often forms early in _____ morning.

C. **Write a sentence using each article. If the article is capitalized, use it as the first word in the sentence.**

21. An   **22.** a   **23.** The   **24.** an   **25.** the

Demonstrative Adjectives

A. Write the demonstrative adjective in each underlined phrase.

1. <u>This year</u> we are studying geometry.

2. My teacher makes <u>that topic</u> easy to understand.

3. You can draw circles with <u>these instruments</u>.

4. Perpendicular lines are <u>those lines</u> that intersect at 90-degree angles.

5. I think <u>this shape</u> is a rhombus.

6. Can you tell if <u>that shape</u> is a polygon?

7. My partner thinks all <u>these rectangles</u> are similar.

8. If you add <u>those angles</u>, they measure 360 degrees.

9. <u>This triangle</u> is equilateral because all three sides are the same.

10. Draw a line with <u>those arrows</u> on the ends.

B. Write the demonstrative adjective in each sentence.

11. I need that ruler to measure the line.

12. These two trapezoids have the same measurements.

13. The teacher drew this angle as an example.

14. I used those sticks to form a parallelogram.

15. This point is called the vertex.

16. The triangle is a right triangle because those sides form a right angle.

17. We were asked to find these shapes in the classroom.

18. I liked that assignment because we were able to move around.

19. We had to find three examples of this shape.

20. This geometry chapter was really fun.

C. Rewrite each sentence by using *this*, *that*, *these*, or *those*.

21. "Please get _____ math tools on the table," Shawna said.

22. "How do I solve _____ problem?" Rod asked.

23. "You can use _____ tools," Shawna answered.

24. "_____ problem looks harder than this one," Rod said.

25. "Don't worry. We'll solve _____ problems together."

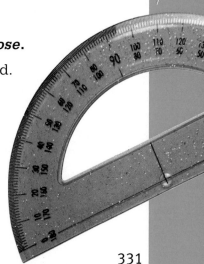

Extra Practice

Proper Adjectives

A. Write the proper adjective in each underlined phrase.

1. <u>Native American peoples</u> live in North America.
2. Jamestown was the first successful <u>British settlement</u>.
3. <u>Spanish conquistadors</u> explored Central America.
4. An <u>Asian emperor</u> sent an explorer to India.
5. <u>Portuguese sailors</u> traveled to South America.
6. <u>English shipbuilders</u> were the most skilled in their trade.
7. <u>French fur traders</u> traveled to western Canada.
8. Many <u>Swedish settlers</u> settled North America.
9. John Cabot, an <u>Italian navigator</u>, discovered Canada in 1497.
10. The Pacific was unknown to <u>European explorers</u>.

B. Write the sentences. Capitalize and underline each proper adjective.

11. The spanish Armada controlled the seas for many years.
12. Southern Mexico was settled by mayan peoples.
13. The Pacific Ocean was reached by dutch ships.
14. A chinese explorer made voyages to East Africa.
15. A french expedition discovered the St. Lawrence River in 1535.
16. chinese exploration stopped when the emperor had sailing ships destroyed.
17. Mounted police maintained order in canadian territories.
18. Lewis and Clark were american explorers.
19. John Ross was a scottish explorer.
20. Alaska was settled by russian explorers.

C. Complete each sentence with a proper adjective formed from the proper noun in parentheses.

21. Zheng He, a _____ explorer made seven voyages. (China)
22. The _____ explorer Columbus sailed to the Americas. (Italy)
23. Ferdinand Magellan, a _____ explorer, led the first voyage around the world. (Portugal)
24. A _____ explorer looked for the Fountain of Youth. (Spain)
25. Powell led the first _____ group through the Grand Canyon. (America)

Comparative and Superlative Adjectives

A. Complete the list by writing the correct comparative or superlative adjective. Use your own sheet of paper.

1. round, rounder, _____
2. green, _____, greenest
3. smooth, _____, smoothest
4. fresh, fresher, _____
5. sad, _____, saddest
6. sweet, _____, sweetest
7. strong, stronger, _____
8. busy, _____, busiest
9. bright, _____, brightest
10. heavy, heavier, _____

B. Write each sentence. Choose the correct adjective from the pair in parentheses.

11. The Mississippi River is the (longer, longest) river in the United States.
12. Lake Michigan is (larger, largest) than Lake Erie.
13. The Pacific Ocean is (bigger, biggest) than the Atlantic Ocean.
14. Rhode Island is the (smaller, smallest) state.
15. The (colder, coldest) temperatures are often in Alaska.
16. The Grand Canyon is (deeper, deepest) than any other canyon in the world.
17. Mount Mitchell is the (higher, highest) point east of the Mississippi.
18. Yellowstone National Park has some of the (prettier, prettiest) scenery in the country.
19. The Appalachians are the (older, oldest) mountains in North America.
20. Death Valley is the (drier, driest) place in the United States.

C. Write each sentence. Use the correct form of the adjective in parentheses.

21. This geography game is (easy) than the last one we played.
22. These are the (hard) question cards!
23. What is the (wide) river in the world?
24. Your question was (tough) than mine.
25. I am the (great) game player in the world!

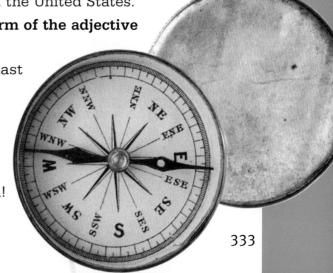

333

Comparing with *More* and *Most*

A. Complete the list by writing the missing form of each adjective. Use your own sheet of paper.

1. interesting, more interesting, _____

2. expressive, more expressive, _____

3. creative, _____, most creative

4. difficult, _____, most difficult

5. stable, more stable, _____

6. dangerous, _____, most dangerous

7. capable, _____, most capable

8. believable, more believable, _____

9. reliable, more reliable, _____

10. creative, _____, most creative

B. Read each adjective. Write the form of the adjective you would use to compare two nouns. Then write the form you would use to compare more than two nouns.

11. crowded

12. educated

13. courageous

14. personal

15. useful

16. imaginative

17. beautiful

18. terrifying

19. amusing

20. spectacular

C. Write each sentence. Use the correct form of the adjective in parentheses.

21. A Michigan winter is (frigid) than a Florida winter.

22. The Great Banks provide some of the world's (plentiful) fishing.

23. Ontario's Point Pelee is one of the (beautiful) parts of southern Canada.

24. The Lowlands area is (suitable) for growing grain than for mining.

25. One of the (rugged) regions in the United States is the Rockies.

Comparing with *Good* and *Bad*

A. Write each sentence. Choose the correct word in parentheses.

1. A computer is one of the (better, best) tools for looking up information.

2. Searching Web sites may be (better, best) than skimming through books.

3. The (worse, worst) computers take several minutes to find information.

4. The (better, best) computers find information fast.

5. Nothing is (worse, worst) than seeing incorrect information on a Web site.

6. It is (better, best) to use several resources than just one.

7. The (better, best) approach is to use both on-line and print resources.

8. The (worse, worst) plan is to use only one source of information.

9. The more resources you use, the (better, best).

10. My work is (better, best) when I use a variety of sources.

B. Write the sentences. Complete each sentence with the correct form of *good* or *bad*.

11. The (good) decision I ever made was to use a computer for my research.

12. I wrote a (good) research report this year than last year.

13. I used to be much (bad) at using the computer.

14. With practice, I got much (good) at it.

15. I use my new skills to find the (good) facts for my report.

16. Some sources are (bad) than others.

17. I had the (bad) time finding Web sites until I used search engines.

18. Search engines made my life a lot (good)!

19. Search engines work the (good) when you input keywords.

20. I used to think research was the (bad) task, but now I love it!

C. Use each of these forms of *good* or *bad* in a sentence. Write the new sentence.

21. good   22. better   23. best   24. worse   25. worst

Combining Sentences: Adjectives

A. Combine each pair of sentences by placing the underlined word in front of the correct noun in the first sentence.

1. Groups of Native Americans lived in North America. The groups were <u>large</u>.

2. They were the settlers of North America. The settlers were <u>first</u>.

3. Some groups caught fish. The fish were <u>freshwater</u>.

4. Sap from trees was used to make sugar. The trees were <u>maple</u>.

5. All the groups made tools. The tools were <u>stone</u>.

6. Some groups included farmers. The farmers were <u>skillful</u>.

7. The Plains Indians followed herds. The herds were <u>buffalo</u>.

8. They rode horses to hunt. The horses were <u>swift</u>.

9. The Hopi lived in homes. The homes were made of <u>adobe</u>.

10. The Iroquois lived in longhouses. The longhouses were <u>wooden</u>.

B. Combine each pair of sentences. Write the new sentence.

11. A scientist found artifacts. The artifacts were Native American.

12. The site is in Arizona. The site is historic.

13. She discovered hunting tools. The hunting tools were ancient.

14. An assistant worked hard to clean the bow. The bow was silver.

15. The bow was near a hogan. The hogan was wooden.

16. A mill for grinding corn was in the hogan. The mill was of stone.

17. The Navajo used corn to make Piki bread. The corn was yellow.

18. The Navajo used tools to make clothes. The clothes were leather.

19. Some tools were used to weave rugs. The rugs were beautiful.

20. The artifacts were given to a museum. The museum was new.

C. Add an adjective to the second sentence of each pair. Then combine the two sentences.

21. Native Americans had their own culture. The culture was _____.

22. Some men were hunters. They were _____.

23. The children fed the animals. The animals were _____.

24. Many groups had traditions. The traditions were _____.

25. Some groups performed dances. The dances were _____.

Abbreviations

A. Write the number of the word in the column at the left next to the correct abbreviation in the column at the right.

1. Monday   Mar.

2. Doctor   Gov.

3. Senior   Mr.

4. January   Sr.

5. Saturday   Jan.

6. Texas   Sept.

7. March   Dr.

8. Governor   Sat.

9. Mister   TX

10. September   Mon.

B. Write the correct abbreviation for the following phrases. Use the correct punctuation.

11. Captain Michael Smith

12. 1315 Dover Street

13. February 12, 2001

14. Thursday, May 4

15. Post Avenue

16. Apartment 3-B

17. Post Office Box 801

18. December 5, 2002

19. Transcontinental, Incorporated

20. Jackson, Mississippi

C. Write each sentence. Use the abbreviation for each underlined word.

21. <u>Mister</u> Mercado teaches mathematics.

22. Last <u>Friday</u>, we used our math skills to bake blueberry muffins!

23. I was asked to bring a <u>teaspoon</u> from home.

24. At 2:00 <u>post meridiem</u>, we measured ingredients and made the muffins.

25. We took the muffins to a shelter on Waveland <u>Road</u>.

Thinking Power

Pronouns and Writing That Compares

In this unit you will learn about pronouns. You will also learn about writing that compares by showing how two things are similar and how they are different.

Math Link *Read about an unusual place called Flatland. Unlike our world of three dimensions, this imaginary place is completely flat. Even its people are Circles, Triangles, Squares, Pentagons, and other flat shapes.*

Y ou lucky people who live in a world of three dimensions are blessed with shade as well as light. You enjoy many colors. You can see an angle and the complete shape of a Circle. But in Flatland, we do not have these blessings. How, then, can I make you understand the difficulty we have recognizing one another?

The first means of recognition is the sense of hearing. Our hearing is keener and more highly developed than is yours....

But feeling is the best way of recognizing another Flatlander. What an "introduction" is to you, feeling is with us.

〜 from *Life in Flatland* by A. Square (Edwin Abbott)

Thinking Like a Writer

Writing That Compares In this paragraph, the author explains how life in Flatland is different from life in our world.

- What are the differences between Flatland and a world of three dimensions?

Pronouns The author used several pronouns in place of nouns. Read the passage again.

QUICK WRITE How do pronouns in place of nouns help the sentences flow together?

Pronouns

THINK AND WRITE

Pronouns

How does using pronouns in place of nouns make your writing flow more smoothly? Write your ideas in your journal.

Pronouns can take the place of one or more nouns and the words that go with the nouns. Use pronouns to avoid repeating the same nouns in your writing.

> *Katy and Pablo talked to the parrot.*
> *Katy walked around the store.*

> *They talked to the parrot.*
> *She walked around the store.*

Guided Practice

Name the pronoun in each sentence. Tell if the pronoun is singular or plural.

EXAMPLE: The clerk took them to the food aisle.
them, plural

1. Pablo said he needed some bird seed.
2. The clerk showed him two kinds of seed.
3. Katy looked at treats for her cat.
4. They each selected the same brand.
5. The clerk said it was a popular brand.

- A **pronoun** is a word that takes the place of one or more nouns.

- Pronouns must match the nouns to which they refer.

More Practice

A. Write the pronoun in each sentence. Then write if the pronoun is singular or plural.

6. The parrot sang a funny song for them.

7. They laughed as the parrot sang.

8. Katy and Pablo fed him a peanut.

9. The parrot's beak was strong enough to crack it.

10. He seemed to like the peanut.

B. Write each sentence. Replace the underlined word or words with a pronoun. Make sure that the pronoun matches the noun to which it refers.

11. Pablo and Katy looked at the fish tanks next.

12. Pablo noticed a large saltwater tank.

13. There were many crabs in the tank.

14. The clerk gave Pablo some advice about taking care of birds.

15. The parrot said good-bye to Katy and Pablo.

C. **Spiral Review** Rewrite each sentence by adding a pronoun, a comparative or superlative adjective, or a proper noun.

Hank and I go to the pet store every week to buy food for our parakeet. (**16.** ____) buy several bags of seed. We always buy the (**17.** ____) brand. If (**18.** ____) has extra money, (**19.** ____) chooses a treat for our parakeet. The bird likes hanging toys the (**20.** ____).

Handbook
page 538

Extra Practice, page 406.

Writing Activity An Advertisement

Create an ad for a new brand of pet food. Compare the new brand to an older one. Give three reasons why the new brand is better.

APPLY GRAMMAR: Draw one line under singular pronouns and two lines under plural pronouns.

Subject Pronouns

RULES

Use a subject pronoun as the subject of a sentence.

We went to the science fair on Saturday.

I, you, he, she, it, we, and *they* are subject pronouns.

Subject pronouns replace nouns that are the subject of a sentence. The subject tells *whom* or *what* the sentence is about.

Gloria went to the science fair, too.
She went to the science fair, too.

The science fair is always held in the auditorium.
It is always held in the auditorium.

THINK AND WRITE

Pronouns

In your journal, write how you can tell if a pronoun is a subject pronoun.

Guided Practice

Name the subject pronoun in each sentence.

EXAMPLE: She enjoyed looking at the projects.
She

1. We enjoyed looking at the waterwheel inventions.
2. They moved water in many different ways.
3. Gloria and I talked about creating our own waterwheel.
4. She told a story about a waterwheel at an old mill.
5. We looked at other projects with a guide.
6. He told us many facts.
7. They were all very interesting.
8. I made a lightning rod for the science fair last year.
9. It won a small prize.
10. You should see it!

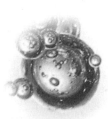

REVIEW THE RULES

- A **subject pronoun** takes the place of a noun or nouns in the subject of a sentence.

More Practice

A. Write the subject pronoun in each sentence.

11. We looked at many projects at the fair.

12. Gloria and I were the first students to try the bubble booth.

13. It was an amusing exhibit.

14. I made a bubble that stretched from my feet to my head.

15. She made hundreds of bubbles with a tiny blower.

B. Write each sentence. Replace the underlined noun or nouns with the correct subject pronoun.

16. Gloria and I went to the design tables next.

17. Several students were building paper structures.

18. One tall structure was carefully built.

19. Simon won a prize.

20. His structures were the tallest at the fair.

C. **Spiral Review** Rewrite each sentence. Replace the subject with the correct subject pronoun. Underline the comparative or superlative adjective in each sentence. Use correct end punctuation.

21. Gloria enjoyed the bubble booth the most

22. Gloria and I stayed at the design tables the longest time

23. Will Mario and Mr. Sung win the largest bubble contest

24. The bubble was bigger than Mr. Sung's car

25. Mr. Sung and Mario had their picture taken for the most popular newspaper in town

Extra Practice, page 407.

Handbook
page 538

Writing Activity A Speech

Write a speech that compares two ways to make bubbles. Vary the length of your sentences to make them interesting.

APPLY GRAMMAR: Underline each subject pronoun that you use.

Object Pronouns

RULES

Use an object pronoun after an action verb or after a word such as *to*, *for*, *with*, *in*, *on*, *of*, *by*, or *at*.

Me, *you*, *him*, *her*, *it*, *us* and *them* are object pronouns.

> *Mrs. Kuralt carries a briefcase. She carries it.*
>
> *She carries it with her.*

You and *it* may be subject pronouns or object pronouns.

> *You are a good artist. (subject pronoun)*
> *I admire you. (object pronoun)*
>
> *It tastes great in a sandwich. (subject pronoun)*
> *Zane will prepare it. (object pronoun)*

THINK AND WRITE

Pronouns

How can you tell if a pronoun is an object pronoun or a subject pronoun? Write your ideas in your journal.

Guided Practice

Name the object pronoun in each sentence.

EXAMPLE: Mrs. Kuralt gave us a group assignment.
us

1. Working in groups worked well for us.

2. Jorge read the instructions to me.

3. I understood them right away.

4. The task was fun for us.

5. Everyone worked on it.

6. Mrs. Kuralt chose him as the timekeeper.

7. The ticking of the clock made them nervous.

8. I took notes with her on each group's progress.

9. Before long, the task was completed by us.

10. I thank you for a job well done.

REVIEW THE RULES

- An *object pronoun* is used as the object of an action verb or after words such as *to, for, with, in, on, of, by,* or *at.*

More Practice

A. Write the object pronoun in each sentence.

11. Kara gave her some great ideas.

12. I took notes on them.

13. Recording the ideas was important to me.

14. Marco watched the time for us.

15. Working together helped you finish on time.

B. Write each sentence. Use the correct pronoun in parentheses.

16. My notes helped (us, we) complete the task.

17. Mrs. Kuralt asked (I, me) to read my notes to the class.

18. I read (them, they) aloud slowly.

19. The members of the class gave (us, we) a round of applause.

20. Kara, Marco, and I thank (you, it).

Handbook
page 538

C. Spiral Review Rewrite each sentence by adding an object pronoun, an article, or an action verb.

21. Our teacher assigned Carla and _____ a science project.

22. _____ few of our projects have won awards.

23. Last year, we _____ a trip to Washington, D.C.

24. Maybe we can _____ a diorama for this science project.

25. The teacher is waiting for _____ to decide.

Extra Practice, page 408.

Writing Activity A Comparison

Write a paragraph that compares a project you did on your own with a project you did with a group. What were the advantages or disadvantages of each method? Give your points in the best order.

APPLY GRAMMAR: Include object pronouns in your paragraph. Underline each object pronoun that you use.

Grammar

Colons and Hyphens

RULES

A **hyphen** shows the division of a word at the end of a line. Always divide the word between syllables.

Paul has always been interested in study-
ing the history of his family.

Hyphens are sometimes used to connect two or more words to form compound words.

great-grandmother   *merry-go-round*   *thirty-five*

A **colon** is used to separate the hour and the minute in the time of day.

3:15   *7:45 A.M.*   *9:00 P.M.*

A **colon** is also used after the greeting of a business letter.

Dear Mrs. Santos: *Dear Sir or Madam:*

THINK
AND WRITE

Colons and Hyphens

Why is it important to know how to use hyphens and colons correctly in your writing? Write your ideas in your journal.

Not all compound words have hyphens. Check your dictionary if you are not sure about using a hyphen in a word.

driveway   *drive-in*
grandfather   *father-in-law*

Guided Practice

Name the word in each sentence that has a hyphen or a colon.

> **EXAMPLE:** Paul interviewed his grandfather at 6:30 in the evening. *6:30*

1. Mr. Cellini wrote a letter to the president about com-ing to America.
2. The letter explained that he had traveled with twenty-five friends and relatives.
3. They first saw the shores of the United States at 8:00 in the morning.
4. The immigrants cheered wildly as they slowly ap-proached the Statue of Liberty.
5. His great-aunt cried for joy as the ship neared the harbor.

- A hyphen is used to divide a word at the end of a line and to join the parts of a compound word.

- A colon is used after the greeting of a business letter and to separate hours and minutes.

More Practice

A. Write each word that has a hyphen or a colon.

6. All the children listened very quietly to their grand-father's stories.

7. Mr. Cellini met his future wife and his brother-in-law on the ship.

8. His sister-in-law was also on board.

9. They all sat together on the deck every afternoon at about 4:00.

10. My grandfather and his half-brother enjoyed these afternoons.

B. Write the sentences. Correctly add hyphens or colons.

11. Paul recorded a tale about his great grandfather.

12. The story he had heard was about a long let ter written in 1919.

13. The words *Dear Sirs* began the letter.

14. In the letter, he had asked for a job in a dry cleaning business.

15. It was 8 15 before the story and Paul's interview were finished.

C. [Spiral Review] **Write the paragraph correctly. Add hyphens, colons, the right form of *good*, or a proper noun.**

Paul went to visit his aunt who lives on (**16.** ____) Street. He says that she makes the (**17.** ____) cookies in the world. Paul likes to visit his aunt at 6(**18.** ____)00 in the evening when the cookies come out of the oven. Paul's aunt tells him hour (**19.** ____) long stories about the old days. He always leaves before 9(**20.** ____)30.

Extra Practice, page 409.

Handbook
page 553

Writing Activity A Journal Entry

Suppose that you have just arrived in this country. Write a journal entry comparing life in your old country with your new experiences. Be sure to show similarities and differences.

APPLY GRAMMAR: Circle each hyphen and underline each colon you use.

Social Studies Link

Mixed Review

REVIEW THE RULES

- A pronoun is a word that takes the place of one or more nouns.

- A pronoun must match the noun that it replaces.

- A subject pronoun replaces a noun or nouns in the subject of a sentence.

- An object pronoun replaces a noun or nouns after an action verb or after words such as *to*, *for*, *with*, *in*, *on*, *of*, *by*, or *at*.

- Use a hyphen to show the division of a word at the end of a line or to join the parts of a compound word.

- Use a colon to separate the hour and the minute in the time of day and after the greeting in a business letter.

QUICK WRITE

Pronouns

Write five sentences that use a proper noun as the subject of the sentence. Then replace each proper noun with the correct subject pronoun.

Practice

A. Write the sentences. Underline each pronoun. Write *SP* above each subject pronoun and *OP* above each object pronoun.

1. I have always been interested in science.

2. Space exploration is very interesting to me.

3. You have just read an article about Mars.

4. What did it say?

5. My friend wants to read it.

6. We would like to do a report about Mars.

7. Mars may have had water on it at one time.

8. They are going to borrow some books about space.

9. The town library has a large collection of them.

10. My father said he will drive us there.

B. Write each sentence. Use a colon or a hyphen to correct each word or group of words in parentheses.

11. My friend and I watched the sun set at (730) last evening.

12. She is interested in learning about solar (flareups).

13. She conducted an experiment using (blowdried) waxed paper.

14. My teacher's (sister in law) works for the space program.

15. She said that the next mission to Mars will (hap pen) soon.

16. I think I will write a letter to NASA to get (up to date) information.

17. I hope to get back a (super duper) letter.

18. I wonder if you can see a (halfmoon) on Mars.

19. I have to finish the letter before (845) P.M.

20. I want to go to bed early so that I can see the sun rise at (627).

C. **Challenge** Rewrite the following part of a business letter. Add pronouns, colons, and hyphens correctly.

Dear Mr. Norell (**21.** _____)

   I know your business publishes books about plan (**22.** _____) ets. The book on Jupiter greatly interests us. Would you have time at 4 (**23.** _____) 00 on Friday to show (**24.** _____) it to (**25.** _____)?

                    Sincerely,
                    Leslie Morris and Rico Santo

Handbook
pages 538, 553

Writing Activity An Essay

   Compare life on Earth with life as scientists imagine it would be on Mars. Point out differences and any similarities. Organize and present ideas in a way that makes sense.

APPLY GRAMMAR: Use a hyphen to separate a word at the end of a line. Circle the subject pronouns in your essay. Underline the object pronouns.

        Science Link

349

Pronoun-Verb Agreement

RULES

Subject pronouns and verbs must agree. A singular subject pronoun takes a singular verb, and a plural subject pronoun takes a plural verb.

She enjoys waterskiing.   *They enjoy* water polo.

Add *-s* to most verbs when you use the pronouns *he*, *she*, and *it*.

He likes water sports.

Do not add *-s* to a verb in the present tense when you use the pronouns *I*, *we*, *you*, and *they*.

We like water sports.

THINK AND WRITE

Pronouns

How does knowing about pronoun-verb agreement help you write clearer sentences? Write your ideas in your journal.

Guided Practice

Name the verb in parentheses that completes each sentence correctly.

> **EXAMPLE:** We (swim, swims) laps together at the public pool.
> *swim*

1. Nadia usually (enter, enters) the swimming pool first.
2. I always (practice, practices) the butterfly stroke.
3. They (complete, completes) the most laps.
4. She (rest, rests) after every ten laps.
5. We (train, trains) for swimming meets.
6. She (wear, wears) swimming goggles.
7. I (use, uses) earplugs.
8. We (believe, believes) in swimming safety.
9. I (like, likes) kickboards very much.
10. They (strengthen, strengthens) my legs.

REVIEW THE RULES

- Subject pronouns and verbs must agree.

- Add -s to most verbs in the present tense when you use the subject pronouns *he*, *she*, and *it*. Do not add -s to a verb in the present tense when you use the subject pronouns *I*, *we*, *you*, and *they*.

More Practice

A. Write each sentence. Use the correct form of the verb.

11. We (like, likes) many different kinds of water sports.

12. In the summer, I (swim, swims) every morning.

13. Every summer, we (stay, stays) in a cottage by the lake.

14. I (learn, learns) a new skill each day.

15. Do you (look, looks) forward to your summer vacation?

B. Write each sentence. Use the correct present-tense form of the verb in parentheses.

16. They (encourage) our interest in sports every summer.

17. I (rise) early during July and August.

18. We (swim) until 10:00.

19. She (water-ski) until noon.

20. He (row) a boat until lunchtime.

C. **Spiral Review** **Write each sentence using the present tense of the verb in parentheses. Circle the subject pronoun. Underline each adjective.**

21. We _____ around the tiny island in canoes. (paddle)

22. She _____ to the huge rock. (swim)

23. He often _____ volleyball in the chilly water. (play)

24. They _____ to the wooden dock. (race)

25. I _____ to play in the rolling waves. (surf)

Extra Practice, page 410.

Handbook
page 539

Writing Activity A Sports Column

Write a newspaper column comparing waterskiing and skiing on snow. Organize your column so that it shows whether you think the two sports have more similarities than differences.

APPLY GRAMMAR: Underline each subject pronoun and the verb with which it agrees.

Combining Sentences: Subject and Object Pronouns

RULES

You can **combine sentences** that have subject pronouns.

He thought of forming a committee. She thought of forming a committee.

They thought of forming a committee.

THINK AND WRITE

Pronouns

How can combining sentences that have pronouns help you vary your sentences? Write your ideas in your journal.

You can use one plural subject pronoun to replace the singular pronouns, or you can join the pronouns with *and* to create a compound subject. In either case, the verb will take a plural form.

I want the job.

We want the job. or

She and I want the job.

She wants the job.

You can also combine sentences when object pronouns share the same action. Replace the singular pronouns with a plural object pronoun (*us* or *them*), or create a compound subject.

The job was given to her.

The job was given to us. or

The job was given to me.

The job was given to her and me.

Guided Practice

Name the compound subject pronoun or the compound object pronoun in each sentence.

EXAMPLE: He and she held the first meeting.
He and she

1. The meeting was led by her and him.

2. He and I took notes on the discussion.

3. She and he listened to our ideas.

4. You and they can join the committee, too.

5. She and I had an idea.

- You can combine two sentences that have pronouns to form compound subjects and compound objects.

- A compound subject can have two pronouns with the same predicate. Subject pronouns and verbs must agree.

More Practice

A. Write the compound subject pronouns or compound object pronouns in each sentence.

6. She and he write some of our ideas.

7. The class gives ideas to her and me.

8. She and I report to the committee.

9. You and we think the meetings are fun.

10. He and they want to join.

B. Combine each pair of sentences by forming compound subjects or objects.

11. She works on the committee. He works on the committee.

12. He told us an idea. She told us an idea.

13. You agree with their plan. I agree with their plan.

14. She plans the menu. We plan the menu.

15. They are happy about the change. I am happy about the change.

C. **Spiral Review** Rewrite each pair of sentences as a single sentence by forming compound subject or object pronouns.

16. She teaches Spanish on Fridays. He teaches Spanish on Fridays.

17. I study French on Tuesdays. You study French on Tuesdays.

18. They give their notes to him. They give their notes to me.

19. You study for the German test. She studies for the German test.

20. The teacher gives them an *A*. The teacher gives us an *A*.

Extra Practice, page 411.

Handbook
pages 538–539

Writing Activity A Letter

Write a letter to your teacher suggesting one way to improve your school. Explain how your idea will make a difference. Stick to your topic.

APPLY GRAMMAR: Combine sentences with pronouns.

Possessive Pronouns

RULES

A possessive pronoun can take the place of a possessive noun. It shows who or what has or owns something.

Alyssa's book is on the table.   *Her* book is on the table.

Some possessive pronouns (*my, your, his, her, its, our, their*) are used before nouns.

my yard   *His* neighbor has a new car.

The possessive pronouns *mine, yours, his, hers, its, ours,* and *theirs* can stand alone and function as nouns.

The car is *hers*.   *Theirs* is a red car.

THINK AND WRITE

Pronouns

Why is it important to know how to use possessive pronouns correctly? Write your ideas in your journal.

Use possessive pronouns to show ownership.

The baseball bat belongs to me.

↓

It is my baseball bat.

↓

The baseball bat is mine.

Guided Practice

Tell which word in parentheses is the correct possessive pronoun.

EXAMPLE: (Our, Ours) school needs money to buy new computers.
Our

1. (My, Mine) class is looking for ways to raise money.
2. Mr. Arnold is making a list of (our, ours) ideas.
3. The first suggestion was (my, mine).
4. I suggested that (our, ours) class hold a yard sale.
5. Stephanie told about (her, hers) plan to hold a raffle.

REVIEW THE RULES

- **Possessive pronouns** show who or what owns something.

- Some possessive pronouns come before nouns. Others stand alone.

More Practice

A. **Write the correct possessive pronoun in parentheses.**

6. Stephanie explained (her, hers) idea for a raffle.

7. Jake and Renée told about (their, theirs) plan for a bake sale.

8. Mr. Arnold liked all of (our, ours) suggestions.

9. Was the plan to vote for the best suggestion (your, yours)?

10. Mr. Arnold said to remember (our, ours) purpose when we vote.

B. **Write each sentence. Replace the underlined word or words with the correct possessive pronoun.**

11. Stephanie's idea received two votes.

12. Jake and Renée's plan got four votes.

13. Three people liked Julio's suggestion best.

14. My idea also received three votes.

15. Jake and Renée's got more votes than most of the other ideas.

C. **Spiral Review** **Rewrite the sentences. Complete each sentence with the correct possessive pronoun, verb form, or plural noun in parentheses.**

(**16.** ____) (My, Mine) class decided to hold a yard sale on Saturday. Stephanie's teachers (**17.** ____) (donate, donated) items. Julio organized a car wash, but Jake and Renée sold (**18.** ____) (loafs, loaves) of bread. Everyone (**19.** ____) (brang, brought) items for the yard sale. We raised two hundred dollars for (**20.** ____) (our, ours) school!

Extra Practice, page 412.

Handbook
page 539

Writing Activity A Paragraph

Compare two ways to raise money for your school. Tell the pros and cons of each method. End your paragraph with a strong conclusion.

APPLY GRAMMAR: Circle each possessive pronoun that you use.

Mechanics and Usage Contractions: Pronoun and Verb

RULES

A contraction is a shortened form of two words.

Subject pronouns can be combined with some verbs to form contractions. Use an apostrophe (') to show that a letter or letters have been left out of a contraction.

they are = *they're*   *it is* = *it's*

Pronoun Plus Verb	Contraction	Pronoun Plus Verb	Contraction
I am	I'm	it is	it's
you are	you're	they are	they're
he/she is	he's/she's	we are	we're

The pronoun-verb contractions *it's, you're,* and *they're* sound the same as the possessive pronouns *its, your,* and *their* but are spelled differently. Remember that unlike contractions, possessive pronouns do not have an apostrophe.

Possessive Pronoun: *Their class loves to read short stories.*

Contraction: *They're interested in mysteries.*

Guided Practice

Name the pronoun-verb contraction for the pair of underlined words in each sentence.

EXAMPLE: It is fun when our book group gets together.
It's

1. All members share the books <u>they are</u> reading.
2. <u>It is</u> always fun to discuss mysteries.
3. Jarod said <u>he is</u> reading a new adventure novel.
4. <u>She is</u> almost finished reading her book.
5. <u>You are</u> welcome to come and talk about books.

REVIEW THE RULES

- A contraction can be a shortened form of a pronoun and a verb.

- An apostrophe is used in place of the letter or letters that have been left out of a contraction.

- Some possessive pronouns sound the same as pronoun-verb contractions, but have a different spelling and meaning.

More Practice

A. Write the correct contraction for the underlined words.

6. <u>It is</u> easy to come up with ideas for the book group.

7. All the students said <u>they are</u> willing to help write a book log.

8. <u>I am</u> making a system to rate the books.

9. <u>You are</u> invited to use the log.

10. <u>We are</u> excited about discovering books in this way.

B. Write each sentence. Choose the correct word in parentheses.

11. _____ fun to be part of the book group. (It's, Its)

12. The members love _____ ideas. (they're, their)

13. Jason said that _____ report was excellent. (you're, your)

14. _____ going to enjoy this book. (Your, You're)

15. I especially liked _____ illustrations. (it's, its)

C. [Spiral Review] **Write each sentence by choosing the correct word. You'll choose between a contraction and a possessive, a plural and a possessive, or two conjunctions.**

16. Wendell and Tara shared (their, they're) opinions about a book.

17. We all like to read about space travel (and, but) astronomy.

18. The (members, members') reading included fiction.

19. The (children's, children) favorite author is Isaac Asimov.

20. Reading takes time, but (its, it's) worth it!

Extra Practice, page 413.

Handbook
page 553

Writing Activity A Book Review

Compare two books you have read. Organize your report so that the similarities and differences between the two books are clear.

APPLY GRAMMAR: Underline pronoun-verb contractions. Circle possessive pronouns.

Mixed Review

REVIEW THE RULES

- **Subject pronouns** and verbs must agree.

- **Add -s** to most verbs when you use the pronouns *he*, *she*, and *it*. Do not add -s to a verb when you use the pronouns *I*, *we*, *you*, and *they*.

- Combine two sentences that have pronouns to form **compound subjects and objects**.

- A **possessive pronoun** shows who or what owns something.

- An **apostrophe** takes the place of the letter or letters that have been left out of a contraction.

- Possessive pronouns never have an apostrophe.

QUICK WRITE

Pronouns

Write five sentences comparing two animals. Use one subject pronoun, one object pronoun, two possessive pronouns, and one pronoun-verb contraction.

Practice

A. Write each sentence. Use the correct form of the verb in parentheses. Draw two lines under any compound subject pronoun.

1. She and I (study, studies) the structure of bridges.

2. The teacher (want, wants) us to build a span across two objects.

3. We (work, works) in small groups.

4. We (uses, use) many different materials to make a bridge.

5. Brian (use, uses) sticks as he builds.

6. Julie (give, gives) him advice.

7. He and she (want, wants) to build a bridge together.

8. You and I (get, gets) ideas from library books.

9. I (find, finds) pictures of old bridges.

10. That group always (review, reviews) the material.

B. **Write each sentence. Choose the correct possessive pronoun or contraction from the pair in parentheses.**

11. That group has many ideas for (they're, their) design.

12. Jamal and Madison want to use (your, you're) idea.

13. (It's, Its) difficult to build a long span.

14. I saw (your, you're) ideas in the notebook.

15. Some group members used glue to fasten (they're, their) bridge.

16. (They're, Their) now ready to test its strength.

17. One bridge fell apart in the middle of (its, it's) construction.

18. Amber's teammates will finish (their, they're) bridge first.

19. "When (your, you're) done," our teacher says, "look at another group's work."

20. (It's, Its) interesting to discuss ways to build a bridge.

C. **Challenge** **Write the sentences. Correct the one error in each sentence.**

21. Jamal's partner work differently from mine.

22. He and I uses different materials.

23. He chooses tubes, but I think their hard to use.

24. After Jamal's partner finishes, they're bridge is four feet across.

25. Our is three feet across.

Handbook
pages 539, 553

Writing Activity **A Photo Essay**

Find pictures of two types of bridges. Examples might include a suspension bridge and a cantilever bridge. Organize your writing and pictures to show how these bridges are like and unlike each other. Provide strong details in words and pictures. Include captions.

APPLY MECHANICS AND USAGE: Underline possessive pronouns in your work.

Science Link

Common Errors with Pronouns

As a writer, you need to pay special attention to how to use pronouns. For example, using object pronouns as the subject of a sentence is a mistake that some writers make. Also, confusing contractions with possessive pronouns is another common error. This chart shows examples of the different kinds of mistakes in pronoun use and how you can correct them.

Common Errors	Examples	Corrected Sentences
Using an object pronoun as the subject of a sentence	My family and me visited New York City last summer.	My family and I visited New York City last summer.
Using a subject pronoun in the predicate part of a sentence	The city looked so big to my sister and I.	The city looked so big to my sister and me.
Confusing contractions and possessive pronouns	We went to the top of it's tallest building.	We went to the top of its tallest building.

THINK AND WRITE

Pronouns

In your journal, write how you know when to use subject and object pronouns.

REVIEW THE RULES

PRONOUNS

- Use a subject pronoun (*I*, *you*, *he*, *she*, *it*, *we*, and *they*) as the subject of a sentence.

- Use an object pronoun (*me*, *you*, *him*, *her*, *it*, *us*, and *them*) after an action verb or after words such as *for*, *at*, *of*, *with*, or *to*.

- Use an apostrophe to show where a letter or letters have been left out of a pronoun-and-verb contraction.

- Remember Possessive pronouns do not have an apostrophe.

More Practice

A. Write the subject pronoun, object pronoun, or possessive pronoun from each sentence.

1. I enjoyed walking through the Central Park Zoo.

2. Central Park gave Mom and me hours of pleasure.

3. Its designer was Frederick Law Olmsted.

4. Another man and he created this park.

5. Central Park's beauty is a tribute to them.

B. Rewrite each sentence. Choose the correct subject pronoun, object pronoun, or possessive pronoun in parentheses.

6. Olmsted's love of parks brought (he, him) to New York City.

7. Before long, the park commissioners gave his friend and (he, him) the job of designing the park.

8. Olmsted grabbed a shovel, and (he, him) began clearing the site.

9. In time, (it's, its) rocky land had 5 million trees and shrubs.

10. Today, this wonderful park is open to you and (I, me).

C. Write each sentence. Use a subject pronoun, an object pronoun, or a possessive pronoun in place of the underlined word or words.

11. New York's Adirondack Park is the largest park in the nation.

12. The state owns about 40 percent of the park.

13. My parents went to Hyde Park last year.

14. Dad showed my brother and me pictures of the trip.

15. Next year, my family and I will visit the battlefield at Saratoga National Historical Park.

Handbook
pages 538–539

Grammar Troubleshooter, pages 518–519

Writing Activity A Paragraph

Write a paragraph that compares two parks that you know. The parks might be ballparks, state or national parks, open fields, or playgrounds. Compare the sizes of the parks, their area, and other information. Organize your writing so that you give all the details of one park and then of the other.

APPLY GRAMMAR: Be sure to use subject pronouns, object pronouns, and possessive pronouns correctly. Do not use an apostrophe with a possessive pronoun.

 Math Link

Mechanics and Spelling

Directions

Read the passage and decide which type of mistake, if any, appears in each underlined section. Choose the letter for your answer. If there is no error, choose "No mistake."

A question ends with a question mark.

When a base word ends with a consonant followed by y, change the y to i when adding an ending that does not begin with i.

Do not capitalize a common noun.

> **Sample**
>
> <u>How can travelers get from Denmark to Sweden.</u>
> **(1)**
> In years past, the only way to travel between these two
> places was by boat or plane. Now, however, motorists can
> travel back and forth between these <u>two countrys by car.</u>
> **(2)**
> A ten-mile highway has been constructed that links
> Denmark and Sweden. <u>Travelers on this Highway go</u>
> **(3)**
> through a tunnel first and then over a long bridge.

1 A Spelling

B Capitalization

C Punctuation

D No mistake

2 F Spelling

G Capitalization

H Punctuation

J No mistake

3 A Spelling

B Capitalization

C Punctuation

D No mistake

Test Tip
Check your work to make sure you haven't skipped any items.

Grammar and Usage

Directions

Read the passage and choose the word or group of words that belongs in each space. Choose the letter for your answer.

Sample

People have been building and using tunnels for many years. Workers __(1)__ one tunnel in the Swiss Alps in 1905. This $12\frac{1}{2}$-mile underground passage connects the countries of Switzerland and Italy. Even though the tunnel was built more than 95 years ago, __(2)__ is still being used today.

The Swiss Alps tunnel __(3)__ new compared to some other tunnels in the world. Long ago in London, workers dug below the Thames River to build an underground passage. This __(4)__ tunnel opened for foot traffic in 1843.

Look at the entire sentence to help you decide which verb tense is correct.

Identify the noun that the pronoun replaces. The pronoun must agree with the noun.

Make sure the verb agrees with its subject.

Use an adjective to tell more about the tunnel.

---

1 A build

   B will build

   C are building

   D built

2 F it

   G they

   H we

   J she

3 A are

   B were

   C is

   D have been

4 F importantly

   G more important

   H most important

   J important

RESEARCH

RESEARCH

Sometimes I like the sound of a word, but I'm not sure what it means. That's when I look it up in the **dictionary**. Once I know its meaning, I can use it to express myself better.

COMPOSITION SKILLS

WRITING WELL

Descriptions are like the icing on the cake. Some words suggest adjectives: monarch butterflies are delicate, fluttering, brilliantly colored. I try to describe the picture that's forming in my head. With my description, I want my reader to see it as clearly as I do. How would you describe a day in the desert?

VOCABULARY SKILLS

USING WORDS

I always think about **word choice** and use vivid verbs and adjectives to describe the sound or the look of a scene. They wake up a reader, as an ice-cold shower shocks you to attention. They bring your writing to life!

Read Now!

As you read the photo essay about winter in Alaska, look for the vivid verbs and adjectives the writer chose and write them down.

TIME

FOR KIDS

PHOTO ESSAY

DENALI
STATE
BANK
-50°
YOUR
LOCALLY OWNED
COMMUNITY
BANK

BRRRRRRR!

Shivering through an Alaska winter

THE BIG CHILL

How cold was it in Alaska one February day? Well, when Ben Dallin, 10, threw boiling water into the air, it never came back down. "It just froze into fog and made a really cool sound: *ssshhh*," he says. (Please don't try this at home!) What kind of weather would do this to hot water? *Verrrrry* cold weather. For more about life in a bone-chilling, toe-curling Alaska winter, read on.

Getting Around What's it like to walk around in weather that's -77° F? "It's hard to talk because your lips kind of go numb," says Abbe Skinner, 14, of McGrath, Alaska.

And get this: Car tires freeze flat on the bottom. It takes a couple of miles of driving for them to get round again. The cold makes cars' fan belts snap and fall to the ground. Alaskans jokingly call them "snow snakes."

Dress for Success Kids stay warm with feathery down coats, oversized snow pants, and "bunny boots"—big white boots with superwarm liners. Some snuggle into soft fur hats and colorful woolly mittens to keep the face and hands from turning into ice cubes. Others wear ski or face masks to keep noses, ears, and cheeks warm and dry.

School Days Schools hardly ever close just because it's cold. In Anchorage, schools start at noon when temperatures plunge to an ice-cubelike -46° F. And until the temperature hits -20° F, students go outside for recess! Becky Campbell of Fairbanks isn't bothered by the cold. "It's part of Alaska," Becky says. "I don't let it get in my way."

It's -50° F as twins Emily and Alison Voss go to school in Fairbanks, Alaska.

Even on the coldest days, some people still try to exercise.

interNET CONNECTION Go to www.mhschool.com/language-arts for more information on the topic.

At 9 a.m. one February day, "ice fog" clouded streets in Fairbanks. Note the temperature on the sign.

WHAT'S THE COLDEST IT HAS EVER BEEN IN YOUR STATE? HERE ARE SOME STATE RECORDS FOR COLDEST TEMPERATURES.

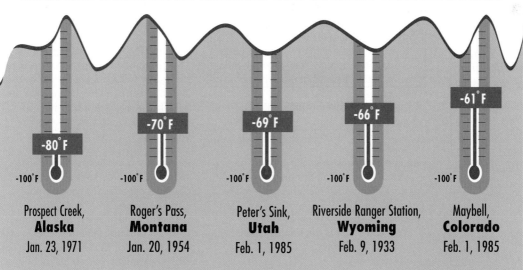

Prospect Creek, **Alaska**	Roger's Pass, **Montana**	Peter's Sink, **Utah**	Riverside Ranger Station, **Wyoming**	Maybell, **Colorado**
-80°F	-70°F	-69°F	-66°F	-61°F
Jan. 23, 1971	Jan. 20, 1954	Feb. 1, 1985	Feb. 9, 1933	Feb. 1, 1985

Write Now!

Take a look at the record-breaking temperatures on the chart. What is the coldest temperature listed? Write to compare the temperatures listed with winter temperatures in your area.

367

Dictionary

The **dictionary** gives the meanings, the pronunciations, and the parts of speech of thousands of words. It also gives other information. Words in a dictionary are listed in alphabetical order. To find a word, look at the first letter. Then turn to that letter in the dictionary to find information. For example, look at the word *contrast* below. You would find it among the *C* words in the dictionary. Notice that the word has more than one meaning. In fact, definitions are given for each of its different parts of speech.

Guide words show you the first and last entry words on the page.

The entry word is in dark type.

Definitions show you each meaning of the word.

The part of speech shows you that the word can be used as an adjective.

The pronunciation tells you how to say the word.

An example sentence shows you how to use the word.

The plural shows you the form for more than one.

The pronunciation key tells you how to say the vowels and consonants.

contralto / convalescent

contralto 1. The lowest female singing voice. **2.** A singer who has such a voice. **con·tral·to** (kən tral´tō) *noun, plural* **contraltos**.

contrary 1. Entirely different; opposite. My cousin's ideas about sports and music are *contrary* to my own. **2.** Liking to argue and oppose. That *contrary* child never agrees with what other people say. *Adjective.*
--Something completely different; the opposite. We thought it would rain, but the contrary happened; it was sunny. *Noun.*
on the contrary. Just the opposite of what has been said. You are not a clumsy dancer; *on the contrary*, you are very graceful.
con·trar·y (kon´trer ē *for adjective, definition 1 and noun*; kon´trer ē *or* kən´trâr´ē *for adjective definition 2) adjective; noun.*

contrast To show differences that are based on comparing. The teacher *contrasted* life in a big city and life on a farm. Red and white *contrast* with each other. *Verb.*
--**1.** A difference. There is a great *contrast* between the weather at the North Pole and the weather in the tropics. **2.** A person or thing that is compared to another and shows differences. Our new car is quite a *contrast* to our old car. *Noun.* **con·trast** (kən trast´ *for verb*; kon´trast *for noun) verb,* **contrasted, contrasting;** *noun, plural* **contrasts**.

contrive To plan or design cleverly. They are *contriving* a surprise party. The inventor *contrived* a car that would run on sunlight.
con·trive (kən trīv´) *verb,* **contrived, contriving.**

control 1. Power, authority, or regulation. The dictator had complete *control* over the country. The car went out of *control*. **2.** The power or ability to hold back or hold in. The police lost *control* of the mob. People do not always keep their anger under *control*. **3.** Something that is used to operate, regulate, or guide a machine or other device. Where is the volume *control* on this television set? The pilot operates the *controls* of an airplane. *Noun.*
--**1.** To command or regulate by using power or authority. Our dog does exactly what it wants; I can't *control* it. The federal government *controls* the handling and delivery of mail. **2.** To adjust or regulate. This knob *controls* the loudness on my radio. **3.** To hold back or hold in. The dam could not *control* the flooded river. I always try *to control* my temper. *Verb.*
con·trol (kən trōl´) *noun. plural* **controls;** *verb.* **controlled, controlling.**

at; āpe; fär; cāre; end; mē; it; īce; pîerce; hot; ōld; sông; fôrk; oil; out; up; ūse; rüle; pull; tûrn; chin; sing; shop; thin; this; hw in white; zh in treasure. The symbol ə stands for the unstressed vowel sound in about, taken, pencil, lemon, and circus.

Practice

A. Use the entry word *contrast* to answer these questions. Write your answers.

1. Which two parts of speech can the word *contrast* be?

2. How many ways can you pronounce *contrast*?

3. In the following sentence is *contrast* a verb or a noun? Her new hairstyle is quite a **contrast** to her old hairstyle.

4. How many different definitions are shown for *contrast* in this entry?

5. Which definition of *contrast* would apply to this sentence? There are a number of **contrasts** between football and soccer.

B. Write an example sentence for each of the following words. If the word can be used as more than one part of speech, give a sentence for each way the word can be used.

6. special

7. probably

8. solve

9. crate

10. sometimes

C. Write a sentence explaining how each of the following can help you find a word in the dictionary or can give you more information about a word.

11. guide words

12. definitions

13. example sentence

14. pronunciation

15. pronunciation key

*inter*NET
CONNECTION

Go to:
www.mhschool.
com/language-
arts for more
information on
the topic.

Writing Activity A Dictionary

Make a special dictionary for a school subject or a special interest or hobby. Be sure to list your entry words in alphabetical order. Include pronunciations and example sentences for your words, as well as their definitions and parts of speech. Use a photograph, an illustration, or a diagram to describe or explain at least one of your words.

Vocabulary: Word Choice

DEFINITION

Writers choose words carefully to paint word pictures for their audiences. Good word choice depends on knowing the definition of many words and on choosing the synonym that best expresses your meaning. One way to choose between synonyms, or words with similar meanings, is to select vivid verbs and adjectives. These words create stronger descriptions and paint a more colorful and exact picture for the reader.

Vague Verbs	Vivid Verbs	Vague Adjectives	Vivid Adjectives
blew	tossed	thin	skinny
watch	study	noisy	clattering
		red	crimson

Word Choice

How does word choice depend on knowing the differences between the meanings of words? Explain your answer in your journal.

Read the paragraph below. Look at the highlighted words.

A fresh breeze *tossed* our hair in our faces as we *studied* the tree planters in the distance. As the tractor chugged along, the tree-planting machine cut a narrow furrow in the soft dirt. The man sitting on the machine dropped a *skinny* sapling down a metal chute about every four seconds. Behind the *clattering* machinery, a row of freshly planted *crimson* oak trees stretched across the field.

Practice

A. Write the sentences. Draw one line under each vivid verb and two lines under each vivid adjective.

1. I wore my crimson boots out to the field.

2. Every time Dad took a step, I lugged the bucket behind him.

3. The water sloshed around my boots.

4. The field had a fragrant smell after the rain.

5. My job was to help my dad plant those delicate trees.

B. Write the sentences. Replace each underlined verb or adjective with a more vivid word from the Word Bank.

slender	drove	gently	marshy	thrusting

6. My dad put the spade into the ground.

7. The wet ground moved.

8. My dad began moving the spade back and forth until a hole was made.

9. I placed a thin tree from the bucket into his hand.

10. He bent and lightly tucked the roots into the ground.

C. Grammar Link Complete each sentence with a vivid verb in the present tense. Make sure that in each sentence the subject pronoun and verb agree.

11. I _____ the weeds from around each little tree.

12. We _____ dead leaves around the trees each fall.

13. Then he _____ the soil so the trees don't get thirsty.

14. They are big enough now that they _____ in the wind.

15. We _____ our healthy trees.

Writing Activity A Paragraph

Write a paragraph that compares a young tree, or sapling, with an old tree. Use vivid verbs and vivid adjectives to explain and describe how these trees are alike and yet different.

APPLY GRAMMAR: Underline the pronouns in your paragraph. Be sure that subject pronouns and verbs agree.

371

Composition: Writing Description

A good description creates a clear, vivid picture of something or someone. It includes details that appeal to the reader's senses and organizes these details logically.

GUIDELINES

- A written description creates a clear and vivid picture of a person, place, or thing.

- Descriptive writing uses sensory details to appeal to the reader's sense of sight, hearing, smell, taste, and touch.

- Use word choice and exact and vivid language to pinpoint exactly how something looks, sounds, smells, tastes, and feels.

- In a description, the details should add up to an overall impression of the subject.

- Organize a description in one of the following ways:
  - Use spatial order, such as describing something from bottom to top.
  - Present important details first or last.
  - Group together similar types of details.

THINK AND WRITE

Writing Description

Why is it important for descriptive writing to be both interesting and accurate? Write your ideas in your journal.

Read this description of winter weather. Notice how the writer compares March in Minnesota to March in Kentucky by grouping together similar types of details.

Sensory details help the reader see a picture.

Vivid adjectives pinpoint exactly how something looks.

The details add up to an overall impression of how spring differs in Minnesota and Kentucky.

It was late March when we moved from Minnesota to Kentucky. In Minnesota, the ground was still blanketed with snow. It was the wet, dirty kind of snow that blends in with the slate gray March sky and the spindly trees. The Minnesota air was cold and damp as we loaded into the car.

In Kentucky, however, it felt like spring. We saw green grass and even some flowers peeking out of the ground. Unlike Minnesota, Kentucky is warm and colorful in March.

Practice

A. For each sentence, write *descriptive* if a sentence creates a vivid picture. Write *not descriptive* if a sentence lacks vivid details.

1. There are flowers in the garden.

2. Leafy ferns stretch across the far corner of the yard.

3. The sweet smell of honeysuckle fills the fragrant air.

4. Tree branches whip in the wind.

5. I walked around the garden.

B. Write a descriptive sentence to compare each pair of topics. Use sensory details and exact, vivid language to describe how the topics are similar or different.

6. a baseball and a basketball

7. a cat and a dog

8. two kinds of cars

9. rain in January and rain in July

10. a ripe peach and a hard peach

C. Grammar Link **11–15.** Choose a descriptive sentence that you wrote in Practice B. Add five sentences to it to create a paragraph that describes and compares. Use a vivid adjective or a vivid verb in each new sentence. Be sure that subject pronouns and verbs agree.

Writing Activity A Letter

What does spring look like where you live? In a letter to a friend, compare your own spring with the one in the photograph. Explain and describe how spring in your area is like or unlike the one shown in the picture.

APPLY GRAMMAR: Draw one line under each pronoun. Draw two lines under the noun to which it refers. Be sure the nouns and pronouns agree.

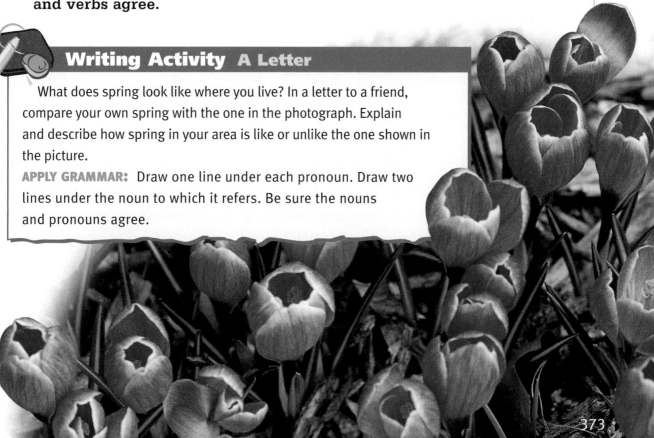

Better Sentences

Directions

Read the passage. Some sections are underlined. The underlined sections may be one of the following:

- Incomplete sentences
- Run-on sentences
- Correctly written sentences that should be combined
- Correctly written sentences that do not need to be rewritten

Choose the best way to write each underlined section. If the underlined section needs no change, choose "No mistake."

A correct sentence may contain several prepositional phrases.

Sample

The Atlantic hurricane season begins in June. From **(1)** then until the end of November, many storms develop into hurricanes. Small storms get bigger and become tropical storms, and then some of these grow into hurricanes. As soon as a storm is classified as a tropical storm. It is **(2)** given a name. The name helps weather forecasters avoid confusion when discussing different storms.

Correct some sentence fragments by joining them with sentences that come before or after them.

1 A From then until the end of November, many storms developing into hurricanes.

  B From then until the end of November. Many storms develop into hurricanes.

  C From then, until the end of November many storms develop they become hurricanes.

  D No mistake

2 F It is when a storm is classified as a tropical storm, it is given a name.

  G As soon as a storm is classified as a tropical storm, it is given a name.

  H It is when a storm is classified as a tropical storm. And is given a name.

  J No mistake

Test Tip
Read the underlined sections carefully.

Vocabulary and Comprehension

Directions

Read the passage. Then read each question that follows the passage. Decide which is the best answer to each question. Choose the letter for that answer.

> **Sample**
>
> While many modern cameras are <u>small</u>, the first cameras were large and heavy. Unlike today's cameras, they did not have shutters. The photographer had to remove a lens cover by hand. In addition, in the past, the chemicals on the film did not work as fast as modern chemicals do. People being photographed had to sit completely still for at least several seconds.

When choosing between synonyms, select the most vivid, precise word to replace a vague one.

1 In this passage, <u>small</u> can be replaced with

   A lightweight

   B short

   C thin

   D narrow

2 Which statement is true?

   F Today's film, unlike film in the past, has no chemicals.

   G The first cameras were smaller than modern cameras.

   H Modern cameras are slow, but the first cameras were not.

   J Modern cameras have shutters, but the first cameras did not.

Seeing Like a Writer

What would you write about these pictures? What are the similarities? What are the differences?

The Referee by Norman Rockwell

Writing from Pictures

1. List similarities between the pictures. Use possessive pronouns in your list.

2. List the details of one picture. Organize the details into categories, and place the information on a chart.

3. Imagine that you had to choose two of the pictures for an art exhibit. Write a short paragraph to explain why they should be displayed together. Is it the differences or the similarities between the two pictures that are the most striking?

Apply Grammar: Include subject and object pronouns in your paragraph. Draw one line under each subject pronoun and two lines under each object pronoun.

Writing That Compares

Have you ever compared two people or things? Then you probably have noticed that the two items were alike in some ways and different in others. In writing that compares, you do the same thing. This type of writing gives you the chance to explain how two items are alike yet also different.

Learning from Writers

Read these examples of writing that compares. What are the writers comparing? Why do you think they used this form of writing to explain their topic?

THINK AND WRITE

Purpose
What reasons might a writer have for comparing two people, things, or ideas? Write your thoughts in your journal.

Is a Doctor Like a Merchant?

For example, suppose I were to see two people coming toward me. Let us say that one is a Merchant (an Equilateral Triangle) and the other is a Doctor (a Pentagon). Both appear to be Straight Lines, so how am I to tell one from the other?

In the case of the Merchant, I see a Straight Line, of course. The center of this line, which is the part nearest to me, is very bright. But on either side, the line fades away rapidly into the Fog. I can tell at once, then, that the line slants back quite sharply from the center.

On the other hand, the Doctor has a slightly different appearance. As with the Merchant, I see only a Straight Line with a very bright center. On either side, the Doctor's line also fades into the Fog, but not as rapidly as the Merchant's line. Thus I can tell at once that the Doctor's line does not slant back as sharply. Because of the slight difference in brightness, I know that one shape is an Equilateral Triangle and that the other is a Pentagon.

—A. Square (Edwin Abbott), from *Life in Flatland*

The Eastern Coral Snake and the Scarlet King Snake

In the United States, there are two kinds of snakes that are red, black, and yellow. One is the eastern coral snake, the most poisonous of all North American snakes. The other is the harmless scarlet king snake.

It is not easy to tell the two snakes apart. Both grow to between two and four feet. Both have bands of bright red, black, and yellow; however, the coral snake has a blunt, black snout, while the king snake has a pointier, red snout.

As you can tell, these two kinds of snakes look very similar. If you see a red, black, and yellow banded snake, think carefully before getting close. The scarlet king snake can do you no harm, but the eastern coral snake may bite, and its venom can be lethal.

–Ryan Smith

PRACTICE AND APPLY

Thinking Like a Reader

1. How does the author explain the difference between the Doctor and the Merchant?

2. What similarities did the author point out between the coral snake and the king snake?

Thinking Like a Writer

3. How did the author of "Is a Doctor Like a Merchant?" organize his comparison?

4. What comparison and contrast words did the author use to compare the two snakes?

5. **Reading Across Texts** Compare the two literature models. Did the authors organize their comparisons in similar ways, or in different ways? Explain your answer.

Features of Writing That Compares

▶ Similarities

Reread "Is a Doctor Like a Merchant?" by Edwin Abbott on page 378. What is the author comparing? What phrase does he use to show you that two items are similar?

> As with the Merchant, I see only a Straight Line with a very bright center.

The phrase "As with the Merchant," lets you know that the writer is pointing out a similarity between the Merchant and the Doctor.

▶ Differences

The author contrasts the Merchant's line and the Doctor's line. How can you tell when he is mentioning a difference?

> On either side, the Doctor's line also fades into the Fog, but not as rapidly as the Merchant's line.

The phrase "but not as rapidly as" points out a contrast, or difference.

▶ Logical Organization

When writing to compare, you should organize your facts and details in a logical way. One way is to move back and forth between two items, comparing details of each. Another way is to give all the details about one item in a paragraph and then all the details about the other in another paragraph. The sentence below shows the method the author uses to compare the Doctor and the Merchant.

> In the case of the Merchant, I see a Straight Line...

Does the writer move back and forth between the Doctor and the Merchant, or does he give all the details about one and then all the details about the other?

▶ Comparison and Contrast Words

When authors use comparison writing, they include words such as *like, both, also, too,* and *in the same way* to show how two things are similar. To show how two things differ, they use words and phrases such as *however, but, while, on the other hand,* and *in the case of.*

> On the other hand, the Doctor has a slightly different appearance.

What words did the author use to show that he was making a contrast, or showing a difference?

PRACTICE AND APPLY

Create a Features Chart

1. List the features of good comparison writing.
2. Reread "The Eastern Coral Snake and the Scarlet King Snake" by Ryan Smith on page 379.
3. Write one example of each feature in Ryan's writing.
4. Do you think that Ryan's essay is a good example of writing that compares? Explain why.

Features	Examples

Prewrite

Writing that compares shows how two things are alike and how they are different. Writing a comparison gives you the chance to compare two items or ideas. It also lets you contrast two items to show their differences.

Purpose and Audience

The purpose of writing that compares is to give your audience information about how two people, places, things, or ideas are like and unlike each other.

Before writing, think about your audience. Will your readers be your classmates and your teacher? How will you clearly explain to them how two things are alike, yet different?

Choose a Topic

Start by **brainstorming** a list of two items that have some things in common and some differences. Think about topics that would interest your audience.

Once you have chosen a topic from your brainstorming list, **explore ideas**. List the features or traits of each thing you will compare. Then use a chart or a diagram to organize your ideas.

THINK AND WRITE

Audience
In your journal, make a list of what your audience may already know about your topic. Then list what they will need to know.

Here is how I explored my ideas.

WHALES	SHARKS
large animal	large animal
sea creature	sea creature
mammal	fish
warm-blooded	cold-blooded
no back legs	several rows of teeth
skin and a few hairs	scales and no hair
have live births	lay eggs
	no bones
	meat-eaters

Organize • Sorting

In writing that compares, writers sort, or classify, information. First, they think about the traits of each item. Next, they compare the two items for likenesses. Then, they think about the differences. Finally, they draw a conclusion about whether the two items are more alike than different. This writer organized the information from his list into a chart. Does his chart show that whales and sharks are more like or unlike each other? What ideas from his list did the writer decide not to put in his chart?

PREWRITE

DRAFT

REVISE

PROOFREAD

PUBLISH

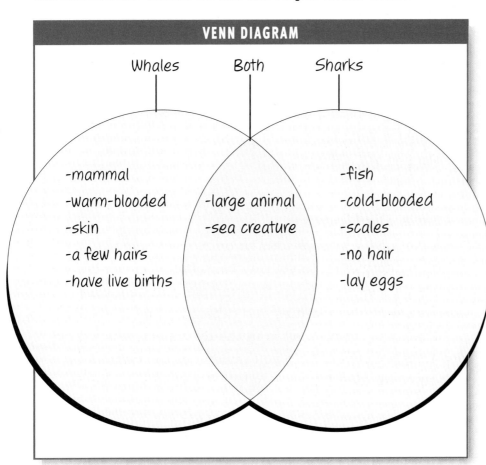

VENN DIAGRAM

Whales — Both — Sharks

Whales:
-mammal
-warm-blooded
-skin
-a few hairs
-have live births

Both:
-large animal
-sea creature

Sharks:
-fish
-cold-blooded
-scales
-no hair
-lay eggs

PRACTICE AND APPLY

Plan Your Writing That Compares

1. Think about your purpose and audience.

2. Brainstorm ideas for two items to compare.

3. Choose a topic, and explore likenesses and differences.

4. Use a Venn diagram to compare and contrast.

Checklist ✓
Prewriting

- Did you think about your purpose and audience?

- Did you choose a good topic and explore ideas?

- Did you make a list of traits, as well as lists of similarities and differences?

- Did you organize your information in a diagram or chart?

- Do you need to do any research?

Prewrite • Research and Inquiry

▶ Writer's Resources

You may have to do research to get more information for your writing that compares. First, make a list of questions. Then decide what resources you will need to answer your questions. If you can, use technology in your research.

What Else Do I Need to Know?	Where Can I Find the Information?
Where can I find the definition and spelling of words related to my topic?	Look in a print or an online dictionary.
Where can I find words that will help me describe similarities and differences?	Look up words in a thesaurus.

▶ Use a Dictionary

A dictionary in book form or online can help you add accurate information to your writing. Defining words from science for a science topic, for example, can help your readers see the similarities and differences more clearly.

When looking up a word in the dictionary, it is a good idea to take notes to help you remember the definition. Add the definition to a vocabulary list of subject words.

The entry word is the highlighted word.

The definition shows the meaning of the word.

The pronunciation tells you how to say the word.

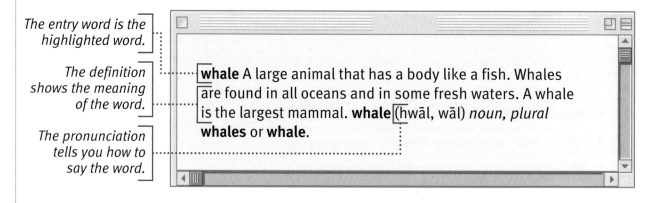

whale A large animal that has a body like a fish. Whales are found in all oceans and in some fresh waters. A whale is the largest mammal. **whale** (hwāl, wāl) *noun, plural* **whales** or **whale**.

Writing PROCESS

▶ Use a Thesaurus

A thesaurus in book form or on computer can help you choose the best words to describe or explain the similarities and differences between two items. A thesaurus lists words with the same or a similar meaning. These words are called *synonyms*. It also gives words with opposite meanings. These words are called *antonyms*. A thesaurus gives synonyms and antonyms for hundreds of words in the dictionary.

▶ Use Your Research

New information gathered from your research can be added to your chart. This writer found some new information. What did he add to his chart?

PREWRITE

DRAFT

REVISE

PROOFREAD

PUBLISH

Handbook
pages 570, 571, 574, 575

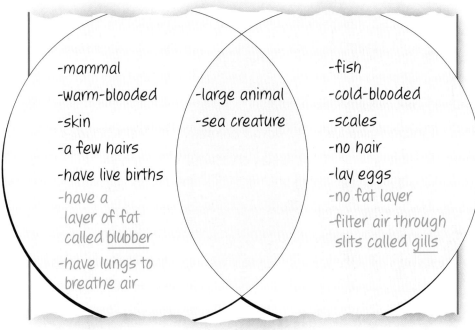

-mammal
-warm-blooded
-skin
-a few hairs
-have live births
-have a layer of fat called blubber
-have lungs to breathe air

-large animal
-sea creature

-fish
-cold-blooded
-scales
-no hair
-lay eggs
-no fat layer
-filter air through slits called gills

PRACTICE AND APPLY

Review Your Plan

1. Look at your chart or diagram.

2. List questions you have about your topic.

3. Identify the resources you will need to find answers to your questions.

4. Add new information you gather to your chart.

Checklist ✓

Research and Inquiry

- ■ Did you list your questions?

- ■ Did you identify possible resources?

- ■ Did you take notes as you found information?

Draft

Before you begin writing your comparison, review your chart or diagram. Think about how you will organize your information. The *point-by-point* method is one way to organize. In this method, a writer moves back and forth between two items, giving similarities and differences of each. The *item-by-item* method is another way to organize information or details. In this method, the writer gives all the information about one item and then all the information about the other. Either method of organizing lets you present your information clearly.

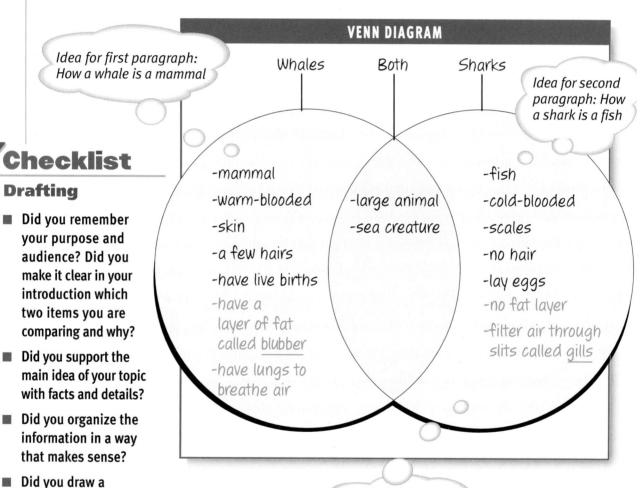

VENN DIAGRAM

Whales   Both   Sharks

Idea for first paragraph: How a whale is a mammal

Idea for second paragraph: How a shark is a fish

-mammal
-warm-blooded
-skin
-a few hairs
-have live births
-have a layer of fat called blubber
-have lungs to breathe air

-large animal
-sea creature

-fish
-cold-blooded
-scales
-no hair
-lay eggs
-no fat layer
-filter air through slits called gills

Conclusion: More differences than similarities

✓ Checklist

Drafting

- Did you remember your purpose and audience? Did you make it clear in your introduction which two items you are comparing and why?

- Did you support the main idea of your topic with facts and details?

- Did you organize the information in a way that makes sense?

- Did you draw a conclusion based on the information you presented?

Better Paragraphs

Regardless of the method you use to compare two items, each of your paragraphs should focus on a main idea, and all the paragraphs should flow together well. If you have chosen the item-by-item method, check to be sure you have used a separate paragraph for each item of your comparison. Read your paragraphs aloud. Have you grouped together the traits for one item in a paragraph and followed it with a paragraph of traits for the other item? Have you also used *analogies* to show how one thing is like another? For example, does the writer show an analogy between the lungs of a whale and the gills of a shark?

PREWRITE

DRAFT

REVISE

PROOFREAD

PUBLISH

Handbook
page 578

As mammals, whales are warm blooded They have
~to control their body temperature~
skin, a few hairs, and a layer of fat called <u>blubber</u>.
~to breathe air~
Mammals also have lungs. Like other mammals,

whales give birth to live babys.
~On the other hand,~
Sharks are cold blooded. They also have scales
~In addition,~
rather than skin. Sharks have no hair or blubber. Like
~through their mouth and gills~
other fish, sharks filter air from water.

TECHNOLOGY

Does the word processing program you are using provide a thesaurus? If so, use this feature to replace repeated or general words with more interesting and exact language.

PRACTICE AND APPLY

Revise Your Writing That Compares

1. Add facts or details to make clear how things are alike and different.

2. Organize your information by grouping it into paragraphs.

3. Use words that compare and contrast.

4. **Grammar** Did you use possessive pronouns to show that someone has or owns something?

Revise • Peer Conferencing

Writing PROCESS

A partner can be of great help when you are revising your writing. Exchange papers with a partner. Then exchange ideas! Your partner may have some new ideas or suggestions that you haven't thought of yourself.

Good opening!

Add a contrast word.

What does "cold blooded" mean?

Make conclusion clearer by summarizing the differences.

Whales and sharks may seem alike, but their different in many ways. Altho both are large sea creatures, whales are mammals. Sharks are fish. As mammals, whales are warm blooded They have skin, a few hairs, and a layer of fat called <u>blubber</u>. Mammals also have lungs. Like other mammals, whales give birth to live babys.

Sharks are cold blooded. They also have scales rather than skin. Sharks have no hair or blubber. Like other fish, sharks filter air from water. They also lay eggs rather than give birth to live babies.

Though whales and large sharks are both sea creatures, they are different in many ways.

Conferencing for the Reader

- Are features of writing that compares included in your partner's work?
  - differences and similarities
  - logical organization
  - words that compare and contrast
  - conclusion based on information presented
- Discuss with your partner the parts of his or her draft that are effective as well as the parts that need revising.

When you revise your comparison-contrast writing, you will want to think about the comments and suggestions your partner made during your conference. This writer made some changes based on his partner's ideas.

REVISE

Is a Shark Like a Whale?

whales and sharks may seem alike, but their

different in many ways. Altho both are large sea

By contrast,

creatures, whales are mammals. Sharks are fish. As

mammals, whales are warm blooded They have skin, a

to control their body temperature

few hairs, and a layer of fat called <u>blubber</u>. Mammals

to breathe air.

also have lungs. Like other mammals, whales give birth

As fish, their body temperature

to live babys.   changes with ocean

On the other hand,   temperature.

Sharks are cold blooded. They also have scales

In addition,

rather than skin. Sharks have no hair or blubber. Like

through their mouth and gills.

other fish, sharks filter air from water. They also lay

eggs rather than give birth to live babies.

Though whales and large sharks are both sea

how they look, breathe, have babies, and control body

creatures, they are different in ~~many ways~~. temperature.

PRACTICE AND APPLY

Revise Your Writing That Compares

1. Read the notes from your peer conference.

2. Use these notes to improve your draft.

3. Add a title that will interest your audience.

4. Add more information, facts, and details that will make your writing clearer, more interesting, and more exact.

Checklist ✔

Revising

- **Does your writing suit your purpose and audience?**

- **Do you need to elaborate on any ideas or details?**

- **Did you use words that compare and contrast?**

- **Did you organize your ideas in a way that makes sense?**

- **Did you write long and short sentences to add variety to your writing?**

- **Did you choose your words carefully?**

- **Did you write a conclusion that summarizes your information?**

Proofread

After you have revised your writing, you will need to proofread it to find and correct any mistakes in mechanics, grammar and usage, and spelling.

STRATEGIES FOR PROOFREADING

- **Reread your revised draft several times.** Each time, look for a different type of error. You'll have a better chance of catching your errors that way.

- **Read each sentence for correct capitalization.** Remember that if a pronoun is the first word of a sentence, it must begin with a capital letter.

- **Reread each paragraph for fluency.** Check to see if each paragraph has a main-idea sentence and facts or details that support it.

- **Read for mechanics and usage.** Be sure your writing has the correct punctuation, including apostrophes in contractions and correct end marks.

- **Check for spelling mistakes.** Use the dictionary or spell checker on the computer to help you.

Spelling

When a root word, or base word, ends in a consonant and *y*, change the *y* to *i* when adding a plural (*-es*) ending (*baby* + *-es* = *babies*).

REVIEW THE RULES

GRAMMAR

- A pronoun is a word that takes the place of one or more nouns. A pronoun must match the noun it replaces, and it must agree with the verb.

MECHANICS

- A hyphen is used to connect two or more words to form a compound word.

- A pronoun-verb contraction, such as *you're*, combines a pronoun (*you*) with a verb (*are*) to make a shortened form of two words. Do not confuse the possessive pronouns *your*, *its*, *their* with pronoun-verb contractions *you're*, *it's*, *they're*.

Look at the proofreading corrections made on the draft below. What does the symbol (SP) mean? Why does the writer want to be sure that he spells his words correctly?

PREWRITE

DRAFT

REVISE

PROOFREAD

PUBLISH

PROOFREAD

Is a Shark Like a Whale?

whales and sharks may seem alike, but ~~their~~ they're (SP)

different in many ways. (SP) Although ~~Altho~~ both are large sea

By contrast,
creatures, whales are mammals. Sharks are fish. As

mammals, whales are warm-blooded. They have skin, a
to control their body temperature
few hairs, and a layer of fat called blubber. Mammals

to breathe air.
also have lungs. Like other mammals, whales give birth
(SP) babies.
to live ~~babys.~~   As fish, their body temperature
changes with ocean
On the other hand,   temperature.
Sharks are cold-blooded. They also have scales
In addition,
rather than skin. Sharks have no hair or blubber. Like
through their mouth and gills.
other fish, sharks filter air from water. They also lay

eggs rather than give birth to live babies.

Though whales and (large) sharks are both sea
how they look, breathe, have babies, and control body
creatures, they are different in ~~many ways.~~ temperature.

Checklist ✓
Proofreading

- Did you indent each paragraph?

- Did you use hyphens and end punctuation correctly?

- Did you correct any mistakes in the use of pronouns or pronoun-verb contractions?

- Did you spell all the words correctly?

PRACTICE AND APPLY

Proofread Your Writing That Compares

1. Be sure to indent paragraphs and to begin each paragraph with a capital letter.

2. Correct any spelling errors.

3. Check for correct punctuation at the end of each sentence.

4. Correct any mistakes in the use of pronouns.

PROOFREADING MARKS

⌗ new paragraph

∧ add

take out

≡ Make a capital letter.

/ Make a small letter.

(SP) Check the spelling.

⊙ Add a period.

Writing PROCESS

Publish

Before you publish your work, read through your writing one last time. Use a checklist to help you focus your efforts.

> ✓ **Self-Check** Writing That Compares
>
> ❑ Did I state my purpose clearly at the beginning?
>
> ❑ Who was my audience? Did I write in a way that will interest them?
>
> ❑ Did I organize my information in a way that makes sense?
>
> ❑ Did I include enough facts and details to show how two items are alike and different?
>
> ❑ Did I choose words to help compare and contrast?
>
> ❑ Did I base my conclusion on the facts I presented?
>
> ❑ Are my sentences varied? Do they flow together easily?
>
> ❑ Did I proofread and correct all errors?

This writer used the checklist to review his writing. Read "Is a Shark Like a Whale?" and discuss the writer's published piece. Is there anything you would have changed or added before publishing? What makes the writer feel that his draft is ready to publish? Do you think it is? Why do you think so?

Is a Shark Like a Whale?

by Simon Vega

Whales and sharks may seem alike, but they're different in many ways. Although both are large sea creatures, whales are mammals. By contrast, sharks are fish.

As mammals, whales are warm-blooded. They have skin, a few hairs, and a layer of fat called *blubber* to control their body temperature. Mammals also have lungs to breathe air. Like other mammals, whales give birth to live babies.

On the other hand, sharks are cold-blooded. As fish, their body temperature changes with ocean temperature. They also have scales rather than skin. In addition, sharks have no hair or blubber. Like other fish, sharks filter air from water through their mouth and gills. They also lay eggs rather than give birth to live babies.

Though whales and sharks are both large sea creatures, they are different in how they look, breathe, have babies, and control body temperature.

PREWRITE

DRAFT

REVISE

PROOFREAD

PUBLISH

PRACTICE AND APPLY

Publish Your Writing That Compares

1. Check your revised draft one more time.

2. Copy your draft over neatly.

3. Add pictures to show your comparisons.

TECHNOLOGY

Does your school have a Web site? Use your school's technology resources to publish your work on the Internet.

Present Your Writing That Compares

Planning ahead will help you make a good presentation. Here are some things you can do to make your presentation a success.

STEP 1

How to Present Your Writing

Strategies for Speaking Plan to present your comparison on audio or video. Remember that your purpose is to give your audience information. Be sure that your points are clear, well organized, and easy to understand.

■ Emphasize the comparisons and contrasts by shifting your tone of voice to signal a change from showing likenesses to showing differences.

■ Tape your speech and play it back for the class.

Multimedia Ideas

You might want to use a sound recording as background music or as an example of the sound of the two items that you are comparing.

How to Show Your Writing

Suggestions for Visuals Add interest to your video presentation by including visuals for your audience to view as they watch and listen to your speech.

- A large poster, diagram, drawing, or chart can help your audience identify and understand the points you are comparing.
- Organize your ideas on a poster to support your points visually.
- Make note cards to remind yourself when to point to or show the visuals.

STEP 3

How to Share Your Writing

Strategies for Rehearsing The more you practice, the more confident you'll feel.

- Practice giving your speech on tape before making your final recording.
- Ask a friend or a family member to watch or listen and to make suggestions.

PRACTICE AND APPLY

Present Your Writing That Compares

1. Refer to note cards as you speak.
2. Make sure you can operate any equipment you need.
3. Present your speech only after you have practiced it.
4. If you are preparing a video of your speech, use appropriate gestures and body movement.

TiP!

Viewing Strategies

- Look carefully at the video and at the visual materials the speaker displays.
- Visuals may give information the speaker does not tell you directly.
- Use critical viewing skills if you are watching the speech on video. Save your comments for later.

397

Writing Tests

On a writing test, you are required to write a composition in response to a prompt. Remember to read the prompt carefully. Look for key words and phrases that describe the topic of your composition and explain how you should present your ideas.

What is the purpose of writing this article?

Think about what kind of writing is appropriate for this audience.

> **Prompt**
>
> Think about what you like and don't like about reading a book.
>
> <u>Write an article</u> for your <u>local library's newsletter</u>. <u>Explain the differences between</u> watching a movie or television program and reading a good book.

This phrase tells you what kind of information to include in your article.

How to Read a Prompt

Purpose Read the prompt again. Look for key words that tell you what your purpose should be. The prompt tells you to write an article, but an article can have several purposes. The word "Explain," however, tells you that the purpose of this article is to inform.

Audience This prompt tells you that your audience is the readers of your local library's newsletter. Be sure your style fits this audience. If a prompt does not name the audience, write for your teacher.

Writing That Compares When you are asked to write about the similarities and differences between two things, you are writing a comparison. When you write a comparison, use words that help you show how the two things are alike and how they are different.

Test Tip
Work at a steady pace so that you can complete the test in time.

How to Write to a Prompt

Here are some tips to keep in mind when you are given a prompt on a writing test.

Before Writing **Content/Ideas**	• Identify your purpose for writing. • Keep your audience in mind. • If you are writing to compare, make a list of similarities and differences. • Stay focused on the topic of the prompt.
During Writing **Organization/** **Paragraph** **Structure**	• State your main idea in a topic sentence. • Organize your ideas in a logical manner. • In writing that compares, use words of comparison and contrast. • End your writing with a strong conclusion.
After Writing **Grammar/Usage**	• Proofread your writing for errors in punctuation. Check that you have used hyphens correctly. • Check for pronoun-verb agreement. • Make sure each pronoun matches the noun to which it refers. • Look for spelling errors.

Apply What You Learned

When you read a writing prompt on a test, look for the answers to these questions: *Why are you writing? Whom are you writing for?* Determine the topic of your composition and the best way to organize your ideas.

> **Prompt**
>
> Every year at school, you have many new experiences.
>
> Write a composition in which you explain how fifth grade and fourth grade are alike and different.

Grammar and Writing Review

pages
340–341

Pronouns

A. Write each sentence. Draw one line under the pronoun and two lines under the noun or nouns it replaces. Above each pronoun, write *S* if the pronoun is singular or *P* if it is plural.

1. Loretta said that she had an idea.

2. Earl asked Loretta to tell him the idea.

3. Earl and Loretta said they would share these ideas with Ernie.

4. The three friends thought they would present the ideas at the PTA meeting.

5. The students gave a persuasive speech, and the adults loved it.

pages
342–345

Subject and Object Pronouns

B. Write each sentence. Use a subject pronoun or an object pronoun in place of the underlined word or words. Then write *SP* above the pronoun if it is a subject pronoun. Write *OP* if it is an object pronoun.

6. My classmates planned Family Fun Day.

7. The festival is an event for the whole family.

8. The event is organized by parents, teachers, and students.

9. My classmates and I help plan the festival.

10. Martha is in charge of planning the games.

11. Tanya and Neil help Martha and I plan the games.

12. Neil asks parents to help.

13. A few parents give Neil excuses.

14. How can Neil get people to help?

15. Perhaps some parents can work in one-hour shifts.

16. Martha asks Otis and you to volunteer.

17. You and Neil need to find out who will help.

18. Neil thanks Martha for helping to recruit volunteers.

19. Martha, Neil, Tanya, and I work out a schedule.

20. The schedule is just the first step in our plan.

Unit 5 Review

pages 346–347

Mechanics and Usage: Colons and Hyphens

C. Write each sentence. Add a colon or a hyphen to make the sentence correct.

21. The meeting is set for 700 on Monday evening.

22. We ask each volunteer to bring a note book to the meeting.

23. The room is jam packed with volunteers.

24. My self esteem rises when everyone applauds our plan.

25. Our successful meeting ends at 815.

pages 350–351

Pronoun-Verb Agreement

D. Write each sentence. Use the correct form of the verb in parentheses.

26. We (begin, begins) setting up booths for Family Fun Day.

27. I (make, makes) a map for the volunteers.

28. They (refer, refers) to the map to set up the games.

29. Martha and I (want, wants) to test the dunk tank.

30. It (sit, sits) at the edge of the playground.

31. She (go, goes) to the dunk tank.

32. You (laugh, laughs) when she falls into the tank.

33. Suddenly, you and Neil (feel, feels) raindrops.

34. Luckily, they (stop, stops) quickly.

35. He (complain, complains) that the fair will be ruined.

pages 352–353

Combining Sentences: Subject and Object Pronouns

E. Combine each pair of sentences by forming compound subjects or compound objects. Change the form of the verb to agree with the pronouns if needed.

36. The planning committee asks her for ideas. The planning committee asks me for ideas.

37. I think about the weather problem. They think about the weather problem.

38. You understand the problem. I understand the problem.

39. She finds solutions. They find solutions.

40. He chooses the best idea. We choose the best idea.

Unit 5 Review

pages
354–355

Possessive Pronouns

F. **Write each sentence. Use the correct possessive pronoun in parentheses.**

41. (My, Mine) friends and I went to the local supply store.

42. We told the salesclerk about (our, ours) problem.

43. The clerk's idea was the same as (our, ours).

44. We went into the storeroom and saw (it's, its) overflowing shelves.

45. The clerk donated hundreds of (his, him) overstocked umbrellas.

46. (Your, Yours) plan was to sell the umbrellas at the festival.

47. Martha's plan was different from (my, mine).

48. Neil liked (her, hers) better.

49. The school approved (your, yours).

50. Neil still liked (her, hers) plan the best.

pages
356–357

Contractions: Pronoun and Verb

G. **Write each sentence. Replace the underlined words with a contraction.**

51. I am sure Family Fun Day will be a success.

52. It is going to be rainy, however.

53. We are ready for our guests in spite of the rain.

54. We have planned games for the whole family to enjoy.

55. You are going to be amazed.

56. I have helped the teachers prepare the food.

57. They have set up a display of tasty treats.

58. He has brought the lemonade.

59. She will bring the potato salad.

60. They are coming, rain or shine.

pages
370–371

Vocabulary: Word Choice

H. Rewrite each sentence by replacing the underlined word or words with a more vivid verb or adjective. Use words that appeal to the reader's sense of sight, touch, taste, smell, or hearing.

61. Our boots <u>splashed</u> in the rain during Family Fun Day.

62. People <u>walked quickly</u> from game to game.

63. The sky looked <u>dark</u> after each shower.

64. The umbrellas formed a <u>safe</u> canopy.

65. The children playing games <u>shouted</u> with delight.

pages
372–373

Composition: Writing Description

I. Write a descriptive paragraph about each topic. Organize the details in your paragraphs logically.

66. The Sound of Traffic

67. The Smell of a Warm Spring Day

68. The Taste of Your Favorite Flavor of Ice Cream

69. The Feel of a Wool Sweater on a Cold Day

70. The View from Your Classroom Window

pages
382–397

Proofreading Writing That Compares

J. Read the following paragraphs. Look for 11 mistakes in capitalization, punctuation, grammar, and spelling. Then write the paragraphs correctly.

Our Family Fun Day this year was a first-rate success. It began in the morning, and hundreds of people attended it. The food court make more money this year than last some people sat in the gym and ate instead of eating they're food in the rain.

Last year, family fun day began at 1200. It was a very hot day and the air conditioning wasnt working. No one felt like eating because it was too hot. Unlike last year, this year's Family Fun Day was a success in spite of the whether.

Project File

A Book Review

Sometimes before you read a book, it's a good idea to read a review of the book. A book review will tell you something about the story. It will also give the writer's opinion of the book. It's up to you to decide whether or not the book is worth reading.

Carlos and the Skunk
by Jan Romero Stevens

Title and Author *Tells your readers the name of the book and who wrote it.*

If a skunk has ever crossed your path, then you know why this book is so funny.

Introduction *Catches your readers' attention and lets them know if the book is funny, exciting, scary, or sad.*

Carlos is a boy who lives in New Mexico. One day Carlos tries to impress his best friend Gloria by catching a skunk. He tells Gloria what he has heard about skunks. "If you pick up a skunk by its tail, it can't spray you," Carlos says. Gloria laughs. She tells Carlos that he shouldn't believe everything he hears. When Carlos tries to pick up the skunk by its tail, something very funny happens.

Body *Gives the setting, the main character or characters, and an important event in the story.*

This book is humorous, and Carlos and Gloria are great characters. It's also amusing to read a story about a skunk instead of a more usual animal, like a dog or cat. If you like funny stories, this is the book for you.

Conclusion *Gives your recommendation about whether or not the book is worth reading.*

Write a Book Review Many magazines and newspapers include book reviews. A book review helps other people decide whether or not they should read a book. What book have you read lately? Was it funny, happy, exciting, or sad? Write a book review for your classmates. Look at the model on page 404 to make sure you include the important parts of a book review.

ACTIVITY 2

A Fact Sheet

The children in "Brrrrrrr!" have learned how to adjust to the climate in Alaska. They have learned how to dress, play, and get around in the extreme cold. How cold or hot does it get where you live? What do you do to adjust to the weather changes?

Make Way for the Weather! Write a fact sheet, comparing Alaska's climate to the climate in your area. Divide your paper into two columns. Begin with an overview of the type of weather in each place. Then give tips about dealing with the climate in each location. Include illustrations that show the clothing and transportation needed to cope with the weather in each area.

Extra Practice

Pronouns

A. Write the underlined pronoun. Next to it, write *S* if the pronoun is singular or *P* if it is plural.

1. Mom told <u>them</u> that today is cleaning day.
2. Kristin and Ben looked at <u>her</u> in surprise.
3. <u>She</u> pointed to the garage with a smile.
4. Ben cringed when <u>he</u> saw junk everywhere.
5. Kristin and Ben needed a plan to clean <u>it</u> up.
6. How could <u>they</u> make the job more fun?
7. "Let <u>me</u> think for a minute," Ben said.
8. "<u>I</u> have the answer," Ben shouted.
9. Kristin, <u>you</u> put on some music, and let's have a race.
10. <u>We</u> can see whose side of the garage looks cleaner.

B. Write the sentences. Draw one line under each singular pronoun and two lines under each plural pronoun.

11. The garage was clean, but it needed to be organized.
12. "We should store similar items together," Kristin suggested.
13. She gathered the empty boxes while Ben got a marker.
14. Ben told her to store household items separately.
15. Kristin, you can put outdoor equipment in that box.
16. Kristin and Ben whistled songs while they worked.
17. Kristin helped him lift heavy boxes.
18. He helped Kristin stack the boxes against the wall.
19. They looked at the clean, tidy garage.
20. "We make a great team," Ben said with a smile.

C. Write each sentence. Replace each underlined word or group of words with a pronoun. Be sure the pronoun matches the noun to which it refers.

21. <u>Kristin and Ben</u> had one more cleaning job to do.
22. Mom handed Pete, the family dog, to <u>Kristin and Ben</u>.
23. <u>Pete</u> did not want a bath, but the dog really needed one!
24. Brother and sister thought of a fun way to bathe <u>Pete</u>.
25. <u>Mom</u> laughed to see Kristin, Ben, and Pete in the sprinklers.

Subject Pronouns

A. Write the subject pronoun in each sentence.

1. We have music class every Tuesday.

2. I like our music teacher, Mrs. Rojas.

3. She plays the flute.

4. We learn how to play different musical instruments.

5. Last week, you met Mrs. Rojas' husband.

6. He is a musician with the local symphony orchestra.

7. I love to hear Mr. Rojas play the clarinet.

8. It is a wonderful instrument.

9. They sometimes play a duet for the class.

10. You wouldn't believe how sweet the music sounds!

B. Write each sentence. Underline the subject pronoun.

11. She is learning to play the tuba.

12. He is learning to play the clarinet.

13. I chose to play the trumpet.

14. We practice together each day.

15. You should hear us play!

16. Every week, we meet with Mrs. Rojas.

17. She demonstrates how to play a favorite song.

18. We practice a new song every week.

19. They ask the teacher for extra help.

20. We learn to play the song beautifully.

C. Write each sentence. Replace the underlined word or words with the correct subject pronoun.

21. Patty and Jacob made their own musical instruments.

22. Patty made an instrument with a can and dried beans.

23. Jacob made an instrument with a box and rubber bands.

24. The instrument looked like a guitar.

25. Patty and I listened to Jacob play the handmade guitar.

Extra Practice

Object Pronouns

A. Write the object pronoun in each sentence.

1. The teacher gave us seeds to plant and test.

2. Aaron asked her for supplies for planting the seeds.

3. The teacher gave him some soil and cups.

4. Everyone used them for planting.

5. Nadia helped me plant some seeds.

6. The teacher told us to write a procedure for the experiment.

7. The task took me a few minutes to complete.

8. Nadia tried it, but she had trouble.

9. Nadia asked us for help.

10. We gave her some suggestions.

B. Write each sentence. Use the correct pronoun in parentheses.

11. That pollution experiment was easy for (I, me).

12. Mr. Thomas asked (I, me) about my experiment.

13. I told (him, he) about using polluted water to grow seeds.

14. I watered (them, they) daily with polluted water.

15. The plants did not enjoy (it, her).

16. I watered (they, them) until they wilted.

17. Students shared their results with (he, him).

18. Our teacher saw (they, them) and summarized the results.

19. Laurie showed (we, us) plants grown in artificial light.

20. It pleased (she, her) to see the results of the tests.

C. Write each sentence. Replace the underlined word or words with the correct pronoun. Then write *SP* if the pronoun is a subject pronoun. Write *OP* if it is an object pronoun.

21. <u>Ms. Tobashi</u> praised the class for a job well done.

22. Ms. Tobashi asked <u>Ramona and me</u> some questions.

23. <u>My classmates and I</u> discussed our discoveries.

24. <u>Joe and Sasha</u> were amazed at the results.

25. The class displayed <u>the plants</u> during Open House.

Colons and Hyphens

A. Write the word in each sentence that has a hyphen or a colon.

1. Our student council had a meeting at 3:00 P.M.

2. We met in the room near the west wing of the li-brary.

3. We had a half-hour meeting to discuss our funds.

4. The council included members from the fifth-grade class.

5. The president, Tabitha, is an eleven-year-old girl.

6. Her half-sister Kate drove us to the meeting.

7. The president called the meeting to order at 3:05.

8. About twenty-five students sat on the floor.

9. Our goal was to settle the mix-up over the money we'd made.

10. It was a nerve-racking meeting.

B. Write each sentence. Add hyphens and colons as needed.

11. I was a bleary eyed onlooker as the council debated.

12. The president was trying to maintain order as the audi ence murmured.

13. By 400 P.M., we still hadn't decided on a plan.

14. This face to face meeting wasn't getting us anywhere.

15. We discussed many important ideas, but we couldn't de cide on the best plan.

16. I suggested writing to the principal for a clear cut solution.

17. Our letter began "Dear Sir We hope you can advise us."

18. The principal would give us some top notch ideas.

19. We will give the money to a start up nursery.

20. It was 545 when we reached our decision.

C. Write each sentence. Use the correct word in parentheses. Underline words with hyphens or colons.

21. Are your problem-solving skills in (tiptop, tip-top) shape?

22. Do you make one-sided or (two sided, two-sided) decisions?

23. We need your decision by (530, 5:30) P.M., or by 6:00.

24. Ask your (brother-in-law, brother in law) or sister-in-law.

25. I like your self-control and your (first rate, first-rate) solution.

Extra Practice

Pronoun-Verb Agreement

A. Write *correct* if the underlined verb agrees with the subject pronoun. Write *incorrect* if it does not.

1. I <u>enjoys</u> the historical farm.

2. We <u>visit</u> this historical site every year.

3. It <u>include</u> a log cabin and a barnyard.

4. Inside the cabin, we <u>see</u> how people lived long ago.

5. She <u>tells</u> my brother historical facts about the tour.

6. He <u>notice</u> the handmade utensils in the kitchen.

7. We <u>asks</u> the tour guide about the tools.

8. She <u>explains</u> that pioneer families ate with wooden utensils.

9. She <u>describes</u> how pioneers made their own furniture.

10. Can you <u>imagine</u> having to make your own furniture?

B. Write each sentence. Use the correct form of the verb in parentheses.

11. We (look, looks) at each room of the old-fashioned cabin.

12. I (show, shows) my father the straw beds.

13. He (notice, notices) bedclothes made of woven fabrics.

14. We (watch, watches) a volunteer role-play a pioneer woman.

15. She (spin, spins) yarn from sheep's wool.

16. I (lead, leads) my brother to the workshop.

17. He (touch, touches) the hoe, the plow, and the other tools.

18. We both (see, sees) the corn mill.

19. I (ask, asks) the guide about this unusual tool.

20. She (demonstrate, demonstrates) how to grind corn.

C. Rewrite each sentence. Use the correct present-tense form of the word in parentheses.

21. I (describe) the tour to my friend.

22. She (help) me present a report to the class.

23. We (ask) the teacher about having a "Pioneer Day" celebration.

24. He (give) us permission to organize a festival.

25. It (become) the best event of the school year.

Combining Sentences: Subject and Object Pronouns

A. Write the sentences. Underline the compound subject pronoun or compound object pronoun in each sentence.

1. She and I decided to put on a play.

2. He and she wrote a script about famous explorers.

3. I asked him and her to hold auditions.

4. Mr. Lee helped them and me assign roles.

5. They and I appreciated the teacher's support.

6. She and he told the actors about the meeting.

7. You and I were filled with excitement.

8. He and I welcomed the actors to the meeting.

9. Sherry and the others asked him and me questions.

10. Devon helped her and them understand our plans.

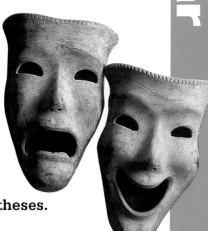

B. Write each sentence. Use the correct word in parentheses.

11. He and (me, I) led the play rehearsals.

12. Actors asked (he, him) and me for help.

13. You and (I, me) know how challenging plays can be.

14. Ms. Reed saw (them, they) and me practice our parts.

15. I showed her and (them, they) the costumes.

16. Sherry reminded him and (me, I) about making sets.

17. (He, Him) and I persuaded Sherry to design the scenery.

18. (She, Her) and I gathered supplies and helpers.

19. Sherry showed them and (I, me) some sketches.

20. The sketches helped (she, her) and us design sets.

C. Combine each pair of sentences by forming compound subjects or compound objects. Write each new sentence.

21. He checked every detail. I checked every detail.

22. Sherry helped him. Sherry helped me.

23. She helped the others dress. I helped the others dress.

24. They were excited about the play. I was excited about the play.

25. The audience applauded for them. The audience applauded for me.

Extra Practice

Possessive Pronouns

A. Write the word in each sentence that is a possessive pronoun.

1. Our science teacher invited two meteorologists to class.

2. Mr. Otto introduced his guests.

3. The guests said their first names, Lorena and Vic.

4. Lorena spoke about her work at the station.

5. Vic explained his job of forecasting weather.

6. I know a coworker of theirs.

7. Vic and Lorena work with my dad.

8. Dad helps the meteorologists write their reports.

9. Our family watches the weather report together.

10. Does your family watch the broadcast, too?

B. Rewrite each sentence by using the correct possessive pronoun in parentheses.

11. Lorena and Vic shared (their, theirs) experiences.

12. Lorena liked (our, ours) questions.

13. I think (my, mine) was the best question of all.

14. I asked about the challenges of (they, their) work.

15. Vic said that (him, his) biggest challenge was waking up at 4:00 A.M.

16. Lorena said (her, hers) was keeping Vic awake.

17. (My, Mine) classmates asked questions about the weather.

18. Lorena and Vic talked about (their, theirs) favorite type of weather.

19. It was the same as (our, ours).

20. (Our, Ours) class thoroughly enjoyed the presentation.

C. Write each sentence. Replace the underlined word or words with the correct possessive pronoun.

21. Vic and Lorena's reports are based on satellite data.

22. Our class wants to visit Lorena's weather station.

23. Your class will visit the station next month.

24. We appreciated Vic's offer to tour the station.

25. The most interesting talk was Lorena's.

Contractions: Pronoun and Verb

A. Write the two words that form each underlined contraction.

1. It's the beginning of a new week.

2. I'm very happy about being in school today.

3. We're planning new projects with our teacher.

4. She's explaining the projects to her aides first.

5. They're listening to her very carefully.

6. Sometimes it's difficult for John to understand.

7. He's sitting in the back of the room.

8. We're asking our teacher if Mrs. Bailey will help us.

9. She's smiling at Mrs. Bailey and us now.

10. You're very pleased to have Mrs. Bailey's assistance.

B. Write each sentence. Replace the underlined words with a contraction.

11. We are starting a fifth-grade buddy system.

12. It is designed to help students in kindergarten.

13. Sometimes they are scared during the first few weeks of school.

14. I am sure the buddy system will be popular.

15. It is a great opportunity for fifth-grade students to help others.

16. She is going to have a "welcome party" to meet our buddies.

17. I know you are hoping to help Jorge.

18. He is a neighbor of mine.

19. I am interested in being buddies with Sumi.

20. I know we are alike.

C. Write each sentence. Use the correct word.

21. (Our, We're) helping Sumi and Jorge learn English.

22. (Their, They're) a bit shy and quiet.

23. (I'm, I) using puppets to teach them some words.

24. (Your, You're) using drawings to share your ideas.

25. (It's, Its) so rewarding being a buddy!

Decide on a Plan

Adverbs, Prepositions, Interjections and Story Writing

In this unit you will learn about adverbs, prepositions, and interjections. You will also learn how to write a fictional story. A work of fiction is a story, or narrative, that a writer creates.

Social Studies Link *Read about the ama, the sea maidens of Japan. Notice how the writer sets up a strong setting, plot, characters, and a problem at the beginning of the piece.*

We are called the ama, the sea maidens of Japan. My mother's mother and even her great-grandmother's mother were fisherwomen who dove to the ocean floor to harvest seafood for the great emperors of Japan.

When I'm older, I'll learn to hold my breath under water for over a minute and gather abalone and seaweed for my family and our village. Okaasan, that is what I call my mama, teaches me to dive and fish along the shallow reefs.

"Kiyomi, when you're older and follow our tradition," she tells me, "you will not have the rope attached to your waist. You must find your own way without me."

from ***The Sea Maidens of Japan*** by Lili Bell

Thinking Like a Writer

Story In a story, the author creates a narrative from imagination. Reread the passage.

• What does the author tell about Kiyomi, the main character?

Prepositions The author used prepositions in her story. Read the sentences again.

QUICK WRITE How do prepositions show direction or location in the story?

Adverbs

— RULES —

An **adverb** is a word that tells more about a verb, an adjective, or another adverb.

Our family drove slowly to the zoo.

Highway safety is a very big problem.

Dad always drives extremely carefully.

An **adverb** can tell *how*, *when*, or *where* an action takes place.

We waited outside for the gates to open. (where)

THINK AND WRITE

Adverbs

Write in your journal how you can tell if a sentence has an adverb.

An adverb is a word that tells more about the verb in a sentence. An adverb can tell *how*, *when*, or *where* an action takes place. Notice that many adverbs end in *-ly*.

How: *Many people waited quietly.*

When: *The gates opened early.*

Where: *The people bought their tickets inside.*

Guided Practice

Name the adverb in each sentence. Tell which verb each adverb describes.

EXAMPLE: I walked quickly to see my favorite animal.
Adverb: quickly; verb: walked

1. I happily watched the polar bears.

2. A polar bear cub lurked nearby.

3. The bear cub looked curiously at me.

4. Another polar bear floated lazily in the water.

5. I always enjoy watching the bears.

REVIEW THE RULES

- An adverb describes a verb, an adjective, or an adverb.

- An adverb tells *how*, *when*, or *where* an action takes place.

More Practice

A. Draw one line under the adverb in each sentence. Draw two lines under the verb it describes.

6. Justin ran quickly to the penguin's pond.

7. The penguins played happily.

8. A crowd gathered nearby.

9. The penguins dove gracefully into the water.

10. The people clapped loudly.

B. Write each sentence. Underline the adverb. Write whether the adverb answers the question *how*, *when*, or *where*.

11. Tyler and Jenny walked ahead.

12. Jenny immediately pointed to a monkey.

13. The monkey tenderly held its baby.

14. The monkey hid swiftly.

15. Tyler waited patiently for the monkey to reappear.

C. **Spiral Review** Write each sentence. Fill in the blank with an adverb. Circle the pronouns. Draw one line under the articles.

16. Have you been to a zoo _____?

17. You _____ have noticed that animals are not kept in cages.

18. Zoos try _____ to make the animals feel at home.

19. The animals live _____ in habitats similar to the way they live in nature.

20. The animals _____ prefer these habitats to a cage of bars!

Extra Practice, page 488.

Handbook
page 540

Writing Activity A Story

Write a story about an experience that could have happened to some friends at the zoo. Use time-order words to organize the events.

APPLY GRAMMAR: Underline the adverbs that you use.

417

Adverbs Before Adjectives and Adverbs

— RULES —

Adverbs describe or tell more about verbs. Adverbs can also tell more about adjectives. Sometimes these adverbs tell to what degree or what extent.

The weather seemed terribly cold.

Adverbs can also tell more about other adverbs.

The ship moved very slowly.

THINK AND WRITE

Adverbs

How can knowing the difference between an adjective and an adverb help you in your writing? Write your ideas in your journal.

Use adverbs to tell more about adjectives or other adverbs.

Storms are a serious problem at sea. → Storms are a *very* serious problem at sea.

The sailors worked quickly. → The sailors worked *extremely* quickly.

Guided Practice

Name the adverb that describes each underlined adverb or adjective.

EXAMPLE: The immigrants sailed in a rather <u>small</u> ship.
rather

1. Families were crowded far <u>below</u>.
2. Many people hoped the trip was almost <u>over</u>.
3. The food and water tasted quite <u>stale</u>.
4. Many passengers waited very <u>patiently</u>.
5. The people were so <u>tired</u> by the end of the trip.
6. Some passengers seemed somewhat <u>excited</u>.
7. The captian of the ship was completely <u>content</u>.
8. His rather <u>precious</u> cargo had reached its destination.
9. Very <u>few</u> problems had occurred.
10. The ship docked fairly <u>speedily</u>.

REVIEW THE RULES

- An adverb can tell more about an adjective.

- An adverb can also tell more about another adverb.

More Practice

A. Write the adverb that describes the underlined word.

11. Some people traveled quite <u>suddenly</u> to America.

12. Religious freedom was very <u>important</u>.

13. Other people wanted a much <u>better</u> chance to earn a living.

14. The United States offered people a fairly <u>better</u> life.

15. The journey to America was extremely <u>difficult</u>.

B. Write each sentence. Write the word that the underlined adverb describes. Tell whether the word is an adjective or another adverb.

16. The ship sailed <u>quite</u> rapidly ahead.

17. The passage to New York could be <u>rather</u> expensive.

18. Decisions to travel were made <u>very</u> carefully.

19. The ship was <u>terribly</u> crowded.

20. The people were <u>finally</u> happy.

Handbook
page 540

C. Spiral Review Write each sentence. Fill in an adverb. Circle the nouns in the sentences. Underline past-tense verbs.

21. _____ suddenly, Colin found himself in a line of people.

22. The crowd seemed _____ unruly.

23. The ship was _____ ready to dock.

24. Passengers scrambled _____ quickly to gather their possessions.

25. The trip ended _____ unexpectedly.

Extra Practice, page 489.

Writing Activity A Paragraph

Write a paragraph about a difficult decision you have had to make. Choose exact words to describe the emotions you felt. Be sure that your "voice" comes through in your writing.

APPLY GRAMMAR: Use adverbs to modify adjectives or other adverbs in your writing.

Comparing with Adverbs

RULES

- An adverb can compare two or more actions.

- Add *-er* to most short adverbs to compare two actions.

    fast ⟶ *faster*

- Add *-est* to most short adverbs to compare more than two actions.

    fast ⟶ *fastest*

- For most adverbs, use *more* to compare two actions if the adverb has two or more syllables.

    eagerly ⟶ *more eagerly*

- For most adverbs, use *most* to compare three or more actions if the adverb has two or more syllables.

    eagerly ⟶ *most eagerly*

THINK AND WRITE

Adverbs

How can you tell when to add *-er* or *-est* or *more* or *most* to an adverb? Write your ideas in your journal.

Either add an ending to an adverb or use *more* or *most*. Do not combine *more* or *most* with *-er* or *-est*.

Guided Practice

Name the adverb form in parentheses that correctly completes each sentence.

> **EXAMPLE:** Carrie spoke (longer, more longer) than Earl.
> *longer*

1. The audience listened (more carefully, most carefully) to Carrie than to Earl.
2. Carrie spoke (more skillfully, skillfulier) than Earl did.
3. Protecting wildlife is debated (more often, more oftener) than any other issue.
4. She presented her arguments (more clearly, more clearer).
5. The audience thought she spoke (more persuasively, most persuasively) of all.

REVIEW THE RULES

- Adverbs that compare two actions use -er or more.

- Adverbs that compare three or more actions use -est or most.

More Practice

A. Write the adverb form in parentheses that correctly completes each sentence.

6. The falcon hunts (more skillfully, most skillfully) than the hawk.

7. Of the falcon and the hawk, the falcon moves (faster, fastest).

8. The hawk (most often, more often) prefers the mouse to the snake.

9. The falcon hunts (more accurately, most accurately) of all large birds.

10. Falcons may be the (more difficult, most difficult) of all birds to train.

B. Write the adverb form that correctly completes each sentence.

11. The cat played (long) than the mouse.

12. A hawk watched the mouse (careful) than the snake did.

13. The snake approached the mouse (slow) than the hawk did.

14. Of the hawk, the eagle, and the falcon, the falcon flies the (fast).

15. Hawks resemble falcons (close) of all birds.

C. Spiral Review Write the sentences. Use the correct form of the adverb. Underline each verb. Circle each pronoun.

16. The hawk cries most loudly than the dove.

17. Of the three, the snake acted the bolder.

18. We now hike most regular than we did last year.

19. You see snakes most often in summer than in winter.

20. I name birds most expertly than my brother does.

Extra Practice, page 490.

Handbook
page 541

Writing Activity A Diary Entry

Write a diary entry from a hawk's point of view. What would it be like to fly above the ground and hunt for your own food? Use strong details to write about a day in your life as a hawk.

APPLY GRAMMAR: Underline adverbs that compare.

Science Link

Negatives

RULES

A **negative** is a word that means "no."

> *Nobody saw me.*
>
> *I have nothing to do.*

Do not use two negatives in the same sentence. This is known as a *double negative.*

Correct a sentence with two negatives by changing one negative to a positive word or by dropping one negative.

We don't help no one.
— *We don't help anyone.*
— *We help no one.*

THiNK AND WRITE

Negatives

How can you correct a double negative in a sentence? In your journal, give two ways.

You can correct a double negative by substituting a positive word for a negative word.

Negative	Positive
no, nothing	am, anything
never	ever
no one, nobody	anyone, anybody
nowhere	anywhere

Guided Practice

Name the negative word in each sentence.

> **EXAMPLE:** No day has ever been so exciting!
> *Negative word: No*

1. The day wasn't windy.

2. We have never been in a hot-air balloon before.

3. No one was as excited as Tony.

4. Kira doesn't know when we will start.

5. Nobody seems as brave as we are.

REVIEW THE RULES

- A **negative** is a word that means "no" or "not."
- Use only one negative word in a sentence.

More Practice

A. Write each sentence. Draw one line under the negative word.

6. Yolanda couldn't see her house from above.

7. Nothing feels as free as this ride.

8. We won't forget this experience.

9. No one thought the trip would be so cold.

10. The descent shouldn't be so fast.

B. Write each sentence. Change one of the negatives in each sentence to a positive word to make the sentence correct.

11. They didn't know nothing about ballooning.

12. Tony couldn't do nothing after the trip.

13. We never did nothing more fun.

14. The balloon couldn't be no more beautiful.

15. No one can't wait until next time.

C. **Spiral Review** **Write each interrogative sentence as a declarative sentence. Then underline each negative in the new sentence. Circle each adjective.**

16. Aren't you going there for a long vacation?

17. Isn't there anyone you would like to take along?

18. Can't you play that sport well?

19. Don't you have a favorite place to visit?

20. Wouldn't you like to fly in a huge balloon?

Extra Practice, page 491.

Handbook
pages 526, 541

Writing Activity A Humorous Anecdote

Write a funny short story about a character who believes that he or she can't do anything right. Create a humorous event that convinces your character that this is not true. Use exact words that will let your audience "see" your character exactly as you do.

APPLY GRAMMAR: Underline negative words. Correct any double negatives.

Punctuation in Dialogue

RULES

Use quotation marks before and after a direct quotation.

"What is that object?" asked Riley.

Begin a quotation with a capital letter.

Kelsey replied, "Maybe it's a tool."

Use a comma or commas to separate a phrase, such as *he said*, from the quotation itself. Place a comma or a period inside closing quotation marks.

"It looks like a toy to me," he said.

"I can see," Riley added, "that it has two wings."

Kelsey said, "Let's take a closer look."

Begin a new paragraph to show that a different person is speaking.

THINK AND WRITE

Punctuation in Dialogue

Why is it important to use quotation marks around someone's exact words? Write your ideas in your journal.

Place a question mark or an exclamation mark inside the quotation marks when it is part of the quotation. Place it outside the quotation marks when it is part of the entire sentence but not part of the quotation.

Kelsey exclaimed, "What a strange object it is!"

Did Riley say, "It's a flying machine"?

Guided Practice

Tell which part of each sentence is a direct quotation.

EXAMPLE: Riley said, "Look at this amazing machine."
Direct quotation: "Look at this amazing machine."

1. Valerie asked, "Do you think that machine could fly?"

2. "I don't know for sure," replied Riley.

3. Riley added, "It was designed by William S. Henson."

4. "Have you ever built a model airplane?" Valerie asked.

5. "No," exclaimed Kelsey, "but it would be fun!"

REVIEW THE RULES

- **Quotation marks** enclose a person's exact words. A new paragraph is used for each new person who speaks.

- A comma or a period goes inside closing quotation marks.

- A question mark or an exclamation mark goes *inside* the quotation marks when it is part of the quotation.

More Practice

A. Write the direct quotation in each sentence.

6. "Do you have any ideas?" asked Jenna.

7. Kelsey replied, "Let's each design our own glider."

8. "I'll make mine look like a jet," stated Riley.

9. Valerie exclaimed, "I want mine to be able to loop."

10. "Mine will definitely go the farthest!" shouted Kelsey.

B. Write each sentence. Use correct capitalization and punctuation, including quotation marks and commas.

11. are we ready for a test flight asked Riley

12. I feel like Orville or Wilbur Wright exclaimed Jenna.

13. Did Jenna say my glider doesn't have an engine?

14. Kelsey screamed my glider went the farthest!

15. When will we do this again asked Jenna.

C. Spiral Review **Write each sentence correctly.**

16. "Have you ever been to kitty Hawk?" asked my teacher.

17. I replied "isn't that where the wright brothers flew the first airplane?"

18. " it was the first motorized flight" added Jenna.

19. "your right! exclaimed my teacher.

20. "Did the Wright brothers build they're own plane" I asked.

Extra Practice, page 492.

Handbook
pages 552–556

Writing Activity A News Article

Write a short news article about a time when you and someone else were speaking while waiting to board a bus, a train, or an airplane. Use words that sound like real dialogue.

APPLY MECHANICS AND USAGE: Use quotation marks correctly.

Mixed Review

REVIEW THE RULES

- An **adverb** tells *how*, *when*, or *where* an action takes place.

- An **adverb** can tell more about an adjective or another adverb.

- **Adverbs** that compare two actions use *-er* or *more*. Adverbs that compare three or more actions use *-est* or *most*.

- A **negative** is a word that means "no" or "not." Use only one negative in a sentence.

- **Quotation marks** set off a direct quotation.

- A comma or commas separate a phrase, such as *she said*, from the quotation itself.

- A comma or a period goes inside closing quotation marks.

- A question mark or an exclamation mark goes inside the quotation marks when it is part of the quotation, and outside the quotation marks when it is part of the entire sentence.

QUICK WRITE

Adverbs

Write five sentences about music. Use an adverb in each sentence.

Practice

A. Write the sentences. Underline each adverb.

1. Tyrone and his family regularly go to outdoor concerts.
2. A pop music concert was recently held at the park.
3. People always take a picnic basket to the concert.
4. Tyrone happily carries the basket of food.
5. The concerts are held nearby.
6. Tyrone's family will thoroughly enjoy themselves.
7. His father listens more closely than he does.
8. Tyrone's mother really likes the music.
9. She thinks the tempo is very upbeat.
10. His mother eagerly awaits the next concert.

B. **Write the sentences. Correct the double negative in each sentence. Underline direct quotations.**

11. Courtney said, "I don't like no new music."

12. Yoko replied, "I haven't never heard this drummer before."

13. No one had no reason to complain.

14. "I haven't never been to an outdoor concert," said Alex.

15. "Haven't you not seen this violinist before?" asked Morgan.

16. Nothing never sounded so lovely.

17. "The weather hasn't never been this warm before," remarked Kay.

18. The concert didn't seem no longer than before.

19. Yoko wasn't sleepy no more.

20. Valerie said, "I won't never forget this experience."

C. **Challenge** **Write the following sentences. Use the correct punctuation for direct quotations.**

21. Grandfather, when did you begin playing the guitar I asked.

22. "I began playing when I was about your age he said.

23. I asked him, how long did it take before you were really good?"

24. He replied I practiced every day for a while.

25. My grandfather then smiled and remarked one day, I just found that I was a good musician!

Handbook
pages 540–541,
552–556

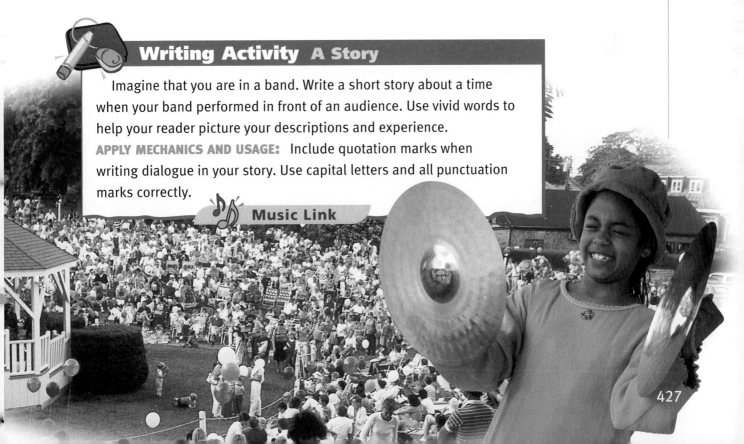

Writing Activity A Story

Imagine that you are in a band. Write a short story about a time when your band performed in front of an audience. Use vivid words to help your reader picture your descriptions and experience.

APPLY MECHANICS AND USAGE: Include quotation marks when writing dialogue in your story. Use capital letters and all punctuation marks correctly.

♪♫ **Music Link**

Prepositions

RULES

A **preposition** is a word that relates a noun or pronoun to another word in a sentence.

This book about bicycles is Ted's.

Common Prepositions

about	among	beside	from	off	to
above	around	between	in	on	under
across	at	by	inside	out	until
after	before	down	into	outside	up
against	behind	during	near	over	with
along	below	for	of	through	without

THINK AND WRITE

Prepositions

In your journal, write how you can recognize a preposition in a sentence.

Guided Practice

Name the preposition in each sentence.

> **EXAMPLE:** We filled the bicycle tires with air.   *with*

1. We drove into the park.
2. Our bicycles were in the car rack.
3. We stopped beside the bike trail.
4. We followed the trail over a hill.
5. The sun was shining through the trees.
6. Billy rode under a bridge.
7. I followed behind him.
8. Suddenly, he stopped by a brook.
9. Near the water, we saw a deer.
10. We watched quietly for a few minutes.

REVIEW THE RULES

- A **preposition** relates a noun or pronoun to another word in a sentence.

More Practice

A. Write the preposition in each sentence.

11. We rode across town.

12. I could see birds along the water's edge.

13. My friend rode beside me.

14. We coasted down a hill.

15. During vacation, we often ride together.

B. Write the sentence. Use a preposition to complete each sentence.

16. The trail went _____ the bridge.

17. _____ the next hour, we enjoyed our ride.

18. People were playing baseball _____ the park.

19. It was difficult riding _____ the wind.

20. We rode _____ dark.

C. **Spiral Review** **Complete each sentence with a possessive pronoun. Then, circle the preposition in each sentence. Underline each of the verbs.**

21. He rode to _____ house on his new bike.

22. _____ new house is by a lake.

23. He parked _____ bike beside mine.

24. "Wear _____ helmet on the ride," my mother said.

25. We had a good time at _____ picnic.

Extra Practice, page 493.

Handbook
page 542

Writing Activity A Paragraph

Write a paragraph about a trip you have taken, perhaps on your bicycle. Write a strong lead and ending. "Build up" your ideas from beginning to end.

APPLY GRAMMAR: Underline each preposition that you use.

Prepositional Phrases

RULES

- A **prepositional phrase** is a group of words that begins with a preposition and ends with a noun or pronoun.

  The heart is an organ in the body.

- The **object of a preposition** is the noun or pronoun that follows the preposition.

  The heart is an organ in the body.

A prepositional phrase can be at the beginning, in the middle, or at the end of a sentence. A *phrase* is a group of words that does not have a subject and a predicate.

Beginning	*During exercise, our heart beats faster.*
Middle	*The heart inside your body beats regularly.*
End	*Swimming and running are examples of exercise.*

Guided Practice

Name the prepositional phrase in each sentence.

EXAMPLE: In our science class, we discuss the heart.
In our science class

1. Veins and arteries are types of blood vessels.
2. The arteries carry blood from the heart.
3. The veins carry blood to the heart.
4. In a minute, your heart beats 70 times.
5. Valves control blood flow through the heart.
6. Your heart is the size of your fist.
7. All animals with backbones have hearts.
8. The heart is divided into two chambers.
9. Your heart is near your lungs.
10. New medicines can guard against heart attacks.

THINK AND WRITE

Prepositions
How does knowing about prepositional phrases help you write clearer and more interesting sentences? Write your ideas in your journal.

REVIEW THE RULES

- A prepositional phrase begins with a preposition and ends with a noun or pronoun. The noun or pronoun is the object of the preposition.

More Practice

A. Write the prepositional phrase in each sentence.

11. Red blood cells carry oxygen through the body.

12. There are four chambers inside the heart.

13. Each chamber in the heart pumps blood.

14. At the top, there are two atria.

15. The bottom of the heart has two ventricles.

B. Write each sentence. Draw one line under the prepositional phrase. Draw two lines under the object of the preposition.

16. Blood follows a path through the body.

17. Blood enters the heart at the right chambers.

18. In the lungs, blood receives more oxygen.

19. Blood then returns to the heart.

20. The heart then pumps blood through the arteries.

C. **Spiral Review** Write the following letter. Use correct capitalization and punctuation. Circle the prepositional phrases.

         21. may 5, 2003

22. Dear Andrea

23.   Did you know that the heart we draw for valentine's day looks nothing like our real heart **24.** Our heart is the size of our fist and it is almost the same shape. I thought you would like to know this information.

         25. Your friend
          Miguel

Extra Practice, page 494.

Handbook
page 543

Writing Activity A Comic Strip

Draw a comic strip about decisions you make to keep your heart healthy. Present your ideas in a logical order.

APPLY GRAMMAR: Use prepositional phrases in your writing.

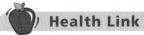 **Health Link**

Object Pronouns in Prepositional Phrases

RULES

An **object pronoun** is the pronoun that follows a preposition in a sentence.

An **object pronoun** can take the place of a noun in a prepositional phrase.

> *My friends planned a surprise party for Sally.*
>
> *My friends planned a surprise party for her.*

Use the object pronouns **me**, **you**, **him**, **her**, **it**, **us**, and **them** as objects in prepositional phrases.

THINK AND WRITE

Prepositions

How can you decide which object pronoun to use in a prepositional phrase? Write your ideas in your journal.

Some sentences have compound objects. To be sure you have used pronouns correctly in a compound object, leave out the other object in the compound and check the pronoun alone.

> *My brother will ride with my mother and me.*
>
> *My brother will ride with me.*

Guided Practice

Name the prepositional phrase in each sentence. Then name the object pronoun in the prepositional phrase.

EXAMPLE: The invitations were sent to them.
Prepositional phrase: to them
Object pronoun: them

1. Kimberly made a coconut birthday cake for us.

2. She has the best recipe for it.

3. Marla gave lemonade to Sally and me.

4. Glen will sing a birthday song to you.

5. The birthday candles will be lit by him.

REVIEW THE RULES

- An object pronoun is the pronoun that follows a preposition in a sentence.

- Use the object pronouns *me, you, him, her, it, us,* and *them* as objects in the prepositional phrases.

More Practice

A. **Write the prepositional phrase in each sentence. Draw two lines under the object pronoun.**

6. The party will start tomorrow for us.

7. My friends prepared food with my mother and you.

8. The room will be decorated by him.

9. Dad will collect the gifts from them.

10. They will be given to her and me.

B. **Write each sentence. Choose the correct pronoun.**

11. Mother gave the flowers to Amy and (she, her).

12. The delivery person placed the balloons beside (he, him).

13. Lloyd arranged the table for (us, we).

14. Yohji patiently held the streamers for (they, them).

15. Dad mixed the salsa with Kimberly and (I, you).

C. **Spiral Review** **Write the sentences. Use the correct object pronoun in place of the underlined noun in the prepositional phrases. Circle the adverbs. Underline each common noun.**

16. Sally arrived somewhat early with Mrs. Smith.

17. We were quite ready for Sally.

18. Sally sat down beside Thomas.

19. The food made by Mr. Smith was excellently prepared.

20. Everyone had a good time at the party for Sally and Jo.

Extra Practice, page 495.

Handbook
page 543

Writing Activity A Dialogue

Write a dialogue between two students who are attending a birthday party. Use vivid words to talk about the fun they are having.

APPLY GRAMMAR: Underline the prepositional phrases in your dialogue. Circle the object pronouns.

Interjections

RULES

An **interjection** is a word or group of words that expresses strong feeling.

> *Oh, that looks delicious.*

Use a **comma** after a mild interjection.

> *Gee, the menu has many interesting dishes.*

Use an **exclamation mark** after an interjection that expresses very strong feeling.

> *Wow! That's my favorite food.*

THINK AND WRITE

Interjections

How can interjections help you express strong emotion in your writing? Write your ideas in your journal.

When an exclamation mark comes after an interjection, the next word in the sentence begins with a capital letter. In this way, the interjection is set off from the rest of the sentence.

> *A new restaurant has opened.*

> *Well, a new restaurant has opened.*

> *Great! A new restaurant has opened.*

Guided Practice

Underline the interjection in each sentence.

EXAMPLE: Look, the new restaurant has opened.
Look

1. Oh, we have heard about this restaurant for weeks.

2. Well, my family wants to eat dinner there.

3. Gee, we should go to dinner early.

4. My, this restaurant serves great food!

5. Oops! Put your napkin in your lap.

REVIEW THE RULES

- An interjection expresses strong emotion.

- Use a comma after a mild interjection and an exclamation mark after a strong interjection.

More Practice

A. **Write the interjection in each sentence.**

6. Wow! Something smells delicious.

7. Oh, will you please sit down!

8. My goodness, I am getting hungry.

9. Well, do you know what you will order?

10. Aha! I see they have chicken in garlic sauce.

B. **Write each sentence. Use the correct capitalization and punctuation.**

11. Yum this chicken tastes wonderful

12. Well I have plenty to eat

13. Hooray they have ice cream for dessert

14. Oh we don't see that on the menu

15. Yikes did you see the check

Handbook
pages 542–543

C. **Spiral Review** **Write each sentence. Circle the interjections. Then use the plural form of the underlined nouns. Draw one line under the adjectives and two lines under the adverbs.**

16. Last week, we went to my favorite restaurant.

17. Well, they always serve exceptionally fine pie.

18. Gee, the table is set with beautiful crystal goblet and silverware.

19. Wow! This restaurant is great for party and wedding!

20. Hooray! What a wonderful restaurant this is for the family in town!

Extra Practice, page 496.

Writing Activity A Review

Imagine that you are a restaurant critic for a local newspaper. Pick one of your favorite restaurants and write a paragraph that gives your opinion about the food, the service, and the decorations. Use opinion words, such as *I believe* or *I feel,* to get across your points.

APPLY GRAMMAR: Underline the interjections that you use.

Combining Sentences: Complex Sentences

THINK AND WRITE

Complex Sentences

How does knowing about complex sentences help your writing? Write your ideas in your journal.

Use these joining words, or conjunctions, to connect two closely related ideas:

More Conjunctions

after	before	than	when
although	if	though	whenever
as	since	unless	where
because	so that	until	while

Guided Practice

Name the conjunction that joins words and ideas in each sentence.

> **EXAMPLE:** I dug a hole before Whitney planted the seed.
> *before*

1. Whitney likes gardening because it is relaxing.

2. I help her since I enjoy gardening, too.

3. We put on gloves before we start.

4. After we plant the seeds, we pat the soil.

5. When we are done, we water the seeds.

REVIEW THE RULES

- A complex sentence has two closely related ideas joined by a conjunction such as: *after, although, as, because, before, if, since, unless, until,* and *when*.

More Practice

A. Write the sentences. Draw one line under each of the two ideas in the sentence. Circle the conjunction that joins them.

6. I like working when the air is cool.

7. Whitney turned the soil before she began to plant.

8. We planted flowers because they are colorful.

9. Whitney wants to work until the sun sets.

10. We will stop after the sun gets hot.

B. Combine each pair of sentences into one sentence. Use the conjunction in parentheses. Write the new sentence.

11. The daisies looked wilted. They were watered. (before)

12. I took a break. The weather was hot. (because)

13. Flowers are expensive. I grow my own. (unless)

14. Whitney made a bouquet. We picked some flowers. (after)

15. We were happy. We were tired. (although)

C. Spiral Review Write the sentences. Complete each sentence by using an adjective or an adverb. Circle the conjunctions. Underline the helping verbs.

16. Bryan walked through the _____ garden gate.

17. Each bush inside had been cut _____ in the shape of an animal.

18. "This is _____," he remarked after he had explored the garden.

19. He thought the garden was _____ although it looked strange.

20. _____ he turned around as he heard a figure approaching.

Extra Practice, page 497.

Handbook
pages 526–527

Writing Activity Instructions

Write instructions about how to grow your own garden. Explain what you would plant and how. Give your steps in a logical order.

APPLY GRAMMAR: Include complex sentences. Draw a circle around the conjunctions that connect two ideas.

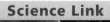

Science Link

Commas with Introductory Prepositional Phrases and Interjections

─ RULES ─

Use a comma after a prepositional phrase at the beginning of a sentence.

For sunburn protection, I wear sunscreen.

Use a comma after a mild interjection.

My, this sunburn is uncomfortable.

Use a comma to invert the order of a sentence that has a prepositional phrase.

Original: *Our skin can be damaged from the sun.*

Inverted: *From the sun, our skin can be damaged.*

THINK AND WRITE

Prepositional Phrases and Interjections

Why is it important to know how to use commas with prepositional phrases and interjections? Write your ideas in your journal.

Guided Practice

Name the prepositional phrase or the interjection that begins each sentence.

EXAMPLE: Well, skin protects the body.
Interjection: Well

1. In the shade, you can still get a sunburn.
2. After a sunburn, our skin is tender.
3. Gee, sunscreen can protect our skin.
4. Before outdoor activity, put on sunscreen.
5. Oh, wear a hat to protect the skin, too.
6. Why, Darla! Apply sunscreen before you play tennis.
7. Below the eyes, the skin is very delicate.
8. With your fingers, apply the cream.
9. Yuck! I hate the smell!
10. On hot days, wear white.

More Practice

A. Write the prepositional phrase or the interjection in each sentence.

11. My goodness, the skin is a large organ.

12. After stretching, our skin would be 15 square feet!

13. Yikes! Our skin is long.

14. By sweating, the skin keeps us cool.

15. Well, without oil glands our skin would be dry.

B. Write each sentence. Draw one line under each interjection or prepositional phrase. Place commas where needed.

16. Look the epidermis is the top layer.

17. Under the epidermis the dermis layer is found.

18. In the dermis layer we find the blood vessels.

19. In the epidermis cells give us our skin color.

20. Wow skin contains many different things!

C. Spiral Review **Write the sentences. Use commas correctly. Circle conjunctions. Underline adjectives.**

21. During July we went to the beach every day.

22. The weather was hot and we enjoyed it.

23. In our bags we had a straw hat a scarf and sunscreen.

24. Gee in the afternoon the sun was strong.

25. Well plan carefully if you want a nice day at the beach.

Extra Practice, page 498.

Handbook
pages 542–543, 554–555

Writing Activity A Story

Write a story about someone who gets a sunburn on the first day of vacation. Be sure your story has a strong beginning, middle, and end.

APPLY MECHANICS AND USAGE: Draw one line under each prepositional phrase and two lines under each interjection.

Mixed Review

REVIEW THE RULES

- A **preposition** is a word that relates a noun or pronoun to another word in the sentence.

- A **prepositional phrase** begins with a preposition and ends with a noun or pronoun.

- The **object of the preposition** is the noun or pronoun in a prepositional phrase.

- An **interjection** is a word at the beginning of a sentence that shows strong feeling.

- A **complex sentence** contains two related ideas joined by a conjunction such as *although*, *because*, *if*, *since*, *until*, and *when*.

QUICK WRITE

Prepositions and Interjections

Write five sentences about what you like about social studies. Include at least three prepositional phrases and two interjections.

Practice

A. Write each sentence. Draw one line under the prepositional phrase. Draw two lines under the preposition in the phrase. Circle the object of the preposition.

1. After the Civil War, many people went West.

2. They came to the gold fields.

3. Homesteaders wanted new lives for their families.

4. For other folks, gold was their goal.

5. Wagon trains traveled across the country.

6. Some wagons went to the Oregon Territory.

7. Other pioneers moved south into California.

8. Over the mountains, the wagons moved.

9. Travel was easiest along riverbeds.

10. Under the stars, people slept.

B. Write each sentence. Add an interjection or phrase to the beginning of each sentence. Underline each prepositional phrase.

11. Many events changed the way of life in the West forever.

12. Gold was discovered in California.

13. Miners unearthed silver in Nevada.

14. The Pony Express carried mail to miners.

15. Inexpensive land brought settlers to the West.

16. Trappers hunted animals for the fur trade.

17. Cattle drives brought meat to the West.

18. A railroad was completed linking East to West.

19. The increase in population caused problems for the Native Americans.

20. Life in the Old West was a challenge!

C. Challenge Write each pair of sentences as a complex sentence. Underline the conjunction that joins the two ideas.

21. Many immigrants came. Work was available.

22. People came in droves. Gold was discovered.

23. Many miners needed supplies. Merchants made a fortune.

24. Families started farms. The government sold land.

25. President Lincoln signed the Homestead Act. People were given acres of land.

Extra Practice, page 499.

Handbook
pages 542–543

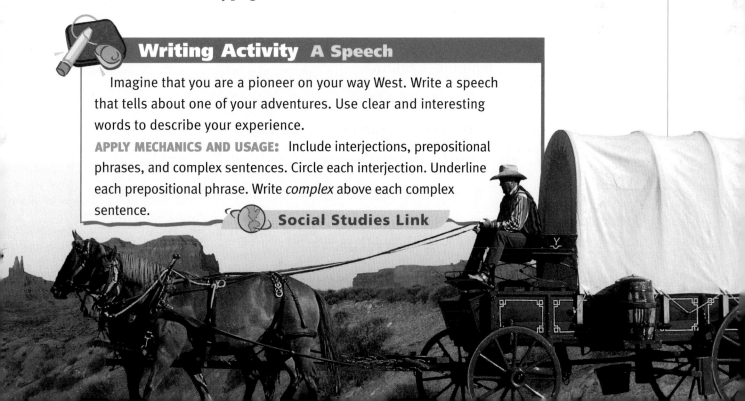

Writing Activity A Speech

Imagine that you are a pioneer on your way West. Write a speech that tells about one of your adventures. Use clear and interesting words to describe your experience.

APPLY MECHANICS AND USAGE: Include interjections, prepositional phrases, and complex sentences. Circle each interjection. Underline each prepositional phrase. Write *complex* above each complex sentence.

Social Studies Link

Common Errors with Adverbs

As a writer, it is important to know the difference between adjectives and adverbs. It is also important not to use a double negative in a sentence. When you revise your own writing, look carefully for double negatives and for adjectives and adverbs that you may have confused. This chart shows examples of the different kinds of errors to look for and how to correct them.

Common Errors	Examples	Corrected Sentences
Using an adjective in place of an adverb	The ship moved slow in bad weather.	The ship moved slowly in bad weather.
Using good *instead of* well	The captain ran the ship good.	The captain ran the ship well.
Using double negatives	The captain won't never desert the ship.	The captain won't ever desert the ship. *or* The captain will never desert the ship.

THINK AND WRITE

Adverbs

In your journal, explain how you can correct a double negative in a sentence.

REVIEW THE RULES

ADVERBS

- An adjective describes or tells more about a noun. An adverb tells more about a verb, an adjective, or another adverb.

- *Good* is always an adjective; *well* is an adverb, except when it means "healthy."

  Jane always does a good job. (adjective)

  She does her chores well. (adverb)

  You felt well this morning. (adjective)

- Do not use two negative words together in the same sentence.

- Remember Some adverbs have an *-ly* ending, which makes them easy to recognize.

- Remember For most adverbs, do not change the spelling of the base word when you add *-ly*.

More Practice

A. Choose *good* or *well* to complete each sentence correctly. Write the word.

1. The Spanish explorers thought Florida was a (good, well) place to land.

2. The trip had been hard, but the sailors did (good, well).

3. They thought their supplies would be (good, well) for many months.

4. A hurricane destroyed their (good, well) planning.

5. The ship did not ride the storm (good, well).

B. Write the sentences. Choose the correct word in parentheses to complete each sentence. Be sure to avoid a double negative.

6. No one from this Spanish ship (never, ever) settled in Florida.

7. It (wasn't, was) no easy task to find a sunken ship at the bottom of the bay.

8. For 450 years, there was no sign (anywhere, nowhere) of the Spanish ship.

9. The waves hadn't scattered (none, any) of the ship's cargo.

10. Archaeologists never (did, didn't) give up the search for the ship.

C. Rewrite each sentence correctly. Remember not to change the spelling of the base word when you add *-ly*.

11. The ship moved direct toward the storm.

12. A hurricane blew fierce, sinking the ship.

13. Archaeologists explored tireless for signs of the ship.

14. Clam and mussel shells held tight to the remains of the ship.

15. Do you think the scientists were real interested in finding the ship?

Grammar Troubleshooter, pages 522–523

Handbook
pages 540–541

Writing Activity A Story

  Imagine that you are one of the scientists looking for the sunken Spanish ship. Write a story about your search. Include action and a strong setting and characters. Give the events in the order in which they could have happened.

  APPLY GRAMMAR: Use adverbs correctly to tell more about your action verbs. Correct any double negatives.

Science Link

Mechanics and Spelling

Directions

Read the passage and decide which type of mistake, if any, appears in each underlined section. Choose the letter for your answer. If there is no error, choose "No mistake."

A sentence always begins with a capital letter.

Be sure that the correct homophone is used in a sentence.

Remember that nouns do not need an apostrophe unless they show possession.

Sample

Last Saturday, my family hiked in the forest.

<u>the</u> shady paths kept us cool. <u>We could here birds</u>
(1)   (2)

chirping excitedly and looked up in a tree to find a

mother bird in the process of building her nest. Then we

heard a soft rustle in the leaves. We turned around and

<u>watched a family of squirrel's</u> scampering under a group
(3)

of oak trees. Finally, we reached a huge waterfall and

jumped into the pond at its base. The cool water felt

refreshing after our long hike.

---

1 A Spelling

   B Capitalization

   C Punctuation

   D No mistake

2 F Spelling

   G Capitalization

   H Punctuation

   J No mistake

3 A Spelling

   B Capitalization

   C Punctuation

   D No mistake

Test Tip
Select only one answer choice for each item.

Grammar and Usage

Directions

Read the passage and choose the word or group of words that belongs in each space. Choose the letter for your answer.

Sample

Montana is known as the Treasure State. How did it get that name? Montana is our country's fourth __(1)__ state. Plenty of wide-open spaces can still be found within its borders. Bighorn sheep, grizzly bear, moose, and elk __(2)__ in the northern part of Montana. The state has copper mines that at one time __(3)__ half of the copper for the United States. The Rocky Mountains and the Missouri River cut an __(4)__ path through the middle of Montana's vast countryside. Montana contains many treasures indeed.

When comparing three or more items, add -est to an adjective that has one syllable.

Look for the subject in the sentence and select a verb that agrees with that subject.

Reread the entire passage to help you decide on its tense.

Use an adjective to modify a noun.

1 A largest

   B larger

   C more larger

   D most largest

2 F lives

   G live

   H is living

   J has lived

3 A is supplying

   B supplies

   C will supply

   D supplied

4 F amaze

   G amazing

   H amazingly

   J amazes

TIME FOR KIDS Writer's Notebook

RESEARCH

RESEARCH

When I do research, I start at the **card catalog** in the library media center. Most books are listed in three ways—by author, by title, and by subject. Everything is in alphabetical order. Whether the catalog is on-line or printed on cards, the filing system is the same. How would you start a search for information about <u>telescopes</u>?

COMPOSITION SKILLS

WRITING WELL

To write good **dialogue** and to capture someone's voice, you have to be a good listener. I pay very close attention to how people sound and what they actually say. Including dialogue that sounds real will spice up any story!

VOCABULARY SKILLS

USING WORDS

Billions of ice-blue stars glitter like diamonds scattered on a black velvet carpet. When I describe the night sky this way, I'm using **figurative language**: words used out of their ordinary meaning to add beauty or force to a description. It helps me write in a way that's out of this world!

Read Now!

As you read the photo essay, look for examples of figurative language and write them down.

446

TIME FOR KIDS

PHOTO ESSAY

Is There Life in Outer Space?

Scientists are searching harder than ever for signs of life on other planets.

Are We Alone?

Are we humans the only ones in the universe gazing up from our planet and asking, "Who else is out there?" It could be that among the billions of stars, there are other planets with other living creatures. And among those creatures, there could be intelligent ones, wondering if there's life on Earth!

People have been wondering if there is life in the big soup pot of the universe for hundreds of years. Only now, in the age of powerful telescopes, can we begin to find out.

In 1996, scientists Geoffrey Marcy and Paul Butler discovered two new planets traveling around distant stars that are similar to our sun. These are the first planets found outside our solar system that could possibly support life. The planets are giant, stormy balls of poisonous gases. But high up in their atmosphere may be the key ingredient for life as we know it: liquid water.

*inter*NET CONNECTION **Go to** www.mhschool.com/language-arts **for more information on the topic.**

If there are living creatures on the planets discovered by Marcy and Butler, they might look like these. Such creatures would float high in the atmosphere, never touching the planets' hot, gaseous surfaces.

The Lowell Observatory in Arizona operates eight telescopes in the U.S. and one in Australia. They are used to learn more about the universe.

Tony & Daphne Hallas/SPL/Photo Researchers

THEY CALL ME AN ALIEN?

Write Now!

You're watching TV when an alien appears on your screen, calls you by name, and starts asking you questions about what kids like to do for fun on Earth. Write to tell about what you did last week for fun.

Use the Card Catalog

The **card catalog** is made up of cards that list every book in the library. These cards may be found in drawers arranged alphabetically. They may also be found on-line. Every book in the library has at least two cards—an **author card** and a **title card**. Some fiction books and most nonfiction books also have a **subject card**. All three cards give the same information about a book. However, the information is arranged differently on the cards.

When you know the author of the book but not the title, use the author card. When you know the name of the book but not who wrote it, use the title card. Use the subject card when you do not have any authors or titles in mind but are looking for a particular topic.

Notice the number in the upper-left-hand corner of the cards. This is the call number. It tells you where to find the book on the library shelf.

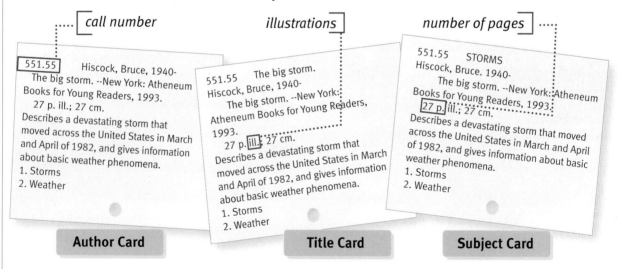

call number

> 551.55   Hiscock, Bruce, 1940-
> The big storm. --New York: Atheneum Books for Young Readers, 1993.
>   27 p. ill.; 27 cm.
> Describes a devastating storm that moved across the United States in March and April of 1982, and gives information about basic weather phenomena.
> 1. Storms
> 2. Weather

Author Card

illustrations

> 551.55   The big storm.
> Hiscock, Bruce, 1940-
>   The big storm. --New York: Atheneum Books for Young Readers, 1993.
>   27 p. ill.; 27 cm.
> Describes a devastating storm that moved across the United States in March and April of 1982, and gives information about basic weather phenomena.
> 1. Storms
> 2. Weather

Title Card

number of pages

> 551.55   STORMS
> Hiscock, Bruce. 1940-
>   The big storm. --New York: Atheneum Books for Young Readers, 1993.
>   27 p. ill.; 27 cm.
> Describes a devastating storm that moved across the United States in March and April of 1982, and gives information about basic weather phenomena.
> 1. Storms
> 2. Weather

Subject Card

Many libraries also have an **on-line catalog**. You can use this computer catalog instead of the card catalog to search for authors, titles, and subjects of books. To find a book on-line, you could do the following:

1. Type in the subject, *storms*.

2. The computer will show a list of all the books in the library on this subject. Each item is numbered.

3. For more information about an item, type in its number.

4. You will see a screen with information about the book. Follow the on-screen directions to use any computer catalog in the library. If you have trouble with your search, ask a librarian for help. Here is how the computer screen for *The Big Storm* might look.

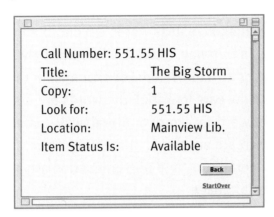

Call Number: 551.55 HIS
Title: The Big Storm
Copy: 1
Look for: 551.55 HIS
Location: Mainview Lib.
Item Status Is: Available

Back

StartOver

Practice

A. **Use the author, title, and subject cards on the opposite page to write answers to these questions.**

1. What is the title of the book?

2. Who is the author?

3. What is the subject?

4. How many pages does the book have?

5. Would *The Big Storm* be in the fiction or the nonfiction section of the library? How do you know?

B. **Write whether you would use an author card, a title card, or a subject card to answer each of the following questions.**

6. How many books in the library are by Bruce Hiscock?

7. Who is the author of *The Wreck of the Zephyr*?

8. Which books about sailing does the library have?

9. Who wrote *An Island Scrapbook*?

10. Does the library have any books about volcanoes?

*inter*NET
CONNECTION

Go to:
www.mhschool.
com/language-arts
for more
information
on the topic.

Writing Activity A Book Review

Use the card catalog in the library to find another book about storms or the weather. Read the book and write a book review about it. Be sure to give a brief summary of the book. Also include your recommendation. Do you think your classmates would like to read the book? Why or why not?

Vocabulary: Figurative Language

THINK AND WRITE

Figurative Language

How does figurative language create pictures in the reader's mind? Explain your thoughts in your journal.

DEFINITION

Figurative language uses words beyond their usual or literal meaning. In this way, figurative language gives added meaning to a word or an expression. For example, in the expression, "I'm up to my ears in work," the words are not supposed to be taken in a word-for-word, or literal, way. Instead, they are meant to create an image, or mental picture, for the reader. Similes, metaphors, and personification are all examples of figurative language.

A simile compares two things that are not alike by using the words *like* or *as*.

Her horse ran like lightning.
Her horse moved as fast as a bolt of lightning.

A metaphor compares two unlike things without using words of comparison. A metaphor doesn't say that one thing is like another. It says that one thing *is* another.

Her horse is a bolt of lightning.

Personification gives human qualities to animals, ideas, and objects.

The horses danced with joy when the oats arrived.

Read the paragraph below. Look at each highlighted example of figurative language.

Our rodeo day began with the promise of excitement. The first event was the wild bull riding. The stone-faced cowboy took his seat on the leering bull. When the gate opened, the bull moved like a bullet into the arena. As quick as a wink, the cowboy was no longer on the bull, but dusting himself off instead.

Practice

A. Write the sentences and underline each example of figurative language.

1. He was as strong as a bull.

2. Her eyes sparkled like diamonds.

3. His eyes were stars in the midnight sky.

4. The bull strutted around the ring.

5. The rodeo clown was as awkward as a donkey.

B. Rewrite each sentence by choosing a word or expression from the Word Bank to replace the underlined description.

> a ray of sunshine
> as swiftly as a diving swallow
> like pools of sparkling green water
>
> ready to rumble
> like a worn trail

6. I darted out of the rain <u>quickly</u>.

7. The cowboy looked <u>tired</u>.

8. His horse seemed <u>lively</u>.

9. The cowboy still had a smile that was <u>cheerful</u>.

10. His eyes were <u>shiny green</u>.

C. **Grammar Link** Rewrite each sentence by using a simile or a metaphor to replace the word or words in parentheses.

11. Wow! The horse in that gate is (white).

12. Gee, that clown has a (wide smile).

13. Oh, that horse ran (quickly) around the barrels!

14. My goodness, the crowd broke out in (loud applause)!

15. Well, the crowd is (leaving in single file).

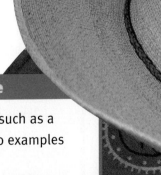

Writing Activity A News Article

Write a brief news article describing an exciting event, such as a rodeo or a circus, that you have seen or attended. Use two examples of figurative language in your writing.

APPLY GRAMMAR: Include interjections to express strong feeling. Circle each interjection that you use.

Composition: Dialogue

Dialogue is the written conversation between two or more characters in a story. It can also show what a character is thinking.

GUIDELINES

- **Dialogue** is the exact words that characters speak in a story.
- Dialogue describes characters and moves along the action of the story.
- Add quotation marks around a speaker's exact words.
- Add details to tell *who* is speaking and *how*.
- Use a comma to separate phrases such as *he said* or *she said* from the quotation itself.
- Place a comma or a period inside closing quotation marks.
- Begin the first word of dialogue with a capital letter.
- Begin a new paragraph each time the speaker changes.

THINK AND WRITE

Dialogue

How can you identify the speaker when you read dialogue in a story? Write a brief explanation in your journal.

Notice how the writer uses dialogue to help you get to know the characters and to move along the story's action.

Dialogue is the exact words that a character speaks.

A new paragraph is used each time the speaker changes.

Quotation marks show a speaker's exact words.

Details tell who is speaking and how he or she is speaking.

A dog had chased my cat, Bubbles, under the porch, and the poor cat was too scared to leave. All afternoon, my neighbor Jim and I tried to coax her from her hiding place.

"Show her a cat toy," Jim suggested.

"I did, but she wasn't even interested," I replied glumly.

"Hey, I know what to do!" Jim cried. He fetched a can of cat food and held it out toward Bubbles. As soon as she heard the sound of the can opening, Bubbles crawled toward us.

"No cat can hold out for dinner!" Jim sang happily.

Practice

A. Write *dialogue* or *not dialogue* to identify if each sentence shows a speaker's exact words.

1. "My cat just had kittens!" exclaimed Julie.

2. Kittens are born with their eyes closed.

3. Bret asked, "Can I have one?"

4. "When they are older," replied Julie.

5. She thought her mother had said that kittens can usually be adopted after six weeks.

B. Write two sentences of dialogue for each situation described below. Write one sentence for each speaker.

6. Alma and Sherry talk about a class field trip.

7. Brendan asks Rosa for help with his homework.

8. A child asks a librarian to get a book from a high shelf.

9. You ask one of your parents to increase your allowance.

10. Grandmother asks Brian what he wants for his birthday.

C. Grammar Link **11–15. Choose one situation from Practice B and add five more dialogue sentences to the conversation. Include a prepositional phrase in at least three sentences to give more information.**

Writing Activity A Dialogue

Write a dialogue in which a character is trying to convince his mother or father to let him have a pet. Be sure to use quotation marks and other punctuation correctly.

APPLY GRAMMAR: Use adverbs in your dialogue to show *how, where,* or *when* about a verb or an action in the dialogue. Underline each adverb that you use.

Better Sentences

Directions

Read the passage. Some sections are underlined. The underlined sections may be one of the following:

- Incomplete sentences
- Run-on sentences
- Correctly written sentences that should be combined
- Correctly written sentences that do not need to be rewritten

Choose the best way to write each underlined section. If the underlined section needs no change, choose "No mistake."

> **Sample**
>
> Plants and animals sometimes predict the weather.
>
> <u>Grasshoppers chirp louder when the weather gets</u>
> (1)
> <u>warmer. Crickets chirp faster when the weather gets</u>
>
> <u>warmer.</u> Dandelion petals close up when it gets colder.
>
> <u>Even cockroaches give weather hints as they scurry</u>
> (2)
> <u>more when a windstorm is coming.</u>

Words that repeat in two sentences may indicate that the sentences should be combined.

When you see a long sentence, check to be sure the sentence is not a run-on sentence.

1 A Grasshoppers chirp louder when the weather gets warmer. Crickets chirp faster.

B Grasshoppers chirp louder and crickets chirp faster when the weather gets warmer.

C Grasshoppers chirp louder than crickets chirp fast when the weather gets warmer.

D No mistake

2 F Even cockroaches give weather hints, they scurry more when a windstorm is coming.

G Even cockroaches give weather hints. As they scurry more when a windstorm is coming.

H Even cockroaches give weather hints as they scurry more. When a windstorm is coming.

J No mistake

Vocabulary and Comprehension

Directions

Read the passage. Then read each question that follows the passage. Decide which is the best answer to each question. Choose the letter for that answer.

Sample

Tracy sat down heavily in her family's cheery yellow kitchen. The sun was streaming through the window, but Tracy didn't feel sunny. She had just remembered that the math project she hadn't started was due today.

"You seem unhappy," commented her brother William. "You look as if you have the weight of the world on your shoulders."

"Everything is going wrong today," Tracy said.

"I guess you're glad it's Saturday," said William.

Tracy had completely forgotten that it was Saturday. "Today won't be so bad after all!" she laughed.

> To decide what a simile means, think about why the two items are being compared.

1 Which phrase does <u>not</u> describe the setting?

  A a family kitchen

  B a kitchen with a window

  C a dark kitchen

  D a cheerful kitchen

2 In this story, the underlined phrase means—

  F you look worried.

  G you look bent over.

  H you look as if you have a fever.

  J you look tired.

Seeing Like a Writer

Look at the pictures. What is happening in them?
What story could you write about each one?

Futbolistas en el Llano by Angel Zarraga

Writing from Pictures

1. Write a two-word phrase that describes the action in each picture. In each phrase, use an adverb to modify a verb.

2. Write a dialogue that could take place between two of the people in one of the pictures. Include information about the event taking place.

3. Choose two of the pictures. Create a title to describe both. Then write a one-paragraph story about them. Use one of the settings, the characters in both pictures, and a series of events that tell a story.

Apply Grammar: Include prepositional phrases in your writing. Underline the prepositional phrases, and circle the prepositions.

A Story

Have you ever written a story that you created yourself? If so, your story probably had a setting, characters, and a plot with a problem that is solved at the end. In some ways, a story is like a personal narrative. However, a story is a work of fiction. It is a narrative that a writer creates from his or her imagination. Like a personal narrative, the main purpose of a story is to entertain an audience.

Learning from Writers

Read the following examples of story writing. Why do you think the authors wrote these stories? As you read, look for phrases that build excitement or add suspense.

THINK AND WRITE

Purpose

Why do you think people write and tell stories? Write your ideas in your journal.

A New Coach

Back in class, Mariah felt she couldn't stand the suspense any longer. Game time was only twenty minutes away. Just as she was about to ask if anybody had been chosen to play, Brandon beat her to it. He would, she thought. He's so smart.

"Mrs. Floyd, are we in the game today?"

"I was beginning to wonder if anybody was interested," Mrs. Floyd answered in a teasing voice.

The class groaned. Mariah let out a low "Aw, no."

Mrs. Floyd went on. "We have three players from our room—Cynthia, Brandon, and Nikki."

Mariah felt everybody's eyes on her. Her stomach felt weak.... She heard the cheers for her classmates. But she was so stunned by not having been chosen, she didn't pay any attention to what else her teacher was saying.

"Even though she's small, she has what in volleyball is called good hands. She hits and passes well.... She moves fast and many times jumps almost as high as she is tall. A hard worker, one hundred percent dedicated to the game, the fifth grade coach, Mariah Metcalf, Room 111!"

The room exploded with cheers. Mariah couldn't believe it. Coach of all fifth grade rooms!

—Mildred Pitts Walter, from *Mariah Loves Rock*

A Narrow Escape

Each wave smashing against the cliffs threw showers of spray into the air. The two children scrambling across the slippery rocks were soaked by the morning spray.

"I can see it now!" shouted Jenny, straining to be heard above the roar of the ocean. She clambered down the steep rock into a shallow pool that was sheltered from the raging sea. Her brother Ben followed.

"Are the flashlights still working?" he asked. Two beams of light pierced the gloom. "Then, let's go," said Ben. They waded into the small opening.

Hidden behind a ridge in the wall was a narrow gap. The children squeezed into a tight, twisty passage of rock.

Ben and Jenny rushed along the passage, finally emerging on the other side. "We made it before high tide," yelled Jenny.

"We're lucky, Sis," Ben smiled.

—Iris Begay

PRACTICE AND APPLY

Thinking Like a Reader

1. Who is the main character in "A New Coach"?

2. What is the setting in "A Narrow Escape"?

Thinking Like a Writer

3. How did the author of "A New Coach" use dialogue to describe the characters?

4. What words did the author of "A Narrow Escape" use to help you picture the setting?

5. **Reading Across Texts** Compare the two literature models. Write about the problem in each model and how it is solved at the end.

Features of a Story

A **story** is a narrative that a writer creates from his or her imagination. A good story:

► has an interesting **beginning, middle,** and **end.**

► describes a **setting,** telling when and where a story takes place.

► has **characters** that move the action along.

► has a **plot** with a problem that is solved at the end.

► often uses **dialogue.**

►Beginning, Middle, and End

Reread "A New Coach" on page 460. Notice the way the story begins and ends.

> Back in class, Mariah felt she couldn't stand the suspense any longer....
>
> The room exploded with cheers. Mariah couldn't believe it. Coach of all the fifth grade rooms!

Think about the way the author builds excitement and suspense. Notice that the exclamation makes you realize how happy Mariah felt at the end. How does the ending let you know what happens?

►Setting

Setting is an important part of "A New Coach." How do the following sentences help you understand where and when the story takes place?

> Back in class, Mariah felt she couldn't stand the suspense any longer. Game time was only twenty minutes away.

This sentence explains that the characters are in class anxiously waiting for a sporting event to begin. The story also takes place in the present.

▶ Characters

The thoughts, words, and deeds of characters help move the action of the story along. The sentences below describe the actions of two characters.

> Just as she was about to ask if anybody had been chosen to play, Brandon beat her to it. He would, she thought. He's so smart.

What do you learn about Brandon from his action? Notice that Mariah's thoughts about him help you to see the character. They also help describe Mariah.

▶ Plot

A good story has a strong plot, or sequence of events, that introduces a problem that is solved at the end.

> But she was so stunned by not having been chosen, she didn't pay any attention to what else her teacher was saying.

How does the sentence show you the story's problem?

▶ Dialogue

Read the teacher's words at the end of "A New Coach."

> "...A hard worker, one hundred percent dedicated to the game, the fifth grade coach, Mariah Metcalf, Room 111!"

How does the dialogue tell you that the problem is solved?

PRACTICE AND APPLY

Create a Story Map

1. List the features of writing a good story.
2. Reread "A Narrow Escape" by Iris Begay on page 461.
3. How does the writer use dialogue to tell her story?
4. Fill in the story map.
5. Write how the problem is solved at the end.

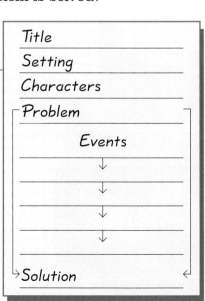

Title

Setting

Characters

Problem

Events

↓

↓

↓

↓

Solution

Prewrite

A story is a narrative that comes from a writer's imagination. A good story has a strong setting, characters, and a plot, or series of events. At the center of the plot is a problem, or conflict, that the main character tries to solve by the end of the story.

Purpose and Audience

The purpose of writing a story is to use your imagination to entertain your readers, or audience.

Before writing, think about the members of your audience. Who will be reading or listening to your story? Think about the kind of story that will amuse them. What will make them smile? What will amaze them?

Choose a Topic

Start by **brainstorming** a list of possible topics. You might think about experiences that have happened to someone you know, or just use your imagination. Then choose the topic that you feel will make the most interesting story for your audience.

After choosing a topic, **explore ideas** by making a list of events of the plot. Your events will need to include a problem and its solution. Also, list characters and a setting. Later, you will organize your ideas.

THINK AND WRITE

Audience

How will your audience affect the way you plan and write your story? Write your ideas in your journal.

Here are some ideas for my story.

My Story About Boy Inventor

Boy likes to experiment with chemistry set.

Boy's mother's flowers die.

Boy tries to find answer to why flowers die.

Boy solves problem with secret formula.

Boy wins a prize.

Boy invents new things.

Writing PROCESS

Organize • Story Elements

The characters, setting, and plot events depend on one another to make a complete story. To put all the "pieces" of a story together, you can use a story map. Not all your ideas may be needed to tell your story. What ideas from her list did this writer leave out of her story map?

PREWRITE

DRAFT

REVISE

PROOFREAD

PUBLISH

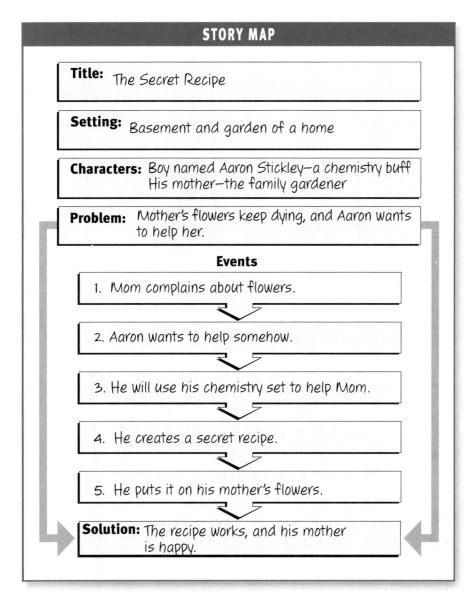

STORY MAP

Title: The Secret Recipe

Setting: Basement and garden of a home

Characters: Boy named Aaron Stickley—a chemistry buff
His mother—the family gardener

Problem: Mother's flowers keep dying, and Aaron wants to help her.

Events

1. Mom complains about flowers.

2. Aaron wants to help somehow.

3. He will use his chemistry set to help Mom.

4. He creates a secret recipe.

5. He puts it on his mother's flowers.

Solution: The recipe works, and his mother is happy.

PRACTICE AND APPLY

Plan Your Own Story

1. Think about your purpose and audience.

2. Brainstorm ideas for a topic, and choose one.

3. Explore ideas for characters, setting, and events.

4. Use the story map to organize your ideas.

Checklist ✓
Prewriting

- ■ Did you think about your purpose and audience?

- ■ Did you choose a good topic and explore ideas?

- ■ Did you think about the characters and setting of your story?

- ■ Did you organize your ideas in a story map?

- ■ Have you checked the order of events and arranged them according to a beginning, a middle, and an end?

- ■ Do you need to do any research?

465

Writing PROCESS

Prewrite • Research and Inquiry

▶ Writer's Resources

You may have to do research to get more information for your story. For example, what do you need to know about wildflowers or chemistry to write your story? First, make a list of questions. Then decide which resources you will need in order to answer them.

What Else Do I Need to Know?	Where Can I Find the Information?
What are some different kinds of flowers?	Visit a library or a media center to do research.
Could ingredients from a chemistry set really be used to make fertilizer?	Look in a card catalog for information, or do an on-line search.

▶ Visit a Library or a Media Center

A library or a media center can provide a variety of sources, such as books, videotapes, audio recordings, and CD-ROM materials. The on-line card catalog can help you find these materials. Suppose that you knew the title of a book about wildflowers. Here is how you would search for it in an on-line catalog in the library.

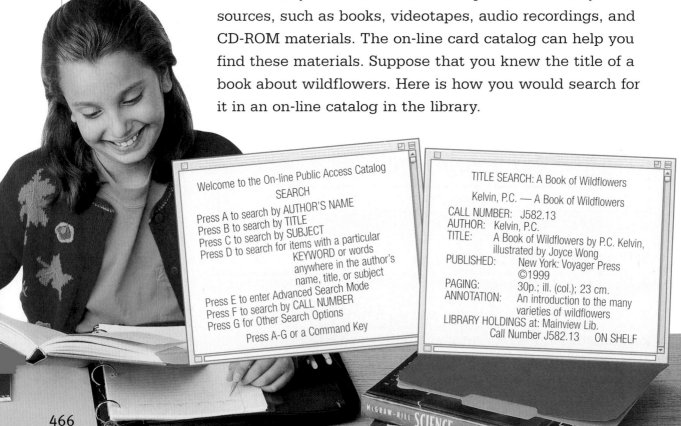

Welcome to the On-line Public Access Catalog
SEARCH
Press A to search by AUTHOR'S NAME
Press B to search by TITLE
Press C to search by SUBJECT
Press D to search for items with a particular KEYWORD or words anywhere in the author's name, title, or subject
Press E to enter Advanced Search Mode
Press F to search by CALL NUMBER
Press G for Other Search Options
Press A-G or a Command Key

TITLE SEARCH: A Book of Wildflowers

Kelvin, P.C. — A Book of Wildflowers
CALL NUMBER: J582.13
AUTHOR: Kelvin, P.C.
TITLE: A Book of Wildflowers by P.C. Kelvin, illustrated by Joyce Wong
PUBLISHED: New York: Voyager Press ©1999
PAGING: 30p.; ill. (col.); 23 cm.
ANNOTATION: An introduction to the many varieties of wildflowers
LIBRARY HOLDINGS at: Mainview Lib.
Call Number J582.13   ON SHELF

▶ Use a Card Catalog

As you know, when visiting the library, you can use the card catalog to find books that will help you in doing research for your story. These cards can be found in drawers or on-line. Each library book usually has three cards in the card catalog: the author card, the title card, and the subject card. Each of these cards gives the same information about the book, but in a different order.

You use the author card when you know the author of the book but not the title. You use the title card when you know the name of the book but not who wrote it. You use the subject card if you do not have any authors or titles in mind but are looking for a book on a particular topic. The call number tells you where to find the book on the library shelf.

▶ Use Your Research

New information gathered from your research can be added to your story map. This writer found some flower names and other information during her research. How did she change her map?

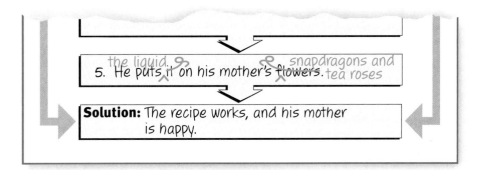

5. He puts ~~the liquid~~ it on his mother's ~~flowers.~~ snapdragons and tea roses

Solution: The recipe works, and his mother is happy.

PRACTICE AND APPLY

Review Your Plan

1. Look at your story map.

2. List questions you have about events in your story.

3. Look in the card catalog in the library or media center to identify the resources you will need to find answers.

4. Add new information you gather to your story map.

PREWRITE

DRAFT

REVISE

PROOFREAD

PUBLISH

Handbook
pages 572, 573, 574

Checklist ✔

Research and Inquiry

- Did you list your questions on index cards?

- Did you identify possible resources?

- Did you take notes or print out helpful information?

Draft

Before you begin writing your story, review the story map you made. Identify the beginning, middle, and end of your story. Consider making a paragraph for each. Also, think about the characters' dialogue. You will need to put each new speaker's words in a separate paragraph.

Beginning: Introduces characters, setting, and problem

✓ Checklist

Drafting

- Is your story well suited to your purpose and audience?

- Have you introduced the characters, setting, and problem of the plot?

- Are the events in your story arranged in a logical order?

- Did you include dialogue that sounds like something the characters would say?

- Does the ending of your story solve the problem in the plot?

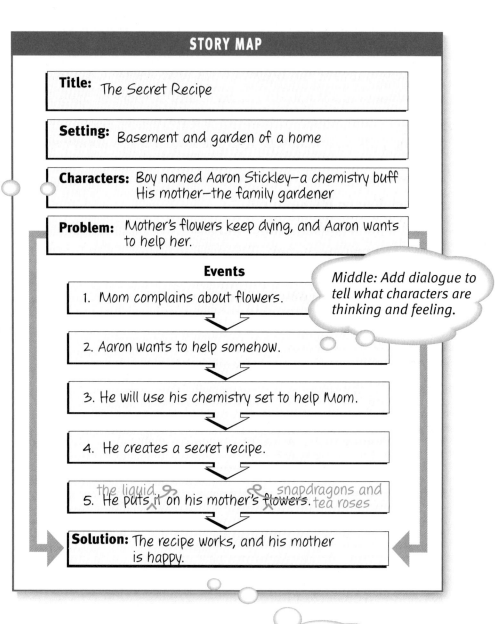

STORY MAP

Title: The Secret Recipe

Setting: Basement and garden of a home

Characters: Boy named Aaron Stickley—a chemistry buff
His mother—the family gardener

Problem: Mother's flowers keep dying, and Aaron wants to help her.

Events

1. Mom complains about flowers.

2. Aaron wants to help somehow.

3. He will use his chemistry set to help Mom.

4. He creates a secret recipe.

5. He puts ~~it~~ the liquid on his mother's ~~flowers.~~ snapdragons and tea roses

Solution: The recipe works, and his mother is happy.

Middle: Add dialogue to tell what characters are thinking and feeling.

Ending: Boy solves problem.

Notice how this writer used the ideas in her story map to write a first draft. She began by introducing the characters and setting in her first paragraph. The writer also used dialogue to express the characters' thoughts and feelings.

PREWRITE

DRAFT

REVISE

PROOFREAD

PUBLISH

DRAFT

The Secret Recipe

Aaron Stickley was experimenting. Suddenly, he heard his mother groan from their backyard.

First paragraph introduces characters and setting.

"What's the matter, Mom." Aaron asked. "My flowers won't grow" Aaron's Mother said.

Dialogue helps state the problem and makes the characters and events come to life.

That's all Aaron needed to hear. Soon he had made a concoction. he knew this would solve his mother's problem.

Aaron's mother looked doubtful, but she fed the flowers with the liquid, anyway.

Gives a possible solution to the problem in the story

Aaron and his mother checked the flowers the snapdragons were blooming and tea roses covered the fence. "You're amazing," his mother exclaimed.

Aaron smiled and thought, "Gee thanks, Mom. Just wait until you need help growing tomatoes!"

Strong, funny ending

PRACTICE AND APPLY

Draft Your Own Story

1. Review your story map.

2. Introduce characters, setting, and a problem.

3. Give events in the order they happened.

4. Use dialogue to describe characters.

TIP!

TECHNOLOGY

Give your document a name that you will remember. You may wish to include the word *draft* in the name.

469

Revise

Elaborate

One way to improve your writing is to elaborate. When you elaborate, you add important ideas and details that will make your writing clearer and more interesting. When you revise your story, you may need to add more vivid and descriptive language.

The details that the writer added, including the prepositional phrase, lets the reader "see" the setting, characters, and events in the story.

> conducting chemistry experiments in the basement
> Aaron Stickley was experimenting.

The writer added the fact that Aaron and his mother checked the flowers the next morning to help readers follow the sequence of events in the story.

> The next morning,
> Aaron and his mother checked the flowers

Word Choice

When you are writing, it is important to choose just the right words for your topic and audience. Vivid verbs and vivid adjectives help give exact meaning and also make a story come alive.

> "My flowers won't grow" Aaron's Mother said. *replied*
>
> That's all Aaron needed to hear. Soon he had made *stirred up*
> *bubbling* "This is your answer, Mom," Aaron announced.
> a concoction. he knew this would solve his mother's
> problem.

DIALOGUE WORDS

said

replied

asked

cried

announced

answered

remarked

exclaimed

suggested

responded

stated

whispered

470

Better Paragraphs

As you continue to revise your draft, check to be sure that you have used a new paragraph each time the speaker changes. Also check to see that each paragraph without dialogue contains a group of related ideas. By indenting your paragraphs, you are signaling to your reader that here is a "chunk" of related material.

Aaron's mother looked doubtful, but she fed the
syripy
flowers with the liquid, anyway.
The next morning,
    Aaron and his mother checked the flowers the
                                        wildly
snapdragons were blooming and tea roses covered the

fence.

PREWRITE

DRAFT

REVISE

PROOFREAD

PUBLISH

Handbook
pages 536, 540, 556

PRACTICE AND APPLY

Revise Your Own Story

1. Add dialogue to bring your characters to life and to make your story more interesting.
2. Group related thoughts into paragraphs.
3. **Grammar** Did you begin a quotation with a capital letter and use quotation marks around a speaker's words?

TiP!

TECHNOLOGY

Do you sometimes forget to indent paragraphs? Many word processing programs allow you to set margins so that the first line of a paragraph indents automatically.

Revise • Peer Conferencing

Writing PROCESS

Get a different view of your writing. Exchange drafts with a partner. Someone else may have some fresh ideas or suggestions that you haven't thought of yourself.

> I think your title could be better.

> Good beginning— include more details about the character.

> Can you describe this in more vivid detail?

> I like this ending. It's funny!

The Secret Recipe

Aaron Stickley was experimenting. Suddenly, he heard his mother groan from their backyard.

"What's the matter, Mom." Aaron asked.

"My flowers won't grow." Aaron's Mother said.

That's all Aaron needed to hear. Soon he had made a concoction. he knew this would solve his mother's problem.

Aaron's mother looked doubtful, but she fed the flowers with the liquid, anyway.

Aaron and his mother checked the flowers the snapdragons were blooming and tea roses covered the fence. "You're amazing," his mother exclaimed.

Aaron smiled and thought, "Gee thanks, Mom. Just wait until you need help growing tomatoes!"

TIP!

Conferencing for the Reader

- Are features of a story included in your partner's draft?
  - strong beginning, middle, and end
  - interesting characters, setting, and plot
  - problem that's solved at the end
  - descriptive words
  - dialogue
  - strong ending
- Make sure to tell your partner what you like about his or her work, as well as what you think needs improvement.

Before you revise your story, think about the comments and suggestions your conferencing partner gave you. This writer made some changes based on her partner's ideas.

REVISE

A Growing Problem
~~The Secret Recipe~~

Brainy conducting chemistry experiments in the basement
Aaron Stickley was ~~experimenting~~. Suddenly, he

heard his mother groan from their backyard.

"What's the matter, Mom." Aaron asked. "My
replied
flowers won't grow" Aaron's Mother ~~said~~.

That's all Aaron needed to hear. Soon he had
stirred up bubbling "This is your answer, Mom,"
~~made a concoction~~. ~~he knew this would solve his~~
Aaron announced.
~~mother's problem.~~

Aaron's mother looked doubtful, but she fed the
syrupy
flowers with the liquid, anyway.
The next morning,
Aaron and his mother checked the flowers the
a sea of pink waves the massive wildly
snapdragons were ~~blooming~~ and tea roses ~~covered the~~
clung to the fence for dear life
~~fence~~. "You're amazing," his mother exclaimed.

Aaron smiled and thought, "Gee thanks, Mom.

Just wait until you need help growing tomatoes!"

PRACTICE AND APPLY

Revise Your Own Story

1. Read your draft aloud, or have your partner read it to you. Listen for the rhythm and flow of your sentences.

2. Use the notes from your peer conference to help improve your draft.

3. Replace plain words with more vivid language.

4. Add a title that will "grab" your audience's interest.

Checklist ✔
Revising

- Will your story entertain your audience?

- Do you need to elaborate on any part of your story to make your ideas clearer?

- Did you choose words that describe?

- Did you write the events in the correct order?

- Do your sentences flow together naturally?

- Did you add an interesting title?

473

Proofread

After you have revised your story, you will need to proofread it to find and correct any mistakes in mechanics, grammar and usage, and spelling.

STRATEGIES FOR PROOFREADING

- **Reread your revised paper.** Look for a different type of error each time you read.

- **Read each sentence and paragraph for correct capitalization and punctuation.** Pay special attention to where dialogue appears.

- **Check that you have indented your paragraphs.** Make sure you have indented to show when a different character is speaking.

- **Check for spelling mistakes.** Use a dictionary or a spell checker to check for errors.

TECHNOLOGY

Remember that a spell checker cannot catch misused words that are spelled correctly. If you type *the* instead of *they*, the mistake will not be caught. Also, a spell checker may not catch misspelled names.

REVIEW THE RULES

GRAMMAR

- An adverb is a word that tells more about a verb, an adjective, or another adverb. Adverbs describe actions more completely by telling *how, when*, and *where*.

MECHANICS

- Capitalize the first word of a direct quotation. A direct quotation gives a speaker's exact words.

- Use a comma to set off a direct quotation from words such as *he said* or *she said*.

- Use quotation marks before and after a direct quotation.

- Place a period or a comma inside closing quotation marks.

- Place a question mark or an exclamation mark inside the quotation marks when it is part of the entire sentence.

- Use a comma after a mild interjection.

Look at the proofreading corrections made on the draft below. What does the symbol ≡ mean? Why does the writer want to start a new sentence?

PROOFREAD

A Growing Problem

~~The Secret Recipe~~

Brainy   conducting chemistry experiments in the basement

Aaron Stickley was ~~experimenting~~. Suddenly, he

heard his mother groan from their backyard.

"What's the matter, Mom," Aaron asked. # "My

replied

flowers won't grow." Aaron's Mother said.

That's all Aaron needed to hear. Soon he had

stirred up bubbling   "This is your answer, Mom,"

made a concoction. ~~he knew this would solve his~~

Aaron announced.

~~mother's problem.~~

Aaron's mother looked doubtful, but she fed the

syripy ⑤ᴾ syrupy

flowers with the liquid, anyway.

The next morning,

Aaron and his mother checked the flowers the

a sea of pink waves, the massive   wildly

snapdragons were blooming and tea roses ~~covered the~~

clung to the fence for dear life

~~fence~~. "You're amazing," his mother exclaimed.

Aaron smiled and thought, "Gee, thanks, Mom.

Just wait until you need help growing tomatoes!"

Checklist ✓
Proofreading

- Did you spell all your words correctly?

- Did you begin and end dialogue with quotation marks?

- Did you capitalize the first word of a direct quotation and end with the correct punctuation mark?

- Did you indent each paragraph?

PROOFREADING MARKS

#	new paragraph
^	add
୬	take out
≡	Make a capital letter.
/	Make a small letter.
⑤ᴾ	Check the spelling.
⊙	Add a period.

PRACTICE AND APPLY

Proofread Your Own Story

1. Correct any spelling errors.

2. Include correct capitalization and punctuation for dialogue.

3. Use the Proofreading Checklist.

Publish

Before you publish your story, review your writing one last time. A checklist can help you focus on your work.

✓ Self-Check   Story

❑ Who was my audience? Did I write in a way that will interest them?

❑ What was my purpose in telling this story? Will my audience be entertained?

❑ Did I begin and end my story in an interesting way?

❑ Did I include enough details so that my audience can "see" my characters, setting, and events?

❑ Did I make my sequence of events clear?

❑ Does my ending include the solution to the problem?

❑ Did I use long and short sentences to make my writing more interesting?

❑ Did I proofread and correct all errors?

The writer used the checklist to review her story. Read "A Growing Problem" and discuss the writer's published work. Do you think it was ready to publish? Why do you think so?

PREWRITE

DRAFT

REVISE

PROOFREAD

PUBLISH

A Growing Problem

by Dara MacKenzie

Brainy Aaron Stickley was conducting chemistry experiments in the basement. Suddenly, he heard his mother groan from their backyard.

"What's the matter, Mom?" Aaron asked.

"My flowers won't grow," Aaron's mother replied.

That's all Aaron needed to hear. Soon he had stirred up a bubbling concoction. "This is your answer, Mom," Aaron announced.

Aaron's mother looked doubtful, but she fed the flowers with the syrupy liquid, anyway.

The next morning, Aaron and his mother checked the flowers. The snapdragons were a sea of pink waves, and the massive tea roses wildly clung to the fence for dear life. "You're amazing," his mother exclaimed.

Aaron smiled and thought, "Gee, thanks, Mom. Just wait until you need help growing tomatoes!"

TiP!

TECHNOLOGY

Experiment with different font styles. Use a font that goes with the humorous mood of your story, but be sure it is easy to read.

PRACTICE AND APPLY

Publish Your Own Story

1. Check your draft one last time.

2. Make a neat, final copy.

3. Make sure the title and your name are easy to read.

4. Add a border, pictures, or a cover.

Present Your Story

To make a good presentation, you need to think ahead. These are steps you can follow to make sure your presentation is a success.

STEP 1

How to Dramatize Your Story

Strategies for Speaking As you plan to act out your story, remember that your purpose is to entertain your listeners.

- Assign character parts to students in your class.
- Write your story in the form of a play.
- Use appropriate gestures, and other dramatic techniques.
- Make eye contact with your audience.

TIP!

Listening Strategies

- Set a purpose. Are you listening to be entertained?
- Listen carefully to the dialogue. Does it help you get to know the characters?
- Follow the sequence of events. Jot down any questions to ask later.
- Keep your eyes on the actors. Pay attention to what they say and to how they say it.

Multimedia Ideas

You might want to videotape your performance. Play back the tape to see how your gestures, body movement, and voice play a part in acting out your story. Make changes based on what you see in the video.

How to Show Your Story

Suggestions for Visuals Make your performance clearer and more interesting by using graphics for your audience to look at as they listen.

- Designing a set for your play can help the audience see the setting and understand the events of the plot.
- Using costumes and props can help your characters and play come alive.

How to Share Your Story

Strategies for Rehearsing The more you practice, the more comfortable you'll feel on the day of your performance.

- Rehearse with the other students in your play.
- Ask a friend, a classmate, a family member, or your teacher to watch a rehearsal and make suggestions.
- Rehearse your lines until you know them without looking at your script.

PRACTICE AND APPLY

Present Your Own Story

1. Write your story in the form of a play.
2. Write dialogue for characters by writing the character's name in capital letters followed by a colon.
3. Write stage directions for actors to follow.
4. Design a set and gather costumes and props.
5. Rehearse your play until all the actors know their lines.

TiP!

Viewing Strategies

- Look carefully at the set, costumes, and props.
- Look for information in the visuals that communicate ideas in the story.
- Save any questions you may have until after the performance.

Writing Tests

On a writing test, you will be asked to write a composition in response to a prompt. Always read the prompt carefully. Look for key words and phrases that identify the topic of your composition and explain how you should present your ideas.

This phrase describes the setting of your story.

Does this prompt name your audience?

Check for clues that tell you the purpose of your writing.

> **Prompt**
>
> Imagine that it is <u>the first day of school</u> for a fifth grade student. As the student enters the classroom, he or she realizes that something is very odd and that this day will be like no other. <u>Write a humorous story</u> about what the student experiences on that unusual first day of school.

How to Read a Prompt

Purpose Look at the prompt again. Find key words that tell you the purpose of your writing. The words "Write a humorous story" tell you that your purpose is to entertain.

Audience Sometimes a prompt identifies your audience. If the prompt does not tell you who your audience is, write for your teacher.

Writing a Story When you are asked to write a story, you are writing a narrative that develops a plot and includes characters and a setting. The phrases "the first day of school," "a fifth grade student," and "this day will be like no other" tell you what the key elements of your narrative should be.

Test Tip
Leave yourself enough time to check your work.

How to Write to a Prompt

Remember these tips when you are given a prompt on a writing test.

Before Writing **Content/Ideas**	• Think about the purpose of your writing. • Keep your audience in mind. • If you are writing a story, list ideas for your plot. • Be sure the story line matches the assignment.
During Writing **Organization/** **Paragraph** **Structure**	• In a story, make sure that you start with an interesting beginning. • Give details about your characters and setting. • Use dialogue to move the story along. • Bring the story to a logical conclusion.
After Writing **Grammar/Usage**	• Proofread your work. • Punctuate dialogue correctly. • Remember to use commas with introductory phrases and interjections. • Spell all words correctly.

Apply What You Learned

When you read a prompt on a writing test, look for key words that tell you the purpose of your writing. Think about the topic and the audience. Then decide on the best way to organize your ideas.

> **Prompt**
>
> Imagine that a brother and sister have mistakenly entered a time machine.
>
> Write a story that tells which time period they visited, what happened to them while they were there, and how they eventually found their way back home.

Unit 6 Review

Grammar and Writing Review

pages 416–417

Adverbs

A. Write each sentence. Underline the adverb.

1. Toby and William left early.
2. They ran quickly to the zoo.
3. Eagerly, they stood in line.
4. The boys hurried inside.
5. They waited excitedly for the show to begin.

pages 418–419

Adverbs Before Adjectives and Adverbs

B. Write each sentence. Underline the adverb. Draw two lines under the adjective or adverb it describes.

6. The wind seemed fiercely cold.
7. The elderly man's clothes were completely damp.
8. He very carefully wrapped a blanket around himself.
9. The man was an unusually patient passenger.
10. He knew the trip was almost complete.

pages 420–421

Comparing with Adverbs

C. Write each sentence. Underline the adverb that compares.

11. The eagle sees more clearly than I do.
12. It spots its prey faster than other birds.
13. The eagle most often prefers the mouse as food.
14. A mouse can hide more easily than a rabbit.
15. Of any bird, I think the eagle hunts most skillfully.

pages 422–423

Negatives

D. Write each sentence. Change one of the negatives into a positive word. Underline the negative in your sentence.

16. We never tried nothing more adventurous.
17. I haven't gone hang gliding at no other time.
18. The wind hadn't never been this calm before.
19. Nothing wasn't going to stop me from trying.
20. No one has never had this much fun!

pages
424–425

Mechanics and Usage: Punctuation in Dialogue

E. **Write each sentence. Add punctuation and capitalization where needed. Underline the direct quotation.**

21. I had a dream I could fly said Riley.

22. You can fly if you take a plane! joked Kelsey.

23. Riley replied that's not what I mean.

24. Did you dream you could fly like a bird? asked Margo.

25. Don't just say fly like a bird!

26. I soared like a glider explained Riley.

27. Riley added I floated above the trees and houses.

28. And then what happened? asked Margo.

29. Did Riley say I woke up?

30. What a great dream that was! shouted Kelsey.

pages
428–431

Prepositions and Prepositional Phrases

F. **Write each sentence. Underline the prepositional phrase. Draw two lines under the preposition.**

31. Jenna and Clarisse rode bicycles to the river.

32. They rode quickly along the trail.

33. The girls leaned their bikes against the railing.

34. Across the river, canoes glided.

35. Jenna put a blanket beside a tree.

36. They placed their picnic basket on the blanket.

37. Clarisse had placed sandwiches inside plastic bags.

38. Jenna ate everything on her plate.

39. A squirrel hid behind a bush and watched them.

40. The squirrel took a grape from the blanket.

pages
432–433

Object Pronouns in Prepositional Phrases

G. **Write the sentences. Change each of the underlined nouns to an object pronoun.**

41. We went to a party after <u>the game</u>.

42. Please give the refreshments to <u>Donald</u>.

43. I helped make the cookies with <u>my mother</u>.

44. The decorations were made by <u>my sister and me</u>.

45. You may sit with <u>Jack and David</u>.

pages
434–435

Interjections

H. **Write the sentences. Underline the interjections.**

46. Oh, today is Jackie's birthday!

47. Wow! Did you decorate that cake yourself?

48. Look, it is a carrot cake.

49. Yum! Carrot cake is my favorite.

50. Well, I certainly had a good birthday.

pages
436–437

Combining Sentences: Complex Sentences

I. **Combine each pair of sentences with the word in parentheses to make a complex sentence. Write the new sentence.**

51. I want to plant tulips. They are beautiful. (because)

52. I dig a hole in the ground. I put the bulb inside it. (before)

53. I water the ground. I plant all the bulbs. (after)

54. The tulips come up in the spring. It is warmer. (when)

55. The flowers are lovely. These bushes need pruning. (although)

pages
438–439

Mechanics and Usage: Commas with Prepositional Phrases and Interjections

J. **Write the sentences. Add commas where needed.**

56. At the beach Alyssa wore sunscreen.

57. Before the trip she applies sunscreen.

58. Good she won't have to worry.

59. After her swim she puts down her blanket.

60. At day's end Alyssa goes home.

pages
452–453

Vocabulary: Figurative Language

K. **Write each sentence. Replace the words in parentheses with a simile or a metaphor to compare the subject of the sentence to something else.**

61. The sun was (very red.)

62. The basketball player was (exceptionally tall.)

63. The joke he told was (old.)

64. The girl's dress was (deep blue.)

65. Life is (wonderful.)

pages
454–455

Composition: Writing Dialogue

L. **Write two lines of dialogue for each of the topics below.**

66. Two friends discuss a basketball game.

67. You ask a friend for a favor.

68. Parents discuss your report card.

69. You win an award at school.

70. A girl orders lunch at a restaurant.

pages
464–479

Proofreading a Story

M. **Write the following story correctly. Correct 14 mistakes in capitalization, punctuation, grammar, and spelling. Indent paragraphs correctly.**

Harvey awoke to the sound of knocking on the front door. when he answered the door he was bombarded by flashes of light and reporters. How does it feel to have won a million dollars   someone asked.

"A million dollars?" Harvey inquired. "I've won a million dollars

The reporters pushed toward Him, shouting more questions.

"Wait! this is my house," Harvey shouted. "You can't come in here!"

The crowd quick swarmed around him and he felt himself waking up. "Well, I guess I am glad it was only a dream," he sighed   himself.

Project File

A Humorous Story

You have probably read or been told more than one humorous story. In fact, you may even have told such a story yourself. Read this humorous story, or anecdote. Think about its funny characters, setting, and exaggerated events. How do they make this story amusing?

A Slippery Character

Lewis is fun to be around, but his sort of fun always gets us into trouble. Once, Lewis got the idea to make a water slide on the grassy slope behind the chicken coop. We rolled plastic sheeting onto the grass and placed a garden hose at the top of the hill. Then Lewis announced, "I really want to try to fly. Add some soap, Lester."

"Uh, I don't know, Lewis. Don't you think that would be too messy?" I asked.

Yet Lewis was not listening. He squirted soap onto the plastic. Then he ran and dove belly-first onto the slide. He was flying, all right, flying right into the chicken-coop fence!

Beginning of a Humorous Story Introduces the unusual characters and setting, and sets up a funny situation.

Dialogue Shows you the characters' personalities and moves along the action of the story.

Ending of a Humorous Story Often has a surprising twist that solves some problem in an unexpected way.

For more information, see Handbook page 587.

486

Write A Humorous Story You see and do funny things all the time. Think of a funny situation you have seen or experienced. Write a humorous story about it. Keep in mind that unusual characters, exaggerated events, and a surprise ending will help to make your story fun to read. Look at the model for writing a humorous story to be sure you have included all the elements that will make your story funny.

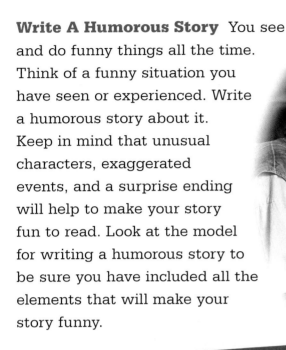

ACTIVITY 2

A Letter of Introduction

"Is There Life in Outer Space?" presents the idea that some scientists think we are not alone in this universe. If you were to travel to another inhabited planet, what do you think it would be like?

Hello Out There! Write a letter that introduces yourself to the ruler of another planet. Tell about yourself, but also give some information about life here on Earth. Be sure to describe the job of one of Earth's leaders, such as the president of the United States.

Adverbs

A. Write whether the underlined adverb tells *how*, *when*, or *where*.

1. The sun was shining <u>brightly</u>.
2. The parrots were squawking <u>loudly</u>.
3. One red bird was <u>nearby</u>.
4. <u>Lately</u>, birds have fascinated me.
5. I <u>happily</u> watched a blue macaw.
6. My sister <u>always</u> wants to see the peacocks.
7. <u>Afterward</u>, we strolled to the reptile house.
8. Mother stared <u>cautiously</u> at the python.
9. We <u>quietly</u> observed the tree snake.
10. We went <u>outside</u>.

B. Write each sentence. Draw one line under the adverb and two lines under the verb it describes.

11. We drove slowly through the jungle area.
12. Monkeys swung playfully from the trees.
13. Parrots screeched loudly at the people.
14. One bright bird flew overhead.
15. Its feathers shone radiantly.
16. I always enjoy the animal park.
17. We saw a pride of lions next.
18. Immediately, a lion roared.
19. Lions can hunt skillfully.
20. The pride rested lazily in the sun.

C. Write each sentence. Draw one line under the adverb. Write whether the underlined adverb tells *how*, *when*, or *where*.

21. A pack of gazelles leaped gracefully.
22. We walked ahead to see more animals.
23. Soon we had seen the whole park.
24. Finally, Dad said that it was time to go.
25. I sadly waved good-bye to the animals.

Adverbs Before Adjectives and Adverbs

A. Write the adverb that describes the underlined word.

1. Families had extremely <u>tight</u> quarters on the ship.

2. The crew moved extraordinarily <u>fast</u>.

3. The children felt utterly <u>frightened</u>.

4. The weather became stormy quite <u>quickly</u>.

5. The winds were outrageously <u>fierce</u>.

6. The wind howled very <u>loudly</u>.

7. Lightning struck the ship almost <u>immediately</u>.

8. Very <u>dark</u> clouds filled the sky.

9. The rain stopped rather <u>suddenly</u>.

10. The storm was completely <u>over</u>.

B. Add an adverb to describe each of the following words. Use an adverb only once.

11. difficult

12. excited

13. tired

14. visible

15. carefully

16. overweight

17. ready

18. slowly

19. dusty

20. damp

C. Write each sentence. Write whether the underlined adverb describes an adjective or another adverb.

21. The ship bumped <u>too</u> heavily against the dock.

22. The passengers were <u>incredibly</u> quiet.

23. The people gathered their things <u>quite</u> slowly.

24. The departure line was <u>extremely</u> long.

25. The crowd was <u>rather</u> noisy.

Comparing with Adverbs

A. **Write the correct adverb form to compare two actions. Then write the adverb form that compares three or more actions.**

1. slowly

2. early

3. quickly

4. swiftly

5. often

6. loudly

7. fast

8. late

9. softly

10. poorly

B. **Write the sentences. Underline the adverb that compares in each sentence.**

11. The eagle can see more clearly than a human can see.

12. Some animals can run longer than other animals.

13. The cheetah runs the fastest of all over short distances.

14. A mare eats grain more often than a pony does.

15. One calf walked more slowly than the other calf.

16. The tree frog hid most carefully of all.

17. The raccoon climbed higher than the bear.

18. The gazelle moved more quickly than the lion.

19. I think the lion hunts most skillfully of all.

20. The crab moves more cautiously than the scorpion.

C. **Write each sentence. Choose the correct comparative or superlative adverb from the parentheses.**

21. The ladybug moved (more slowly, most slowly) than the ant.

22. The beetle moved the (fastest, faster) of all the insects.

23. The housefly flew (most quickly, more quickly) than the moth.

24. The trap-door spider hunts (most skillfully, more skillfully) than the common house spider.

25. The spider spins its web (more skillfully, most skillfully) of all.

Negatives

A. Write the negative in each sentence.

1. No one in the group had flown before.

2. Nobody wanted to board the plane.

3. Briana doesn't have the tickets.

4. Never had we been so confused.

5. Scott didn't have the tickets, either.

6. I don't know where the tickets are.

7. They weren't in anyone's pocket.

8. No solution could be found.

9. "Aren't those the tickets?" asked Sandy.

10. Nothing more needed to be said.

B. Choose a word from the Word Bank to rewrite each sentence.

no	wasn't	never	weren't	hadn't
couldn't	None	No one	nowhere	Nothing

11. We _____ wait for our ride in the glider.

12. A glider has _____ motor.

13. The plane_____ as noisy as I had expected.

14. _____ else is quite like a ride in a glider.

15. _____ wanted to get off the plane.

16. I had _____ done anything more exciting.

17. Our town was _____ in sight.

18. The clouds _____ far above us.

19. We _____ been flying long when it was time to land.

20. _____ of us regretted the trip.

C. Write each sentence. Change one of the negatives in each sentence to a positive word so that the sentence is correct.

21. Nobody doesn't want the trip to end.

22. We didn't have no more money.

23. They didn't know nothing else to do.

24. I don't want to do nothing more.

25. I haven't no more ideas.

Extra Practice

Punctuation in Dialogue

A. Write the sentences. Underline the name of the person who is speaking in each sentence. Circle the quotation marks.

1. "Let's make paper helicopters," announced Kelsey.

2. Riley asked, "What do we need?"

3. "First, we need paper," answered Jenna.

4. "We also need scissors," added Mario.

5. "Did Mario say we also need scissors?" asked Graciela.

6. "Yes," answered Jenna. "Now let's each make a helicopter."

7. "What do we do first?" asked Riley.

8. "Fold your paper in half," said Mario.

9. "Don't just say to fold it in half!" exclaimed Jenna.

10. "Then unfold it," confirmed Mario, "and cut along the fold on each side."

11. "Do I cut it only a third of the way?" asked Riley.

12. Mario said, "Yes, and then fold in each side."

13. "Wow!" said Riley. "Now it looks like a giant letter *T*."

14. "Cut the top down to the fold line and in half," said Graciela.

15. "It looks like rabbit ears now," laughed Mario.

16. Jenna continued, "Fold one flap back and one forward."

17. "Put a paper clip on the bottom," instructed Kelsey.

18. "Hold it up high," said Mario, "and release it."

19. "Oh," Graciela noticed, "it spins like a helicopter now!"

20. "What fun this is!" Jenna shouted.

B. **Write each sentence. Draw one line under the direct quotation.**

21. Mom said, "We're going to the Smithsonian Institution."

22. "Will we go during vacation?" I asked.

23. "Yes," she answered, "we leave next Tuesday."

24. "What will we see?" inquired my sister.

25. My brother answered, "Nothing fun will be there, I bet."

26. "We will go to the National Air and Space Museum," said Dad.

27. "What do they have there?" asked my brother.

28. "They have a model of the Wright brothers' plane," Mom replied.

29. "They have one of the space capsules," I added.

30. "Do they have a capsule from a lunar landing?" my brother asked in surprise.

C. **Write each sentence. Use capitalization and punctuation correctly.**

31. the museum really has a space capsule said Dad.

32. I said they also have the *Spirit of St. Louis*.

33. is that Charles Lindbergh's plane? asked my brother.

34. yes I replied and they also have many uniforms.

35. my brother cried what fun this is going to be!

36. now do you want to go? I asked.

37. My brother responded when do we leave?

38. go pack your bag said Mom.

39. did Mom say go pack your bag?

40. I think we're going to enjoy this trip commented Dad.

Extra Practice

Prepositions

A. Write the sentences. Underline each preposition.

1. My friend and I stopped at the park.

2. We ate lunch on the grass.

3. I had ice in my juice.

4. My friend poured water into a bottle.

5. We sat beside a maple tree.

6. The sun peeked through a cloud.

7. The birds flew among the branches.

8. Cyclists rode by us.

9. People were jogging around the track.

10. Children stood between their parents.

B. Write the sentences. Choose a preposition to complete each sentence.

11. Two girls played catch _____ us.

12. A ball rolled _____ the fence.

13. The team _____ the infield wore red.

14. Blue hats were _____ the team at bat.

15. One player hit the ball _____ the park.

16. The player jumped _____ the fence.

17. He returned _____ the home run was scored.

18. We sat _____ home plate.

19. We stayed _____ noon.

20. Then we ate hamburgers _____ lunch.

C. Use each preposition in a sentence. Write the new sentences.

21. across

22. beside

23. over

24. between

25. among

Prepositional Phrases

A. Write the prepositional phrase in each sentence. The preposition is underlined to help you.

1. The heart is located <u>inside</u> the rib cage.

2. The ribs protect the heart <u>from</u> damage.

3. The heart is a muscle <u>in</u> the circulatory system.

4. The heart is positioned <u>under</u> the breastbone.

5. You feel your heart beat <u>against</u> your chest.

6. <u>After</u> a race, your heart beats rapidly.

7. Your heart beats more slowly <u>during</u> sleep.

8. Blood carries oxygen <u>to</u> your cells.

9. Blood carries wastes <u>from</u> the cells.

10. The heart is an important part <u>of</u> the body.

B. Write each sentence. Draw one line under the prepositional phrase.

11. Our teacher showed us a video about exercise.

12. During exercise, you should check your pulse.

13. Put your finger on your pulse.

14. You can count how many times your heart beats in one minute.

15. After exercise, your heart beats faster.

16. Blood is pumping more quickly through your veins.

17. Exercise is good for your body.

18. I like to run around the school track.

19. My best friend likes to play basketball inside the school gym.

20. My mom likes to jog near our house.

C. Write each sentence. Draw one line under the prepositional phrase. Draw two lines under the preposition.

21. Exercise takes care of your heart.

22. With exercise, your body is healthier.

23. You can choose from many different exercises.

24. Less oxygen is needed during rest.

25. Exercise is necessary for good health.

Object Pronouns in Prepositional Phrases

A. Write the object pronoun of the underlined prepositional phrase in each sentence.

1. Chelsea is moving <u>near them</u>.

2. We planned a class party <u>for her</u>.

3. Winston thought <u>of it</u> first.

4. We gathered <u>around him</u>.

5. Tiffany sat <u>beside me</u>.

6. She suggested games <u>to us</u>.

7. Bingo was a suggestion <u>from her</u>.

8. Everyone agreed <u>except him</u>.

9. Winston really seemed <u>against it</u>.

10. The class disagreed <u>with him</u>.

B. Write each sentence. Draw one line under the prepositional phrase. Draw two lines under the object pronoun.

11. The teacher served apple juice to us.

12. We will play bingo without him.

13. Hector brought balloons for her.

14. Michelle was happy about it.

15. Felicia spilled juice on me.

16. Tiffany danced around us.

17. Tucker brought streamers with him.

18. He hung balloons under them.

19. He set two chairs behind me.

20. I put a table beside you.

C. Write each sentence. Choose the correct object pronoun in parentheses.

21. We had a fun time at (them, it).

22. Chelsea was glad the party was for (him, her).

23. She thanked (us, it).

24. The students hope that Chelsea will remember (him, them).

25. She said good-bye to (it, him).

Interjections

A. Write the interjection in each sentence.

1. Wow! We are going to Ricardo's Restaurant for my birthday.

2. Gee, that's Andy's birthday, too.

3. Yuck! Dad says that I have to wear a tie.

4. Yum! Ricardo's Restaurant has the best pasta.

5. Oh, maybe I can have ice cream for dessert.

6. Oops! I can't eat too much.

7. Well, I should get ready.

8. Wait! Has anyone seen my shoes?

9. Aha! They are under the bed.

10. Hooray! We're ready to go.

B. Write each sentence. Use the correct capitalization and punctuation.

11. Wow this is a beautiful restaurant.

12. My goodness did you see the flowers?

13. Look that waiter spilled the soup.

14. Yum the food looks delicious.

15. Oh each table has candles.

16. Oh no I tripped over my chair.

17. Shh here comes the waiter.

18. Oops I dropped my napkin.

19. Hooray they have spaghetti and meatballs.

20. Hmm do they have blue cheese dressing?

C. Use each interjection in a sentence. Write the sentence, using the correct capitalization and punctuation.

21. Yum

22. Wow

23. Yikes

24. Oh

25. Gee

Extra Practice

Combining Sentences: Complex Sentences

A. Write the conjunction that joins the two ideas in each complex sentence.

1. We made a plan when we planted our vegetables.

2. We planted carrots because we like them.

3. I brought radish seeds since they grow easily.

4. Pearleen planted peas before she watered the ground.

5. Peas grow well unless the weather is hot.

6. We raked rocks although some pebbles remained.

7. We patted the soil after we placed the seeds.

8. We worked hard until it was noon.

9. We would take a break if we could.

10. I stopped working as the heat became unbearable.

B. Write each sentence. Circle the conjunction. Draw one line under each of the two ideas in the sentence.

11. Pearleen adds compost because it helps the plants to grow.

12. I watered the ground after the seeds were soaked.

13. I can't wait until the vegetables are ready.

14. We can pick them as they mature.

15. Tomatoes are ripe when they are red.

16. The peas will be ready after the pods are full.

17. Pearleen added a trellis where she knew the plants would climb.

18. Radishes are ready more quickly than you think.

19. The carrots won't be ready if we watch them grow.

20. We will pull out the plants after the first frost arrives.

C. Combine each pair of sentences into one complex sentence. Use the conjunction in parentheses. Write the new sentence.

21. I won't plant beets. I don't like them. (because)

22. Plants grow fast. The weather is hot. (when)

23. The garden needed water. The heat wave was over. (after)

24. I added fertilizer. I raked the soil. (before)

25. I like to garden. I really am not a gardener. (although)

Commas with Prepositional Phrases and Interjections

A. Write each sentence. Underline the prepositional phrase or the interjection. Circle the commas.

1. During the afternoon, the sun is hot.

2. Before the game, I get my sunscreen.

3. Wow, the sun is hot!

4. At midday, I rested.

5. To our picnic, we brought an umbrella.

6. Gee, too much sun might give me wrinkles.

7. Inside the park, I touched poison oak.

8. On my hand, I began to itch.

9. In a few minutes, the poison oak spread.

10. For my rash, my mother applied lotion.

B. Write each sentence. Underline the prepositional phrase or the interjection.

11. Oh! Goose bumps look funny.

12. During cold weather, I get goose bumps.

13. Gee, I better wear a sweater.

14. Well, I don't have goose bumps anymore.

15. Oh my, what happens if I cut my skin?

16. In a cut, a clot seals the wound.

17. With white blood cells, the infection is attacked.

18. At the edges, skin cells begin to grow.

19. Over time, new skin cells close the wound.

20. Wow, skin is amazing!

C. Write each sentence. Add a comma to prevent misreading.

21. After stretching skin holds its shape.

22. On skin wrinkles are found.

23. Look oil keeps our skin waterproof.

24. To our skin pigment gives color.

25. With sunscreen protection starts.

Unit 1 Sentences

A. Write each sentence correctly. Add capital letters, end punctuation, and commas where needed.

1. have you ever gone skiing

2. let me teach you how to do it

3. what a great day for skiing it is

4. my boots are new and my poles help me turn

5. i like to ski but my friend likes to ice-skate

B. Write each sentence. Draw a line between the complete subject and the complete predicate. Then draw one line under the simple subject and two lines under the simple predicate.

6. The man threw his line into the water.

7. A hook attaches to the line.

8. The yellow cork floats in the water.

9. Suddenly, a fish tugs on the line.

10. My father takes a deep breath.

Unit 2 Nouns

A. Write whether each noun is singular or plural. Then write the singular possessive form and the plural possessive form of each noun.

11. puppy

12. women

13. foxes

14. formulas

15. horse

B. Write each group of words. Capitalize proper nouns and add punctuation where needed.

16. january 5 2001

17. dear mr smithson

18. stanford university

19. yours truly

20. north valley ave

Unit 3 Verbs

A. Write each sentence. Use the correct form of the verb in parentheses. Add commas where needed.

21. We (go, goes) hiking on Sunday Monday and Tuesday.

22. Carla (walk, walks) in the lead.

23. She (is, are) carrying a pack a rope and water.

24. Our team members (climb, climbs) to the top.

25. Gee these trips (is, are) exciting.

B. Write each sentence. Complete the sentence with the past-tense form of the verb in parentheses.

26. Luke (try) to finish his work on time.

27. His friends (bring) him a snack yesterday.

28. He (know) the time would pass quickly.

29. His mom (speak) from the other room.

30. Ben's assignment (be) late.

Unit 4 Adjectives

A. Draw one line under each adjective, including each demonstrative adjective. Draw two lines under each article.

31. A successful author visited this school.

32. She read an interesting poem to us.

33. I have the first book she wrote.

34. The book about a timid pig is funny.

35. The talented author has written these five books.

B. Write each sentence. Use the correct form of the adjective in parentheses to compare.

36. Plums taste _____ than nectarines. (good)

37. To me, watermelon is the _____ fruit of all. (refreshing)

38. Currants are _____ than raisins. (small)

39. The lemon is the _____ of all fruits. (good)

40. A pineapple can be _____ than a bag of apples. (expensive)

C. **Write each sentence. Correct the capitalization and punctuation where needed. Underline each proper adjective.**

41. the mexican flag is red white and green.

42. july 4 1776 is an important date for the american people.

43. the french revolution put an end to rule by kings and queens.

44. on may 18, we will be in san diego california.

45. the louisiana purchase doubled the size of our country.

D. **Combine the adjectives in each pair of sentences. Write the new sentence. Draw one line under each adjective. Do not underline articles.**

46. I live in a large house. I live in a white house.

47. Amanda looked for her special book. Her book is new.

48. Mrs. Armstrong is our young teacher. She teaches English.

49. Colin found a lost kitten. The kitten is calico.

50. Dominique looked in her small room. Her room was messy.

Unit 5 Pronouns

A. **Write each sentence. Choose the correct pronoun in the parentheses. Write *SP* if the pronoun is a subject pronoun. Write *OP* if the pronoun is an object pronoun.**

51. The sailboat belongs to (we, us).

52. Renee knows how to sail, and (she, we) will take us.

53. Mother and (I, me) will take lessons this summer.

54. The instructor gave life jackets to (we, us).

55. The boat only had room for mother and (I, me).

B. **Write each sentence. Choose the correct word in parentheses. Be sure that pronouns and verbs agree.**

56. (Your, You're) going to enjoy this musical.

57. They (watches, watch) the show with pleasure.

58. The musical has Andrea Taylor as (its, it's) star.

59. At the bell the audience took (they're, their) seats.

60. She (make, makes) the show worth watching.

C. Combine the pronouns in each pair of sentences to form a compound subject or a compound object. Write the new sentence.

61. He wrote a plan. I wrote a plan.

62. Mom drove me to school. Mom drove her to school.

63. You make a list. He makes a list.

64. Now you agree with me. Now she agrees with me.

65. I want to hear him. I want to hear them.

D. Write each sentence. Use correct punctuation, word usage, and capitalization. Use apostrophes correctly in contractions.

66. we drove them to the train station at 900.

67. hes leaving for portland.

68. the train doesnt arrive until 1130.

69. patrick is going to attend camp at they're university.

70. he wont be coming home until you're wedding.

Unit 6 Adverbs and Prepositions

A. Write each sentence. Draw a line under the adverb in each sentence. Write whether the adverb tells *how*, *when*, or *where*.

71. The rain fell rapidly.

72. Later, a rainbow appeared.

73. The sun shone brightly through the clouds.

74. We ran outside to play.

75. We quickly ran to get our equipment.

B. Write each sentence. Use the correct form of the adverb in parentheses to compare.

76. Kerry and he play tennis (good, well).

77. Kerry serves the (faster, fastest) of all the players.

78. I play (more skillfully, most skillfully) than Jared does.

79. Mickey can return a serve (harder, hardest) than Jared can.

80. Kerry wins the (more frequently, most frequently) of all.

Grammar

C. Write each sentence by using only one negative.

81. The neighbors haven't no place to keep the dog they found.

82. Kirk never had no dog before, but he wanted one.

83. He didn't have no money to buy one.

84. His neigbors didn't want no payment for the dog.

85. The dog didn't take no time to become Kirk's loyal pet.

D. Write each sentence. Draw one line under the prepositional phrase. Draw two lines under the preposition.

86. Birds flew over our heads.

87. The boats sailed silently on the lake.

88. A shiny red balloon floated above us.

89. A duck floated lazily across the surface.

90. My favorite class is in the late afternoon.

E. Use the word in parentheses to combine each pair of sentences. Write the new sentence.

91. I returned the cassette. It was broken. (because)

92. I wanted to buy it. It was my favorite band. (since)

93. The tape wouldn't play. I put it in the recorder. (after)

94. The tape was working. I left the store. (when)

95. I returned home. I noticed a crack in the case. (before)

F. Write each sentence. Add punctuation where needed.

96. Ramona did you finish your homework asked Mother.

97. Yes I finished it she replied.

98. Wow what a difficult assignment it was said Ramona.

99. Dont complain that it was a difficult assignment said Mother.

100. I know chuckled Ramona. Learning isn't easy.

Troubleshooter

Contents

Correcting Sentence Fragments

Remember!

- A sentence is a group of words that expresses a complete thought.

- A sentence fragment does not express a complete thought.

Problem 1

A sentence fragment that does not have a subject

Sentence Fragment: *Visited the gardens.*

> Who or what visited the gardens?

Solution 1

You need to add a subject to the sentence fragment to make it a complete sentence.

Sentence: *My class visited the gardens.*

Problem 2

A sentence fragment that does not have a predicate

Sentence Fragment: *My teacher, Mrs. Santos.*

> What about your teacher, Mrs. Santos?

Solution 2

You need to add a predicate to the sentence fragment to make it a complete sentence.

Sentence: *My teacher, Mrs. Santos, had never seen so many beautiful flowers.*

Problem 3

A sentence fragment that does not have a subject and a predicate.

Sentence Fragment: *At the front gate.*

Who or what is this about? What did they do?

Solution 3

Add a subject and a predicate to this fragment to make it a complete sentence.

Sentence: *The tour guides gave us a map at the front gate.*

Practice Rewrite the sentence fragments to make complete sentences.

1. Decided to get out the map.
2. A big painted sign.
3. Walked down the path.
4. Next, Sam and I.
5. A beautiful smell in the air.
6. The rest of the class.
7. Followed the sounds of their voices.
8. Never caught up to the class.
9. Our teacher and all our classmates.
10. Had been looking for us everywhere.

Need More Help? For more help, see Sentences on pages 2–7 and Handbook page 526.

507

Correcting Run-on Sentences

Remember!

- A sentence is a group of words that expresses a complete thought.

- A run-on sentence contains two or more sentences that should stand alone.

Problem 1

Two sentences joined with no punctuation between them

Run-on Sentence: *Everyone wrote a report my report was about the desert.*

> **Are these two complete thoughts?**

Solution 1

Separate the two complete thoughts into two sentences, and add the necessary capitalization and punctuation.

Sentences: *Everyone wrote a report. My report was about the desert.*

Problem 2

Two sentences joined only by a comma

Run-on Sentence: *The desert seems like an empty place, many plants and animals live there.*

> **Aren't these two different sentences?**

Solution 2

Place a comma at the end of the first complete thought. Then add *and*, *but*, or *or* to connect the two thoughts.

Compound Sentence: *The desert seems like an empty place, but many plants and animals live there.*

Problem 3

Three or more sentences joined with *and*, *but*, or *or*

Run-on Sentence: *The desert has a harsh climate, and the temperatures can be extreme, and there is very little rain.*

> Does this sentence include three separate thoughts connected by *and*?

Solution 3

Create more than one sentence by separating ideas and using correct end punctuation. Join two closely related ideas to form a compound sentence.

Separate Sentences: *The desert has a harsh climate. The temperatures can be extreme, and there is very little rain.*

Practice Rewrite these run-on sentences correctly.

1. My family took a vacation last summer, and we went to the desert, but we stayed cool in a hotel.
2. Our trip was to Santa Fe, it is the capital of New Mexico.
3. My family and I saw the sights we visited every museum in town.
4. We enjoyed the shops, and my mother shopped for jewelry, but my brother and I were more interested in the food.
5. I had fun, I learned a lot about New Mexico.

Need More Help? For more help, see Combining Sentences on pages 8–9 and Handbook page 527.

Confusing Plurals and Possessives

Remember!

- A *plural noun* names more than one person, place, thing, or idea and usually ends in *s* or *es*.

- A *possessive noun* shows who or what owns or has something.

- To form the possessive of most singular nouns, add an apostrophe and an *s* ('*s*).

- To form the possessive of a plural noun that ends in *s*, add only an apostrophe ('). To form the possessive of a plural noun not ending in *s*, add an apostrophe and an *s* ('*s*).

Problem 1

Using an apostrophe in a plural noun

> *Incorrect Plural Form:* Two fifth-grade student's interviewed a new classmate.

> Do the students have or own anything?

Solution 1

Remove the apostrophe. Do not use an apostrophe in a plural noun.

> *Correct Plural Form:* Two fifth-grade students interviewed a new classmate.

Problem 2

Leaving out an apostrophe in a singular possessive noun

> *Incorrect Possessive Form:* The new students name was Kathryn.

> Doesn't the name belong to the student?

Solution 2

Correct a singular possessive noun by adding an apostrophe before the *s* ('*s*).

> *Correct Possessive Form:* The new student's name was Kathryn.

Troubleshooter

510

Putting the apostrophe in the wrong place in a plural possessive noun

Incorrect Form: *Kathryn knew all the student's names at her old school.*

Are we talking about the names of one student or of many students?

Solution 3

Correct a plural possessive that ends in *s* by moving the apostrophe after the *s* (*s'*). To correct a plural noun not ending in *s*, move the apostrophe before the *s* (*'s*).

Correct Form: *Kathryn knew all the students' names at her old school.*

Practice Rewrite each sentence correctly. Use the correct plural or possessive form.

1. Kathryn enjoyed the classes' at her new school.

2. It took a couple of days to learn her five teacher's names.

3. Kathryns new bus driver seemed very nice.

4. She even met some girl's on the bus.

5. One friends' house was right next door to hers.

6. Amandas parents invited Kathryn to their house.

7. The familys' dog had just had seven puppies.

8. Kathryn wrote letter's to tell her friends about the puppies.

9. They wrote back, and Kathryn read the childrens' notes.

10. She missed her friends', but she liked her new home, too.

 Need More Help? For more help, see Plural Nouns on pages 90–93, Possessive Nouns on pages 100–103, and Handbook pages 530–531.

Troubleshooter

Lack of Subject-Verb Agreement

Remember!

- The *subject and verb must agree* in a sentence.
- The subject and verb agree when both are singular or both are plural.

Problem 1

Using a singular verb with a plural subject or a plural verb with a singular subject

No Agreement: Sheila take piano lessons on Mondays.

Is the subject singular or plural? What about the verb?

Solution 1

Change the plural verb to match the singular subject.

Subject-Verb Agreement: Sheila takes piano lessons on Mondays.

Problem 2

Using a singular verb with a compound subject joined by *and*

No Agreement: Jesse and Lee gives Sheila piano lessons.

Is this subject plural or singular? What about the verb?

Solution 2

Change the singular verb to match the compound subject.

Subject-Verb Agreement: Jesse and Lee give Sheila piano lessons.

Problem 3

Using the wrong verb form with a compound subject joined by *or*

No Agreement: Tina or Marta help her in pottery class.

No Agreement: Her sister or her friends helps, too.

> **Is *Marta* singular or plural? Is *friends*?**

Solution 3

When a compound subject is made up of two subjects joined by *or*, the verb agrees with the subject that is closer to it.

Subject-Verb Agreement: Tina or Marta helps her in pottery class.

Subject-Verb Agreement: Her sister or her friends help, too.

Practice Rewrite each sentence correctly so that all subjects and verbs agree.

1. Dancing and skating is Sheila's favorite activities.
2. She dance the best of all the students.
3. Larry or two other boys offers to be her skating partner.
4. Her friends asks to see the dance steps.
5. Her mother and teachers admires her talent.

 Need More Help? For more help, see Subject-Verb Agreement on pages 174–175 and Handbook page 533.

Incorrect Verb Forms

Remember!

- The past tense of a regular verb is formed by adding -*d* or -*ed*.

- The past participle of a regular verb is formed by adding -*d* or -*ed*.

- Irregular verbs have special forms that do not add -*d* or -*ed* in the past or the past participle.

Problem 1

Forming irregular verbs incorrectly

Incorrect Verb Form: *Nick heared about a poster contest.*

> **What is the past tense of *hear*?**

Solution 1

Replace the incorrect form of the irregular verb with the correct irregular form. Check the dictionary if you are not sure of the correct form.

Correct Verb Form: *Nick heard about a poster contest.*

Problem 2

Using an incorrect irregular verb form for the past tense

Incorrect Verb Form: *Nick drawn a design for his poster.*

> **What are the verb forms of *draw*? When is each one used?**

Solution 2

Replace the past participle with the simple past-tense form of the irregular verb. Past participles are used with a helping verb such as *have*, *has*, or *had*.

Correct Verb Form: *Nick drew a design for his poster.*

514

Problem 3

Using the incorrect irregular verb form with *have*

Incorrect Verb Form: *His grandmother had gave him a set of supplies.*

> What form of *give* do you use with the helping word *had*?

Solution 3

Replace the past-tense form with the past participle.

Always use the past participle form of the verb after *has*, *have*, or *had*.

Correct Verb Form: *His grandmother had given him a set of supplies.*

Practice Rewrite the sentences correctly. Use the correct verb forms.

1. Nick drawed his poster on the computer.
2. He run into a small problem with the lettering.
3. He taked the picture to his computer teacher for help.
4. She seen a way to correct it.
5. Nick knowed exactly what to do.
6. He finished the poster and written his name on the back.
7. He was sure he had did his best work.
8. He brung his poster to the teacher.
9. She has sended it in to the contest.
10. She has saw many students win in contests like these.

 Need More Help? For more help, see Irregular Verbs on pages 188–191 and Handbook page 535.

Incorrect Use of Adjectives That Compare

Remember!

- Add *-er* or *more* to adjectives to compare two nouns.

- Add *-est* or *most* to adjectives to compare three or more nouns.

- Do not use *more* and *-er* at the same time, and do not use *most* and *-est* at the same time.

Problem 1

Using *-er* or *-est* instead of *more* or *most*

Incorrect Form: *Teisha wanted this project to be creativer than her last one.*

> **How do you make comparisons with a long adjective such as *creative*?**

Solution 1

To compare adjectives of more than two syllables, use *more* or *most*. Remove the *-er* and use *more* before the adjective.

Correct Form: *Teisha wanted this project to be more creative than her last one.*

Problem 2

Using *-er* or *-est* with *more* or *most*

Incorrect Form: *She thinks that the Internet is the most quickest way to get information.*

> **Should you use *most* and *-est* when comparing with the adjective *quick*?**

Solution 2

With shorter adjectives, add *-er* or *-est* to compare people, places, or things. Never use *more* or *most* with *-er* or *-est*.

Correct Form: *She thinks that the Internet is the quickest way to get information.*

Problem 3

Using the incorrect form when comparing with *good* or *bad*

Incorrect Form: *She was sure her report would be the goodest in the class.*

> **What are the comparative forms of *good*?**

Solution 3

The comparative forms of *good* and *bad* are *better* and *worse*. The superlative forms of *good* and *bad* are *best* and *worst*. Rewrite this sentence by using *best* instead of *goodest*.

Correct Form: *She was sure her report would be the best in the class.*

Practice **Rewrite the sentences correctly. Use the correct form of adjectives that compare.**

1. As Teisha worked, she came up with the most greatest idea.

2. She found a gooder source of information than she had before.

3. She interviewed a person who was ten years more older than Teisha.

4. Then Teisha added photographs to make her project interestinger.

5. Everyone thought that Teisha's project was more better than her last one.

Need More Help? **For more help, see Comparative and Superlative Adjectives on pages 270–275 and Handbook page 537.**

Incorrect Use of Pronouns

Remember!

- A **pronoun** is a word that can take the place of one or more nouns.

- Use a **subject pronoun** when the pronoun is the subject of a sentence.

- Use an **object pronoun** when the pronoun is the object of a verb or the object of a preposition.

Problem 1

Using a pronoun that does not match the noun to which it refers

Pronoun Does Not Match: *Mary Beth likes inventions so she chose to write about it.*

> **To which noun does *it* refer?**

Solution 1

Replace the incorrect pronoun with a pronoun that clearly matches the noun to which it refers.

Pronoun Match: *Mary Beth likes inventions so she chose to write about them.*

Problem 2

Using an object pronoun as the subject of a sentence

Incorrect Pronoun: *Them are photographs of her grandfather.*

> **Should the pronoun *Them* be used as the subject?**

Solution 2

Replace an object pronoun that appears as the subject of a sentence with a subject pronoun. Subject pronouns are *I, you, he, she, it, we,* or *they.*

Correct Pronoun: *They are photographs of her grandfather.*

Troubleshooter

Problem 3

Using a subject pronoun after an action verb or a preposition.

Incorrect Pronoun: *Grandfather showed Dina and I pictures of his inventions.*

> Should the pronoun *I* be used after the action verb *showed*?

Solution 3

Use an object pronoun after an action verb or preposition. Object pronouns include *me*, *you*, *him*, *her*, *it*, *us*, and *them*.

Correct Pronoun: *Grandfather showed Dina and me pictures of his inventions.*

Practice **Write each sentence. Use the correct pronoun in parentheses.**

1. Grandpa invited (us, we) to come for a visit.

2. (We, Us) came over the next day.

3. Grandpa and (I, me) got out his old photo albums.

4. (He, Him) smiled as he turned each of the pages.

5. Dina asked (he, him) to talk about his early inventions.

6. He had invented a car, and (it, she) had won an award.

7. My brothers came over, and they showed Grandpa and (we, us) their latest invention.

8. Grandpa's cars didn't run on gas. (They, Them) ran on electricity.

9. We and (he, him) definitely have something in common.

10. We're interested in inventions since (they, it) improve the world.

For more help, see Pronouns on pages 340–345 and Handbook page 538.

Apostrophes

Remember!

- An **apostrophe** is used in possessive nouns to show ownership.

- An **apostrophe** is used to show where a letter or letters have been left out of a contraction.

- An **apostrophe** is not used in a possessive pronoun.

Problem 1

Leaving out the apostrophe in a contraction

> Incorrect Form: *Burt couldnt sleep because he heard a strange noise.*

What is the contraction? What letters have been left out?

Solution 1

Place an apostrophe in a contraction to show where a letter or letters have been left out of the contraction.

> Correct Form: *Burt couldn't sleep because he heard a strange noise.*

Problem 2

Using an apostrophe with a possessive pronoun

> Incorrect Form: *Burt had no flashlight, so his sister let him use her's.*

Is her's a contraction? Is it a noun showing ownership?

Solution 2

Remove the apostrophe. The possessive pronouns *my, mine, your, yours, his, her, hers, its, our, ours, their,* and *theirs* do not contain apostrophes.

> Correct Form: *Burt had no flashlight, so his sister let him use hers.*

Problem 3

Confusing contractions and possessive pronouns

Incorrect Word: *He saw an animal, and it's eyes were shining.*

> Should it be *it's* eyes or *its* eyes? Is the pronoun a contraction or a possessive?

Solution 3

Replace the contraction *it's* with the possessive pronoun *its.*
Possessive pronouns do not have apostrophes.

Correct Word: *He saw an animal, and its eyes were shining.*

Practice Rewrite the sentences. Use apostrophes correctly.

1. His dad said, "It's you're turn to call the Animal Rescue Department."

2. Burt quickly agreed and said, "Ill make the call immediately."

3. He talked to a worker and explained that he didnt have a trap.

4. The man asked Burt if he wanted to borrow their's.

5. "Yes," said Burt. "Now, heres how you get to our location."

6. The rescue team arrived and said, "Lets put food in this cage."

7. Then they quickly propped open it's door.

8. Once the animal reached the food, it wasnt able to escape.

9. "Hes going to be a lot happier in his new home," Burt said.

10. "Your a great friend to animals," the workers told Burt.

Need More Help? For more help, see **Possessive Pronouns on pages 354–355, Contractions on pages 356–357, and Handbook page 539.**

Adverbs and Double Negatives

Remember!

- An adverb is a word that tells more about a verb, an adjective, or another adverb.

- An adverb can tell *how*, *when*, or *where* an action takes place.

Problem 1

Confusing adjectives and adverbs

Incorrect Form: *We acted helpful toward the dancers.*

> Is the word *helpful* telling more about a noun or a verb?

Solution 1

Replace the adjective *helpful* with the correct adverb.
Use an adjective only when describing a noun.

Correct Form: *We acted helpfully toward the dancers.*

Problem 2

Using *good* instead of *well*

Incorrect Form: *I don't think I dance very good.*

> Is *good* supposed to be used as an adjective or an adverb?

Solution 2

Replace *good* with *well*. *Good* is always an adjective.
Well is usually an adverb.

Correct Form: *I don't think I dance very well.*

Troubleshooter

Using double negatives

Incorrect Form: *I didn't know no one in the dance class.*

> Are there two negatives in this sentence?

Solution 3

Do not use two negatives in one sentence. Replace one of the negative words with a positive word.

Correct Form: *I didn't know anyone in the dance class.*

Practice **Rewrite each sentence correctly.**

1. The class was fun, and she finished it easy.

2. She didn't know nothing about the program.

3. She and Justin danced good together.

4. She said she had never met no one as talented.

5. The audience clapped loud at the end of the performance.

 Need More Help? For more help, see Adverbs on pages 416–419, Negatives on pages 422–423, and Handbook pages 540–541.

Troubleshooter

Commas

**Remember!**

- Use a comma to separate items in a series.

- Use a comma after a mild interjection.

- Use a comma after a long introductory prepositional phrase.

- Use a comma after an introductory word such as *yes* or *no*.

Problem 1

Using commas incorrectly

Incorrect Form: *I brought a tape recorder a pencil and a notebook.*

Incorrect Form: *After the basketball game we planned a trip.*

Incorrect Form: *Well what will you be reporting on next?*

Incorrect Form: *Yes you should do that story.*

> Are there items in a series? Is there an introductory phrase? Is there an interjection?

Solution 1

Insert commas between items in a series, after introductory prepositional phrases, after mild interjections, and after introductory words.

Correct Form: *I brought a tape recorder, a pencil, and a notebook.*
Correct Form: *After the basketball game, we planned a trip.*
Correct Form: *Well, what will you be reporting on next?*
Correct Form: *Yes, you should do that story.*

Practice Rewrite the sentences. Use commas correctly.

1. I learned to use a computer a camera and a tape recorder.

2. On the desk in front you will find your supplies.

3. No we forgot to take pictures during the class trip.

4. Gee it was a lot of hard work.

5. During the summer this job was much easier.

Need More Help? For more help, see Commas on pages 438–439 and Handbook pages 554–555.

Handbook

Contents

Sentences and Sentence Fragments

- A **sentence** is a group of words that expresses a complete thought.

    The children went on a picnic.

- A **sentence fragment** is a group of words that does not express a complete thought.

    The boy in the red jacket.   (needs a predicate)

    Carried the largest basket.   (needs a subject)

Practice Write *sentence* or *fragment* for each group of words. Rewrite each fragment to make a complete sentence.

1. Began to fall.
2. The sky was filled with clouds.
3. We picked up our picnic supplies.
4. The entire group of friends into a shelter.
5. Picnic in the shelter.

Types of Sentences

- There are four different types of sentences.

Type of Sentence	Examples
A **declarative sentence** makes a statement and ends with a period.	*Sue goes to the lake often.* *The beach was crowded with people.*
An **interrogative sentence** asks a question and ends with a question mark.	*Have you been there this year?* *Can Tom give me directions?*
An **imperative sentence** tells or asks someone to do something and ends with a period.	*Let me borrow your rowboat.* *Push the boat into the water.*
An **exclamatory sentence** expresses strong feeling and ends with an exclamation mark.	*Wow, what a beautiful day!* *Oh, no, I dropped the oar!*

Practice Write each sentence. Add the correct end punctuation. Write whether the sentence is *declarative*, *interrogative*, *imperative*, or *exclamatory*.

1. Have you ever been sailing

2. I took lessons last summer

3. Hey, it was the easiest thing I've ever learned

4. Hold this rope tightly

5. Don't let it slip through your hands

6. Oops, I almost tipped over

7. Do you want to steer for a while

8. The lesson lasts for one hour

9. Does it cost much money

10. Lessons are not very expensive

RULE 3 pages 8–9

Compound Sentences

- A compound sentence contains two simple sentences that have similar ideas. They are joined by a comma and the word *and*, *or*, or *but*.

  We went hiking, and we camped overnight.

  You can carry your pack, or you can bring the tent.

  Hiking is hard work, but I enjoy the exercise.

Practice Combine each pair of sentences by using a comma and the word *and*, *but*, or *or* to create a compound sentence.

1. The trail is long. We should finish in two hours.

2. We can follow the trail. We could take a short cut.

3. It began to rain. The wind began to howl.

4. I saw bear tracks. I didn't see a bear.

5. We can stop here. We can eat lunch at the top.

 **QUICK WRITE**   Write five compound sentences. Use the proper punctuation for each one.

Handbook

RULE 4
pages
14–15

Complete Subjects and Complete Predicates

- The complete subject of a sentence includes all the words that tell *whom* or *what* the sentence is about.
- The complete predicate of a sentence includes all the words that tell what the subject *does* or *is*.

  The new museum opens at nine o'clock.

  Complete subject: The new museum

  Complete predicate: opens at nine o'clock.

Practice Write each sentence. Draw one line under the complete subject. Draw two lines under the complete predicate.

1. Hector's class went to the museum.
2. All of the children were excited about the trip.
3. The tour guides taught them a lot about ancient times.
4. They studied pottery that was thousands of years old.
5. The boys and girls learned about the people who made the pottery.

RULE 5
pages
16–19

Simple Subjects and Simple Predicates

- The simple subject is the main word in the complete subject. It tells exactly whom or what the sentence is about.

  The helpful volunteer showed us a movie.

- The simple predicate is the main verb in the complete predicate. It tells exactly what the subject does or is.

  All of the students thought that the movie was interesting.

Practice Write each sentence. Draw one line under the simple subject and two lines under the simple predicate.

1. Many paintings hang on the walls.

2. Picasso painted in a unique style.

3. My favorite painting is the one by Picasso.

4. The colors glow under the lights.

5. The museum offers painting lessons.

6. The next class begins tomorrow.

7. I like my art class.

8. The instructor teaches about the artists.

9. He shows us many colors.

10. New art classes start every month.

 RULE 6 pages 20–23

Compound Subjects & Compound Predicates

- A compound subject has two or more simple subjects that are joined by the same predicate and by the word *and* or *or*.

  Stewart and Laura **went to the museum.**

- A compound predicate has two or more simple predicates that share a subject and are joined by the word *and* or *or*.

  We **stopped and visited** *the insect exhibits.*

Practice Write each pair of sentences as one sentence with a compound subject or a compound predicate.

1. Spiders were on display. Insects were on display.

2. The tarantula has eight legs. The black widow spider has eight legs.

3. Stewart observes the beetles. Stewart takes notes on the beetles.

4. A boy notices the colorful butterfly. His mother notices the colorful butterfly.

5. The girl found an ant fram in the store. The girl bought an ant farm in the store.

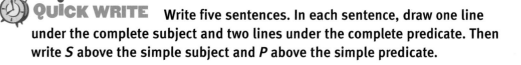 **QUICK WRITE** Write five sentences. In each sentence, draw one line under the complete subject and two lines under the complete predicate. Then write *S* above the simple subject and *P* above the simple predicate.

Handbook

RULE 1
pages 88–89

Nouns

- A noun is a word that names a person, place, thing, or idea.

  The festival was held on Monday.

RULE 2
pages 104–105

Combining Sentences: Nouns

- Sentences with related information about two different nouns may be combined by using the conjunction *and* or *or* to join the nouns.

  Music will be presented.   Dance will be presented.

  Music and dance will be presented.

Practice Combine the nouns in each sentence by using *and* or *or* to create one sentence. Underline each noun, and write whether it names a person, place, thing, or idea.

1. Many girls performed dances. Many boys performed dances.

2. The stage in our school had lights. The stage had props.

RULE 3
pages 90–93

Singular and Plural Nouns

- A singular noun names one person, place, thing, or idea.
- A plural noun names more than one person, place, thing, or idea.
- Most plural nouns are formed by adding -s or -es.

Singular	Plural	Singular	Plural
vegetable	vegetables	sandwich	sandwiches
valley	valleys	pastry	pastries
knife	knives	woman	women

Practice Write each sentence. Draw one line under singular nouns and two lines under plural nouns.

1. Sandwiches were sold at booths next to the sidewalk.

2. The woman tasted a dish made with noodles.

RULE 4
pages 94–95

Common and Proper Nouns

- A common noun names a person, place, thing, or idea.
- A proper noun names a particular person, place, thing, or idea and begins with a capital letter.

Practice Write each sentence. Draw one line under each common noun and two lines under each proper noun.

1. The women admired the costumes from India.
2. A Native American wore moccasins of leather and beads.
3. The fabrics from Africa have bold colors.

RULE 5
pages 100–103

Possessive Nouns

- A possessive noun is a noun that shows who or what owns or has something.

Description	Examples	
A singular possessive adds 's to a singular noun.	*horse's tail* *leaf's color*	*fox's tracks* *child's toy*
A plural possessive adds ' to a plural noun that ends in *s* and 's to a plural noun that does not end in *s*.	*two horses' tails* *many leaves' colors*	*many foxes' tracks* *two children's toys*

Practice Write each sentence. Use the correct possessive form of the words in parentheses ( ).

1. I admired the (saddle of the Arabian horse).
2. The (daughter of the woman) clapped her hands.
3. The (tricks of the clowns) made everyone laugh.
4. The (floats of the parade) were very colorful.
5. The (weather of the day) was perfect for a parade.

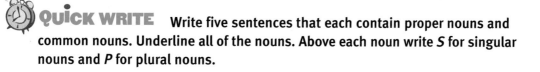 **QUICK WRITE** Write five sentences that each contain proper nouns and common nouns. Underline all of the nouns. Above each noun write *S* for singular nouns and *P* for plural nouns.

531

Handbook

RULE 1
pages
168–171

Action Verbs and Direct Objects

- An action verb is a word that tells the action of the subject.

  I wrote a story.

- A direct object is a noun or pronoun that tells *what* or *who* receives the action of the verb.

  She read the story.

Practice Write each sentence. Underline and write *AV* above the action verb. Underline and write *DO* above the direct object.

1. My story told an adventure.
2. I needed some paper.
3. My sister borrows my pencils.
4. I bought a notebook.
5. I finished my story.

RULE 2
pages
172–173

Verb Tenses

- The tense of a verb tells when something happens.

Description	Examples	
A present-tense verb shows something is happening now.	*dances*	*carries*
A past-tense verb shows something has already happened.	*danced*	*carried*
A future-tense verb shows something is going to happen.	*will dance*	*will carry*

Practice Rewrite each sentence using the correct tense of the verb in parentheses ( ).

1. Tomorrow we (watch) a play.
2. Yesterday the actors (perform) a comedy.
3. Now Rene (like) comedies better than mysteries.
4. Mrs. Thomas (want) to see a musical tonight.
5. Last year she (act) in a drama.

Handbook

RULE 3
pages
176–177

Spelling Present- and Past-Tense Verbs

- The spellings of some verbs change when *-es* or *-ed* is added.

Rules for verbs ending in:	Examples
consonant + *y* : change the *y* to *i* and add *-es* or *-ed*.	*Mavis tries to help Mom.* *Mavis tried to help Mom.*
one vowel and one consonant: double the final consonant before adding *-ed*.	*Rylie mopped the floor.*
e: drop the *e* before adding *-ed*.	*Harrison baked a cake.*

Practice Write each sentence. Use the past-tense form of the verb in parentheses ( ).

1. My classmates and I (hope) everyone would like the show.

2. The girls (skip) to the music.

3. The audience (copy) our motions.

RULE 4
pages
174–175

Subject-Verb Agreement

- A singular verb is used with a singular subject.

  Sue wants to find a book.

- A plural verb is used with a plural subject.

  The customers want the new bestseller.

- Add *-s* to most verbs if the subject is singular and present tense.

- Do not add *-s* to the verb if the subject is plural or if the pronouns are *I* or *you*.

Practice Rewrite each sentence using the correct form of the verb in parentheses ( ).

1. The bookstore (sell, sells) hundreds of books.

2. My friends (want, wants) a book of poetry.

3. Pam and Bob (look, looks) for the comic books.

 QUICK WRITE Write five sentences that each contain an action verb. Underline the verb. Then write if the verb is in the past, present, or future tense.

Handbook

RULE 5
pages
182–185

Main Verbs and Helping Verbs

- The main verb in a sentence shows what the subject does or is.

    The horse is leaping over the fence.

- A helping verb helps the main verb show an action or make a statement.

    The horse is leaping over the fence.

- Use a form of the verb *be* with the *ing* form of verbs.
- Use a form of the verb *have* with the past participle.

Practice: Write each sentence. Complete the sentence with a helping verb.

1. I _____ waiting for the race to begin soon.

2. The horses _____ meeting at the starting line.

3. The winner _____ finished in the fastest time.

RULE 6
pages
186–187

Linking Verbs

- A linking verb links the subject of the sentence to a noun or an adjective in the predicate. Linking verbs do not show action. The noun that follows a linking verb renames the subject, such as *coach* below.

    Patricia was a coach.

- The adjective that follows a linking verb describes the subject, such as *strong* below.

    The gymnast is strong.

Practice Complete each sentence with the correct form of the the linking verb in parentheses ( ). Draw one line under the noun that renames the subject. Draw two lines under the adjective that describes the subject.

1. The student _____ a champion. (be)

2. Her coach _____ skillful. (be)

3. His parents _____ supportive. (be)

4. James _____ excited. (look)

5. The team _____ ready to compete. (seem)

RULE 7
pages
181–191

Irregular Verbs

- An irregular verb is a verb that does not add *-d* or *-ed* to form the past or the past participle.
- The helping verbs *has, have,* and *had* are used with irregular verbs in the present and past participle.

Description	Examples
Present Tense	*Sarah runs to the park.* *She buys new shoes.*
Past Tense	*Sarah ran to the park.* *She bought new shoes.*
Past Participle	*She has run to the park before.* *She already has bought new shoes.*

Practice: Rewrite each sentence using the correct form of the verb in parentheses ( ).

1. Last night we (choose) the path around the lake.
2. Several geese had (fly) above us.
3. We (go) slowly around the path that night.
4. I have (ride) my bike here before.
5. Dan (bring) bottles of water last night.
6. He had (give) a bottle to each of us.
7. Later Sarah (throw) a stone across the water.
8. Afterwards I (drink) the rest of my water.
9. That evening, we (see) the sun go down.
10. I have never (see) a more beautiful sight.

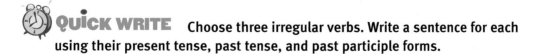

QUICK WRITE Choose three irregular verbs. Write a sentence for each using their present tense, past tense, and past participle forms.

Handbook

RULE 1
pages
260–263

Adjectives and Articles

- **Adjectives** are words that describe nouns or pronouns. Many adjectives tell *what kind* or *how many*.

    Mount St. Helens had a violent eruption in 1980. (what kind)

    Before 1980, the volcano had few eruptions. (how many)

- *A*, *an*, and *the* are special adjectives called articles. Use *a* or *an* to refer to any person, place, thing, or idea. Use *the* to refer to a particular person, place, thing, or idea. *The* can refer to plural as well as singular nouns.

    an eruption   a volcano   the lava

Practice Write each sentence. Complete each sentence with an article or another adjective.

1. Mount St. Helens is part of _____ Cascade Range.

2. _____ volcanoes are inactive and cause no harm.

3. Some volcanic eruptions have caused _____ damage.

RULE 2
pages
264–265

Demonstrative Adjectives

- A **demonstrative adjective** tells which one or which ones.

- **This** and **these** are demonstrative adjectives that refer to something nearby.

    According to these records, this volcano erupts often.

- **That** and **those** are demonstrative adjectives that refer to something farther away.

    Look in the distance at that volcano among those hills.

Practice Write each sentence. Complete each sentence with *this, that, these,* or *those*.

1. Can I see _____ brochures in your hand?

2. _____ brochure has more information than this one.

3. _____ facts about volcanoes are amazing!

Comparative and Superlative Adjectives

- Use comparative adjectives to compare two nouns or pronouns.

  taller **than**   *more active* **than**   *better* **than**

- Use superlative adjectives to compare more than two nouns or pronouns.

  tallest **of all**   *most active* **of all**   *best* **of all**

Practice Write each sentence. Use the correct adjective from the pair in parentheses ( ).

1. The volcano was (large, larger) than Kayla expected.

2. It was the (more amazing, most amazing) sight she had ever seen.

3. It was the site of the (worse, worst) natural disaster in 100 years.

Combining Sentences with Adjectives

- Two sentences that tell about the same noun can be combined by adding an adjective to one of the sentences.

  There was hot *lava. The lava was* black.

  There was hot, black *lava.*

Practice Combine each pair of sentences by adding an adjective to one of the sentences. Write the new sentence.

1. Kayla showed us pictures. There were several pictures.

2. She told about the volcano. The volcano was impressive.

3. It was a big volcano. The volcano was inactive.

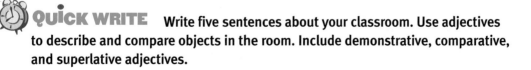 **QUICK WRITE** Write five sentences about your classroom. Use adjectives to describe and compare objects in the room. Include demonstrative, comparative, and superlative adjectives.

Handbook

Handbook

RULE 1
pages 340–341

Pronouns

- A **pronoun** is a word that takes the place of one or more nouns. A pronoun must match the noun that it replaces.

Singular Pronouns	*I, you, he, she, it, me, him, her*
Plural Pronouns	*we, you, they, us, them*

Practice Write each sentence. Replace each underlined word or words with a pronoun. Make sure that the pronoun matches the noun to which it refers.

1. <u>Maddie and Claire</u> decide to attend the meeting.

2. <u>The meeting</u> is about recycling and conservation.

3. Mr. Alden gives <u>the girls</u> permission to attend the meeting.

RULE 2
pages 342–345

Subject Pronouns and Object Pronouns

- A **subject pronoun** can take the place of a noun that is the subject of a sentence. I, you, he, she, it, we, and they are subject pronouns.

   Mario runs the meeting.   *He runs the meeting.*

- An **object pronoun** can be used as the object of an action verb or after words such as *to, for, with, in*, or *at*. The words me, you, him, her, it, us, and them are object pronouns.

   Mario tells us how to protect the environment.

Practice Write each sentence. Replace the underlined noun or nouns with the correct subject or object pronoun. Underline each subject pronoun.

1. <u>Mario</u> presents information about recycling.

2. Mario asks <u>Claire and me</u> to help set up a video.

3. <u>The video</u> shows how discarded plastic can harm wildlife.

4. Students ask <u>Mario</u> questions about recycling.

5. Mario tells <u>the students</u> how to conserve natural resources.

538

Pronoun-Verb Agreement

- Subject pronouns and verbs must agree. Singular subjects go with singular verbs. Plural subjects go with plural verbs.
- Add *-s* to most verbs when you use *he, she,* or *it*. Do not add *-s* to a present-tense verb when the subject is *I, you*, or a plural pronoun.

    She asks questions.   *They ask* questions.

- A compound subject can have two pronouns with the same predicate. The verb agrees with the plural subject.

    She and I ask questions.

Practice Rewrite each sentence with the correct present-tense form of the verb in parentheses ( ).

1. He _____ the principal about our meeting. (tell)

2. He and I _____ the principal to start a recycling program. (convince)

3. She _____ that our school can help the environment. (know)

Possessive Pronouns

- A possessive pronoun shows *who* or *what* owns something.

    Mario's poster has information.   His poster has information.

- *My, your, his, her, its, our, your*, and *their* are possessive pronouns that come before nouns. *Mine, yours, his, hers, its, ours, yours*, and *theirs* are possessive pronouns that can stand alone.

    I liked your poster.   That poster is a favorite of mine.

Practice Write each sentence. Replace the underlined word or words with the correct possessive pronoun.

1. The program succeeds due to <u>the students'</u> hard work.

2. Mr. Alden is <u>the program's</u> faculty advisor.

3. <u>Mario's</u> poster convinces others to recycle.

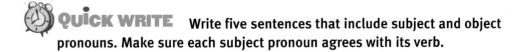 **QUICK WRITE**   Write five sentences that include subject and object pronouns. Make sure each subject pronoun agrees with its verb.

Handbook

Handbook

RULE 1
pages 416–417

Adverbs

- An adverb tells more about a verb. An adverb tells how, when, or where an action takes place.

  Theresa jogs slowly. (how)

  The race begins soon. (when)

  The fans gather nearby. (where)

- Many adverbs end in *-ly*.

  carefully   sweetly   happily   softly

Practice Write each sentence. Draw one line under the adverb. Write whether the underlined adverb tells *how*, *when*, or *where* the action takes place.

1. One runner lifted her knees high to stretch her legs.

2. Another runner sat down and stretched.

3. Theresa walked around to keep her legs limber.

4. Sometimes Theresa hopped on one foot or the other.

5. Anna hummed quietly while she waited for the race to begin.

RULE 2
pages 418–419

Adverbs Before Adjectives and Adverbs

- Adverbs can describe adjectives as well as verbs.

  Theresa felt awfully nervous.

- Adverbs can also tell more about other adverbs.

  Her heart was beating very quickly.

Practice Write each sentence. Write whether the underlined adverb describes an adjective or another adverb.

1. Theresa was extremely nervous about the race.

2. She was too excited to notice the cheering crowd.

3. She bolted very quickly at the sound of the whistle.

4. She ran quite well during the race.

5. Theresa was rather happy with her progress.

RULE 3
pages
420–421

Comparing with Adverbs

- Adverbs can compare two or more actions.

To Compare Two Actions

Add -er to most short adverbs.	*longer, higher, slower*
Use *more* with an adverb that has two or more syllables.	*more quietly, more patiently*

To Compare Three or More Actions

Add -est to most short adverbs.	*longest, highest, slowest*
Use *most* with an adverb that has two or more syllables.	*most quietly, most patiently*

Practice Write each sentence. Choose the correct comparative or superlative adverb from the parentheses ( ).

1. Theresa ran (more quickly, most quickly) than the others.

2. Theresa had trained (harder, more hard) than her competitors.

3. Of all the fifth-graders, Theresa ran (more swiftly, most swiftly).

RULE 4
pages
422–423

Negatives

- A negative is a word that means "no." Do not use a double negative in one sentence. Correct a double negative by changing one negative into a positive word.

    She didn't want no one to feel bad about the race.

    She didn't want anyone to feel bad about the race.

Practice Write each sentence correctly, using only one negative.

1. Before long, there wasn't no one left on the track.

2. After the race, Theresa didn't have no energy to celebrate.

3. Theresa didn't want to do nothing but sleep.

 QUICK WRITE Write six sentences with adverbs. Include a least one comparative adverb and one superlative adverb. Also include at least one negative.

Handbook

RULE 1
pages
434–435

Interjections

- An interjection is a word or group of words that expresses strong feeling.

    Oops! We forgot to put film in the camera.

- A comma is used after a mild interjection.

    Gee, I guess we should have checked the camera.

- An exclamation mark is used after an interjection that expresses very strong feeling.

    Hey! Maybe there is film in our backpacks.

Practice Rewrite each sentence using correct capitalization and punctuation.

1. Look there is film in my backpack
2. Hooray we will have pictures to remember our trip
3. Well should we start on our hike
4. Oh no the flash doesn't seem to be working
5. Yikes we forgot to replace the batteries

RULE 2
pages
428–429

Prepositions

- A preposition is a word that relates a noun or pronoun to another word in a sentence.

    My family enjoys traveling during the summer.

Common Prepositions

about	among	beside	from	off	to
above	around	between	in	on	under
across	at	by	inside	out	until
after	before	down	into	outside	up
against	behind	during	near	over	with
along	below	for	of	through	without

542

Practice Write each sentence. Choose a preposition to complete the sentence.

1. Our family enjoys spending time _____ each other.

2. We drive _____ the mountains.

3. We hike _____ the trails.

4. The trails curve _____ the river.

5. The view _____ the mountains is beautiful.

RULE 3
pages 430–433

Prepositional Phrases

- A prepositional phrase begins with a preposition and ends with a noun or pronoun.

    We love to explore near the river.

- The object of a preposition is the noun or pronoun that follows a preposition.

    There is a bridge over the river.

- When the object of a preposition is a pronoun, use an object pronoun, such as *me, you, him, her, it, us,* or *them.*

    You can see over it to the other side.

Practice Write each sentence. Draw one line under the prepositional phrase. Draw two lines under the object of the preposition.

1. My brother walked across the bridge.

2. He looked at the clear, blue water.

3. My parents brought a picnic for us.

4. After lunch, we spread out a blanket and relaxed.

5. Everyone rested under a large, shady tree.

QUICK WRITE Write five sentences with interjections and prepositional phrases. Underline each prepositional phrase, and circle the object of the preposition.

Titles and Names

- An abbreviation is a shortened form of a word. An initial is the first letter of a name. Titles and initials begin with a capital letter and end with a period.

Title	Abbreviation	Title	Abbreviation
Mister	Mr.	Doctor	Dr.
Governor	Gov.	Senator	Sen.

Name	Initials
John Robert	J. R.
Nancy Jane	N. J.

Organizations

- In both formal and informal writing, use abbreviations for certain organizations and government agencies. These abbreviations usually have all capital letters and no periods.

  United Nations   *UN*   *Federal Bureau of Investigations*   *FBI*

Internet Addresses

- Use abbreviations at the end of Internet addresses.

commercial	.com	educational	.edu
organization	.org	network	.net

Practice Rewrite each sentence. Change each word or group of words in parentheses ( ) to an abbreviation or initials.

1. Our class contacted the (Department of Natural Resources).
2. We talked to a man named (Doctor) (Paul James) Donahue.
3. We asked about (Doctor) Keller, a famous botanist.
4. Our class was told to contact her at www.geese. (organization).
5. (Doctor) Keller works for the (Environmental Protection Agency).

Time

- Use abbreviations to indicate time before noon and after noon. These abbreviations are capitalized with periods after each letter.

Abbreviation	Meaning
11:00 A.M.	11:00 ante meridiem (before noon)
11:00 P.M.	11:00 post meridiem (after noon)

Days and Months

- In informal writing, use abbreviations of the days of the week and the months of the year. These abbreviations begin with a capital letter and end with a period.

Day	Abbreviation	Month	Abbreviation
Monday	Mon.	January	Jan.
Tuesday	Tues.	February	Feb.
Wednesday	Wed.	March	Mar.
Thursday	Thurs.	April	Apr.
Friday	Fri.	May	May
Saturday	Sat.	June	June
Sunday	Sun.	July	July
		August	Aug.
		September	Sept.
		October	Oct.
		November	Nov.
		December	Dec.

Addresses

- Address abbreviations are capitalized and followed by a period.

Avenue	Ave.	Drive	Dr.
Street	St.	Road	Rd.
Boulevard	Blvd.	Post Office	P. O.

Handbook

States

- **United States Postal Service** abbreviations for the names of states consist of two capital letters. No period follows these abbreviations.

State	Abbreviation	State	Abbreviation
Alabama	AL	Montana	MT
Alaska	AK	Nebraska	NE
Arizona	AZ	Nevada	NV
Arkansas	AR	New Hampshire	NH
California	CA	New Jersey	NJ
Colorado	CO	New Mexico	NM
Connecticut	CT	New York	NY
Delaware	DE	North Carolina	NC
Florida	FL	North Dakota	ND
Georgia	GA	Ohio	OH
Hawaii	HI	Oklahoma	OK
Idaho	ID	Oregon	OR
Illinois	IL	Pennsylvania	PA
Indiana	IN	Rhode Island	RI
Iowa	IA	South Carolina	SC
Kansas	KS	South Dakota	SD
Kentucky	KY	Tennessee	TN
Louisiana	LA	Texas	TX
Maine	ME	Utah	UT
Maryland	MD	Vermont	VT
Massachusetts	MA	Virginia	VA
Michigan	MI	Washington	WA
Minnesota	MN	West Virginia	WV
Mississippi	MS	Wisconsin	WI
Missouri	MO	Wyoming	WY

Units of Measure

- Use abbreviations for units of measure. The abbreviation is the same for singular and plural units.

   in.—inch(es)   lb.—pound(s)   km—kilometer(s)   l.—liter(s)

Handbook

First Words

- Capitalize the first word of a sentence.

    My sister is going to camp.

- Capitalize the first word of a direct quotation. Do not capitalize the second part of an interrupted quotation.

    Dan cried, "Please stop the presses!"
    "I am leaving," Jan declared, "as soon as I can."

- When the second part of a quotation is a new sentence, put a period after the interrupting expression and capitalize the first word of the new sentence.

    "I know that song," said Lisa. "We learned it last week."

- Capitalize all words in the greeting of a letter.

    Dear Sirs: *Dear Friend,*

- Capitalize the first word in the closing of a letter.

    Sincerely,   *Yours truly,*

- Capitalize the first word of each line of poetry unless the word is not capitalized in the original piece.

    I shot an arrow into the air,
    It fell to earth, I know not where;
    For, so swiftly it flew, the sight
    Could not follow it in its flight.

Practice Rewrite the friendly letter correctly. Use capital letters where needed.

(1) dear friend,

(2) how are you? Let me just say, **(3)** "here is a poem for you."

(4) roses are red.

    Violets are blue.

    Sugar is sweet.

    And so are you.

                    (5) your friend,

                        Michael

Proper Nouns: Names and Titles of People

- Capitalize the names of people and the initials that stand for their names.

  James Robert Perry   *J. R. Perry*

- Capitalize titles or abbreviations of titles when they come before or after the names of people.

  Mr. James Perry, Jr.   General J. P. Perry   Dr. Ellen Mahoney

- Capitalize words that show family relationships when used as titles or as substitutes for a person's name.

  Then Dad and Grandma Ellen cooked dinner.

- Do not capitalize words that show family relationships when they are preceded by a possessive noun or pronoun.

  Diane's grandmother is a good cook. Her dad is a good cook, too.

- Capitalize the pronoun *I*.

  Can I help cook dinner?

Practice Rewrite each sentence correctly. Capitalize the names and titles of people where needed.

1. p. j. and i made brownies for the family party.
2. My uncle, general steven ross, loved them.
3. My uncle and i ate five brownies each.
4. Father helped grandpa make pasta.
5. Grandpa said that mr. matthews gave him the recipe.

Proper Nouns: Names of Places

- Capitalize the names of cities, states, countries, and continents. Do not capitalize articles or prepositions that are part of the name.

City	*Austin*
State	*Texas*
Country	*United States of America*
Continent	*North America*

- Capitalize the names of bodies of water and geographical features.

  Atlantic Ocean   *Niagara Falls*

- Capitalize the names of sections of the country.

  the South   *the Pacific Northwest*

- Do not capitalize compass points when they just show direction.

  New York is east of Cleveland.

- Capitalize the names of streets and highways.

  Elm Street   *Santa Ana Freeway*

- Capitalize the names of buildings, bridges, and monuments.

  Sears Tower   *Brooklyn Bridge*   *Jefferson Memorial*

- Capitalize the names of stars and planets.

  The closest star to our planet is Proxima Centauri.

  The planet closest to the sun is Mercury.

- Capitalize *Earth* when it refers to the planet. Do not capitalize *earth* when preceded by *the*. Do not capitalize *sun* or *moon*.

  One moon revolves around Earth.

  The earth revolves around the sun.

Practice Rewrite each sentence correctly. Use capital letters where needed.

1. Our class drove through titusville, florida, to visit the john f. kennedy space center.

2. The bus drove south along cheney highway.

3. We looked at the atlantic ocean, and then we went inside to learn about space.

4. We learned about the crab nebula, an exploding star far from earth.

5. We also learned about mars, the fourth planet from the sun.

Other Proper Nouns and Adjectives

- Capitalize the names of schools, clubs, businesses, and political parties.

  Albright Middle School   *Explorers' Club*

  Reynold's Pharmacy   *Democratic Party*

- Capitalize the names of historic events, periods of time, and documents.

  Battle of Bunker Hill   *Colonial Period*

  Declaration of Independence

- Capitalize the days of the week, months of the year, and holidays. Do not capitalize the names of the seasons.

  We started school on Tuesday, September 1.

  Our first vacation is on Labor Day.

  My favorite season is autumn.

- Capitalize abbreviations.

  Dr.   *Ave.*   *Sept.*   *Ln.*

- Capitalize the names of ethnic groups, nationalities, and languages.

  The French won the war.   *I speak Japanese.*

- Capitalize proper adjectives that are formed from the names of ethnic groups and nationalities.

  Italian bread   *Egyptian cotton*

- Capitalize the first word of each main topic and subtopic in an outline.

  I.   Products and exports

  A.   Natural resources

  B.   Manufactured goods

Practice Rewrite each sentence correctly. Use capital letters where needed.

1. The fifth graders at jefferson elementary are studying the louisiana purchase.

2. The jeffersonville historical society has helped them gather information.

3. The Louisiana Territory had been changing hands since the seven years' war.

4. spanish, french, and british troops had all occupied the territory.

5. The students wondered if the troops spoke english.

Titles of Works

- Capitalize the first, last, and all important words in the title of a book, play, short story, poem, film, article, newspaper, magazine, TV series, chapter of a book, and song.

    I can't wait to read *Roll of Thunder, Hear My Cry.*

    Did you see *Peter Pan* at the community theater?

    A clever short story is "Rip van Winkle."

    My favorite poem when I was young was "Old King Cole."

    You should read "Cars of the Future" in this month's *Vehicles Monthly.*

    My dad reads *The Los Angeles Times* every morning.

    Did you watch *Newsbreaker* last night?

    Chapter one of that book is titled "The Long Night."

    I sang the "Star-Spangled Banner" before the big game.

Practice Rewrite each sentence correctly. Capitalize all titles of works.

1. Our school newspaper, *the titan times*, prints entertainment reviews.

2. One writer liked the book *stuart little*.

3. Her favorite chapter was titled "a narrow escape."

4. Another writer reviewed a play titled *the great divide*.

5. He compared it to the short story titled "opposite ends."

6. One writer reviewed the choir's performance of "somewhere over the rainbow."

7. I remember that song from the film *the wizard of oz*.

8. Next month, I'll write a review for the television series titled *karate man*.

9. The article's title will be "getting your kicks."

10. Maybe I'll write a review of my favorite magazine, *kidsports*, too.

End Punctuation

- Use end punctuation at the end of a sentence.
- A period ends a declarative sentence. A declarative sentence makes a statement.

  I have a cold.
- A period ends an imperative sentence. An imperative sentence makes a command or a request.

  Keep yourself warm.
- A question mark ends an interrogative sentence. An interrogative sentence asks a question.

  Will I get well?
- An exclamation mark ends an exclamatory sentence. An exclamatory sentence expresses strong emotion.

  I finally feel better!

Periods

- Use a period at the end of an abbreviation (in informal writing).

  Dr.   St.   Tues.   Jan.
- Use a period in abbreviations for time (in both formal and informal writing).

  12:00 A.M.   12:00 P.M.
- Use a period after initials.

  P. J. Reynolds
- Use a period after numbers and letters in an outline.

  I.   Margaret Mead
  A.   Famous anthropologist
  B.   Summary of her work

Practice **Write each sentence. Use correct punctuation.**

1. Do you have any chicken soup

2. At 10:00 AM, some ladies brought chicken soup to my house.

3. I liked Mrs Nelson's chicken soup best.

4. "AJ Jones," she said, "you'll feel better soon."

5. How hot it was

Colons

- Use a colon to separate the hour and the minute when you write the time of day.

    12:45   *1:15*   *6:30*

- Use a colon after the greeting of a business letter.

    Dear Sirs: *Dear Mr. Franklin:*

Hyphens

- Use a hyphen or hyphens in certain compound words.

    drive-in   *merry-go-round*

- Use a hyphen to show the division of a word at the end of a line. Always divide the word between syllables.

    Jennifer wants to go camping and canoe-
    ing this weekend.

- Use a hyphen in compound numbers.

    twenty-two students   *forty-nine stairs*

Apostrophes

- Use an apostrophe and an *s* (*'s*) to form the possessive of a singular noun.

    Jason's book   *my mom's bike*   *the car's horn*

- Use an apostrophe and an *s* (*'s*) to form the possessive of a plural noun that does not end in *s*.

    children's books   *men's shoes*   *geese's feathers*

- Use an apostrophe alone to form the possessive of a plural noun that ends in *s*.

    ladies' purses   *donkeys' brays*   *lilies' scent*

- Use an apostrophe in a contraction to show where a letter or letters are missing.

    we + are = we're   *he + is = he's*   *would + not = wouldn't*

- Do not use an apostrophe in a possessive pronoun.

    its good points   *their friends*   *your idea*

Handbook

Commas

- Use a comma between the name of the city and state in an address.

    Boston, Massachusetts

- Use a comma after the name of a state or a country when it is used with the name of a city in a sentence.

    We visited San Francisco, California, on our vacation.

- Use a comma between the day and year in a date.

    April 20, 2002   *July 4, 1776*

- Use a comma before and after the year when it is used with both the month and the day in a sentence. Do not use a comma if only the month and the year are given.

    June 4, 2000, is our last day of school.

    We will begin middle school in September 2001.

- Use a comma after the greeting in a friendly letter and after the closing in all letters.

    Dear Tyler,   *Sincerely,*

Practice **Rewrite the following friendly letter. Place commas where needed.**

                              124 Higgins Street

(1) Pittsburgh PA 15212

(2) September 4 2001

(3) Dear Mariela

(4) On September 30 2001 I will be coming to town.

                              (5) Your friend

                              Grace

Commas

- Use commas to separate three or more items in a series.

    Our flag is red, white, and blue.

    You are kind, patient, and helpful.

- Use a comma before *and, but,* or *or* when it joins simple sentences to form a compound sentence.

    We like to play softball, but the field is often used.

    My mother can drive us, or we can take the bus.

Practice Rewrite each sentence correctly. Add commas where they are needed.

1. We unloaded the balls bats and catcher's equipment for the big game.

2. I hope I'll be pitcher but I'm not sure whether I'll be chosen.

3. A pitcher has to be smart fast and accurate.

4. Our games are exciting and many people cheer.

5. We score early in the game or we depend on good pitching.

Commas

- Use a comma after introductory words or phrases in a sentence.
    Yes, I enjoy science class.
- Use a comma to set off a noun of direct address.
    Greta, please pass the mustard.
- Use a comma to set off a direct quotation.
    "I'll be right there," I said.
    "Will you please," I added, "pass the salt?"
- Use a comma after an introductory prepositional phrase.
    To the right of the tree, you'll see the monument.
    Behind the house, my family is waiting.
- Use a comma to prevent misreading.
    To a tall girl like Joan, Taylor seems really short.

Practice Rewrite each sentence. Add commas where needed.

1. Mom are you ready for the family reunion?

2. Yes I'm ready.

3. Well I'm not.

4. As you know we haven't prepared anything for the potluck supper.

5. On the table you'll find the recipe for the beans.

6. Over the stove you'll find the ingredients.

7. Yes Mom I'll make the beans.

8. Like my mom I enjoy cooking.

9. "You are both great cooks"my dad said.

10. "I think"I replied "you're right!"

Handbook

Quotation Marks

- Use quotation marks before and after a direct quotation, the exact words that a speaker says.

  "Someday I'm going to Brazil," said Paul.

  "Someday," said Paul, "I'm going to Brazil."

- Use a comma or commas to separate a phrase, such as *he said*, from the quotation itself. Place the comma outside the opening quotation marks but inside the closing quotation marks.

  Veronica asked, "Would you like to go to China?"

  "When I get older," replied Adam, "I'd love to go there."

- Place a period inside closing quotation marks.

  Pam added, "I hear Singapore is beautiful, too."

- Place a question mark or an exclamation mark inside the quotation marks when it is part of the quotation.

  "Where do you want to travel?" asked Maria.

  "I want to go on safari in Kenya, of course!" shouted Lily.

- Use quotation marks around the title of a short story, song, short poem, magazine or newspaper article, and chapter of a book.

  "Jack and the Beanstalk"   "Yankee Doodle Dandy"

  "How Valentine's Day Came to Be"   "Little Miss Muffet"

  "Hurricane Floyd Rocks the Southeast"   "A Mysterious Visitor"

Practice Rewrite each sentence correctly. Add punctuation where needed.

1. Are you ready for Around-the-World Day asked Mrs. Lee.

2. I want to learn about Jamaica said Isabel.

3. Will we asked Kevin learn about Ireland?

4. Yes replied Mrs. Lee we will.

5. Michael exclaimed What fun this day will be!

6. Did you enjoy the story titled Best Player?

7. Yes, it reminded me of the poem Casey at the Bat.

8. It made me think of the song Take Me Out to the Ballgame.

9. I read an article titled Greatest Baseball Players in History.

10. Now I look for books with chapter titles such as Home Run Kings.

Italics (Underlining)

• Use italics or underlining for the title of a book, film, television series, play, magazine, or newspaper.

The Secret Garden	<u>The Secret Garden</u>
Dumbo	<u>Dumbo</u>
Reading Rainbow	<u>Reading Rainbow</u>
Fiddler on the Roof	<u>Fiddler on the Roof</u>
Sports Illustrated	<u>Sports Illustrated</u>
The New York Times	<u>The New York Times</u>

Practice Rewrite each sentence correctly. Underline titles where needed.

1. Did you know that the movie Alice in Wonderland was based on a book?

2. Yes, the book was titled Alice's Adventures in Wonderland.

3. The author's life was described on a TV show called Great Authors.

4. Articles about the author also appeared in newspapers such as the Chicago Tribune .

5. The author's biography was published in Cricket magazine, too.

Sentence Structure: Diagramming Guide

A **sentence diagram** shows how the words in a sentence go together. The diagram shows capitalized words but not sentence punctuation. The most important words in the sentence are put on a horizontal *base line*. The other words are written on lines connected to the base line. First, you will learn how to diagram the most important words in a sentence. Later, you will learn how to diagram the other words.

RULE 1
pages 16–19

Simple Subjects and Simple Predicates

- The simple subject and the simple predicate are written on the base line of a sentence diagram. The simple subject is written on the left side of the base line, and the simple predicate is written on the right side. An up-and-down line separates the simple subject from the simple predicate.

Miners dig minerals.

Miners | dig

In an interrogative sentence, the simple subject often comes between the two parts of a verb phrase.

Have you seen the mine?

you | Have seen

In an imperative sentence, there may not be a named subject. In this case, the subject is *you*.

Watch that miner.

(you) | Watch

Practice Make a sentence diagram of the simple subject and the simple predicate in each sentence.

1. Minerals come from the earth.

2. Coal is formed between layers of rock.

3. Miners blast minerals out of the ground.

4. Does copper come from mines in Arizona?

5. Close that mine now.

Handbook

RULE 2
pages
20–23

Compound Subjects and Predicates

- A sentence with a compound subject has two or more simple subjects with the same predicate. A sentence with a compound predicate has two or more simple predicates with the same subject. The simple subjects or simple predicates are joined by *and* or *or*. In a sentence diagram, the word *and* or *or* is written on a dotted up-and-down line connecting the subjects or the predicates.

Rice and pasta provide energy for the body.

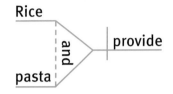

Humans work, play, and sleep.

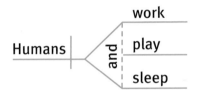

Practice Diagram the compound subject or the compound predicate in each sentence. Include in each diagram the simple subject and the simple predicate that goes with each compound.

1. Bones and teeth need calcium.
2. Some fats and oils help the body.
3. Vitamin A strengthens and improves vision.
4. Starches and sugars are carbohydrates.
5. Toddlers and women require extra iron.
6. Good food and exercise are important.
7. Oxygen and food are needed by the body.
8. A healthy body repairs and replaces damaged cells.
9. Babies, children, and teenagers need healthy food.
10. Children eat, sleep, and exercise to stay healthy.

Handbook

Handbook

RULE 3
pages
170–171 — **Direct Objects** —

- A direct object is a noun or pronoun in the predicate that receives the action of the verb. It answers the question *Whom?* or *What?* In a sentence diagram, the direct object is written after the simple predicate on the base line. An up-and-down line separates the direct object from the simple predicate. This vertical line does not cross the base line.

Many students join the band.

students | join | band

A verb can have more than one direct object. Look at the following example to see how a compound direct object is diagrammed.

Many students join the band, choir, or orchestra.

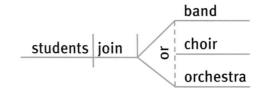

Practice Diagram the simple subject, the simple predicate, and the direct object or objects in each sentence.

1. Mrs. Jacobsen encouraged Daniel.

2. She explained the requirements for joining the drama club.

3. Daniel joined the club.

4. The students brought costumes and props.

5. The principal planned a stage set.

6. The crew cleared the stage.

7. Some art students painted the scenery.

8. Another group designed a program.

9. Dad took photographs.

10. Mom fed the cast and crew.

RULE 4

pages 260–265

pages 416–421

Adjectives and Adverbs

• **Adjectives**, including the articles *a*, *an*, and *the*, describe nouns. Adjectives tell *what kind, which one(s)*, and *how many*. **Adverbs** describe verbs, adjectives, or other adverbs. Adverbs answer *how, when, where*, or *why*. In a sentence diagram, adjectives and adverbs are placed on slanted lines below the words they describe.

The talented drummer played loudly.

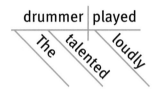

An adverb does not always appear next to the verb it describes. In the following sentence, an adverb describes another adverb.

The drummer struck the instrument very quickly.

The adverb **very** describes the adverb **quickly**. Notice how the adverbs are diagrammed.

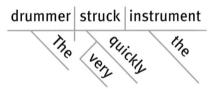

Notice how the two adjectives are diagrammed in the following example.

The bass drum boomed loudly and deeply.

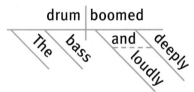

Practice Diagram every word in these sentences.

1. A single kettledrum echoes forcefully.

2. Felt covers the tenor drumsticks.

3. Ancient civilizations probably played drums.

4. Military and marching bands often play tenor drums.

5. Many famous composers wrote musical arrangements.

Handbook

RULE 5
pages
430–433

Prepositional Phrases

- **Prepositional phrases** begin with a preposition such as *to, for, from, at,* or *in* and end with a noun or pronoun. In a sentence diagram, a prepositional phrase is written on a slanted line below the word that it modifies. The object of the preposition is written on a connecting horizontal line.

Sound and pictures are recorded separately in movies.

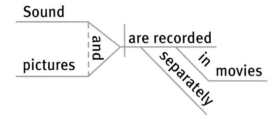

The words that describe the object of the preposition are written on slanting lines below it.

Some sounds are added to the completed film.

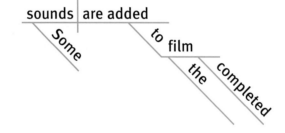

Practice **Diagram every word in these sentences.**

1. Many movies are filmed in Europe.
2. The producer and director work on the film.
3. The director talks to the cast.
4. The actors and crew listen to the director.
5. The script is written by a screenwriter.
6. Film is added to the camera.
7. The sets are created by a set designer.
8. Some costumes are repaired by the wardrobe person.
9. The music is recorded in a sound studio.
10. The movie studio pays for the movie.

RULE 6
pages
8–9

Compound Sentences

- A compound sentence joins two or more simple sentences with a comma and the conjunction *and*, *or*, or *but*. Diagram each part of a compound sentence separately. Write the conjunction on a line between the two parts. Draw a dotted line connecting this word to each part.

Honeybees live throughout the world, but no bees live in Antarctica.

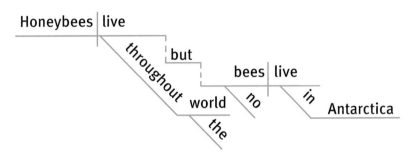

Practice Diagram every word in these compound sentences.

1. Bees are insects, and they are related to wasps.
2. A bee has two pairs of wings, but the wings are joined.
3. Pollen sticks to the bee, and it nourishes the young bees.
4. Bees sting an enemy, or they fly away.
5. Most bees attack often, but a honeybee stings only once.
6. Worker bees work, but the queen bee rules.
7. The stinger contains poison, and many people have allergic reactions to the stinger.
8. Honeycombs have rows of wax cells, and they have a pattern of holes.
9. The queen bee lays eggs, and the worker bees care for the hive.
10. Some people keep beehives, and they collect the honey.

Handbook

Note-Taking and Summarizing

DEFINITIONS AND FEATURES

- You can take notes from written material or from listening to a speaker.
- When taking notes, record only important facts. Use your own words instead of the author's or speaker's words.
- Record the sources of your notes, including the book title, the author, and the page number.
- You can summarize your notes to be sure that you understand the material. A summary includes only the most important ideas.

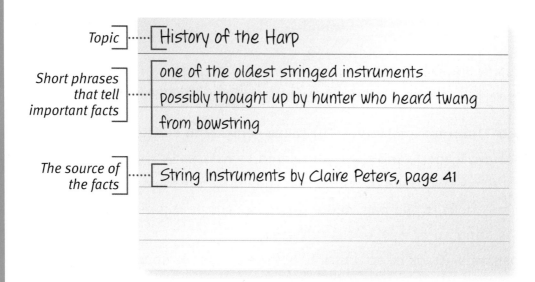

Topic .... [History of the Harp

Short phrases that tell important facts ...... [one of the oldest stringed instruments
possibly thought up by hunter who heard twang from bowstring

The source of the facts ...... [String Instruments by Claire Peters, page 41

Practice Take notes on the following article, listing five facts on a sheet of paper. Then write a summary using your notes and your own words. Give your summary a title.

The modern concert harp is the only instrument in an orchestra that is played entirely by plucking the strings. Harpists use their fingers to pluck the 47 strings. Modern concert harps have seven foot-pedals. Each pedal has three possible positions. These pedals change the pitch of the strings. This allows the harpist to play in any key.

 inter NET CONNECTION Go to www.mhschool.com/language-arts for more information on the topic.

Choosing Reference Sources for Research

Handbook

— DEFINITIONS AND FEATURES —

- Use two or more sources when researching information for a research report.
- Sources could include nonfiction books, periodicals (magazines and newspapers), encyclopedias, interviews, and videotapes.
- Choose the source that matches your topic. For current information, use a magazine. For statistics, use an almanac.
- Include a bibliography, or list of sources, at the end of the report. Include title, author, and date of publication of each source.

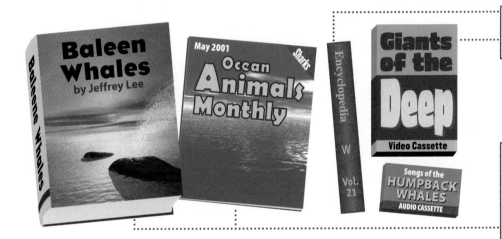

Use two or more sources when researching.

List the title and author, as well as the date of publication and page numbers, in a bibliography.

Practice Read the following topics. Write *book, periodical, encyclopedia, videotape, audiocassette,* or *interview* to name the best source of information for that topic.

1. A local architect's plan for a new park in your town
2. A brief article on elm trees
3. Large amounts of specific, in-depth information about baseball
4. The local weather report for the week
5. The most current information about campgrounds
6. Instructions for building a birdhouse
7. A diagram of the anatomy of a fish
8. A recording of a poet reciting nature poems
9. The life of a famous author
10. How to make a specific recipe created by your mother

Handbook

Parts of a Book

DEFINITIONS AND FEATURES

- The table of contents lists chapter titles and page numbers. It can give you an idea of the chapters' main ideas.
- The copyright page tells the company who published the book and the date and place of publication.
- The glossary is a dictionary that lists words found in a particular book.
- Use the index to find specific information in the book. The index lists topics and subtopics in alphabetical order.

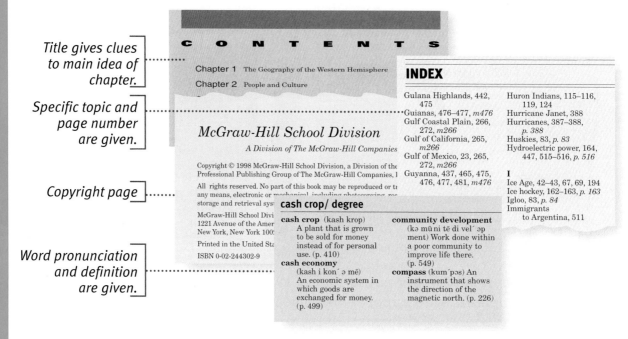

Title gives clues to main idea of chapter.

Specific topic and page number are given.

Copyright page

Word pronunciation and definition are given.

Practice Write *table of contents, copyright page, glossary,* or *index* to tell where in a book you would locate the following information.

1. The meaning of the word *thorax*

2. Page numbers for information about the red ant

3. A date to tell whether a book is more than 5 years old

4. Page numbers for information about air pressure

5. Where a book was published

inter NET CONNECTION Go to www.mhschool.com/language-arts for more information on the topic.

Bibliography

---— **DEFINITIONS** AND **FEATURES** —---

- A bibliography is a list of all the sources you have used to research and write a report. It may include books, articles, or other media resources.
- The bibliography tells your readers where you found your information and provides them with a guide to find out more.
- Entries are normally listed alphabetically by author. When no author is given, list an entry by its title.
- The bibliography gives the names of the authors, the title of the book or article, the publisher, the place of publication, and the copyright date of the material.

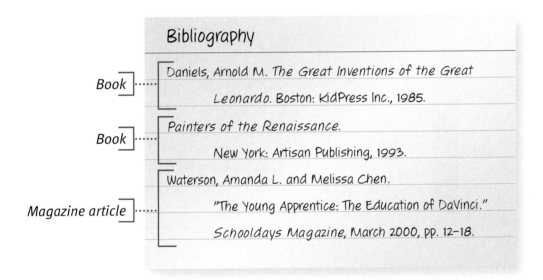

Bibliography

Book ..... Daniels, Arnold M. *The Great Inventions of the Great Leonardo.* Boston: KidPress Inc., 1985.

Book ..... *Painters of the Renaissance.* New York: Artisan Publishing, 1993.

Magazine article ..... Waterson, Amanda L. and Melissa Chen. "The Young Apprentice: The Education of DaVinci." *Schooldays Magazine,* March 2000, pp. 12–18.

Practice Use the sample bibliography to answer the following questions.

1. In what year was Arnold M. Daniels's book published?
2. Why is *Painters of the Renaissance* listed by title?
3. In which source did the author find information about Leonardo DaVinci's education?
4. Who wrote "The Young Apprentice"?
5. Where was *Painters of the Renaissance* published?

Handbook

Time Lines and Historical Maps

DEFINITIONS AND FEATURES

- A time line shows the order in which events happened. Dates are written on a time line to show the period of time between events.
- A historical map shows land features and places from long ago. It may show where historical events occurred. Historical maps often include labels or symbols that convey important information.

The title tells the topic of the map.

This time line covers a period of 50 years.

The time line is divided into five parts, one for each decade.

The key identifies the meaning of the map symbols.

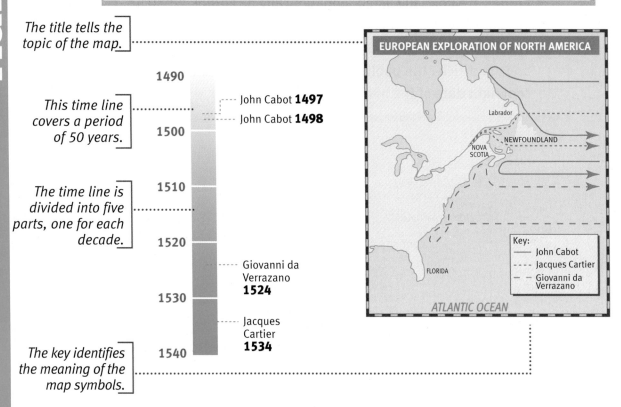

1490

John Cabot **1497**
John Cabot **1498**

1500

1510

1520

Giovanni da Verrazano **1524**

1530

Jacques Cartier **1534**

1540

EUROPEAN EXPLORATION OF NORTH AMERICA

Labrador
NEWFOUNDLAND
NOVA SCOTIA

FLORIDA

Key:
—— John Cabot
------ Jacques Cartier
– – Giovanni da Verrazano

ATLANTIC OCEAN

Practice Use the time line and map to answer the questions.

1. What European explorer was the first to sail to North America during this time period?

2. Did you use the time line or the map to answer question 1? Why?

3. What explorer followed the most southerly route?

4. Why can't you use the time line to answer question 3?

5. Which explorer sailed to North America twice? How do you know?

Go to www.mhschool.com/language-arts for more information on the topic.

568

Graphs

DEFINITIONS AND FEATURES

- A graph is a visual way to show information. Graphs help readers compare different types of information, or data.
- The title tells what information can be found on the graph.
- Labels on graphs give more information about the data.
- There are many types of graphs. Circle graphs show how a group can be divided into smaller groups. Bar graphs show numbers. Each bar represents a number of items.

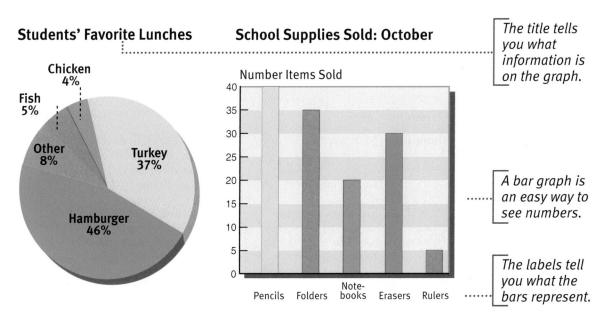

Students' Favorite Lunches

Chicken 4%
Fish 5%
Other 8%
Turkey 37%
Hamburger 46%

School Supplies Sold: October

Number Items Sold

Pencils Folders Note-books Erasers Rulers

The title tells you what information is on the graph.

A bar graph is an easy way to see numbers.

The labels tell you what the bars represent.

Practice Use both graphs to answer the questions.

1. Which lunch do students like the most?
2. Which lunch do students like the least?
3. Which lunches do students like about the same?
4. Do more students like hamburger, or do more students like chicken, fish, and other lunches combined?
5. What clue helps you answer question 4 without adding?
6. How many notebooks were sold during October?
7. Which item had the highest sales?
8. Which item had 30 sales?
9. How many more notebooks were sold than rulers?
10. How are the two graphs different from each other?

Handbook

Dictionary

DEFINITIONS AND FEATURES

- A dictionary can help you learn the meaning, spelling, and pronunciation of an unfamiliar word.
- The words in dark type are called entry words. They show the spelling and syllables of the words.
- The two guide words at the top of a dictionary page identify the first entry word and the last entry word on that page.
- Entry words are arranged in alphabetical order.
- The pronunciation is shown in parentheses.
- Some words have different meanings. Each definition of an entry word is numbered.

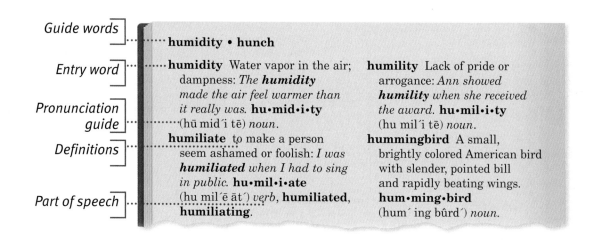

Guide words

Entry word

Pronunciation guide

Definitions

Part of speech

humidity • hunch

humidity Water vapor in the air; dampness: *The* **humidity** *made the air feel warmer than it really was.* **hu•mid•i•ty** (hū mid´i tē) *noun.*

humiliate to make a person seem ashamed or foolish: *I was* **humiliated** *when I had to sing in public.* **hu•mil•i•ate** (hu mil´ē āt´) *verb,* **humiliated,** **humiliating.**

humility Lack of pride or arrogance: *Ann showed* **humility** *when she received the award.* **hu•mil•i•ty** (hu mil´i tē) *noun.*

hummingbird A small, brightly colored American bird with slender, pointed bill and rapidly beating wings. **hum•ming•bird** (hum´ ing bûrd´) *noun.*

Practice Use the above entries from part of a dictionary to answer these questions.

1. What part of speech is the word *humidity*?

2. How many syllables does the word *humiliate* have?

3. What word could you look up to further understand the meaning of *humility*?

4. Which of these words would appear elsewhere on this dictionary page: *hunch, human, humus, hunger, hurdle*?

5. Why are the words *humiliated* and *humiliating* shown after the entry word *humiliate*?

Go to www.mhschool.com/language-arts for more information on the topic.

Thesaurus

DEFINITIONS AND FEATURES

- A thesaurus is a reference source that lists synonyms and antonyms. Synonyms are words that have the same or similar meanings. Antonyms are words that have opposite meanings.
- Use a thesaurus to help you choose more interesting and more exact words to use in your writing.
- Synonyms are listed after entry words in a thesaurus. Entry words in dark type are listed in alphabetical order.
- Some entries include a cross-reference, which refers you to other words in the thesaurus.
- A computer or an on-line thesaurus can usually be found under "Tools" in the menu bar of a word-processing program.

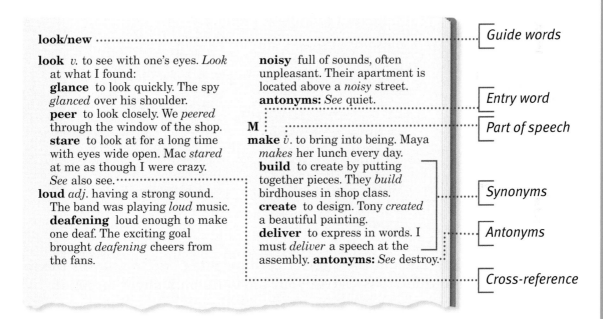

look/new ·· Guide words

look *v.* to see with one's eyes. *Look* at what I found:
glance to look quickly. The spy *glanced* over his shoulder.
peer to look closely. We *peered* through the window of the shop.
stare to look at for a long time with eyes wide open. Mac *stared* at me as though I were crazy. *See* also see.
loud *adj.* having a strong sound. The band was playing *loud* music.
deafening loud enough to make one deaf. The exciting goal brought *deafening* cheers from the fans.

noisy full of sounds, often unpleasant. Their apartment is located above a *noisy* street.
antonyms: *See* quiet. ······················· Entry word

M ·· Part of speech
make *v.* to bring into being. Maya *makes* her lunch every day.
build to create by putting together pieces. They *build* birdhouses in shop class. ·········· Synonyms
create to design. Tony *created* a beautiful painting.
deliver to express in words. I must *deliver* a speech at the assembly. **antonyms:** *See* destroy. ········ Antonyms

··· Cross-reference

Practice Write each sentence. Replace the underlined word with a synonym or an antonym shown in the thesaurus entries on this page. Use a different word each time.

1. Amy was <u>making</u> a collage.

2. She heard a <u>loud</u> voice.

3. She <u>looked</u> out the window.

4. A man was <u>making</u> a speech.

5. The crowd around him was <u>loud</u>.

Handbook

Card Catalog

┌─── **DEFINITIONS** AND **FEATURES** ───────┐

- A card catalog provides information about each library book. It may be a set of cards or a computer database.
- The cards in the catalog are listed in alphabetical order.
- Each book has three cards stored in separate files: an author card, a title card, and a subject card.
- The author card lists the name of the author first. The title card lists the title of the book first. The subject card lists the general subject of the book first.
- The call number tells where to find the book on the shelf.

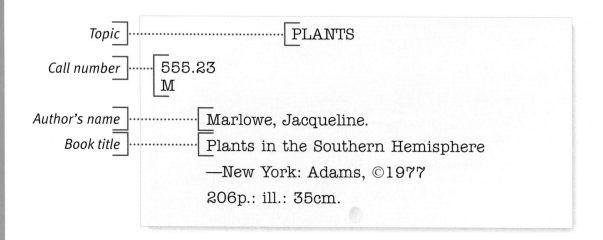

Topic ················ PLANTS

Call number ······ 555.23
M

Author's name ········ Marlowe, Jacqueline.

Book title ········ Plants in the Southern Hemisphere

—New York: Adams, ©1977

206p.: ill.: 35cm.

Practice Look at the subject card on this page to answer the following questions. Write your answers on a sheet of paper.

1. Who is the author of the book?
2. What is the title of the book?
3. What is the call number of the book?
4. What is the subject of the book?
5. What year was the book published?

inter**NET** **CONNECTION** Go to www.mhschool.com/language-arts for more information on the topic.

Library or Media Center

── DEFINITIONS AND FEATURES ──

- A library or a media center includes a variety of materials and resources that are arranged in different sections.
- Fiction books are arranged on shelves alphabetically by authors' last names. Nonfiction books are arranged by subject.
- The circulation desk is where you check out books.
- The reference section includes books for research such as encyclopedias, atlases, and almanacs. The reference section may also include computers for Internet and CD-ROM research.
- A media center may include videotapes, audiotapes, VCRs, tape recorders, and software.
- The card catalog contains information about library books. It may be in drawers or on a computer database.
- The periodicals section includes magazines and newspapers.

Library Floor Plan

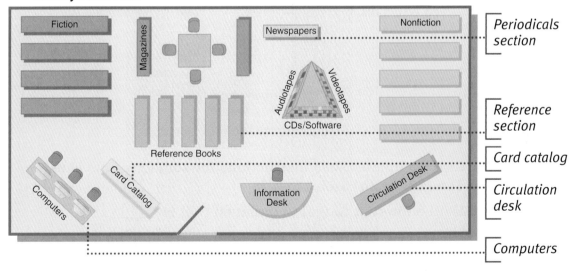

Practice Look at the floor plan shown on this page. Write where you would find each of the following items in the library.

1. the *A* volume of an encyclopedia
2. a list of Roald Dahl books that can be found in the library
3. a Web site on how to play chess
4. an issue of *Sports Illustrated for Kids*
5. a copy of *The Giver,* a novel by Lois Lowry

573

Handbook

Using the Internet

DEFINITIONS AND FEATURES

- The Internet is an up-to-the-minute, current source of information about many topics.
- You can use a search engine to find information about a specific topic. Narrow your search by using keywords.
- On-line encyclopedias contain the same type of information as print encyclopedias. They are often arranged alphabetically by keyword.
- You can find daily news on the Internet by searching through on-line newspapers.
- At some Web sites, you can send e-mail to experts to ask specific questions about topics.

You can use a search engine to find information about a topic.

Kids Info

Topic [_____] DOWNLOAD SEARCH

- Homework Help
- Sports
- Science
- All Over the World
- Technology and Games
- Entertainment News

HELP!

Practice Complete these instructions for someone who is using the Internet to do research.

1. Use the Internet to find information that is _____.

2. Use a _____ to find Web sites about a certain topic.

3. If you want to interview an expert on-line, you can _____ him or her.

4. Use _____ to find Web sites and encyclopedia articles on specific topics.

5. If you want to find out what has happened in a certain city on a certain day, check out an on-line _____.

*inter*NET CONNECTION Go to www.mhschool.com/language-arts for more information on the topic.

574

Periodicals and Media Resources

DEFINITIONS AND FEATURES

- **Periodicals** are magazines and newspapers published at regular intervals, such as weekly, monthly, and quarterly.
- Periodicals provide current information about various topics.
- The Readers' Guide to Periodical Literature is a set of books or an electronic database that alphabetically lists, by topic or author, articles published in magazines. It identifies the magazine, issue, and pages where the article can be found.
- Media resources are nonprint resources that you can use to find information, such as CD-ROMs, videotapes, and audiotapes.

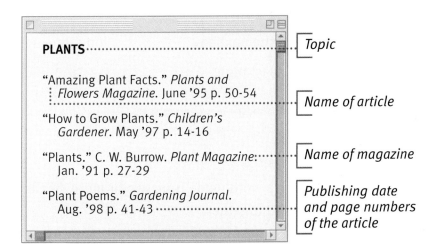

PLANTS ······· *Topic*

"Amazing Plant Facts." *Plants and Flowers Magazine.* June '95 p. 50-54 ········· *Name of article*

"How to Grow Plants." *Children's Gardener.* May '97 p. 14-16

"Plants." C. W. Burrow. *Plant Magazine:* ······ *Name of magazine*
Jan. '91 p. 27-29

"Plant Poems." *Gardening Journal.* Aug. '98 p. 41-43 ·········· *Publishing date and page numbers of the article*

Practice Use the *Readers' Guide* entries on this screen to answer the following questions.

1. How many magazines include articles about plants?
2. What magazine has an article titled "Plants"?
3. What article is in the magazine *Children's Gardener*?
4. When was the article "Amazing Plant Facts" published?
5. On what pages will you find the article titled "Plant Poems"?

Handbook

RULE 1
pages 38–39

Time-Order Words

- A time-order word tells when events happen and in what order they happen.

- Use time-order words to show how ideas are related to each other and to make your writing flow more smoothly.

- Sometimes a phrase can show time order in a piece of writing.

first	yesterday	now
next	today	before
then	tomorrow	after
last	as soon as	in the meantime
finally	one day	meanwhile
second	the next day	a long time ago
third	last night	

RULE 2
pages 120–121

Compound Words

- A compound word is a word made from two or more smaller words that have been joined together.
- You can often tell the meaning of a compound word by looking at the words that make up the compound word.
- A compound word may be written as one word, two or more words separated by a hyphen, or as two separate words.

Two Words	Compound Word	Meaning
fire + truck	fire truck	truck that fights fires
back + pack	backpack	pack worn on the back
space + shuttle	space shuttle	shuttle that flies into space
fish + hook	fishhook	hook that catches fish
pot + roast	pot roast	roast made in a pot
wall + paper	wallpaper	paper placed on the wall
double + park	double-park	park two cars next to each other

RULE 3
pages
206–207

Prefixes and Suffixes

- **Prefixes** and **suffixes** are word parts added to the beginning or end of a **root word** or base word.
- A **prefix** is a word part added to the beginning of a base word.
- A **suffix** is a word part added to the end of a base word.
- Adding a prefix or suffix changes the **meaning** of the base word to which it is added.

Prefix	Meaning	Suffix	Meaning
re-	again, back	-ful	full of
un-, dis-, non-	not, the opposite of	-able, -ible	capable or worthy of, fit for
mis-	wrongly, badly	-ness	state, condition, or quality of
pre-	before	-less	without, not having
bi-	having two of; twice	-ist	one who does or makes
im-, in-	not, without, in, into	-ment	the act, state, quality, or result of

RULE 4
pages
292–293

Synonyms and Antonyms

- **Synonyms** are words that have the **same** or almost the same meanings.
- **Antonyms** are words that have **opposite** meanings.
- A word may have **more than one** synonym or antonym.

Word	Synonym	Antonym
strong	powerful	weak
careful	cautious	careless
fix	repair	destroy
untrue	false	true
possible	likely	impossible

Handbook

RULE 5
pages
370–371

Word Choice

- Carefully choose words to create vivid pictures for your readers. To be as precise as possible, use words with the exact meanings you intend.
- Choose a synonym that best expresses your meaning.
- Select vivid verbs and vivid adjectives to create stronger and more exact descriptions.

Vague Verbs	Precise Verbs	Vague Adjectives	Precise Adjectives
ask	invite	big	mammoth
do	perform	cold	frigid
fix	remodel	dark	foggy
fly	soar	dull	uninteresting
get	reach	fast	speedy
hang	drape	fine	splendid
look	peer	hard	puzzling
melt	liquefy	late	overdue
move	dance	nice	agreeable
say	shout	noisy	ear-splitting
		old	outmoded
		sweet	honeyed

RULE 6
pages
452–453

Figurative Language

- **Figurative language** uses words in ways beyond their usual or literal meanings.
- Writers use figurative language to create images for readers.
- Figurative language can make writing more vivid, precise, and interesting.
- Similes, metaphors, and personification are three specific types of figurative language.

Figurative Language	Definition	Example
simile	compares using the word *like* or *as*	The beach was *as hot as an oven*. The students' footsteps sounded *like thunder*.
metaphor	compares two unlike things without using words of comparison	The beach *was an oven*. The students' footsteps *were thunder* on the stairs.
personification	gives human qualities to animals, ideas, and objects	The cool water *invited* me to jump in. The stairs *complained* when the students ran up them.

Handbook

Problem Words

- The English language includes some confusing words that are often misused. The following charts will help you understand how to use these words properly.

Words	Correct Usage
accept	*Accept* means "to receive" or "to agree to." It is a verb. *I accept your apology.*
except	*Except* means "other than." It is usually a preposition. *I like all fruits except bananas.*
bad	*Bad* is an adjective. It means "the opposite of good." *My brother is a bad cook because he never reads directions.*
badly	*Badly* is an adverb. It means "in a bad manner." *The boy treated his sister badly because his feelings were hurt.*
beside	*Beside* means "on the side of." *The book is beside the lamp.*
besides	*Besides* means "in addition to." *Besides Joel, Carl and Ellen were cast in the play.*
can	*Can* tells about an ability. *I can play the flute.*
may	*May* expresses permission. *You may spend the night at Harold's house.*
fewer	*Fewer* is used for things that can be counted. *I have fewer crayons than Todd does.*
less	*Less* is used for things or ideas that cannot be counted. *I am less organized than Sherry is.*
good	*Good* is an adjective that describes something positive. *I had a good steak at the restaurant last night.*
well	Well is usually an adverb. It gives more information about the verb by telling "how." *My sister swam well last summer.*

Problem Words

Words	Correct Usage
lay	*Lay* means "to put something down." *Lay the papers on my desk.*
lie	*Lie* means "to recline or rest." *Seth lies on the floor in front of the fireplace.*
loose	*Loose* means "not secured." *Maggie had her first loose tooth.*
lose	*Lose* means "to misplace." It is a verb. *Did you lose your house key?*
set	*Set* means "to put something down or in a certain place." *I set my pencil on the table.*
sit	*Sit* means "to be seated." *Our class should sit in the front of the auditorium.*
their	*Their* is a possessive pronoun meaning "belonging to them." *The Murphys are gone so Ryan will feed their dog this week.*
they're	*They're* is a contraction meaning "they are." *We aren't sure when they're coming back from vacation.*
your	*Your* is a possessive pronoun that means "something that belongs to you." *Is that your cat?*
you're	*You're* is the contraction for "you are." *You're a wonderful artist, Sam.*
whose	*Whose* is an adjective showing possession. *Whose paper is this on the floor?*
who's	*Who's* is a contraction for "who is." The apostrophe takes the place of the *i* in *is*. *I don't know who's coming to the festival next week.*

Handbook

RULES

▶ **Silent e** When words *end in silent e*, drop the *e* when adding an ending that begins with a vowel. *(rule + es = rules)* When adding an ending that begins with a consonant, keep the silent *e* (*love + ly = lovely*).

▶ **Spelling with y** When a base word *ends with a consonant followed by y*, change the *y* to *i* when adding any ending except endings that begin with *i*. *(fly + es = flies; fly + ing = flying)* When a base word *ends with a vowel followed by y*, do not change the *y* when adding endings. *(donkey + s = donkeys)*

▶ **Vowel and Final Consonant** When a one-syllable word *ends in one vowel followed by one consonant*, double the consonant before adding an ending that begins with a vowel. *(jog + ing = jogging)*

▶ **The letter q** is always followed by *u*. *(quaint, quitter)*

▶ No English word ends in *j*, *q*, or *v*.

▶ **Plural and Verb Tense** Add *-s* to most words to form plurals or to change the tense of verbs. Add *-es* to words ending in *x, z, s, sh,* or *ch*. *(cup + s = cups; wish + es = wishes; class + es = classes)*

▶ **Plural: f and fe** To make plurals of words that end with one *f* or *fe*, usually change the *f* or *fe* to *v* and add *-es*. *(wife + es = wives)*

▶ **ie and ei Word** When choosing *ei* or *ie*, remember that *i* comes before *e* except after *c* or when it sounds like /ā/ as in neighbor or weigh.

▶ **The /s/ Sound** When the /s/ *sound* is spelled *c*, it is always followed by *e, i,* or *y*. *(place, circle, fancy)*

▶ **When /j/ is Spelled g** *g* is always followed by *e, i,* or *y*. *(gem, giant, energy)*

▶ **The /ch/ Sound** If the /ch/ sound immediately follows a short vowel in a one-syllable word, it is spelled *tch*. *(clutch, batch)* There are a few exceptions in English: *much, such, which,* and *rich*.

▶ **The /f/ sound** at the end of a word may be spelled *f, ph,* or *gh*. *(brief, graph, tough)*

RULES

Use these strategies to help you become a better speller.

▶ **Homophones** Learn common homophones and make sure you have used the correct homophone in your writing. *(They're going to their house. They live over there.)*

▶ **Rhyming Words** Think of a word you know that has the same spelling pattern as the word you want to spell, such as a rhyming word. *(stew, blew, knew)*

▶ **Use words that you know** how to spell to help you spell new words. *(blower + sock = block)*

▶ **Make up clues** to help you remember the spelling. *(ache = a cat has ears; u and i build a house; a piece of pie; Al has morals)*

▶ **Related Words** Think of a related word to help you spell a word with a silent letter or a hard-to-hear sound. *(sign-signal; relative-related)*

▶ **Syllables** Divide the word into syllables. *(re mind er)*

▶ **Prefixes and Suffixes** Learn to spell prefixes and suffixes you often use in writing.

▶ **Word Chunks** Look for word chunks or smaller words that help you remember the spelling of the word. *(hippopotamus = hippo pot am us)*

▶ **Change the way you say the word** to yourself to help with the spelling. *(knife = /k nīf/; beauty = /bē ū tē/)*

▶ **Visualizing** Think of the times you may have seen the word in reading, on signs, or in a textbook. Try to remember how it looked. Write the word in different ways. Which one looks correct? *(~~havy~~, ~~hevy~~, heavy)*

▶ **Use the Spell-Check Program** If you are working on a computer, use the spell-check program. Remember, though, that spell-checkers are not perfect. If you write *your* instead of *you're*, a spell-checker will not catch the mistake.

▶ **Personal Word List** Keep an alphabetical Personal Word List in your Spelling Journal. Write words you have trouble spelling.

Handbook

Easily Confused Words

- Some words are easily confused because they are spelled similarly or because they sound alike. These words have different definitions, so you need to be sure you use the correct one.

accept	any more	desert	loose	taut
except	anymore	dessert	lose	taunt
accuse	approve	expect	midst	than
excuse	improve	suspect	mist	then
adapt	breath	farther	personal	though
adopt	breathe	further	personnel	through
afar	cloth	finale	picture	very
affair	clothe	finally	pitcher	vary
alley	close	formally	quiet	weather
ally	clothes	formerly	quite	whether
all ready	conscience	hour	recent	your
already	conscious	our	resent	you're
all together	costume	later	respectively	
altogether	custom	latter	respectfully	
angel	dairy	lay	sink	
angle	diary	lie	zinc	

Frequently Misspelled Words

- For many writers, some words are difficult to spell. You can use this list to check your spelling.

a lot	doesn't	heard	our	surprised
afraid	especially	hero	people	tried
again	everybody	instead	piece	truly
already	everyone	into	probably	until
always	except	knew	radio	upon
athlete	excited	know	really	usually
beautiful	family	knowledge	right	vacation
because	favorite	library	said	we're
before	field	maybe	separate	weird
believe	finally	minute	should	were
caught	friend	myself	since	when
clothes	getting	of	sincerely	where
control	government	off	something	which
different	grabbed	once	successful	whole
disappear	happened	one	sure	you're

Common Homophones

- Homophones are words that sound the same but have different spellings and meanings. *Whole* and *hole* are examples of homophones.

ad	currant	heal	mail	threw
add	current	heel	male	through
aisle	days	herd	main	throne
I'll	daze	heard	mane	thrown
isle				
allowed	dew	higher	missed	to
aloud	do	hire	mist	too
				two
base	die	hole	pair	toad
bass	dye	whole	pear	towed
boar	find	in	peak	wade
bore	fined	inn	peek	weighed
brake	flew	its	rap	wail
break	flu	it's	wrap	whale
capital	foul	knew	ring	waist
Capitol	fowl	new	wring	waste
cell	grate	knot	some	weave
sell	great	not	sum	we've
chews	hair	lead	stationary	wrung
choose	hare	led	stationery	rung
coarse	hall	lessen	their	
course	haul	lesson	there	
				they're

Word Study Steps

Be a better speller by following these steps.

1. Study each letter in the word.
2. Picture the word in your mind.
3. Write the word carefully.
4. Check the spelling of the word.

Handbook

Poem

A **poem** is a form of writing that allows you to express yourself.

The *title* of a poem tells what the poem is about. Be sure to capitalize the first letter of each important word in the title.

A poem can be about any *topic*, but many poems are about nature.

Spring is Full of Wonders

Spring is full of wonders.

Sometimes it is as mysterious as a little girl

Who doesn't want to talk,

Sometimes as simple and familiar as a

garden fence.

Or like old apple trees blossoming from

time immemorial

Or like a blue swallow returning under

the eaves.

Sometimes happy

Sometimes sad

But always interesting.

Spring as usual,

Common and familiar.

However never repeating itself completely.

—Gordana Danicic

This poem uses similes. A *simile* compares two unlike things by using the words *like* or *as*.

This poem uses *sensory words* to describe what the poet saw and felt.

GUIDELINES

- Choose a *topic* that you would like to write about.
- Give your poem a *title*.
- Think of ways to use *sound* in your poem. Will it rhyme? Will it use repeated consonant or vowel sounds? Will it imitate a sound?
- Think about the pattern, or *form*, of your poem. Your poem can have a certain shape or be divided into stanzas, for example.

Practice Observe the world around you. What do you see and hear? Choose a topic that interests you. Then write your own poem.

Humorous Play

A **humorous play** tells an amusing story through dialogue, characters, stage directions, and props.

<u>Cinderella Meets Snow White</u> .... A play needs a "catchy" *title*.

<u>Characters</u>
CINDY: An 11-year-old girl
SNOW: An 11-year-old girl
PRINCE: An 11-year-old boy .... A list of *characters* includes a brief description of each one.

Setting: A sunny day on a fairy-tale street .... The *setting* tells when and where the story takes place.

Props: a hand mirror ....

Scene 1:

Prince is in the center of the street practicing some dance steps. Cindy and Snow enter. .... *Props* and *costumes* are important to the story line.

SNOW: Prince, is it true you're taking Cindy to the dance tonight?

CINDY: I heard you asked Snow to the dance. Is that true?

PRINCE: Well, it's like this, I...

SNOW: Why wouldn't he ask me? Watch this. *(Speaking to her hand mirror)* Mirror, mirror in my hand, who's the fairest in the land? *(She gets no response.)* Mirror? Come in, mirror. I must have a bad connection. .... *Stage directions* are included whenever you want the characters to perform any physical action.

CINDY: Have you thought of getting cable?

SNOW: Well, Prince, who is it going to be?

PRINCE: Well, um...

CINDY: Wait a minute. Why are we arguing over him? .... The *dialogue* is the characters' spoken words.

SNOW: You're right. Who wants a guy who can't keep his word?

PRINCE: Well, now wait a minute. I...

SNOW: *(Speaking to Cindy as they walk off together)* I'll meet you at 7:00.

PRINCE: Wait! Girls?? Somebody?? Yipes!!

Practice Write a humorous play based on a familiar story. Include the setting, plot, characters, dialogue, and stage directions.

Handbook

Friendly Letter

A **friendly letter** is a letter that you would write to a friend or a family member. The tone of a friendly letter is familiar and casual. A friendly letter has these parts:

The heading gives the address of the person writing the letter.

2245 Beacon Street
Providence, Rhode Island 02906
January 23, 2003

Dear Amy,

The greeting begins with Dear and includes the name of the person to whom the letter is written.

 Hi! How are you? Is it snowing in Providence? It snowed here last night. We had almost two inches of snow! My brother and I went outside this morning to build a snowman, but the snow had already turned to rain. Instead, we got out a puzzle and went to work.

The body is the main part of the letter.

 When we got to the last piece, we couldn't find it. It turns out that Shep, our dog, had snatched it off the table and chewed it. We took the puzzle apart and put it away.

 Tonight we're going to the mall to look for a new desk. The desk in my room is nice, but it's so small that I can't spread out my schoolbooks. I hope I can find a yellow one like yours.

The closing is a way of saying good-bye. It is followed by a comma.

 Are you still coming to visit this summer? I'm excited that we'll be going to the water park. We'll have a great time! I hope to hear from you soon.

Your friend,

The signature is the signed name of the writer.

Julia

Practice Write a letter to a friend or a relative. Describe something you did on your last vacation, or an interesting hobby that you have. Be sure to include the correct letter form.

Editorial

An **editorial** is a form of writing that expresses a writer's opinion about a topic. Editorials are usually found in newspapers or magazine.

Bat Alert!

The Indiana Bat is in danger! In 1967, these flying mammals were added to the list of endangered species. Unfortunately, logging in our area has caused the Indiana Bat population to drop by 60% since the 1960s. Although some logging in nearby counties has been put on hold, everyone knows that the number of bats will continue to decrease until all logging in the area is stopped.

The only way to save these innocent creatures is to work together to help preserve their natural habitat. Otherwise, the Indiana Bat will surely vanish from the face of the earth.

State your opinion in a topic sentence.

Support your opinion with facts and details.

Use opinion words to convince your audience.

Save your strongest argument for last.

GUIDELINES

- Brainstorm a list of topics about which you have a strong opinion.
- Think about your audience. Will your classmates read your editorial? Will the community read it?
- Consider your purpose for writing. Are you writing to persuade?
- Research your topic. Use reference sources.
- Organize your ideas in a logical order.

Practice Think of an issue that concerns you, such as building parks, keeping streams clean, or recycling. Research information, and write your own editorial.

589

What Is a Thesaurus?

A **thesaurus** is a writer's reference that provides synonyms—
and sometimes antonyms—for many common words. Synonyms are
words that mean the same or almost the same thing. Antonyms
are words that have opposite meanings. Use a thesaurus when you
are looking for a more interesting, vivid, or exact word to use in
your writing. Read this sentence:

The sunset was pretty.

Pretty is not a very interesting or exact word. If you check the
word *pretty* in the thesaurus, you will find these words: *attractive,
beautiful,* and *gorgeous.* These words are more vivid and precise.

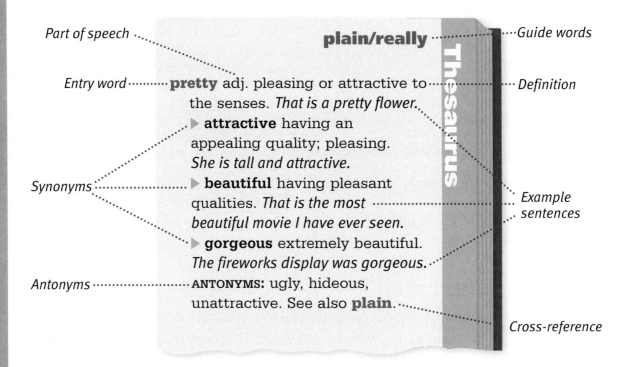

- The guide words at the top of each page show the first and last
  entry word on that page.
- The word *pretty* is the entry word. The information that follows
  is called the entry.
- The part of speech of each entry word is given.
- A definition tells what the entry word and each synonym mean.
- An example sentence shows you how to use each word.
- A cross-reference sends you to additional information.

Practice

A. Answer the questions below by using the Thesaurus beginning on page 594.

1. What are the guide words on the page with the entry word *big*?

2. What is the part of speech for the entry word *big*?

3. Which synonym has exactly the same definition as the entry word *big*?

4. Write a new example sentence for the word *enormous*.

5. Which of the following words would you find on a page with the guide words *neat/peer*? *nice, old, many, plain, often*

DEFINITIONS AND FEATURES

- Synonyms are words with similar meanings.
- There may be different shades of meaning among the synonyms listed within a single entry. For example, the entry for the word *good* includes the synonyms *excellent, fair,* and *fine*.
- Look at the definitions and example sentences for each word. They will help you figure out whether the synonyms have slightly different meanings.
- Near the bottom of some entries you will find a list of antonyms, or words that mean the opposite of the entry word.
- In some cases you will find cross-references. For example, under the entry word *small*, you might find the cross-reference: "See *little*." This means that you should look up the word *little*; the word *small* will be listed under *little*.

B. Use the thesaurus to replace each underlined word with a more exact word.

1. The <u>dry</u> climate is perfect for cactus to grow.

2. I used to think that studying the desert was <u>dull</u>.

3. My teacher, Ms. Gomez, is <u>great</u>.

4. She makes the desert seem <u>interesting</u>.

5. She went with other teachers on a new <u>journey</u> to take pictures and collect materials in the desert.

Practice

C. Use the thesaurus to rewrite the editorial. Use this key: (A) replace the word with an antonym; (S) replace the word with a synonym, or more exact word.

> I listened to the mayor's speech yesterday, and I am surprised (S) by his latest proposal. He thinks elementary school students should no longer be allowed to ride their bicycles to school. He says it is too dangerous and suggests that all students be forced (S) to ride the bus. I think this is a great (A) idea! There are many of us who live very many (A) blocks from the school. Why would we want to wait fifteen minutes for a bus and then ride for another twenty when we can be home five minutes after school is out? There are crosswalks and sidewalks all over the neighborhood, so nobody rides in the street or darts in front of traffic. I think it is important for all of us to write our mayor today. He needs to know how right (A) he is.

D. When you write poems, you want to choose words that will paint a picture. A thesaurus may help you find just the right words to make your poem interesting. Rewrite the poem below. Replace the underlined words with synonyms from the thesaurus.

Lone Goose

The cold nights become longer.
A quiet scene as I peer out my window.
The geese have begun their yearly journey.
But one remains on my lawn.
Maybe he wasn't ready for winter.

E. Dialogue in a play needs to be realistic, and stage directions need to be clear. Use the thesaurus to replace underlined words in this play. When you have finished, read the play out loud or perform it with some classmates.

Ready for School?

CHARLIE (*waking and yawning*): I always have a <u>hard</u> time waking up, but today I am going to surprise everyone by being ready for school on time.

MOM (*outside Charlie's door*): Charlie, are you up?

CHARLIE: Yeah, yeah, I'm up.

MOM: Don't forget...

CHARLIE (<u>*answers*</u>, *cutting her off*): I know Mom. I'll be ready on time today.

CHARLIE (*thinking to himself*): I'm really <u>smart</u> today!

CHARLIE: Maria, have you seen my backpack?

MARIA: Charlie, why do you...

(*Charlie runs into the kitchen and begins packing lunch.*)

CHARLIE (*happy with himself*): Well, I'm quick today. I'll be the first one ready for school!

MOM: But Charlie...

CHARLIE: I know, Mom. You're really excited. For once, I am ready for school early!

MOM AND MARIA (*loudly*): But Charlie, that is what we are trying to tell you! Today is Saturday!

CHARLIE (<u>*surprised*</u>): What a silly <u>mistake</u>!

QUICK WRITE Write a friendly letter to a relative or friend. Tell about something in which you are involved right now (a sport, a class project, a club activity). Use the thesaurus to help you use precise, exact words.

Thesaurus

adventure n. something that a person does that is difficult or exciting. *The camping trip was an adventure for the whole family.*

▶ **exploit** a brave deed or act. *The newspaper article described the latest exploit of the rescue squad in great detail.*

▶ **feat** an act or deed that shows great courage, strength, or skill. *Crossing the river on horseback was a feat for even the strongest rider.*

▶ **venture** a task or under-taking that involves risk or danger. *Taking part in a venture such as the search for a sunken ship needs great courage.*

allow See **let**.

angry adj. feeling or showing anger. *Don's remark made me angry.*

▶ **enraged** filled with rage; angry beyond control. *The enraged lion growled loudly.*

▶ **furious** extremely angry. *Marty was furious when he found out I ruined his bike.*

answer v. to give a spoken or written response. *I wonder whether Celia is going to answer my letter.*

▶ **reply** to say in response. *If he insults you, don't reply. Just walk away.*

▶ **respond** to give an answer. *James did not respond to my question.*

ANTONYMS: See **ask**.

appear v. to come into sight. *As soon as the first buds appear, she thinks it's spring.*

▶ **emerge** to come into view. *In the night sky, the moon was trying to emerge from behind the clouds.*

▶ **show** to be in sight, to be visible. *If you use thin cloth for the curtains, the light will show through them.*

ANTONYMS: disappear, vanish

argument n. a discussion of something by people who do not agree. *They had an argument about who was better at solving problems.*

▶ **conflict** a strong disagree-ment. *Sometimes a minor problem can lead to a more serious conflict.*

▶ **disagreement** a difference of opinion. *We resolved our disagreement by taking turns.*

▶ **fight** an angry disagree-ment. *We had a fight over which movie to see.*

▶ **quarrel** an angry argument or disagreement. *The broken window set off a quarrel over who should get it fixed.*

ANTONYMS: agreement, accord, settlement, understanding

ask v. to put a question to. *Let's ask for directions.*

▶ **inquire** to seek information by asking questions. *Please inquire at the desk.*

▶ **question** to try to get infor-mation (from someone). *Bill's mother questioned him about where he had been.*

ANTONYMS: See **answer**.

Thesaurus

awful adj. causing fear, dread, or awe. *The tree made an awful noise when it fell.*

▶ **dreadful** causing great fear. *I am in shock from the dreadful experience.*

▶ **terrible** causing terror or awe. *Jason received some terrible news.*

 B

---

beautiful

adj. very nice to look at

attractive	ideal
exquisite	lovely
fair	pleasing
good-looking	pretty
gorgeous	radiant
graceful	splendid
handsome	

ANTONYMS: ugly, beastly, terrible-looking

---

big adj. of great size. *He works on a big farm.*

▶ **enormous** much greater than the usual size. *We saw an enormous elephant at the zoo.*

▶ **huge** extremely big. *That is a huge tree!*

▶ **large** of great size; big. *What large feet you have!*

ANTONYMS: See **little**.

brave adj. willing to face danger; without fear. *The brave firefighter raced into the burning house.*

▶ **bold** showing courage; fearless. *The bold explorer walked into the dark jungle.*

▶ **courageous** having courage.

A courageous woman dove into the icy water to save the child.

▶ **daring** willing to take risks. *The daring boy stood ready at the edge of the cliff.*

ANTONYMS: afraid, fearful

break v. to come apart; to separate into pieces. *These glass animals break easily.*

▶ **crack** to break without fully separating. *The shell cracked as the eggs were hatching.*

▶ **fracture** to break or split a bone. *Juan fractured his ankle and had to leave the game.*

▶ **shatter** to break suddenly into many pieces. *The vase will shatter if you drop it.*

bright adj. filled with light; shining. *Is that light bright enough to read by?*

▶ **brilliant** shining or sparkling with light. *The crown was decorated with brilliant gems.*

▶ **shiny** shining; bright. *Her blue coat has shiny silver buttons.*

ANTONYMS: dark, dull

 C

---

carefully adv. paying close attention to avoid danger or risk. *The tourists stayed carefully away from the edge of the cliff.*

▶ **cautiously** using care. *The bicyclist cautiously avoided the potholes.*

▶ **gingerly** with great delicacy or care. *Gingerly, I pulled the cactus spine from my thumb.*

▶ **warily** with care and caution. *The mouse warily poked its nose*

Thesaurus

out of the cupboard in case the cat was near.

ANTONYMS: carelessly, heedlessly, recklessly

chore n. something that has to be done regularly. *Setting the table is a chore I have to do every evening before I watch television.*

▶ **duty** an action or service assigned to someone. *It's my duty to check that the plants are watered every day.*

▶ **job** a specific piece of work. *The chart shows each student's job for the week.*

▶ **task** a piece of work to be done. *Cleaning the chalkboard is my favorite task.*

cold adj. having a low temperature. *There is cold water in the refrigerator.*

▶ **chilly** uncomfortably cool. *You need a sweater on a chilly night.*

▶ **icy** very cold. *You could see your breath in the icy room.*

ANTONYMS: See **hot**.

cook v. to prepare food for eating, using heat. *Dad will cook dinner.*

▶ **bake** to cook in an oven. *Alice put the cake in the oven to bake.*

▶ **broil** to cook by exposing to a flame or another source of heat. *Let's broil the hamburgers on the grill.*

▶ **roast** cook with little moisture in the oven or over a fire. *Roast the turkey for six hours.*

> **create**
>
> v. to bring into being
>
> | | |
> |---|---|
> | build | generate |
> | compose | invent |
> | design | originate |
> | dream up | plan |
> | fashion | produce |
> | form | shape |
>
> ANTONYMS: destroy, copy

cry v. to shed tears. *The sad movie made me cry.*

▶ **sob** to cry with short gasps. *The lost child sobbed until his parents found him.*

▶ **weep** to show grief, joy, or other strong emotions by crying. *The letter made Sofia weep with homesickness.*

ANTONYMS: See **laugh**.

---

discussion n. the act of talking something over, often to exchange ideas.

▶ **chat** a friendly, informal talk. *Margarita had a chat with her friends before the game.*

▶ **conversation** talk between two or more people. *They interrupted their conversation to give their tickets to the conductor.*

▶ **talk** an exchange of spoken words. *My uncle said he wanted to have a talk about our vacation plans.*

do v. to carry out. *Some days I can't do anything right.*

▶ **execute** to complete; to put into effect. *The President's job is to execute laws.*

▶ **perform** to carry out to completion. *The acrobats will now perform a triple backflip.*

drag v. to move something along slowly or heavily. *The horse strained to drag the overloaded hay wagon.*

▶ **haul** to pull or move with effort. *It took three people to haul the file cabinet up the stairs.*

▶ **tow** to pull or drag behind. *I can hardly believe this little truck can tow an entire bus!*

dry adj. not wet; free of moisture. *Is the paint dry yet?*

▶ **arid** dry as a result of having little rainfall. *Nothing grows here because the land is so arid.*

▶ **parched** dried out by heat. *The drink felt good to my parched throat.*

ANTONYMS: See **wet**.

dull adj. not interesting. *They walked out of the dull movie before it ended.*

▶ **boring** lacking in interest. *I almost fell asleep during the boring program.*

▶ **tedious** long and tiring, boring. *Checking all the addresses was a tedious task.*

▶ **tiresome** causing boredom or weariness. *Mrs. Rodriguez does not want to hear any more tiresome excuses.*

ANTONYMS: interesting, exciting, fascinating

easy adj. requiring little mental or physical effort; not difficult. *The math problems were so easy that Sheila finished them in five minutes.*

▶ **facile** not hard to do or achieve. *There is no facile solution to the problem of global warming.*

▶ **simple** not complicated. *The kit came with simple directions that were easy to follow.*

ANTONYMS: See **hard**.

explore v. to look through closely. *The class will begin to explore the history of space travel next week.*

▶ **investigate** to look into carefully in order to get information. *Each group will investigate a desert animal.*

▶ **research** to study carefully in order to find facts; investigate. *My sister researched our family tree on the Internet.*

▶ **study** to try to learn about. *Next year, we will study geometry and world history.*

far adj. being a long way off; not near. *The farms are in the far regions of the country.*

▶ **distant** extremely far. *Many sailors went to sea to visit distant lands.*

▶ **remote** faraway, in an out-of-the-way place. *It took us three days to climb to the remote mountain village.*

ANTONYMS: near, close

fast adj. moving or done with speed. *A fast car can travel at 100 miles per hour.*

▶ **quick** done in a very short time. *She gave a quick response.*

Thesaurus

▶ **rapid** with great speed, often in a continuing way. *Jeff kept walking at a rapid pace.*

▶ **swift** moving at great speed, often said of animals or people. *A swift runner warned the nearby villages.*

ANTONYM: slow

fasten v. to put two things together firmly. *We used a bolt to fasten the tire swing to the chain.*

▶ **attach** to connect one thing to another. *They used glue to attach the badges to our notebooks.*

▶ **bind** to tie or join together. *Our teacher will bind our stories into a class book.*

▶ **connect** to join together. *The driver connected the trailer to the truck.*

ANTONYMS: unfasten, detach, separate, disconnect

force v. to make someone do something. *Don't force Yuka to go if she doesn't want to.*

▶ **coerce** to make someone act in a given manner. *The bully tried to coerce the younger children to walk on the other side of the street.*

▶ **compel** to force. *The storm will compel us to cancel the game.*

▶ **require** to demand in a way that can't be refused. *The laws require drivers to stop at red lights.*

funny adj. causing laughter. *I heard a funny story on the radio.*

▶ **amusing** causing smiles of enjoyment or laughter. *Harriet found the monkeys amusing.*

▶ **comical** causing laughter through actions. *The baby made all kinds of comical faces.*

▶ **hilarious** very funny and usually noisy. *Hilarious laughter came from the party next door.*

get v. to go for and return with. *Did you get the package at the post office?*

▶ **acquire** to come into possession of through effort. *How did she acquire so much money?*

▶ **obtain** to get as one's own, often with some difficulty. *First, you'll have to obtain a permit.*

gigantic

adj. very big and powerful, like a giant

colossal	monumental
enormous	mountainous
huge	towering
immense	tremendous
mammoth	vast

ANTONYMS: tiny, minute, microscopic

give v. to turn over possession or control of, to make a present of. *I want to give you this book.*

▶ **confer** to give as an honor. *The college will confer a degree upon the guest speaker.*

▶ **contribute** to give in common with others. *We are asking each person to contribute $10.*

▶ **grant** to give in response to a request. *Please grant me this favor.*

▶ **present** to give in a formal way. *Miss Kingsley presented a check for $5,000 to the Disaster Fund.*

ANTONYMS: See **take**.

good adj. above average in quality. *He wanted a good meal.*

▶ **excellent** extremely good. *This is an excellent book.*

▶ **fair** somewhat good; slightly better than average. *He was a fair musician but a very good composer.*

▶ **fine** of high quality; very good. *Fine jewelry is usually very expensive.*

ANTONYMS: bad, poor

great adj. of unusual quality or ability. *Picasso was a great artist.*

▶ **remarkable** having unusual qualities. *The actors did a remarkable job.*

▶ **superb** of greater quality than most. *That was a superb dinner.*

ANTONYMS: terrible, awful
See also **good**.

happy adj. having, showing, or bringing pleasure. *Their visit made Mrs. Johnson very happy.*

▶ **glad** feeling or expressing joy or pleasure. *We are glad you were able to join us.*

▶ **joyful** very happy; filled with joy. *A wedding is a joyful occasion.*

▶ **merry** happy and cheerful. *Suzanne is such a merry person that she cheered me up right away.*

▶ **pleased** satisfied or content. *Was he pleased with his presents?*

ANTONYMS: See **sad**.

hard adj. not easy to do or deal with. *These problems are hard.*

▶ **difficult** hard to do; requiring effort. *The hikers planned a difficult climb.*

▶ **tough** difficult to do, often in a physical sense. *We had a tough time pulling the boat out of the water.*

ANTONYMS: See **easy**.

harmful adj. causing loss or pain. *Keep harmful substances away from the baby.*

▶ **destructive** causing or bringing injury or harm. *The destructive winds knocked down trees.*

▶ **hurtful** causing pain. *Hank apologized for the hurtful things he had said.*

ANTONYM: safe

help v. to provide with support; to be of service to. *Mom will help me with my homework.*

▶ **aid** to give help to someone in trouble. *The Red Cross will aid flood victims.*

▶ **assist** to help, often in a cooperative way. *The whole class will assist with the project.*

hidden adj. put or kept out of sight. *Sean searched to find the hidden image in the painting.*

▶ **concealed** kept out of sight. *Margo's fingers felt the concealed lock in the darkness.*

▶ **secret** known only to one-self or a few. *George finally found the papers in a secret drawer hidden in the desk.*

ANTONYMS: open, clear, obvious

Thesaurus

high adj. located or extending a great distance above the ground. *The eagle nested on a high cliff.*

▶ **lofty** very high; of grand or inspiring height. *Above the valley rose a range of lofty mountain peaks.*

▶ **tall** having a height greater than average but with a relatively narrow width. *Over the years, the pine trees grew to be very tall.*

▶ **towering** of great or imposing height. *The city's towering buildings made Luis feel small.*

ANTONYMS: low, short

hoist v. to pull up. *The movers used a rope to hoist the piano into the van.*

▶ **lift** to move from a lower to a higher position. *Let's lift the lid, so we can see what's inside.*

▶ **raise** to put in a higher position. *Oliver raised the window to let some air into the room.*

hot adj. having a high temperature; having much heat. *This pan is hot.*

▶ **fiery** as hot as fire; burning. *Inside the volcano was a fiery pool of lava.*

▶ **scalding** hot enough to burn, often said of liquids. *I got a bad burn from the scalding water.*

▶ **scorching** hot enough to cause burning or drying. *The desert sun was scorching.*

▶ **torrid** extremely hot, often said of weather. *Much of Africa has a torrid climate.*

ANTONYMS: See **cold**.

---

howl

n. a loud, wailing cry

bellow	**screech**
shriek	**wail**
scream	**yell**
shout	**yowl**

ANTONYMS: whisper, murmur

---

hurt v. to cause pain or damage. *I fell out of bed and hurt myself.*

▶ **harm** to do damage to. *An early frost will harm the crops.*

▶ **injure** to cause physical damage. *Warm up before you exercise, or you might injure yourself.*

imagine v. to picture something in one's mind. *Imagine what it would be like to live in another time in history.*

▶ **guess** to form an opinion without having enough knowledge or facts to be sure. *Harold couldn't guess the number of jellybeans in the jar.*

▶ **suppose** to think about something as if it is possible or really happening. *Suppose that you had four oranges and Carly had two.*

interesting adj. arousing or holding interest or attention. *Mr. Wu gave an interesting talk.*

▶ **captivating** capturing and holding the attention by beauty or excellence. *The tourists found the village a captivating place.*

▶ **fascinating** causing and holding the interest through a special quality or charm. *I just read a fascinating book about the space program.*

▶ **inspiring** having a rousing effect; arousing interest. *Her inspiring example gave courage to others.*

ANTONYMS: dull, boring.

journey n. a long trip. *We took a journey across the country.*

▶ **expedition** a long trip made for a specific reason. *The scientists will collect rocks on the expedition.*

▶ **excursion** a short trip made for a specific reason. *The bus left for the excursion to the zoo.*

▶ **trek** a long trip, especially when slow or difficult. *It seemed as if our trek would never end.*

▶ **trip** the act of going from one place to another. *The class will take a trip to the state park.*

large See **big**.

laugh v. to make the sounds and facial movements that show amusement. *They sang songs to make the baby laugh.*

▶ **chuckle** to laugh softly, especially to oneself. *Reading the comic strip made me chuckle.*

▶ **giggle** to laugh in a silly, high-pitched, or nervous way.

The two friends giggled over their joke.

▶ **guffaw** to laugh loudly. *When Rick guffawed, everyone looked to see what was so funny.*

let v. to give permission. *Will Kyle let me borrow his bike?*

▶ **allow** to grant permission, usually in relation to rules. *Talking is not allowed in the library.*

▶ **permit** to allow to do something. *The club members decided to permit him to join.*

ANTONYMS: deny, refuse, forbid

like v. to take pleasure in (something); to feel affection for (someone). *They like cats.*

▶ **admire** to have affection and respect for (someone). *All the team members admire their coach.*

▶ **enjoy** to take pleasure in (something). *They enjoy playing chess together.*

▶ **love** to like (something) a lot; to feel great affection for (someone). *The children love that old mutt.*

ANTONYMS: dislike, hate

little adj. small in size; not big. *I have two large dogs and one little one.*

▶ **small** not large. *Violets are small flowers.*

▶ **tiny** extremely small. *A watch has many tiny parts.*

ANTONYMS: See **big**.

look v. to see with one's eyes. *Look at what I found!*

▶ **glance** to look quickly. *The spy glanced over his shoulder to be sure he wasn't being followed.*

▶ **peer** to look closely. *We peered through the window of the shop.*

▶ **stare** to look at for a long time with eyes wide open. *Mac stared at the television during his favorite program.* See also **see**.

loud adj. having a strong sound. *The band was playing loud music.*

▶ **deafening** loud enough to make one deaf. *The exciting goal brought deafening cheers from the fans.*

▶ **noisy** full of sounds, often unpleasant. *Their apartment is located above a noisy street.* ANTONYMS: See **quiet**.

lure v. to attract strongly. *We hoped the seeds on the floor would lure the gerbil from his hiding place.*

▶ **attract** to cause to come near. *If you don't want flies, don't leave out food that will attract them.*

▶ **draw** to cause to move toward, to attract. *The clowns make noise to draw a crowd.*

▶ **tempt** to appeal strongly to. *The offer of samples tempted customers into the store.* ANTONYM: repel

manufacture v. to make or process something, especially using machinery.

▶ **assemble** to make something by putting the parts together. *Workers in the plant assemble cars.*

▶ **produce** to make or create something. *The workers produce a car every 20 minutes.*

many adj. consisting of a large number. *Jenna has many friends.*

▶ **numerous** a great many. *I have numerous chores to get done today.*

▶ **plenty (of)** enough, or more than enough, suggesting a large number. *There is plenty of food for lunch.*

▶ **several** more than a few but less than many. *Harold checked out several books from the library.* ANTONYM: few

mean adj. lacking in kindness or understanding. *Maya felt bad about being mean to her sister.*

▶ **nasty** resulting from hate. *The villain wore a nasty sneer.*

▶ **selfish** concerned only about oneself. *Pattie is so selfish that she never shares anything.*

▶ **spiteful** filled with ill feelings toward others. *It's best to leave Dan alone when he's feeling spiteful.* ANTONYMS: See **nice**.

mistake n. something that is not correctly done. *I corrected the mistake I made on the test.*

▶ **blunder** a careless or stupid mistake. *It was a serious blunder to forget the time of the game.*

▶ **error** something that is wrong. *The students found only one spelling error in their article.*

▶ **fault** a weakness or mistake. *The lack of light was a fault in the room's design.*

neat adj. clean and orderly. *Her homework is always very neat.*

▶ **tidy** neat and clean, often said of a place. *We raked the yard to make it look tidy.*

▶ **well-groomed** carefully dressed and groomed. *He is a well-groomed young man.*

ANTONYMS: messy, untidy, sloppy

new adj. having just come into being, use, or possession. *They are building a new house.*

▶ **fresh** new or seeming new and unaffected by time or use. *We put a fresh coat of paint on the old table.*

▶ **modern** having to do with the present time; up-to-date. *Technology is important in modern American life.*

▶ **recent** referring to a time just before the present. *Critics have praised her most recent book.*

ANTONYM: old

nice adj. agreeable or pleasing. *Her parents are extremely nice.*

▶ **gentle** mild and kindly in manner. *Grandpa's gentle words made Lisa feel much better.*

▶ **kind** gentle and friendly; good-hearted. *It is kind of you to offer to help.*

▶ **pleasant** agreeable; giving pleasure to. *Georgia and Scott are always such pleasant company.*

▶ **sweet** having or marked by agreeable or pleasing qualities. *He wrote a sweet thank-you note.*

ANTONYMS: See **mean**.

obey v. to carry out wishes, orders, or instructions. *The dog obeyed and rolled over.*

▶ **comply** to act in agreement with a rule or request. *The people who comply with the order will be dismissed first.*

▶ **follow** to act according to wishes, orders, or instructions. *If you follow the directions, you'll do it right.*

ANTONYMS: ignore, defy, disobey

often adv. many times; again and again. *James is often late.*

▶ **frequently** happening again and again. *The two families get together frequently.*

▶ **regularly** happening at fixed times. *It is a good idea to exercise regularly.*

ANTONYMS: seldom, rarely

old adj. having lived or existed for a long time. *The old car broke down.*

▶ **aged** having grown old. *Our aged dog sleeps most of the time.*

▶ **ancient** of great age; very old; of times long past. *We visited the ruins of an ancient city.*

ANTONYM: young. See also **new**.

peer v. to look hard or closely so as to see something clearly. *I tried to peer through the grime on the window to see what was inside.*

▶ **gaze** to look long and attentively at. *They stopped to gaze at the toys displayed in the window.*

▶ **look** to use one's eyes to see. *Look at the pictures, and choose the one you like best.*

▶ **stare** to look very hard at. *Their aunt told them it was rude to stare at people.*

plain adj. not distinguished from others in any way. *The meal was plain but hearty.*

▶ **common** average or standard; not distinguished. *Mumps is a common childhood illness.*

▶ **ordinary** plain; average; everyday. *Super Food is just an ordinary grocery store.* ANTONYM: special. See also **unusual**.

pretty adj. pleasing or attractive to the senses. *That is a pretty flower.*

▶ **attractive** having an appealing quality; pleasing. *She is tall and attractive.*

▶ **beautiful** having pleasant qualities. *That is the most beautiful movie I have ever seen.*

▶ **gorgeous** extremely beautiful. *The fireworks display was gorgeous.* ANTONYMS: ugly, hideous, unattractive. See also **plain**.

quiet adj. with little or no noise. *The woods were quiet tonight.*

▶ **calm** free of excitement or strong feeling; quiet. *Sue remained calm as she waited to be rescued.*

▶ **peaceful** calm; undisturbed. *He spent a peaceful morning fishing.*

▶ **silent** completely quiet; without noise. *The room was silent while the principal spoke.*

▶ **still** without sound; silent. *The house was still and dark.* ANTONYMS: loud, noisy

raise v. to pick up or move to a higher place. *Raise your hand if you have any questions.*

▶ **boost** to push or shove up. *Give me a boost, so I can reach the window ledge.*

▶ **heave** to lift, raise, pull, or throw, usually with effort. *The farm workers will heave the hay bales into the wagon.*

▶ **lift** to pick up. *Can they lift the table by themselves?* ANTONYMS: lower, bring down, take down, drop

ready adj. fit for use or action. *Is your costume ready?*

▶ **prepared** ready or fit for a particular purpose. *We were not prepared for our cousins' visit.*

▶ **set** ready or prepared to do something. *Everything was set for the picnic.*

really adv. in fact. *Was your dad really in the Olympics?*

▶ **actually** in fact; really. *Grandpa says he's 100 years old, but he's actually only 70.*

▶ **indeed** really; truly. *The person you met was indeed my sister.*

▶ **truly** in fact; really. *She was truly a great woman.*

Thesaurus

receive v. to take or get. *I hope to receive a letter from my pen pal soon.*

▶ **accept** to take something that is given. *Our neighbor asked us to accept the gift with her thanks.*

▶ **acquire** to get or gain as one's own. *They hope to acquire more books for the library.*

▶ **get** to come to have or own. *That swimmer will get a ribbon at the end of the race.*

▶ **obtain** to get through effort. *They wrote to the director to obtain more information.*

ANTONYMS: give, discard, abandon, donate, distribute

return v. to come or go back. *The visitor promised to return soon.*

▶ **recur** to happen or appear again. *The pain in your knee will recur if you don't rest the knee.*

▶ **revisit** to come to the same place again. *They plan to revisit the place where they first met.*

ANTONYMS: leave, depart, go away

right adj. free from error; true. *Her answers are always right.*

▶ **accurate** without errors or mistakes. *The witness gave an accurate description of the thief.*

▶ **correct** agreeing with fact or truth. *Is this the correct way to put it together?*

▶ **exact** very accurate; completely correct. *Get exact change for the bus.*

ANTONYMS: wrong, mistaken

rude adj. not polite; ill-mannered. *Rude people never say "thank you."*

▶ **discourteous** without good manners. *It is discourteous to keep people waiting.*

▶ **impolite** not showing good manners. *Randy's impolite remarks made Mr. Parsons angry.*

ANTONYMS: polite, courteous

run v. to go quickly on foot. *Milo can run very fast.*

▶ **dash** to go very fast; to run with sudden speed. *Lou dashed to the telephone to report the accident.*

▶ **race** to run very fast; to run in competition with. *Sharon raced Mitch to the corner.*

▶ **scurry** to move hurriedly. *Mr. Flynn scurried about town to finish all of his errands.*

▶ **sprint** to run at top speed for a short distance. *Janet sprinted after the departing bus.*

sad adj. feeling or showing unhappiness or sorrow. *I know you're sad that they moved away.*

▶ **downcast** low in spirits; sad. *Ollie was downcast about the rain.*

▶ **miserable** extremely unhappy. *Peg was miserable until she made some friends in her new school.*

ANTONYMS: See **happy**.

same adj. being just like something else in kind, quantity, or degree. *They both gave the same answer.*

Thesaurus

▶ **alike** similar, showing a resemblance. *All three of the kittens look alike.*

▶ **equal** the same in size, amount, quality, or value. *Each child got an equal share of the cake.*

▶ **identical** the same in every detail. *The chair is identical to the one in the museum.*

ANTONYM: different

say v. to make known or express in words. *Candidates always say they will be fair and honest.*

▶ **declare** to make known publicly or formally. *The umpire declared that the game was canceled.*

▶ **pronounce** to say formally or officially that something is so. *The jury pronounced him guilty.*

▶ **speak** to express an idea, a fact, or a feeling. *Dr. García will speak to the class about health habits.*

▶ **state** to express or explain fully in words. *Mr. Jones stated his plan.*

▶ **talk** to express ideas or information by means of speech; to speak. *We often talk about sports.* See also **tell**.

scared adj. afraid; alarmed. *"I'm not scared of bats," he said.*

▶ **afraid** feeling fear, often in a continuing way or for a long time. *Nick is afraid to fly in a plane.*

▶ **fearful** filled with fear. *The child is fearful of strangers.*

▶ **frightened** scared suddenly or for a short time. *They were frightened until the storm ended.*

▶ **terrified** extremely scared; filled with terror. *I've always been terrified of dogs.*

see v. to receive information, impressions, etc., through the use of the eyes. *She could see the river from her window.*

▶ **observe** to notice. *Did you observe her leaving by the side door tonight?*

▶ **perceive** to become aware of through the sense of sight or other senses. *I perceive that you are unhappy.*

▶ **view** to see or look at, usually for some purpose. *Hundreds of people visited the gallery to view the artist's work.* See also **look**.

shy adj. uncomfortable in the presence of others. *Van was too shy to ask Angie to dance.*

▶ **bashful** easily embarrassed; very shy. *Don't be bashful— come in!*

▶ **timid** showing a lack of courage; easily frightened. *Deer are timid animals.*

ANTONYM: bold

sick adj. having poor health. *Tom was sick, but now he is well.*

▶ **ill** not healthy; sick. *He was so ill that he could not eat.*

▶ **unwell** not feeling well. *You should lie down if you are unwell.*

ANTONYMS: well, healthy

small See **little**.

smart adj. intelligent; bright; having learned much. *There are many smart students in her class.*

▶ **clever** mentally sharp; quick-witted. *He gave a clever answer.*

▶ **intelligent** able to learn, understand, and reason. *Dolphins seem to be intelligent animals.*

▶ **shrewd** clever or sharp in practical matters. *The woman's shrewd decisions have made her a success.*

▶ **wise** able to know or judge what is right, good, or true, often describing a person with good sense rather than one who knows a lot of facts. *In this folk tale, a boy is guided by a wise woman.*

ANTONYM: stupid

smile v. to show a smile, in a happy or friendly way. *Our neighbor smiled and waved.*

▶ **beam** to smile joyfully. *Dan beamed when he received the award.*

▶ **grin** to smile broadly with real happiness or amusement. *Walter grinned when he saw the picture.*

▶ **smirk** to smile in a silly or self-satisfied way. *Nina smirked foolishly.*

ANTONYMS: frown, scowl

sort v. to separate according to kind or size. *We need to sort the laundry by color.*

▶ **categorize** to group or classify things. *The librarian is categorizing the magazines by topic.*

▶ **classify** to arrange in groups. *We will classify the animals according to where they live.*

▶ **file** to put away in an arranged order. *His job was to file papers in alphabetical order.*

special

adj. different from others in a certain way; not ordinary.

choice	rare
distinguished	remarkable
exceptional	superior
noteworthy	uncommon
outstanding	unique

ANTONYMS: ordinary, common, usual, unremarkable

strange adj. differing from the usual or the ordinary. *We heard a strange noise in the basement.*

▶ **odd** not ordinary. *Jo has an odd pet.*

▶ **weird** strange or odd, in a frightening or mysterious way. *Kids say the weird house is haunted.*

See also **unusual**.

strong adj. having great strength or physical power. *It took four strong men to move the piano.*

▶ **muscular** having well-developed muscles; strong. *That shirt makes you look muscular.*

▶ **powerful** having great strength, influence, or authority. *Their new car has a powerful engine.*

ANTONYM: weak

Thesaurus

sure adj. firmly believing in something. *I'm sure I'll have a good time once I get there.*

▶ **certain** free from doubt; very sure. *Roy was certain he had left the key on the counter.*

▶ **confident** firmly trusting; sure of oneself or of another. *Wendy is confident of winning the prize.*

▶ **definite** positive or certain. *They have not made any definite plans.*

ANTONYMS: doubtful, unsure

surprised adj. feeling sudden wonder. *He was surprised at how cold it was outside.*

▶ **amazed** overwhelmed with wonder or surprise. *Daria was amazed to learn her father had once been in the circus.*

▶ **astonished** greatly surprised; shocked. *Everyone was astonished to see Mrs. Buford at the meeting.*

▶ **astounded** greatly surprised; stunned. *The judges were astounded by the gymnast's performance.*

take v. to get into one's hands or possession; to obtain. *May I take this book?*

▶ **grab** to take roughly or rudely. *Brian grabbed the phone and said, "What do you want?"*

▶ **seize** to take suddenly and by force. *The rebel army seized the tower.*

▶ **snatch** to take suddenly and quickly, often in secret. *He snatched the letter when she wasn't looking.*

ANTONYMS: See **give**.

talk See **say**.

tell v. to put or express in written or spoken words. *May I tell you an interesting story?*

▶ **announce** to state or make known publicly. *The principal will announce a new school program at the assembly.*

▶ **narrate** to tell about events, especially a story. *Mr. Bell will narrate Peter and the Wolf.*

▶ **relate** to tell or report events or details. *Each boy related his side of the argument.* See also **say**.

think v. to have in mind as an opinion or attitude. *What do you think of our new math teacher?*

▶ **believe** to accept as true or real. *The police did not believe the man's story.*

▶ **consider** to regard; to believe. *We consider her one of the family.*

unusual adj. not usual, common, or ordinary. *Jon writes unusual stories.*

▶ **extraordinary** very unusual; beyond the ordinary. *Monica is an artist of extraordinary talent.*

▶ **rare** seldom happening, seen, or found. *Some rare plants are protected by law.*

▶ **uncommon** rare or unusual. *Such a heavy rain is uncommon for July.*

See also **strange**

Thesaurus

upset adj. feeling uneasy; distressed. *Ben is upset about the math test.*

▶ **anxious** uneasy about or fearful of what may happen. *The family is anxious about Grandma's health.*

▶ **concerned** troubled or worried. *We are concerned about the flood.*

▶ **worried** uneasy or troubled about something. *Gene had a worried look on his face.*

ANTONYM: calm

very adv. to a great extent. *The basketball player was very tall.*

▶ **considerably** to a large or an important degree. *It will be considerably colder tomorrow.*

▶ **extremely** greatly or intensely. *May Ling is an extremely talented musician.*

▶ **somewhat** a little, to some extent. *We are somewhat tired today.*

walk v. to move or travel on foot. *She takes the bus, but we walk.*

▶ **march** to walk with regular steps. *The band will march in the parade.*

▶ **stride** to walk with long steps, usually with a purpose. *Just stride right in, and tell him.*

▶ **stroll** to walk in a relaxed or leisurely manner. *Why don't we stroll around the block?*

want v. to have a desire or wish for. *Craig wanted to see you.*

▶ **desire** to have a strong wish for. *The group desired a leader.*

▶ **wish** to have a longing or strong need for. *I wish I were taller.*

▶ **yearn** to feel a strong and deep desire. *The boy yearned for rest.*

wet adj. covered or soaked with water or another liquid. *Be careful—the floor is wet.*

▶ **damp** slightly wet. *The clothes in the dryer were still damp.*

▶ **moist** slightly wet; damp. *The grass was moist from the dew.*

▶ **sopping** extremely wet; dripping. *Linda took off her sopping shoes.*

whole adj. made up of the entire amount, quantity, or number. *How could you eat a whole melon?*

▶ **complete** having all its parts. *Make sure the kit is complete.*

▶ **entire** whole; having all its parts. *The entire week was rainy.*

▶ **total** whole, full, or entire; often referring to numbers. *The total bill was $14.27.*

research for, 134–135
revising, 138–141
signature in, 72–73
strongest argument in, 130–131, 132–147

***but,* combining sentences with,** 8–9, 12–13, 20–21, 22–23, 26–27, 77, 82–83, 527, 529

Call number, 467
Capital letters, 10–11, 12–13, 78, 96–97, 98–99, 142, 160, 228, 544–552
  for family names, 96–97, 98–99, 142, 160
  for first word of sentence, 10–11, 12–13, 60, 78, 228, 547
  for proper adjectives, 266–267, 268–269, 314, 332
  for proper nouns, 96–97, 98–99, 142, 160
  for titles of people, 96–97, 98–99, 142, 160, 548
  for titles of works, 96–97, 98–99, 142, 160
  in abbreviations, 278–279, 280–281, 337, 544–546
  in friendly letters, 588
  in initials, 544
  in outlines, 294–295
  in quotations, 424–425, 426–427, 474, 492, 556
Card catalog, 450–451, 487, 572
Characters, 462–463, 464–475
Charts
  beginning, middle, ending chart, 49
  compare and contrast chart, 381, 383, 385, 386–387
  features chart, 131
  flow chart, 217, 219, 221, 222–223

reason and explanation chart, 133, 135, 136–137. *See also* Prewriting organizers, Study skills.
Closing, of letter, 72–73, 588
Colons, 72–73, 346–347, 348–349, 409, 553
  between hour and minute, 346–347, 348–349, 409, 553
  in business letters, 72–73, 346–347, 348–349, 409, 553
Commas
  after closing of letter, 142, 554, 588
  after greeting of letter, 142, 554, 588
  after introductory words, 178–179, 180–181, 555
  after time–order words, 228
  after *yes, no,* and *well,* 178–179, 180–181, 554–555
  before quotations, 424–425, 426–427, 474, 492, 556
  between city and state, 554
  between day and year, 554
  in business letters, 72–73
  in compound sentence, 10–11, 12–13, 60, 78, 228
  in direct address, 178–179, 180–181, 555
  in introductory interjections, 438–439, 440–441, 499, 555
  in introductory prepositional phrases, 438–439, 440–441, 499, 555
  in sentence combining with *and, but, or,* 8–9, 12–13, 20–21, 22–23, 26–27, 77, 82–83, 467, 527, 529, 554

rules for using, 178–179, 180–181, 438–439, 440–441, 524, 554–555
  to prevent misreading, 555
  to separate a phrase from the direct quotation, 556
  to separate words in series, 178–179, 180–181, 554
  with name, in direct address, 178–179, 180–181, 555
Common errors, 28–29, 110–111, 196–197, 282–283, 360–361, 442–443
  adverbs, 442–443
  comparative and superlative adjectives, 282–283
  plurals and possessives, 110–111
  pronouns, 360–361
  sentence fragments and run–on sentences, 28–29
  subject verb agreement, 196–197
Comparison
  adjectives for, 270–271, 280–281, 333, 536
  adverbs used in, 420–421, 426–427, 490, 541
  details in, 380–381, 382–391
  in writing, 378–379, 382–391
  simile as type of, 586
  using graphs in, 569
  with *good* and *bad,* 274–275, 280–281, 335, 537
  with *more* and *most,* 272–273, 334, 537
Composition skills, 40–41, 122–123, 208–209, 294–295, 372–373, 454–455
  leads and endings, 122–123
  main idea and supporting details, 40–41
  organization, 208–209
  outlining, 294–295

Index